Lawyers Making Meaning

Jan M. Broekman • Larry Catà Backer

Lawyers Making Meaning

The Semiotics of Law in Legal Education II

Springer

Jan M. Broekman
Dickinson School of Law
Penn State University
Carlisle, PA, USA

Larry Catà Backer
Dickinson School of Law,
School of International Affairs
Penn State University
State College, PA, USA

ISBN 978-94-007-5457-7 ISBN 978-94-007-5458-4 (eBook)
DOI 10.1007/978-94-007-5458-4
Springer Dordrecht Heidelberg London New York

Library of Congress Control Number: 2012954528

Printed on acid-free paper

Springer is part of Springer Science+Business Media (www.springer.com)

LAW DOES NOT SIMPLY DISTORT THE WORLD—OR EVEN MERELY REPRESENT IT CORRECTLY; RATHER IT MAKES A WORLD, ONE IN WHICH AND THROUGH WHICH WE LIVE, ACT, IMAGINE, DESIRE AND BELIEVE.

J. M. Balkin:
The Promise of Legal Semiotics, 1991

Preface

"Law ... *makes* a world", the motto of this book declares. But the riddle of law is *how* law does so! The answer is the major theme of this book: through understanding and awareness of how lawyers make meaning. Yet this world, thus made, in turn makes law, and constrains it within its logic and the cultural habits it inculcates. Law makes the world, is made in the reflection of that world and derives its meaning from the assimilation of legal subjects (you and me), those who are meant to incarnate both law and world. Moreover, law sometimes imposes a class structure in the world it makes—distinguishing between subjects and objects of law. The world law makes is populated by a diverse and dizzying variety of objects, subjects, aggregations, personalities, and presumptions whose interactions, constructions, and objectifications are the stuff of meaning making for lawyers as well.

Law, then, does not merely make the world within which it exits; it does more. To make a world requires two distinct actions. The first, the usual object of lawyers, is to fill the world with substance—and lawyers spend their time making meaning of this substance and sometimes making the substance itself. The second, sometimes the object of lawyers, and central to the tasks of judges and legislators in their engagement with law, is the task of making and protecting the boundaries of this world law makes. Beyond law exist other worlds, sometimes as complex as that of law, and always in communication with it; these other forms of compulsion—the "not-law" fields of governance with which lawyers have an increasingly uncertain relationship include, beyond religious, moral, and ethical "worlds", the worlds of psychology, of economics and philosophy. Lawyers make meaning, and a world, by making law; they also make meaningful boundaries that separate what is allocated to the law-world and everything else. Lawyers serve the structures within which meaning is made, but they also subvert those structures as they make meaning. The legal structures are now stacking side-by-side and atop one another in a world in which meaning has acquired a global dimension. That last has both broadened and changed the parameters for meaning making and the toolkit available for lawyers engaged in their work.

This complex substantive and systemic inter-relationship comprises theory and practice of the law—both are subject of study at various levels. Law schools offer one of them; the study of legal semiotics in legal education offers another. This book provides a guideline to enhance semiotic sensitivity, which is neither the one nor the other. "We have no power of thinking without signs", the US philosopher Charles Sanders Peirce once noticed. Our guideline follows him in this regard and enhances semiotic sensitivity to criticize and to level our reflections.

Fragments of the book have been tested and used during the last 5 years in various Course Books written for students of the "Roberta Kevelson Seminar on Law and Semiotics" at the Pennsylvania State University's Law School. Initial experiences and student papers have been published in an earlier volume on that subject.[1] This book provides sufficient materials for other 'Law & Semiotics' courses in relevant institutions.

The focus of this book is perhaps unexpected or even surprising. The issue is not how lawyers learn semiotics or are taught to apply semiotic subtleties in their legal practices. They already know the basics of what could be called semiotics and apply them within the strictly determined boundaries of their legal discourse. Molière's Mr. Jourdain was not aware that he 'spoke prose', lawyers as well as law students are not aware how studying law equals to learn speaking semiotics. There is consequently less need for lawyers to acquire additional knowledge called 'semiotic' as there is a strong need to enhance and intensify awareness of the semiotic dimensions in legal handiwork. So listening to and reflecting upon what the Godfathers of semiotics offer could assist lawyers and law students to focus on what their self-understanding and practice requires. Such an exercise in self-understanding adds a level of rigor to the work of making meaning within the law-world in accordance with its logic, and the lawyer's role as interpretant, symbol, and sign. Lawyers sensitive to the semiotic foundations of their work come to see and understand what they are told to do *differently*—a difference that will ultimately determine the face of law in modern society.

As may be fitting for a book touching on semiotics and law, this study is organized in four parts. The chapters are tightly integrated into a whole, but each might be read independently; the same is true of their parts and paragraphs. Each stands alone yet also closely intertwined with the others. Part I, entitled "Face-to-face with Legal Semiotics" (itself a semiotic play on meanings better understood after reading Chaps. 5 and 12) serves as a foundation. Chapter 1 introduces the reader to the idea of semiotics in general and legal semiotics in particular. It also introduces the major actors and shapers of the field. Chapter 2 then delves into the heart of the matter—signs.

Part II, entitled "Godfathers of Semiotics", then introduces to the development of the strains of thinking that together now define semiotics. Chapter 3 focuses on the Americans, Charles Sanders Peirce, Roberta Kevelson, including the pragmatics of legal semiotics. Chapters 4 and 5 then consider de Saussure, Greimas, and European approaches to the ordering of meaning. The important concept of layering and boundaries, through the semiotic square, is also considered. Lastly, Chap. 6 looks to

---

[1] Jan M.Broekman & Francis J. Mootz III (Eds): *The Semiotics of Law in Legal Education*, Springer 2011. See also: Jan M. Broekman & Anne Wagner (Eds): *Prospects of Legal Semiotics*, Springer 2010.

the psychology of semiotics through the thought of Lacan. Language, the principal currency of the lawyer comes into its own here as well the idea of the delirium of the self is the particular object of this chapter. Chapter 7 amalgamates our semiotic Godfathers through the medium of language.

Part III, entitled "Jurisprudence and Legal Semiotics", then turns to the business of legal semiotics. Chapters 8 and 9 look into the connection between legal theory and semiotics. It starts with a discussion of the origins of legal semiotics. It then considers semiotics theory and the practice of law. It ends with Chap. 10 considering the relationship between legal semiotics and the critical legal studies movement in the United States. Chapter 11 then looks into the application of these insights, considering first the self, and the state in the organization of meaning, and then in Chap. 12 turning to the semiotics of politics between persons and things. The object of the latter is to consider the evolution of semiotic worlds of law beyond the state. It considers the law and semiotics of this new world of meaning. Its central focus is on the construction of legal meaning around the object–symbol embodied in the corporation. Chapter 13 then turns to structuralism. The possibility of multiple structures for framing meaning, existing together and apart (the state and the corporation within globalization) provides the opening for a reconsideration of structuralism as a foundation of law systems and the production of meaning.

Part IV, entitled "Doing and Saying Legal Semiotics," then ties together strands of legal semiotics. Chapters 14, 15 and 16 focuses on the specifics of "doing" and "saying" in legal semiotics. That requires a close look at the semiosis of the lawyer's toolkit—text, names, and meaning relationships. The Socratic discussion of Cratylus is central to this discussion. Lastly, Chap. 17 touches on the unpredictable in meaning. The focus is on Fortuna/Tyche and its role in legal discourse and the production of meaning and structure in law, and brings us back full circle to the essence of the semiotic project in law. Chapter 18 then concludes the study, providing a vocabulary of semiotic terms and a bibliography.

Together, the materials in this book provide a structure for understanding and exploring the semiotic character of law and law systems. Cultivating a deep understanding for the ways in which lawyers make meaning—the way in which they help make the world and are made, in turn by the world they create, can provide a basis for consciously engaging in the work of the law and in the production of meaning.

But beyond that, the object of semiotics in law is to provide a space to understand the larger frameworks within which lawyers operate on meaning. That task goes to utility and efficiency. A useful lawyer is one that is conscious of his/her role, and of the limits of that role. But the efficient lawyer is also the one conscious of the ways in which that role must be necessarily subverted through the application of forms of meaning that are at once a sign of fidelity to the structures of the legal system within which she operates and at the same time an effort to remake it. The lawyer, who questions, seeks to extend or to narrow precedent, the lawyer who works with administrative agencies on the interpretation of regulations, or who works on the making of statutory texts—these are all examples of the lawyer as a semiotician.

Contents

Part I
Face-to-Face with Legal Semiotics

Chapter 1
Semiotics: A Fresh Start for Law

"I Was an Under-Age Semiotician", Steven Johnson writes in his October 2011 article for *The New York Times Book Review.* How could he? Did he know, and does he know today, what semiotics means? The word comes from the Greek *seme* for 'sign', so that *sem*iotics should be understood as "the science of signs", which always comes with parallels like symbols, meanings or significations. The concept is mentioned in the Jeffrey Eugenides 2011 novel *The Marriage Plot*[1] and functions there *as a sign* in the novel. The novel recaptures the spirit of US Universities in the early 1980s, in particular the struggle to better understand and firmly fixate a youthful self. The novel does not unveil much about that sign concept; a sign is in the novel little more than an element of western culture in the final days of structuralism, existentialism, phenomenology, deconstructionism in the 1980s of the last century, as many reviewers skillfully highlight.[2] Though the students in the semiotics seminar at the foundation of *The Marriage* Plot were English majors in humanities programs—they were by no means law students—they incarnate the three-part relationship at the heart of meaning.

All that is reflected in the novel's title. The plot thrives on *love in the light of semiotics* as understood during the 1980s and the philosophical question about its true meaning. Is love more than or different from a construct of the human mind, to which we assign psychic values we cannot overcome? The title bears the expression *plot* not by accident. A *plot* is a story element and equals a fable, an argument, a design, a motif, and is sometimes conceived as the ultimate *deus ex machina.* Is love plotted as an intrigue, a future or a maneuver? If marriage and love have anything to do with each other, is that the result of a plot, or the construction of a couple within the coordinates of a cultural pattern? No wonder that Roland Barthes' 1977 *A Lover's Discourse* plays an eminent role in the book: if being in love, or being married is solely an idea engendered by your mind, then you can liberate yourself from its tyranny or fascination and regard marriage as an issue for lawyers! No wonder that

[1] Jeffrey Eugenides: *The Marriage Plot*, New York 2011.

[2] Consider for example, Sam Sacks: "Sense & Semiotics" in *The Wall Street Journal,* Oct. 8/9 2011, W. Deresiewicz: "The Graduates", Steven Johnson: "I Was an Under-Age Semiotician" in *The New York Times Book Review*, Oct. 16, 2011 or Michael Greenberg: "The Mania of Love" in *The New York Review of Books*, Nov. 2011.

J. M. Broekman, L. Catà Backer, *Lawyers Making Meaning*,
DOI 10.1007/978-94-007-5458-4_1, © Springer Science+Business Media Dordrecht 2013

the Dutch translation of Eugenides' novel leaves the word *plot* out and simply titles *Huwelijk* (Marriage) and the German follows suit with *Die Liebeshandlung* (The Act of Love). The issue remains untouched in those titles, whereas the Spanish as well as the Italian translation write correctly *La Trama del Matrimonio* (The Marriage 'Plot', or 'Intrigue'). The *plot* is the semiotic hinge which gives the novel its widely spread attention; it emphasizes the dynamics and power of the human mind and its constructs and can relate semiotic insights dated some forty years ago with recent insights, not in literature but this time in law.

Flanked by fashionable interpretations of Derrida's texts and Parisian structuralism, the English major students were taught to understand *life as a text*: poems, novels, *belles letters* i.e. 'literature' in its entirety functioned as a representation of life within a multitude of cultural phenomena. Signs, a major component of semiotics, provided a pathway from the reduction of flesh as text to its abstraction as sign. Semiotics itself was the ultimate abstraction of meaning, in which the interpretant sought a distilled and denatured object from out of which to construct a sign.

> Semiotics . . . drew a line; it created an elect; it was sophisticated and Continental, it dealt with provocative subjects, with torture, sadism, hermaphroditism—with sex and power. (. . .) If Restoration drama was getting you down, . . . there was another option. You could sign up for Semiotics 211 and find out what everyone else was talking about[3].

Signs, in this sense, were *not* the objects to focus, and law was *not* at the horizon. Law and politics is a far more recent development; legal practices and their political implications (both the result of meaning making by specific professionals) are not included if one reflects upon the essence of one's life with an eye on bookmarks! Remembering the fads of those years, its components dated back to Levi Strauss, Foucault, Derrida, eventually Husserl or Heidegger, the US philosopher Peirce, or the Swiss linguist Ferdinand De Saussure, perhaps in our days Umberto Eco.

Traces of deconstructionism or structuralism can still surface in literary texts, but they do not play a leading role anymore. But the problem of meaning remains critically important, and semiotics serves that inquiry well. So the question remains what semiotics has to do with law, and in particular with a legal education program in the second decade of the twenty-first century? The answer lies in the changing, and to some large extent, the expanding character of law; as law moved from in the world to a position where it makes the world, the problem of meaning becomes critical. Consider marriage. The step from marriage as a religious bond incarnating notions of love to a civilian bond providing a space for the state in the marriage bed was made exemplary in the Napoleonic Code, 1804—a Code that confirmed the triumph of legal thinking about social order: marriage is a contract between partners, which

---

[3] See: Jeffrey Eugenides: *The Marriage Plot*, New York 2011, p. 24 and Sam Sacks: "Sense & Semiotics" in *The Wall Street Journal,* Oct 8/9 2011, W. Deresiewicz: "The Graduates", and Steven Johnson "I Was an Under-Age Semiotician" in *The New York Times Book Review*, Oct 16, 2011. Eugenides, together with authors like Franzen or Wallace, belongs to a generation of recent writers that has been educated in semiotics, deconstructionism and related Foucaultian and Derridian subtleties, which put basic ideas about writing, reading, text or authorial emotions in perspective.

close that contract in freedom. Not lovers, but bearers of rights and duties marry! Even in interrelations between Common Law and Sharia Law, the issue is important. In *Zawahiri v. Alwattar* (No. 07AP-925), a US Court held that the Muslim marriage contract, if understood to embody a prenuptial agreement, was not enforceable; however, the court also held that a Muslim marriage contract could be enforceable as a simple contract. What is fable, or construct of the human mind, or language and meaning made socially effective—and what is nature beyond the human construct? The lawyers' meaning-making capacity decides!

A *first* semiotic insight that forms a possible foundation for tracking changes from literature to law is that each fable, fiction, argument or motif functions as a source of meaning and an originator of significations. They should mainly be accepted, appropriated and made come true by means of rule following, as Anglo-Saxon legal theory emphasizes. Any founding norm is in essence *a semiotic power, which is not recognized as such in legal practice*. The meaning-making power in a lawyer's handwork thus remains in the dark. Indeed, lawyers do not relate to what semiotics unfolds.

A *second* semiotic insight is, that legal theory does not display semiotic sensitivity: concepts such as meaning, sign and signification remain in legal theory, legal philosophy and mostly in general jurisprudence subordinated to rules and/or principles. Traffic lights are an example here: a red traffic light is a *signal* to stop in conformity with rules, and there are resemblances between command and social order—a semiotic issue in its own right. Meanings of the red traffic light are narrated by lawyers during the performance of their legal practice and are then offered to the Court as a fact—not as a fable or a fiction. The rhetoric of behavior can depend upon rules and appear as rule-following, but never without a wider linguistic basis of human conduct: language, speech, verbal as well as non-verbal communication are indispensable for rules to be in effect. Legal meanings always emerge in a discourse, which expresses culture as human artifice par excellence.

The two insights show that legal education on both sides of the Atlantic needs to be completed with knowledge and understanding of semiotics in law and legal discourse. However, the step from (English) literature to semiotics of law in legal education is not made until now. Yet, the question remains what semiotics has to do with law, and in particular with a legal education program in the second decade of the twenty-first century[4].

Long before the semiotic question in law became recognized, the question was at home in medicine[5]. Galen of Pergamos, the eminent Roman physician of Greek origin emphasized that the human body emits *signs* and produces specific *tokens* with regard to its health and wellbeing. Physicians have to read them, and create their diagnosis and therapy accordingly. Reading and interpreting were already in that period a necessary performance of each physician. "The principal SEMEIOTIKOS for

[4] Jan M. Broekman & Francis J. Mootz III (Eds): *The Semiotics of Law in Legal Education*, Op. Cit., 2011.

[5] See: Thomas Sebeok: "Galen in Medical Semiotics" in: *Global Semiotics,* Indiana UP, 2001, p. 44 f.

classical philosophers was thus the physician seeking to determine a hidden disease in order to apply a cure", Clark concludes[6]. They persist in law today: clients provide narratives about everyday life occurrences, which have to be read and interpreted by lawyers. Client stories and lawyers' activities belong to a process of encoding and decoding a human environment. Many meanings from medicine and law shape our material and spiritual landscape, draw lines and mark languages, so that information about how we relate to each other, our environment and manners to understand reality, constantly refer to such meanings. Are lawyers our contemporary SEMEIOTIKO?

Semiotics

Semiotics in the context of law gives way to at least four aspects:

(a) *Signs* are abundantly present in law and legal discourse but law in itself is also a specific and outstanding *sign* in society;
(b) Rather than a *thing* law is a social *process* in its own right—it shows how a process can also possess *sign* character;
(c) This *process* is an ensemble of preconditions or prescripts about how lawyers have to act and to think, but it shows in addition most clearly how lawyers *make meaning*;
(d) The *freshness* of this perspective of law and the activity of lawyers was already clear in the 1930s when Charles Morris introduced the concept of "legal discourse" as a notation for "law" and as an opening of law for semiotic views.

Since Morris' days *freshness* has been understood as a virtue. One can hardly escape fresh meaning; one finds many authors claiming to develop a fresh look at law. The case of Herbert L. Hart in his well-known "The Concept of Law" impresses in this regard. The book served as the foundation of the legal education of an entire generation UK law students; it was mentioned in a blog of Lawrence Solum as "the most important work of legal theory in the twentieth century". He wrote sixty pages in his famous book to expose some of the most important features of a legal system, which determine the major properties of law. But those were based on one of the preferred features of Anglo-Saxon legal literature: law as based on an original 'command' from either a Divine or a human authority. His book became in hindsight famous for what came *after* those sixty pages: the "fresh start". This would set us free from the fable of an original speech act, the *command* as a foundational norm that works as a *terra nova*. That move has an important meaning: it makes us witness the fact that "the simple model of law as the sovereign's coercive orders failed to reproduce some of the salient features of a legal system ... The root cause of the failure is that they do not include ... the idea of a rule, without which we cannot hope to elucidate even the most elementary forms of law"[7]. There are various reasons

[6] D.S. Clarke: *Principles of Semiotic*, London/New York 1987, p. 13.

[7] H.L.A, Hart: *The Concept of Law,* [2nd Ed.] Oxford UP 1994. p. 79 f.

to appreciate this turn, which leads Hart to his distinction between primary and secondary rules in legal theory, i.e. between rules of conduct and power conferring rules: rules about how to make and manage rules of conduct. But what has this to do with semiotics in law and legal discourse?

A *first* semiotic insight is that each fable, fiction or foundational thought functions as a dominant source of meaning and originator of significations. They should mainly be accepted, appropriated and made come true by means of rule following, as Anglo-Saxon legal theory emphasizes. Any founding norm is in essence *a semiotic power, which is not recognized as such in legal practice*, despite Hart's secondary rules. The argument in legal practice is, that 'facts are as they are' and the world of facts 'is not made by lawyers who only have to judge what is unfolding before their eyes'. Lawyers are *not* face-to-face with semiotics, because it seems more appropriate *not* to cultivate awareness about the multiplicity of meanings inherent to the "law-job", as Llewellyn wrote 1941 in his "My Philosophy of Law", and later describes as how the law's mood is too craft-conscious and the need for the clean line too great for the renovation to smell of revolution or, indeed, of campaigning reform. The semiotic potentiality of law as well as its meaning-making power implied in a lawyer's handwork thus remains in the dark. Indeed, lawyers do not relate to what semiotics unfolds.

There is *secondly* a need to make another fresh start *after* Hart's *first* fresh start! How do we have to understand that? Hart displays no semiotic sensitivity: concepts such as meaning, sign and signification remain subordinated to rules or principles. Traffic lights are an example here: Hart underlines that a red traffic light is a *signal* to stop in conformity with rules. But there are resemblances between command and social order—an unrecognized semiotic theme in its own right. Meanings of the red traffic light are narrated during performances of legal practices, and are then offered as a fact—not as a fable or a fiction. The rhetoric of a 'fresh start' is fascinating but in the light of legal semiotics not convincing. Behavior can depend upon rules and appear as rule-following, but never without a wider linguistic basis of human conduct: language, speech, verbal as well as non-verbal communication are indispensable for rules to be in effect. That is equally true for his new start: legal meanings do always emerge in a discourse, which is the necessary context of featuring the interplay of primary and secondary rules. Both types of rules express culture as human artifice par excellence. His emphasis on rules shows the unrealized opening to *a real fresh start*: the recognition and understanding of semiotic dimensions in law.

Semiotics focuses on signs and satellites of signs such as symbols, directives, rules and the like—altogether components, which *make* legal meaning. Legal semiotics received the status it has today during the last decades of the twentieth century at Penn State University Berks Campus, where Roberta Kevelson established the Penn State Center for Semiotic Research in Law, Government and Politics. She was deeply involved in the philosophy of Charles Sanders Peirce and laid the foundations for legal semiotics in the US and abroad with many publications on the theme. The law schools produced another, more doctrinally connected, vein in the last decade of that century.[8] The imaginative recognition of similarity and difference in seemingly disparate areas of law has always been the mark of the skilled lawyer. But legal semiotics goes beyond the ordinary lawyer's tools. It systematizes and organizes the process of discovery in legal analysis."[9]

Semiotics focuses on signs and satellites of signs such as symbols, directives, rules and the like—altogether components, which *make* legal meaning. Meaning is made legally valid and accepted by institutional approval and checking. This is the foundation for the "=" in the formula "teaching law = teaching semiotics". As Jack Balkin explained:

> The legal semiotician is interested in legal ideology, and she sees the way that people argue for moral and legal positions as central to this study. Rather than viewing ideology as a smokescreen for illicit motivation, the legal semiotician takes the language of the law very seriously indeed. For her, ideology is constituted in part by the very patterns of argument and factual characterization that persons within the legal culture adopt. (Jack M. Balkin: "The Promise of Legal Semiotics," Op. Cit, p. 1831, 1842.)

But it is now necessary to move beyond the obsession with doctrine and politics that have tended to constrain a lawyer's efforts to transfigure critical legal studies into legal semiotics. It is necessary to start from semiotics and progress into law, as Roberta Kevelson suggested, than to squeeze a semiotic sensitivity into a doctrinal construct that seeks methodologies to confirm its own prejudices and ideologies.

Legal Semiotics

One could conclude at first glance, that *law* is an important *area of application* for semiotic insight in signs and symbols. That application would then be incorporated in legal practice. At the initiative of Kevelson and many others, semiotics of law started its development with this intuition. But several issues widen that theme considerably and allow for new formulations today.

(1) Lawyers perform insightful and well-informed operations with signs and symbols when they *practice* law, without unveiling why, how, in what (textual) forms and where they do so! They characterize their activities not as semiotics, but as legal science, legal practice or legal theory. But below the surface of law and legal texts are semiotic operations at work. Their discovery completes the legal handwork in more than one way.

(2) Lawyers tend to neglect semiotics because of their legal attitude or professional ideology, which refers in the first place to their own institutionally protected understanding and maintenance of what is called 'law'. Judith Shklar underlined in her 1964 study on *Legalism* how "Modern legal theory would be incomprehensible if it were forgotten that its creators are themselves lawyers and that professional habits of mind exercise a real influence upon them...". And her more probing phrase is

---

[8] Jeremy Paul: "The Politics of Legal Semiotics," 69 *Texas L. Rev.* 1779 (1991).

[9] Jack M. Balkin: "The Promise of Legal Semiotics," 69 *U. Texas L. Rev.* 1831, 1841 (1991).

still valid in our days: "Law is endowed with its own discrete, integral history, its own 'science', and its own values, which are all treated as a single 'block' sealed off from general social history, from general social theory, from politics, and from morality"[10]. The question for future developments in law and semiotics is, how the latter breaks this ideological fortress down so that it causes awareness about how law is necessarily involved in a process of enforcing inescapable legal forms upon society.

(3) Thought patterns of legal practices seem to constitute legal discourse and its social acceptability. Law's practice determines in that case *what is law* and what is *correctly defined* as legal. If indeed practice dominates the definition of law, then the creation of legal meanings is also the result of practices, which constitute legal discourse. Let us not forget that legal practitioners emphasize the *applicative nature of law* and disregard any legal science or theory without those practical dimensions. Insight in the semiotic dimensions of law will, however, not lead to accept semiotics as exclusively a matter of law's practices.

(4) *Semiotics and Legal Practice* is a theme of considerable importance for each fragment of knowledge pertaining to law. Legal signs, symbols and meanings are materials for engendering legal knowledge in a practice-directed sense. The expression "legal semiotics" becomes pleonastic: issues managed by lawyers are *semiotic* because they bear the meaning of *legal* facts.

(5) *Defining legal semiotics* is not a simple theoretical or scientific act. Various dimensions come to the fore. The defining involves (a) *specific meanings* which lawyers create to establish social order, (b) a *general view on law*—especially the dynamics of law—and (c) a defining of law which relates importantly with *legal practice*, so that (d) *hermeneutic* dimensions appear important, including the fine tuning of justice and wisdom, and makes us consider (e) whether *truly measured* legal activity supports the technical meanings law instills in daily life.

A more profound insight into these dynamics of managing "meaning in law" suggests that one should differentiate between semiotics *in* law as exercised by lawyers, and semiotics *of* law, which is in the hands of linguists, philosophers, or politicians.

Semiotics and Communication

Semiotics became appreciated during the second half of the twentieth century as one of the most sophisticated and complex theories of human communication, even in the shadows of deconstructionism or structuralism. That appreciation has, however, some serious implications in the case of *legal* semiotics. Apart from its legal/technical vocabulary and its doctrine-ridden engineering, law is generally recognized as a special means to communicate in a specific social order and with limited goals. But that recognition requires a special involvement of philosophical nature: one must rely upon socio-political conditions, which in particular enable citizens to enhance their *power of expression* to achieve social order. In doing so, one must be aware of how

[10] Judith Shklar: *Legalism. Law, Morals, and Political Trials*. Harvard UP 1986(2), p. 3

all language acts presuppose more than a simple speaker-hearer relation. The *subject* position in speech act a context is consequently far more complex than the singular concept of a speaker or hearer suggests. And the position of a subject in society, in the form of *citizenship* as created in western culture by law and state, is as a consequence by no means a simple parallel. Law on the one hand and semiotics on the other may originally have very different appreciations of the position of subject and citizen today. How do they come together in the approach to social reality in the form of legal semiotics? If semiotics is the word that indicates a trendy attitude of the 1970s and 1980s, its essence is indeed in the observation that meaning is never an objective fact but that all meanings show our lives as having the format of to the mental and cultural situation we live in. Many nuances of the personages in Eugenides' *The Marriage Plot* show how difficult it is to accept this discovery. The novel is not about the type of semiotics we have in mind when we speak about "legal semiotics" or "law-and-semiotics". It is about the psychological costly and energy devouring attempts we all must make to cope with existing, fixated, inherited meanings. These are engendered in our education so that we are expected to live with them. That expectation is in our age perhaps the foundational norm of occidental citizenship.

Lawyers must be aware that words carry forever and a day meanings, which *are* 'meanings' because they are by definition destined to others. To find meaning in the self alone is in this sense meaningless (without meaning) precisely because it is neither communicated nor performed. Even to reference the self requires a context within which the self is identified among others, that is a referent (an other). Among these *others* are those who mark spoken and documented words of law. That is a cornerstone of the legal semiotic context: since all words include the presence of *others* (other people, other individuals, other human beings), also words of law must do so in order to not pervert their word-character. Behaviors in law and legal discourse are apparently not limited to authoritarian features of words and meanings, or to what philosophers already in the seventeenth century evocated as 'command'. To say for instance, that 'command' is a source of law implies that law is based on predominantly vertical human relations. But vertical dimensions of social relations seem a form of *power* and not an appropriate means of human communication—not even appropriate in law!

Any traditional definition of semiotics includes the science of *signs* and *symbols*, its *auditorium* (individuals, groups and social institutions) and its *logic*. One should, however, notice how semiotics underlines the importance of social issues even in the context of more abstract linguistic views. Peirce became for instance influential in legal semiotics through defining the *semiotics*-project already in 1907 as determined by a specific triad of *signs*, their *object* and their *interpretants*; this tri-relative influence, as he said, not being in any way resolvable into actions between pairs. The triad consolidates how relating signs and their object is never without a third party, named: "the Other". None of the actual encompassing social issues such as citizenship, the political implications of transgressing the borderlines between private- and public money, the global desire for joint decision-making, the diverse policies pertaining to environmental problems are entirely without legal semiotic relevance. Yet none of this can be understood within semiotics until the focus moved from individual triadic relations to systems of such relations. It is to that project that Roberta Kevelson's contributions were foundationally important.

Roberta Kevelson

Roberta Kevelson was inspired to conclude that modern semiotics analyzes structures of communication as a *complex system of sign relationships*. Law as a system, she suggests, should be recognized as an important branch of general semiology. *Communicating in terms of law means communicating with/within law as a system of signs*. That idea is a major contribution to perceive law as a social process: not only subjects, and others understood as 'other subjects' are involved, but also the systemic features of law as laid down and studied in legal science and doctrine. A problem to grasp this complexity—at the origin of legal semiotics—is, whether communication *with* law does or does not mean communication *within* law. "Is there law outside law?"—Luhmann questioned as a central issue of any legal theory. Legal rhetoric as well as law's argumentation could be understood as examples for how semiotics function in a legal system. The idea that semiotics *in* legal discourse also counts for semiotics *of* legal discourse is, however, problematic and seldom explicitly formulated.

Among Kevelson's published works are: *High Fives; The Inverted Pyramid; The Law as the System of Signs* and, possibly her most significant work: *Peirce and the Mark of the Gryphon*. She never wrote jurisprudential work, and not many legal semioticians after her did so. After her death in 1998, legal semiotics remained a theme for philosophers, sociologists, linguists and some legal theorists but it did not directly enter jurisprudence, legal practice or legal education to any appreciable degree.[11] At best it was sometimes viewed as an adjunct to the critical legal studies movement in American academic circles or as an esoteric form of jurisprudential philosophy best left to Europeans.[12] This aggravates the difficulties in legal education around the 'Law & Semiotics' theme[13] and moved Kevelson, and her legal semiotics project as such, to the academic sidelines. Her approach to legal semiotics shows the tendency to link human and natural sciences, mind and brain, human reality and the virtual. Thomas A. Sebeok's widely read 2001 *Global Semiotics* forms an example of that tendency. The book parallels in spirit but not in proportion his 1994 *Encyclopedic Dictionary* with 380 contributions from 132 authors. A close reading of his attempt to envisage semiotics on a global scale shows, however, that specific fields of semiotic exploration and application were not appropriately represented. Among these is legal semiotics.

[11] Consider Bernard S. Jackson: *Semiotics and Legal Theory* (Liverpool, UK: Deborah Charles Pub, 1997) (emphasis of philosophy and ethics over law).

[12] For example, Duncan Kennedy: "A Semiotics of Legal Argument," 42 *Syracuse Law Review* 75 (1991) (an American project of radicalizing legal realism).

[13] Jan M. Broekman & William A. Pencak: "Lawyers Making Meaning: The Roberta Kevelson Seminar on Law and Semiotic" *IJSL*, Vol. 22, No. 1, 2009.

Sebeok emphasized in his global overview *medicine* rather than *law* as an exemplary semiotic discourse—an issue Kevelson developed whilst favoring legal discourse. In contrast to Kevelson, he treats culture as a matter of consciousness and cognition rather than of politics and social order. It interests how his assessment of semiotics in global perspective includes *woman in semiotics*. He mentions in the first place Lady Victoria Welby, and then three North American pioneers: Susanne K. Langer, Margaret Mead and Ethel M. Albert, without a word about Roberta Kevelson. She laid the foundations for *legal* semiotics in the US and abroad with many publications in the Philosophy Department of Penn State University, in particular *The Law as a System of Signs* (1988). The international journal that exists since that very same year under the name *The International Journal for the Semiotics of Law* is of such a legal-semiotic importance that it should already in 2001 be incorporated in a book on global perspectives published in that year—but it was not! Is legal semiotics appreciated as a niche activity?

Legal semiotics studies all legal areas and disciplines on a global scale, as one concludes from the global map of legal systems. Common Law and Civil Law cover a large number of citizens living in either system; they function less and less separately (as often suggested in the juridical discipline named 'comparative law') but reinforce each other by means of creating *mixed* legal systems. The latter closely fit to a great variety of cultural and socio-political circumstances, and are appropriate in view of the many dimensions of growth around the globe. When paying attention not only to debates among lawyers but also to discussions of linguists, neurologists and other scientists about the appropriate definition of semiotics, we should evaluate all semiotic activity as an *ongoing debate* and not a debate on one particular denomination. Today, more and more studies in semiotics unfold new perspectives in human sciences, medicine and biology as well as in new visions on virtual dimensions and nanotechnology, so that the *basso continuo* of semiotics becomes more important in our society[14]. They reach from foundational interpretations of the '*sign*' towards a general theory of *meaning*. The latter is of primordial relevance for any theory of knowledge in the midst of newly established sciences.

Jourdain's Bewilderment

Can we, and do we indeed enter a world, which is made like a lawyer's world? And in this lawyer made world, is the lawyer made also, as the position of world and lawyer shifting in the process of making and being made? Consider in that context the personal awareness of a lawyer and the question whether he is or is not prepared to understand his professional activity and his thought patterns in a semiotic sense. Can

[14] Several of these are impressively represented in the "Semiotics Institute Online" at projects.chass.utoronto.ca/semiotics/cyber.html.

he do that? Read a world famous fragment of the conversation between Monsieur Jourdain and his "The Philosophy Master", central figures in Molière's theatre piece *The Would-be Gentleman* (*Le Bourgeois Gentilhomme*) from 1670[15], which shows affinities to a lawyer—not only a lawyer of his days, but in particular of ours. Their words should be studied carefully and go as follows—they report a discovery each of us should make! A "fresh start" could be in a bewildering discovery about our self, the language we speak and the presuppositions we make come true!

M. Jourdain	. . . But now I'm going to tell you something in confidence. I am very much in love with a great lady of rank, and I want you to help me to write a little note, which I shall drop casually at her feet.
Philosophy Master	Very good.
M. Jourdain	I want it done in the most gallant style.
Philosophy Master	I understand. Do you wish to write to her in verse?
M. Jourdain	Oh no. Not in verse.
Philosophy Master	You want just prose.
M. Jourdain	No. I don't want either verse or prose.
Philosophy Master	But it must be one or the other.
M. Jourdain	Why?
Philosophy Master	Because, Sir, there are only two ways of expressing oneself, in prose or verse.
M. Jourdain	There's nothing except prose or verse?
Philosophy Master	No, Sir. Whatever is not prose is verse, and whatever is not verse is prose.
M. Jourdain	What is ordinary speech then?
Philosophy Master	Prose.
M. Jourdain	What! When I say: 'Nicole, fetch me my slippers, and give me my nightcap', is that prose?
Philosophy Master	Yes, Sir.
M. Jourdain	Good Heavens! Then I have been speaking prose for more than forty years without knowing it. I couldn't be more grateful to you for teaching me that. Now what I want to put in the note is: 'Fair Marquise, your beauty makes me die of love.' But I want it said prettily, put in an elegant way.
Philosophy Master	You can say that the sparks from her eyes reduce your heart to ashes; that, because of her, you are suffering night and day the agonies of a. . .
M. Jourdain	No, no, no. I don't want any of that. I want only what I have just said: 'Fair Marquise, your beauty makes me die of love'.
Philosophy Master	But you must embroider it a bit.

[15] The comedy-ballet in five acts was performed in a room of the castle of Chambord in Touraine, France, on October 14, 1670. Molière himself played the role of M. Jourdain.

M. Jourdain	No, I tell you. I want nothing else in the note but just those words, but arranged in a smart and up-to-date way. Let me hear the various ways in which they can be put, so that I can choose which I like best.
Philosophy Master	Well, first of all you can put them as you have said: 'Fair Marquise, your beauty makes me die of love'; or you can say 'Of love makes me die, fair Marquise, your beauty'; or: 'Your beauty of love makes me, fair Marquise, die'; or: 'Die your beauty, fair Marquise, of love makes me'; or: 'Makes me your beauty die, fair Marquise, of love'.
M. Jourdain	But which is the best of all those?
Philosophy Master	The one you said: 'Fair Marquise, your beauty makes me die of love'.
M. Jourdain	Yet it was without studying. I did all that at the first go off. I thank you from the bottom of my heart. Please come again early tomorrow.
Philosophy Master	I won't fail.

Is Jourdain like a lawyer? Think about it: Jourdain as good as any lawyer depends on language and its possibilities of expression: no more, no less! And both want their words to achieve the best results. Mastering the language is a central issue of the life situation of both, and they regard language as the major instrument to achieve success. What is more: Jourdain wants to know all the rules that govern what he finally will say, write or declare—those rules have strictly to be followed, as each lawyers is prepared to do. And Jourdain gradually discovers that he does *not* know all dimensions and properties of his own speech. The desire to follow rules brings him to the discovery of the extreme limitations when using a language's means of expression. In his case, there are only two: 'prose' and 'poetry'—what else is there? Can one avoid prose? Can one avoid poetry? Or are the possibilities to qualify behaviors so limited? These questions lead us to the Philosophy Master, who guides Jourdain but only within the discoursive space within Jourdain is willing to operate. Is Jourdain being made by the Philosophy Master or is the Philosophy Master made by Jourdain, with whom the Philosophy Master is playing (and mocking). All this throws another light on speech, action and meaning. Those problems are inherently a lawyer's problem and the central issue in legal education. Is *any* lawyer fully and technically correct aware that she speaks 'prose'?, Is the lawyer making prose or being made by it? This is semiotics speaking, constraining, making and connecting speech, action, meaning, consequence.

One should perhaps venture to say that 'practicing law IS practicing semiotics'! Emphasis is in that case on understanding how essential semiotics is in law. There is no lawyer or legal scholar who is not vaguely aware of that. Law is a discourse, which manages meaning. Signs, signals, symbols play a constitutive role in legal thought formation, legal decisions and jurisprudential approaches. Specific for law is, that its signs are only accepted if law proper has the power and the authority to define them.

Study Semiotics and Law

An introduction of legal semiotics is seldom in line with commonly accepted ground lines of legal education. The objects of study and reflection in legal education are different from semiotics; the attitude of the student who encounters the theme of semiotics differs considerably from the classical themes in legal education. Melina M. Zamora, underlining the rational and emotional complexities of participating in the 2009 Penn State Seminar on Law and Semiotics, writes in her opinion paper[16]:

> Semiotics in general and this class 'Law & Semiotics' in particular, have been very difficult for me to comprehend and understand. Most of the time this class has felt like someone is speaking Chinese, a foreign language, in which I do not even know how to say "hello". The reason I believe that it has been so difficult is because it has been so engrained in our heads as law students to accept legal rules from case book readings and from professor's teachings that I have never looked beyond these rules for a more complex understanding of the law. Because law school to begin with is intimidating and foreign to most incoming students, it is hard for them to imagine yet another "foreign language", an alternative way to look at the law.
>
> Prior to law school, most students never question the teachings of their professor. In schools, most students are taught to accept things the way the teacher presents them, instead of reaching for foundations and more complex meanings. Even in grade school, if the teacher tells you that this animal is a "cat," then children believe the teacher and accept that animal as a cat without searching for more complex meanings. Even as we grow older, we conform to a lot of laws without knowing really what we are complying with. Citizens of a community do not speed through town because it is against the law. Few citizens ever look deeper into, for instance, *why* it is against the law. Citizens must conform or else face the punishment of a speeding ticket.

When Roberta Kevelson was asked in 1996 why she had studied semiotics, believed in it and had been teaching it, she answered in a comparable pitch[17]:

> ... the greatest thing about semiotics is the recognition that we communicate not in a hierarchical fashion where an authority speaks downward but in a dialogic fashion among people who create a universe that is not finished, but open. What we take as law or a fixed judgment is always provisional. We are open to the world; the self is a dynamic sign in play that continually creates something genuinely new. Semiotics can keep freedom alive—it is experimental and anti-authoritarian; it is never under anyone's control; there are no masters or slaves, only equals in relationships.

Reflecting upon her own task as a university teacher, she said:

> I am not there to give students anything. I am there to interact and get them to know that the way we can interact is through an idea, which is something you hold on to at both ends.

The first line focuses on how encountering semiotics in law provokes a specific attitude and openness in communication, which puts in perspective the narrow sender/receiver framework in legal thinking and legal education, together with its

---

[16] Melina M. Zamora: "A Deeper Understanding of Law" in: *IJSL*, Vol. 23, No. 1, Op. Cit.: *Signs of Law*, (Broekman & Pencak, Eds) 2010.

[17] William A. Pencak: "A Conversation with Roberta Kevelson", in: Pencak & Lindgren (Eds): *New Approaches to Semiotics and the Human Sciences*, 1998.

institutional implications. Since meanings are always manifold, a viewpoint or fragment of knowledge is not a private property, and teaching or learning becomes an experience, which participants have in common, and not a linear transfer of facts[18]. A contrast with semiotics emerges because the place and situation of an author or speaker relates to a spoken or written text—together with the multiple discourses to which words, expressions and meaning belong. Richard Vanlandingham noticed in that context the institutional power of legal discourse, which could override legal semiotics, and wrote about legal texts, words, expressions and meanings, saying that[19]:

> ... even when a student believes that he or she understands the texts and therefore understands the signs, his or her understanding is still reliant on the interpretation as put forth by those with the institutional authority to give their interpretation the force of law. For until that interpretation by a judge is finally made, the lawyer cannot be sure if his understanding is correct, meaning it has the force of law. Even when someone who has the institutional authority to give texts the force of law puts a text forth, a lawyer still may not understand the text in the same manner as those who are institutionally authorized, have interpreted it. This isbecause, if the interpretation is put down in a text itself (such as in a statute) that text may be interpreted differently. And that is why lawyers charge by the hour.

"Law as a system of signs", Kevelson's expression, means already *before* it is involved in this or any other semiotic consideration, that law is envisaged as a language. What does that mean? "Law is a profession of words"—but the bridge from word to meaning is often in poor condition. Meaning is always and for everyone and in each different social setting a central issue, but how can lawyers focus on the study of meaning (as semiotics proposes) when they have to work with words (as the law professors initiate and guide)? This fact underlines the *system*-character of language (as made visible in traffic signs) and the *communicative* features of law (there is no society without "signs of law"). Has semiotics an answer to that question, law students will ask.

The question why law students should study semiotics is intriguing in all regards. There is no student of law who has to follow a mandatory course on legal semiotics and there is no US Bar Exam or EU Legal Education requirement that focuses on legal semiotics. Even in Courts is the expression unknown, so that legal semiotics seems an issue at considerable distance to normal legal life and its principles. However, law's language forms a special environment of which lawyers should be aware of: signs, symbols, meanings and doctrinal forms are most important elements of their language and the work to be performed. Students are taught to understand and to practice that language called 'law' through their study of jurisprudence, doctrines, judgments, precedents and cases, which function mostly as crucial names in society.

---

[18] Students often experience the AV component of the Penn State Dickinson School of Law education as no more than an instrument for linear transference of facts—how does one discuss and reach out to each other beyond the linearity of legal data and legal facts?

[19] Richard C. Vanlandingham: "'Signs of Law' in Student Perspective", *IJSL*, Vol. 23, No. 1, Vol. 23, No. 1: *Signs of Law*, (Broekman & Pencak, Eds) 2010.

To study law often is taken to mean: to study all building blocs of the legal discourse. Students must furthermore master legal writing, legal argumentation, understand the legal hierarchy and its function in discourse (as speech acts) as well as in society (as social institutions)—but all this remains vague and void without semiotic insight. Who cares, who knows or even understands this as long as legal instruments function well? A law student must indeed understand the complexity and plural structure of legal texts and law's discourse. Semiotics reaches beyond a law student's primal interest in acquiring new and effective legal instruments.

And why would lawyers study legal semiotics? Most certainly to leave one's naïveté behind and enjoy the complexity of human life and law! But that is a goal too far from legal practice. Experience how the expression 'legal semiotics' is *pleonastic* because it says that there is no law that does not manage meaning in context! This thus pertains to a lawyer's *self-understanding*: if she is a manager of meaning in the widest sense of the word, then she manages meanings of legal discourse with their place in society in general. Drawing on the writings of Charles Sanders Peirce, George Herbert Mead and others[20], one could argue that any *self*—particularly the 'self' of a lawyer or law student—should be understood as an internal conversation among a present self ("I") and another, most likely future self ("you") concerning a past self ("me"). So there is a mutually supportive relation between a self, the legal system, democracy and modern culture—an observation of utmost interest for any lawyer[21].

[20] See Norbert Wiley: *The Semiotic Self,* Chicago UP 1994, p. 18 f.

[21] Stephen Breyer: *Active Liberty. Interpreting Our Democratic Constitution,* New York 2005, wrote a clarifying text on that supportiveness.

Chapter 2
Signs, and Signs in Law

Law and semiotics seem worlds apart. The two embrace a different attitude, their practices unfold in a different spirit, and the goals of both discourses differ considerably. Yet *law and semiotics belong together*; the emphasis is on *signs* demonstrates this togetherness. A variety of arguments consider *the place and function of signs in law.* We refer to a scale that spans from abstract philosophical considerations to those who are immediately relevant for legal practice. The keywords of that scale are: the *concept of sign* itself, the importance of *culture*, signs as a power of *merging* law and semiotics, a *community* as precondition for signs, signs in *legal practice*, for example the Cf. citation as a sign in law, and the most needed expansion of knowledge in law.

What is a Sign?

We first consider some peculiarities pertaining to the concept of a *sign* in general. What is a sign? The question seems difficult to answer straightforwardly. There are at least four aspects worth noticing.

First: a sign is not a thing. Signs stand for objects or things, but the "stand for..." is predominant. A sign on itself is not a sign; there is always a context, a community, a language or at least another person needed to cause a sign to be a sign! Yet, we all talk about signs as if they were things. Dictionaries and encyclopedias do not give the information to prepare us for the surprises, which this concept has prepared for us. They provide descriptions about a sign *as if* it is an object, a thing to understand via fixed data and properties. A sign is in a Webster "that by which anything is shown, made known, or represented". It is thus presented to its readers as an expression, an action, a motion or a gesture, a symbol, an emblem, a standard or cognizance in a more general sense. All this does, however, not definitively cover the essence of a sign. We can only be alive when we accept the "as if" fable as the foundation for our thoughts and knowledge, our social contacts and languages: this is in harmony with the fictitious character of legal narratives. Legal fictions are as old as Western culture, Civil Law tells us.

Second, *every*thing can become a sign. Signs unfold amidst *all there is*—not in correspondence to the way *it is*, but rather as a *potential* for *what there is*. In each

J. M. Broekman, L. Catà Backer, *Lawyers Making Meaning*,
DOI 10.1007/978-94-007-5458-4_2, © Springer Science+Business Media Dordrecht 2013

process of becoming a sign is *the change from potentiality to reality* involved. That change is not a narration of 'what is' but on the contrary of 'what functions in a change'. The 'is' appears in this light as *a sign/name for change*. That has important semiotic consequences. We encounter the making of a particular meaning when we perform a speech act, which indicates an: 'that is'. That meaning functions as a prescript for, and not only as a description of our behavior, our thoughts and our actions. *The name:* 'is' functions in that case as a *sign*, which is decisive in semiotic perspective. It functions in a broader cultural view as a means-in-law, since lawyers tend to determine a 'what *is*' as their ultimate purpose: 'this *is* a breach of contract' or: 'this *is* voluntary manslaughter'. A confirmation of this insight is in the thought that there is no*thing* in life that is *not* embedded in what we notice as potentially significant, and here lays the foundation for the many ways in which meaning is generated in law. Peirce wrote 1885 in that context:

> A sign is in a conjoint relation to the thing denoted and to the mind. If this triple relation is not of a degenerate species, the sign is related to its object only in consequence of a mental association, and depend upon a habit. Such signs are always abstract and general, because habits are general rules to which the organism has become subjected. They are, for the most part, conventional or arbitrary. They include all general words, the main body of speech, and any mode of conveying a judgment.

So there 'are' no signs and there 'is' no meaning beyond an omnipresent energy of transformation. Semiotics is therefore in Peirce's view *a method,* which includes an *attitude* in view of the flow of life's dynamics, which in its turn regenerates the most essential signifying processes continuously.

Third, things *must act upon one another*—otherwise there is no meaning, no *no*thing. That means for semiotics: signs must be in a relation to other signs, sign systems, and eventually language in its entirety, to bear meaning. Meaning is the result of relations between elements, and those relations—not unlike human relations—are dynamic and differentiating, so that meaning will never be static, neither in social life nor in the sciences. That is essential, and the concept of a sign is only located in the midst of relations, in networks we say today. This tells us that meaning and sign never result from a soloing constitutive power of an individual subject.

Fourth, we should pay attention to two more aspects: (a) *before* a sign could be uttered it had already to be present in a human consciousness. So the thought is itself a sign and should itself find its utterance through encountering an ego in a previous event, and: (b) *after* a sign has been interpreted for a first time, it will remain in the consciousness of its interpreter, where it will also be a sign, which as a sign should have in its turn an interpreter, and so on. Hence another remark of Peirce, saying in 1903:

> "A sign is supposed to have an object or meaning, and also to determine an interpretant sign of the same object. It is convenient to speak as if the sign originated with an utterer and determined its interpretant in the mind of an interpreter." And ". . . every thought proper involves the idea of a triadic relation. For every thought proper involves the idea of a sign. Now a sign is a thing related to an object and determining in the interpreter an interpreting sign of the same object. It involves the relation between sign, interpreting sign, and object." (See Umberto Eco: *The Role of the Reader*, Indiana UP 1979, Ch. 7: "Peirce and the Semiotic Foundations of Openness".)

Signs, then, are both fixed and contingent—the fixity and contingency itself serves as a sign. Complexity and meaning arises from the inter-relations of aggregations of signs, their objects and the shifting community, which functions as the hotbed for interpretants around which signs arise. This is, in other words, an apt description of law and its system. Inter-relation speaks to communication, a point taken up next.

Communication

Speakers, voices, mediators, interpreters change position in their communication. All communication between human individuals depends on a sign-activity, which is embodied in what we call a speaker-interpreter relationship. Signs without an actual speaker or interpreter are by no means beyond human relation: they are often perceived as signals, symbols and the like. These are signs that (other) signs exist! Signs thus convey human intelligence—an intelligence that cannot otherwise be conveyed. This underlines the cultural character of semiotics and highlights legal semiotics as one of the most important features among them. Do not forget how legal cases and other constitutive elements of law's discourse and institution function as a main speaker in a modern society. Lacan characterized in that context law as a master discourse because of law's specific character perceivable in its discourse, texts and institutions.

It fascinates that Peirce was not the only thinker who underlined the specific meaning and function of signs, He was in agreement with highly esteemed colleagues like William James, but his ideas had also remarkable forerunners. The Italian philosopher Georgio Agamben[1] published in 2008 a study *on method* (not unlike Peirce), which referred to such a forerunner, named Paracelsus (1493–1541), a Renaissance physician, botanist, alchemist, astrologer, and general occultist. He wrote in Book 9 of his *De natura rerum* "Nichts ist ohn ein Zeichen" [nothing is without a sign]. Paracelsus argues how "nature does not release anything in which it has not marked what is to be found within that thing". Man can thus know by means of signs what has been marked in each thing. Signs reveal in this regard the qualities, forms and figures of that which is in them. Are lawyers for that very same reason fascinated by signs?

Culture, Law and Medicine

One remembers how medicine and semiotics were intertwined since the Ancient Greek, because one could not imagine symptoms of illness without noticing (even reading) its signs. And our medical practitioners followed until half a century ago a

[1] Georgio Agamben: *The Signature of all Things. On Method.* (Engl. Ed.) New York 2009.

course in *medical semiology*, which provided the basis for their diagnostic skills.[2] The medical attention for signs was in that ancient tradition accompanied by the philosophical and the linguistic—the three demonstrate that an interdisciplinary approach is an inherently feature of semiotics because of the universal function of the sign. Law and legal discourse have—in contrast to medicine—never incorporated a course on semiotics in legal education, although the relation between law and semiotics was and still is important.[3]

Roland Barthes mentioned in a 1985 essay that semiotics has been part of our occidental culture for a long time, and in particular in medicine. Signs were once used to direct troops in the battlefield, so that they apparently emerged beyond language. That was also the case in medicine: signs of the patient were not produced in a well-articulated language, but they became elements of a sign-related context, which had to make the understanding and treatment of an underlying illness possible. 'Semiotics' and 'illness defined by a clinical picture' unfolded a corresponding scientific basis, which was also the basis for medicine as a social institution. An illness was in that approach the expression of a scientific rather than an existential experience. Social problems in need of a legal solution are today in parallel with this change from existential to scientific experience. Ethics forms a field of intermediate understanding between law and medicine, and is therefore in constant danger to perform either in a purely scientific or in a purely existential spirit.

Signs, Symptoms, Names

A central theme is the relation between *sign* and *symptom*. The theme refers to the status of facts in medicine and law. Both are *institutional* discourses, and their facts are solely recognized as facts within discourses of their institutional frameworks. A symptom is generally understood as the form in which the illness presents itself—so what is the status of an illness when we ask 'are you ill?' What 'being' is involved here? That is also the form within which legal problems present themselves to lawyers, judges and courts—so what is the status of a legal issue as symptom? What is the relation between facts, as symptom, their aggregation (as sign) and their consequence (given a construction and consequence by the interpretant)? Foucault[4] often refers to symptoms as the form in which an illness or a social problem presents itself. However, medical and legal literature locates symptoms in the frame

[2] Roland Barthes: "Sémiologie et medicine", in: *L'aventure sémiologique*, Paris 1985, Jan M. Broekman: "Semiology and medical discourse" in; *Methodology and Science*, International Journal for the Empirical Study of the Foundations of Science and their Methodology, 1988, -Id.-: *Intertwinements of Law and Medicine*, Leuven UP 1996.

[3] Jan M. Broekman & Francis J. Mootz III (Eds): *The Semiotics of Law in Legal Education.* Springer 2011.

[4] Michel Foucault: *Naissance de la Clinique – Une Archéologie du regard medical.* Paris PUF 1963 (*The Birth of the Clinic*)

of *causality* and thus determines a symptom as the *cause* of an illness or a social/legal problem—a problematic determination in semiotic context.

Medical doctors often conclude that a symptom is in a given case not clear or even contradictory. This feeling is not alien to lawyers; they experience the same, which often is the source for their alerted attention for (legal) interpretation. Legal thought patterns coagulate with medical: the interpretation of the illness or the clinical picture is abandoned in favor of a contractual bond between doctor and patient. That leads every semiotic analysis into depth structures of speech, text and action, which are juridical in essence, as the 'bond' or 'contract' between physician and patient shows. The founding schema of such legal/medical knowledge is in this case: (1) there is a particular impression of an x, which (2) impresses a physician or another person who observes the patient, and this (3) refers to a particular some*thing* that forms the material basis for (4) the medical, the psychopathological or/and the scientific examination. It interests to observe how (1), (2) and (3) deliver scientific certainty and the justification for (4). Be aware: there is a circular relationship between (1), (2) and (3) on the one hand and (4) on the other, since medical practice is unthinkable without the first three steps. The legal analogue follows a similar path. A bundle of facts is discovered as privileged by lawyers who observe these facts and derive a particular something from them that forms a basis for their examination and treatment. Again circularity, since legal practice is incomprehensible in the absence of the excavation of facts, their investment in symbol and the interpretation of the complex of object and symbol within a system that is itself a cluster of pathways (legal rules and processes) of object-symbol interpretation.

However, in cases of unclear symptoms in law and/or medicine, facts do not always receive full attention for their sign-function. It shows how fundamental *the transition from facts to signs* is for law and medicine, if not for lawyers. Barthes formulates: " (. . .) the confusion of symptoms (. . .) does not mean that there is an obscurity of signs, but on the contrary that the obscurity of facts did not yet reach the nature of signs." That definition is important, because if she is correct, "it says that the word 'symptom' did not immediately express the idea of signification, whereas the connotation of that word in its metaphorical sense already did—when we speak metaphorically of a 'symptom' we are already in the field of semantics."[5]

Does illness, or socio-legal conflict (or for that matter: love) ever "reach the high nature of a sign"? It seems difficult to answer straightforwardly. First, there are the circumstances, but then there is the culture and then there is the mirror stage in the development of each of us, and finally there is the metaphysical embedding of it all. Indeed, the circumstances are always there. They are never totally clear, because there are concealed issues in each situation so that we live in parts and in a light that hardly breaks through darkness, leaving shadows that never completely disappear. We encounter these features in Eugenides' novel, which focuses on the sign-symptom issue, so typical for most human circumstances.

---

[5] Roland Barthes: *Sémiologie et Medicine,* Op. Cit., p. 275 f.

Barthes' considerations on the latter are by no means irrelevant. They face the interpretation of signs in all inter-human situations. In order to be someone somewhere, one has always to read signs—however, the character of the intertwinements of sign and symptom is a matter of concern. Leonard, a major personage in the novel, is manic-depressive. When the depression is flooding once again, he ends his relationship with Madeleine who does not know or suspect anything about his genetic predisposition. When studying semiotics, one would conclude that his symptoms did for her not even become a sign! She lived with the idea that Leonard enjoyed himself elsewhere with someone else although he was in a psychiatric hospital. Objectivity is apparently beyond any circumstance. Barthes, as well as the Eugenides novel, shows us that this determines even (romantic) love! Barthes' 1977 book plays a crucial role in the minds of 1980 US University students, circles of broken-hearted youngsters. His words echoed all around among the semio-grads of those days[6]: in love, I am a fool, I even cannot say that because I cannot de-double my own image; I am crazy in my own eyes, senseless when I talk about it to others: "every lover is mad, we are told. But can we imagine a madman in love?"[7] Those ideas were captivated without understanding their semiotic weight. They show how symptoms of a state of mind are like all other symptoms: once they become a sign, they reach out to others who interpret them accordingly in a sense of inter-subjectivity and even objectivity—just the way cultural constructions are! This move seems to be one of the fascinating features of the semiotic attitude, resulting in a form of bewilderment from which we have to become emancipated.

Illness or conflict as a text need more than oppositions and differences of meaning in order to be appropriately read. That text needs a determinate place in the semiotics of meaning-oppositions; the physician needs the body as the place of meaning as the lawyer needs society as such a place to embed fact and meaning. Is legal or medical discourse a body of knowledge in themselves, with a specific practice that is able to show such signs and to elucidate this appearance? Body and society successively seem to be the only place for medicine and law where such processes of reading could be meaningful. A circular access to legal and medical knowledge comes to the fore: how the body thinks itself, so the medical discourse; how medical discourse thinks/defines the body, so the body itself; how a society thinks itself (for instance as discordant), so the legal discourse; how legal discourse thinks/defines itself, so a society itself. The essential question does not pertain to the essence of facts but whether facts-symptoms-meanings can be transformed or transited.[8] Understanding a medical or a legal symptom is in the light of semiotics a self-interpretation of a conceptual system called 'medicine' or 'law'.[9] That is one of the foundational issues of modern society as unfolded by legal semiotics.

---

[6] Paul Greenberg: "The Semio-grads" in: *The Boston Globe,* 2004 (May 16).

[7] R. Barthes: *Fragments d'un discours amoureux*, Paris Du Seuil 1977. p. 141 [First Engl. Ed. 1987]

[8] Jan M. Broekman: "Semiology and the Medical Discourse" in: *Methodology & Science. Op. Cit.,* 1988.

[9] Jan M. Broekman: *Intertwinements of Law and Medicine,* Leuven UP, 1996, p. 159 f.

Symptoms seem to find only a place in legal discourse when they belong to the totality of legal concepts represented in jurisprudence, law or legal discourse. The relation between sign and symptom is *additional* in that case. Legal institutions decide whether the concept that articulates such a symptom will be accepted or not. Their decision belongs to the corpus of jurisprudence itself, is strongly anchored in a lawyer's mind and is incorporated in all legal articulations that function as precedent.

If this circularity between symbol and sign refers to foundations of science and society, what function gives semiotics then to the *name*? Connections between sign, symbol and name have already been put on record. Judgments, precedents or cases in law do indeed also function as names in society. Moreover, there is a strong articulation at hand when the verb '*is*' seemed a name for *change:* a name in its own right also called '*sign*'. Is this a confusion of concepts? No, there is no confusion at hand but perhaps a specific secrecy. What is the secret in law's maintaining terms such as symptom, sign and name? Various elements of a possible answer are possible. Consider that *signs in law* are *names* for a conceptually conceived social reality—names, which are carefully admitted in the discourse concerned and systematized in the Common Law's jurisprudence and equally well in the Civil Law's legal doctrinal body. It is clear: without those names, there exists no legal reality. And without them, there exist no legal facts.

Lawyers do not apply rules to facts in a neutral and detached manner. They *create* legal facts by means of applying a precisely defined game of differentiation of rule and application of principles. Their 'name-giving' is a substantial part of the legal process.[10] Lawyers tend to consider the connection between facts and rules as a linguistic relation. If law creates its facts, then such a creation is the result of law's language, of its speech activity as well as logical reasoning. So there exists no legal reality without institutionally recognized names. Legal thought formation as influenced by linguistic expressiveness, legal action as influenced by causality and legal speech acts as influenced by institutions lead to the lawman's job. He or she has to interpret facts by means of creating their legal names and thus, via this name giving, to appropriate legal interpretation. This is again quite circular because it resembles the reading of a self-conceived text. Brute facts and institutional facts cooperate in secrecy: they do not make publicly clear that brute facts are solely called 'brute facts' as the result of a *qualification performed by the institution*. The suggestion of Roland Barthes could in this perspective be the opinion of a lawyer. He tells us, that the medical doctor is the one who transforms by means of a mediating language (...) the symptom into a sign. But neither medical doctors nor lawyers transform symptoms as if they were natural data into signs, which now appear as a natural datum, as a purely descriptive authority. Legal issues receive their identity not from a pure description but through an explicit *making* of meaning.

---

[10] Jan M. Broekman: "Legal Discourse and Legal Facts" in: *EYSL—European Yearbook in the Sociology of Law*, Giuffrè, Milan 1996, p. 181 f.

Signs Merge Law and Semiotics

What emerges, then, is the systemic quality of semiotic analysis, one beyond its application within a particular body or conflict to one that embeds that action within the universe in which *semiosis* attains its form. Returning to our *Bourgeois Gentilhomme*, systemicity is embodied in the Philosophy Master, who both mocks and structures the semiotic universe within which Jourdain may become both self-aware and produce contingent meaning. Kevelson's suggests that *law is a system of signs* in terms of legal semiotics, so that law can be broadly (and not solely technically) understood as a "process of communication or message exchange by means of signs and sign systems".[11] Kevelson highlights several fundamental issues in this context.

The *first* is, that there is no legal argumentation with a purely formal character. Premises of legal arguments, she writes, are neither true nor false, but hypothetical. So it was believed for a long time that analysis of legal discourse must necessarily be much looser and less conclusive than discourses proceeding from truth propositions.

The *second* is in Kevelson's discussion with O.W. Holmes' famous essay *The Path of Law,* that in each legal case is a legal event, in which legal discourse is one kind of legal act among others, and that legal procedures are exchanges of official messages by means of *signs*.

The *third* is that semiotic perspectives incorporate hitherto unattended views on law, as Kevelson notices[12], because with semiotics

> one has introduced for further inquiry the strong possibility that should our social system of law, economics, and politics ... be understood against the theoretical background of a dynamic, "motion-picture" universe that is continually becoming, that is infinitely developing and changing in response to genuinely novel elements that emerge as existent, *then the basic concepts of rights, resources, and reality take on new dimensions of meaning in correspondence with n-dimensional, infinite value judgments or truth-like beliefs which one holds*.

In the second half of the twentieth century, semiotics became appreciated as one of the most sophisticated and complex theories of human communication—as Eugenides' novel *The Marriage Plot* underlined. Apart from its legal/technical vocabulary and its doctrinal engineering, law is also (in approximately the same period) recognized as a special means to communicate social meaning. Emphasis is here on meaning. The novel shows that a large variety of circumstances in life can be highlighted through semiotics only because that approach clarifies their *meaning*. However, to focus meaning one must focus expressivity, and in doing so, understand how words are always in need of an addressee. Words incorporate meanings destined to others. Words of the law (especially those, which are spoken by an authority first and then read in the specialized discourse) are strongly marked by the presence of the *other*, and that is an essential feature of semiotics.

---

[11] Roberta Kevelson: *The Law as a System of Signs,* Plenum Pres, New York and London, 1988.

[12] Kevelson, -Id.- p. vii.

Community

A further confrontation with the *sign* as a constitutive element in law and legal discourse finds again a foundation in the philosophy of Peirce. As long as things do not act upon one another, there is no meaning, he wrote. Signs must be in a relation to other signs, sign systems and eventually language in order to be meaningful, so that meanings result from relations. Peirce writes 1905:

> A sign is plainly a species of medium of communication

The position of an active semiotic subject is an issue of special consideration in Peirce's philosophy. It teaches us how to perceive a lawyer's activity[13]:

> When we think, then, we ourselves, as we are at that moment, appear as a sign. Now a sign has, as such, three references: first, it is a sign to some thought which interprets it; second, it is a sign for some object to which in that thought it is equivalent; third, it is a sign, in some respect or quality, which brings it into connection with its object.

Signs are, generally spoken, a something that represents for someone something else within the framework of a view or a quality. Peirce's words are more precise in his well known and often quoted formulation:

> A sign, or representamen, is something, which stands to somebody for something in some respect or capacity. It addresses somebody, that is, creates in the mind of that person an equivalent sign, or perhaps a more developed sign. That sign which it creates I call the interpretant of the first sign. The sign stands for something, its object. It stands for that object, not in all respects, but in reference to a sort of idea, which I have sometimes called the ground of the representamen. (Peirce, CP. 2. 228)

The impact of signs forms the foundation for lawyers' activities and their discourses: if ever signs represent reality, if ever signs are agreed upon, then humans within the boundaries of their cultural pattern confirm not only those individual issues, but all possible judgments of mankind as for instance expressed in concepts of justice or—more modern—human rights. It means, that concrete knowledge is always based upon semiotic transformations, which in their turn cannot function without community:

> ...The real, then, is that which, sooner or later, information and reasoning would finally result in, and which is therefore independent of the vagaries of 'me' and 'you'. Thus, the very origin of the conception of reality shows that this conception essentially involves the notion of a COMMUNITY, without definite limits, and capable of a definite increase of knowledge. (Peirce, CP. 5. 311)

The idea of community is fundamental, but brings problems of order and logic with it, as Peirce notices in the context of his outline of pragmatism:

> A medium of communication is something, A, which being acted upon by something else, N, in its turn acts upon something, I, in a manner involving its determination by N, so that I

[13] Charles Sanders Peirce (1931–1935, Charles Hartshorne and Paul Weiss, Eds.) *The Collected Papers of Charles Sanders Pierce I–VI*, Cambridge Mass, Harvard University Press. (Abridged as C.P.) CP. 5. 238.

> shall thereby, through A and only through A, be acted upon by N. [...] A Sign, on the other hand, just in so far as it fulfills the function of a sign, and none other, perfectly conforms to the definition of a medium of communication. It is determined by the object, but in no other respect than goes to enable it to act upon the interpreting quasi mind; and the more perfectly it fulfills its function as a sign, the less effect it has upon that quasi-mind other than that of determining it as if the object itself had acted upon it.

A community demonstrates semiotic relevance through its unity of interpretation and experience[14]. Peirce speaks about the central issue that is contained in the word "community": whoever speaks about *words*, speaks about '*Together*' the word 'community' points on the one hand to *semiotics* because of its social practice to engender consistency in interpretation of signs and meanings, and on the other to *logic* because of the structure of its experiences.

Peirce defined *semiotics*—his name for any form of activity, conduct, or process that involves signs, including the production of meaning, which is a sign process—as specifically determined by a triad: *signs*, their *object* and their *interpretants*;

> this tri-relative influence not being in any way resolvable into actions between pairs... *Semeíosis*, if I remember rightly, meant the action of almost any kind of sign; and my definition confers on anything that so acts the title of "sign". (Charles S. Peirce: *The Essential Peirce, Selected Philosophical Writings*, The Peirce Edition Project (Ed.) Indiana UP 1998, Vol. 2, p. 411.)

Modern semiotics analyzes structures of communication, which are complex systems of sign relationships. The system of law is such a system, and this leads to a more profound understanding of law and legal discourse—the ultimate goal of each law student focusing on semiotics. Indeed, communicating is in terms of legal acts a communication within law as a system of signs. The idea that semiotics in legal discourse also counts for a semiotic analysis of legal discourse, follows consequently but is seldom mentioned in the observations of lawyers. As if Peirce focuses on the social activities of lawyers, he describes 1909 how

> A Sign is anything, which represents something else (so far as it is complete) and if it represents itself it is as a part of another sign, which represents something other than itself, and it represents itself in other circumstances, in other connections. A man may talk and he is a sign of that he relates, he may tell about himself as he was at another time. He cannot tell exactly what he is doing at that very moment. Yes, he may confess he is lying, but he must be a false sign, then. A sign, then, would seem to profess to represent something else. Either a sign is to be defined as something, which truly represents something or else as something, which professes to represent something.

We exemplify this by means of Ira Robbins'[15] observations on the semiotic implications of the "Cf." citation in legal texts. They are altogether a concrete example for signs in legal discourse, a subject to which we turn to next.

---

[14] Marcel Danesi: *Messages, Signs, and Meanings*. Toronto UP 2004.

[15] Ira P. Robbins: "Semiotics, Analogical Legal Reasoning and the Cf. citation", in: *Duke Law Journal*, Vol. 48, 1043, 1999.

The Cf. Citation as a Sign

The major thesis is, that the Bluebook's introductory citation signals are essential for any subtype of legal discourse. The choice of signal can influence not only the interpretation of cited cases, but also the path of the law as imagined by the players in context. However, what is called *signal* appears to be precisely a *sign* in the Peircean and general semiotic sense of the word. It becomes clear that Cf. formulas are instrumental in constructing cohesion and rationality in legal discourse. Semiotic interest in discourse precedes semiotic interest in speech acts, because the latter always unfold in the context of the first. Hence Robbins:

> This notion of closeness is also inherent in legal citation practice, for introductory signals indicate the purposes for which the citations are made and the degree of support the citations give. In this way, citation signals help to pave the path of the law.

Paving the path of law is a respectable goal, but it needs instrumental support that fits with the linguistic character of law's discourse: words, and signs.

> By helping to assign the degree of support and the strength of distinctions and reconciliations, they help to articulate the degree of departure from existing law. If the signposts are bad, so too may be the destination. We must therefore take utmost care to be true to the intended development of the law. Put differently, careless citation practice can lead to haphazard consequences that should be controlled to the extent desired and to the extent possible. Despite the laudable goals of citation practice, the cf signal is viewed with skepticism. One reason is that practical definitions and uses of the signal vary widely.
> The Bluebook authors explicitly grant the cf. signal the terrain of analogical legal reasoning. Other writers implicitly do the same, reserving cf. for cited authorities that involve substantially different facts, law, or both. Black's Law Dictionary effectively portrays the cf. as a catchall for any point the author wishes to make.' Cf. might be short for "cipher"-it is a nebulous introductory signal, practically devoid of meaning without further explanation by the authors Or cf. might simply mean "can't find": aware that a particular proposition requires support, the author, unable to locate anything close, just cites a book, article, or case that is "close enough.

The semiotic dimensions of a citation sign are difficult to determine. The form of legal discourse is at stake rather than the substance. Is the substance of that discourse identical to what lawyers gave the name 'law'? This becomes more important if one considers how

> ... few would contend that analogical thinking is not essential to the development of law. If the function of the cf signal relates to analogical reasoning, then the use of the signal must be accepted as an integral, organic part of legal discourse. This relationship may be conveyed in terms of semiotics, the study of systems of symbols and signs that have communicative value.

That legal semiotics must, moreover, explain what role specific meanings fulfill as a *sign* in law's discourse along the lines of legal thinking in general. The sign-role appears essential in law, and defines the events and circumstances in which legal rules should be applied. There is no legal semiotics without focus on signs in law, and there is no law without institutionally embedded sign functions. The many varieties of the Cf. citation as a legal sign indicate the truth of this conclusion. Important is therefore Robbins' remark:

> When the nation's highest court fails to explain cryptic cf. citations, the clarity and predictability of American law suffers profoundly.

An example that completes this remark is in Stone v. Powell[16], which is

> . . . a case that many lower federal courts and commentators have analyzed extensively. Perhaps the Court deliberately utilized a cf. citation in order to avoid having to define its terms, to provide needed flexibility to lower court decision makers, or to avoid expansion of the Fourth Amendment. It is impossible to know. The result has been time-consuming construction, deconstruction, and extrapolation of re-inventive analogies.

Important for any judgment about the function and importance of a legal semiotic sign as constituent of law is Robbins' suggestion:

> The Stone Court limited the relief available to prisoners asserting Fourth Amendment violations on collateral review of their convictions. It stated: "[W]here the State has provided an opportunity for full and fair litigation of a Fourth Amendment claim, a state prisoner may not be granted federal habeas corpus relief on the ground that evidence obtained in an unconstitutional search or seizure was introduced at his trial." Footnote thirty-six, which followed this assertion, contained only a cf. citation to the entire case of Townsend v. Sain. The Court thus failed to clarify the significance of the Townsend opinion to Stone. Nor did the concurring opinion or either of the two dissenting opinions include any discussion of the inscrutable reference to Townsend.

One perceives here the embedding of a legal sign in the total construction of legal discourse. Various Courts, judges and legal commentators underlined furthermore, how the use of a sign, in this exemplary case a Cf. citation, showed that the citation was an example for the hermeneutic dimensions at work in the course of constructing legal discourse. That is a truly legal semiotic observation.

Signs exercise important social functions in a large diversity of discourses. Their meaning depends on their context in which they unfold a meaning and create social bonds. This general observation is very concrete in law and legal discourse. The logic of signs, not in the sense of a formal logic but rather of legal rhetoric[17], is essential for lawyers, which they tend to master constantly. Especially in a Civil Law discourse, signs with the character of "general principles" are important as a source of law. Legal standards are signs that have been set for all participants in the discourse. The same importance of the sign-character of law is in the Common Law world, where "precedent" fulfills a comparable function. The discussion about legal rules, developing at both sides of the Atlantic and thus uniting Civil and Common Law, focuses on the application of signs with rule character. The logic of signs, which support law's institutional hierarchy, is particularly important for the construction of the legal narrative, as James Boyd White explained in many publications.

---

[16] 428 US, 465 (1976).

[17] Ch. Perelman & L. Olbrechts-Tyteca: *The New Rhetoric: A Treatise on Argumentation*. Notre Dame UP 1969. Also: Francis J. Mootz III: *Rhetorical Knowledge in Legal Practice and Critical Legal Theory*, Alabama UP 2006.

It is in its sign-character, one could add to White's observations, that the logic of narrative codification is clarified. This semiotic chain of arguments and language uses has direct practical effect, since lawyers are supposed and educated to master their profession of words and to control and influence their meanings in view of their social effects. They do this by institutionally accepting the uses of words, word clusters etc, up to cases, which are given a specific name, as well as of principles. All these activities focus the coherence of legal signs, which has to be adopted by any legal practitioner. The acceptance of the specifically legal practice based on the use of words makes it possible for lawyers to fathom the problem that everyday language and legal language are no identical but belong together functionally.

General Considerations

Legal semiotics is repeatedly defined as the study of law focusing on signs and symbols as well as the construction of meaning in law in legal discourse. Law's communicative structures are essential in that context. Recent large-scale economic, political and social developments in the Western hemisphere have increased the need to expand our knowledge about law, and semiotic studies sustain that need. That has various implications for legal semiotics.

a. There are today intensive and varied theoretical discussions and debates on *changing patterns of legal knowledge* implied in law and its practices (Posner, Dworkin, Fisch, Summers, Sunstein, Luhmann, Teubner, Hart, McCormick). They contribute ultimately to a new general knowledge about law rather than to new laws or legal techniques.
b. The social relevance of legal knowledge is furthermore challenged by the rapid growth of multicultural contexts in which Western law has to function. This adds to new perspectives on law rather than to new components of existing law.
c. Those implications are reinforced by the fact that the expansion of legal knowledge is paralleled by a host of fundamental changes in general knowledge. Lawyers confronted with semiotics must also consider patterns of knowledge in the emerging e-communication (which is a new field of human communication), or in cyberspace and nanotechnology, where not only hitherto unknown signs and symbols, but also new meaning processes are created.
d. Consequences of expansion and change in legal knowledge should not only be registered in view of actual practices of law, but also in legal education. Education introduces new forms of knowledge, and lawyers are particularly targeted where education relates to changing forms of knowledge. Legal practitioners acquire an awakened awareness of their influence on the lives of citizens and the profiles of a newly emerging social self, which result from those changes. Semiotics, the study of signs, symbols and meanings in legal discourse appears to be of essence in legal education. Law students study how law and lawyers function in fields that exploit legal terms such as ownership, privacy, constitutionality or Human Rights and policies such as care, consent or lawful allocation of social means.

What sign-characters are used here, and could one venture the idea that a diversity of signs and their subsequent ideologies are favored in lawyers' practices?

e. The relation between law and semiotics as part of academic disciplines and as sociopolitical practices is a central theme. It is the cornerstone of a society that protects the lives of its citizens. Students must acquire sufficient material knowledge to understand and debate those questions, in particular pertaining to views on men and society as well as on justice and knowledge as developed in the course of the last decades of the twentieth century and the first of the twenty-first century. This directs their attention (emotional, professional, cultural and pertaining to their individual pattern of knowledge) to at least two issues, which will determine their position of a lawyer in our society: (a) what is a sign and what is a sign's meaning in the context of law and legal discourse; (b) explanations about a sign in legal discourse as a strong unity—a system, as a legal system, perceived as a unity, or a fragmented whole, or a social construct of different nature.

The latter is particularly important for law, because the *unity* of a legal system relates to the problem of *reference*. The thesis about unity claims that a legal *system* fits to law and its language/expressiveness, and functions as a structured discourse of a nation-state, including all manifestations of an ideological nature. Such a system embraces the paradigm called *legal positivism* and is the basis for safe acts of reference. Are all lawyers positivists when they perform their legal task? But legal positivism itself is suffused with semiotic ambiguity—grounded in symbolic constructs ranging from command, compulsion, authority and hierarchy within norm structures that may be more or less resistant to distinct styles of interpretation;[18] "difference or slippage between the textually affirmed determinacy of the rule as signifier and the signified–a particular instance of rule application – is inevitable".[19] Positivism, thus understood, would deny the differences between the multiple types of signs in law, and such denial functions when one considers legal discourse as constructed in accordance with means of (formal) logic—an issue Peirce, Husserl and others, lawyers as well as philosophers, have been wrestling with. It is interesting to research whether they did have an eye for the inherently *semiotic* dimensions[20].

---

[18] Candace J. Groudine: "Authority: H.L.A. Hart and the Problem of Legal Positivism," IV *The Journal of Libertarian Studies* 273 (1980) (considering law as a system of command or of social rules in the context of authority and H.L.A. Hart: *The Concept of Law* (Oxford 1961); David Richards, *The Moral Criticism of Law* (Encino, California: Dickenson 1977).

[19] Duncan Kennedy: "A Semiotics of Legal argument," Op. Cit., p. 87.

[20] Frederik Stjernfelt: *Diagrammatology – An Investigation on the Borderlines of Phenomenology, Ontology, and Semiotics*. Synthese Library, Vol. 336, Springer, Dordrecht 2007.

Part II
Godfathers of Semiotics

There are three godfathers of semiotics, without whom nobody could ever have developed the idea of a semiotics of law, or legal semiotics. None of them had law as profession or field of study or research, although they achieved in preparing for a wide interest in law analyzed and understood by means of semiotics. One of them is the highly esteemed American philosopher Charles Sanders Peirce (1839–1914), who was also logician, mathematician, scientist and founder of semiotics. The others, who hardly studied Peirce's philosophy, were Jacques M.E. Lacan, (1901–1981), psychologist, philosopher and psychoanalyst, and the linguist and philosopher Algirdas J. Greimas (1917–1992). It means that one American and two Europeans laid the basis for semiotic activities, which developed into our actual *legal* semiotics. One worked in an English and two in a French mother tongue—ironically, their main works are today accessible in English, but not in French. A philosopher, a linguist and a psychoanalyst—how do we ever trace the ground patterns of semiotics that lead us to semiotics of law and legal discourse? That is the leading question of this second part of the book.

We should, when operating semiotics in law and legal discourse, keep in mind that none of these godfathers were lawyers or had any fundamental insight in legal procedures and practices. They were looking at jurisprudence as outsiders, like Peirce or Greimas, and had little or no knowledge about operating legal questions. In other words, the three were in the case of law and legal practice *enablers* and by no means *executors*. Their enabling future lawyers by offering subtleties of the semiotic method focused in the first place on an understanding of signs, and via such an understanding *how lawyers make meaning*—even where they are not educated to understand the meaning making process, or ever dealt in practice with this socially important issue.

More interesting still is that the course of history of the last century has developed two different traditions in the field of *legal* semiotics: one strong US tradition, which honors the work of Charles Sanders Peirce, and another equally strong European tradition, which refers to the work of the linguist Greimas. Both acknowledge many aspects of Jacques Lacan's insight in the typology of discourses we daily use, and his surprising ideas on identity formation and language acquisition in a cultural setting. It is most evident, that the US tradition, primarily in reference to Peirce, finds its roots in pragmatism, a philosophical mainstream that favors the contextual and situational characteristics of meaning. Exemplary for its first beginnings are the works of Ch. W. Morris, W. James and Ch. S. Peirce, with Roberta Kevelson as the dominant *executor* of a US oriented legal semiotics. The European tradition focuses language and social action in many guises, and some of them are directly connected to the works of their European godfathers, Greimas and Lacan.

Chapter 3
Peirce and Legal Semiotics

Peirce Elucidates Legal Language

The magic of law has a name—the name is 'language'. Its magicians have studied to handle it carefully and exploit all its possibilities. Court decisions do not only decide cases, but they also give them names, and those names symbolize a meaning. Names, not case materials are quoted in arguments and recited in legal-political debates. The names name the legal materials; observe how candidates for official functions are asked to express an opinion about a name—their answers consider *the name as a symbol*. That symbol/name is generally known in the public but only lawyers know and understand all the subtleties of the case. The name that functions as a symbol is rather a political issue than an index for the precise legal content of that well-known case. Doctrines are symbols: a breach of contract is a sign in legal language and the meaning of that sign determines a rich variety of legal consequences. The relations between symbols, signs and names are always dominating a discussion on legal issues.

This fascinating view on law and legal discourse is by no means common knowledge. Lawyers consider language as their precious instrument but mingle signs and words, fuse doctrine and expressiveness, mix names and symbols. They have a mastery of their language, but one could ask whether having such mastery is something that effects life whilst uttering a sentence? They seldom know an answer. In other words: is the utterance of a Court decision the happening of the decision's material subject, so that one could say that the decision is the technique of precisely using command words? Jurists generally hold it that expressions describe or represent reality, which is not a legal but a philosophical perspective.

Apparently, only an outsider can inform lawyers about the multiple implications of their own words! That is the task of legal semiotics. Names, doctrines and other legal expressions are in Peirce's view a *sign*, a core concept of each process of meaning formation. A sign is for Peirce a something that relates to something else for someone in some respect or capacity. This is general and precise at the same time and could help jurists, among many others, to clarify their magic in social life.

J. M. Broekman, L. Catà Backer, *Lawyers Making Meaning*,
DOI 10.1007/978-94-007-5458-4_3, © Springer Science+Business Media Dordrecht 2013

Daniel Chandler[1] formulates in 2002:

> Semiotics is concerned with everything that can be taken as a sign. 'It' involves the study not only of what we refer to as 'signs' in every day speech, but of anything which 'stands for something else'. Signs take the form of words, images, sounds, gestures and objects.' Signs can be something active and positive, or something negative, so that an absence of an action may also be seen as a sign. Semiotics is also the 'study of how meanings are made and how reality is represented.' Making of meaning and representation can take place in the form of 'texts' and 'media'. Legal and legislative texts provide one category of text. . . .a 'text can exist in any medium and may be verbal, non-verbal, or both (. . .). The term 'text' usually refers to a message, which has been recorded in some way (e.g. writing, audio- and video- recording) so that it is physically independent of its sender or receiver. A text is an assemblage of signs (such as words, images, sounds, and/or gestures) constructed (and interpreted) with reference to the conventions associated with a genre and a particular medium of communication.

One should emphasize that such descriptions are either literal quotations or paraphrases of lines Peirce wrote. Peirce notes 1902:

> A Sign does not function as a sign unless it be understood as a sign. It is impossible, in the present state of knowledge, to say, at once fully precisely and with a satisfactory approach to certitude, what is to understand of a sign. . . ., it does not seem that consciousness can be considered as essential to the understanding of a sign. But what is indispensable is that there should, actually or virtually, bring about a determination of a sign of the same object of which it is itself a sign. This interpreting sign, like every sign, only functions as a sign so far as it again is interpreted, that is, actually or virtually, determines a sign of the same object of which it is itself a sign. *Thus there is a virtual endless series of signs when a sign is understood; and a sign never understood can hardly be said to be a sign.* (*italics* JMB)

The *Routledge Companion to Semiotics and Linguistics* informs about sign and semiotics in the spirit of Peirce[2]:

> Signs can be seen as comprising three components: 'representamen', which is 'what usually goes for a sign in everyday talk'; an 'object' to which the representamen is related, and an 'interpretant' (meaning) reflecting the link between the first two.
> Peirce classified signs into various types: 'icon', 'index' and 'symbol'. The *icon* interrelates with its semiotic object by virtue of some resemblance or similarity with it. An *index* interrelates with its semiotic object through some actual or physical or imagined causal connection and a *symbol* is a linguistic sign whose interrelation with its semiotic object is conventional.So there is no necessary natural link (as with the index) or a link due to some resemblance or similarity (as with the icon) between the representamen and the semiotic object.

Peirce acclaims not unlike the French linguist Ferdinand de Saussure that signs (strung together in a manner prescribed by rules) communicate meaning. Coded texts are thus signs to decode for a reader, and that decoding touches the essence of the magic of legal language.

---

[1] Chandler, Daniel: *Semiotics: The Basics*, Routledge, Abingdon (2002), p. 2 See also Colin Robertson: *Semiotics and EULaw*, Mss. 2008, Ch. 2: *EU legislative texts as signs*.

[2] Merrell, Floyd*: Charles Sanders Peirce's Concept of the Sign*, in: *The Routledge Companion to Semiotics and Linguistics*, P. Colbry (Ed.), London/New York 2001, p. 28 ff.

Roberta Kevelson gave law a Peircean frame when highlighting in various publications how

> ... the entire notion of a legal system, consisting of interrelating communicative processes between legal discourse and legal practice, functions almost universally as a model of dialogic thought development... law is a prototype of intersubjective social change of value as a whole... in view of Peirce's 'expanded logic' ... it is nothing new to regard logical terms and modes or patterns of reasoning as signs and sign systems. Aristotle speaks of signs in this sense. The legal argument is not a formal argument. Its hypotheses are neither true nor false, but hypothetical. Therefore it was believed for a long time that analysis of legal discourse must necessary much looser and less conclusive that discourse proceeding from true propositions. Yet it was Peirce's genius to recognize that at bottom all propositions are hypothetical.... (Kevelson Roberta: *The Law as a System of Signs*, Plenum Press New York 1988)

Max H. Fisch indicates connections between Peirce and American legal pragmatism, in particular represented by jurists like Holmes, who in dealing with various forms of life and law proved to possess notions of semiotic relevance when writing on liability, tort, contract, possession and the like.

Peirce knew from conversations with legal colleagues in the Philosophical Clubs he established in Cambridge and in Boston—to which Holmes belonged—about the problems with legal interpretation, reference activities in legal discourse, causality in the law and about the philosophical debates on the status of facts in law. But that is certainly not enough to describe any strong, direct, non-philosophical and jurisprudentially relevant thought pattern of Peirce on *legal* semiotics. In his philosophy, as is the case with many authors of articles in the IJLS[3], the semiotic background remains general and one even does not know whether semiotics can correctly be applied to law, in particular to everyday practices of law.

In a fascinating essay at the end of his book on *Peirce, Semeiotic and Pragmatism*, Fisch deals with what he judges to be the range of Peirce's relevance. Semiotics is of course the first theme of all studies, and Peirce's focus on a general theory of signs matches that plan, which brings him near to De Saussure—the two had predecessors in the ancient Greek culture as well as in our modern times: "Peirce's most fundamental published papers go back to 18677–1871, a decade before Saussure's *Mémoire* and half a century before his *Cours.*Those early papers of Peirce were first *re*published, and much of his relevant later work was first published, in 1931–1935, in the first six volumes of his *Collected Papers* (...)"[4] Closely intertwined with semiotics are his studies in logic, whereby it seems in hindsight of extreme importance how he developed in early years the idea of a triadic logic. Peirce describes in an essay *The Art of Reasoning Elucidated* (1910) how he seeks "a midway between the two rational Modals, as the modified forms are called by all old logicians". That idea of triadic relations will later play a major role in the reception and perception

[3] See for example how the entire third issue of the IJSL 2008 remains in a dualism between semiotics and law, and leaves the relationship between the two undecided.

[4] Max H. Fisch: *Peirce, Semeiotic, and Pragmatism* (Ketner & Kloesel, Eds) Bloomington Indiana UP 1986, Ch. 2 & 22.; Vincent Colapietro: "Peircean Semeiotics and Legal Practices", in: *International Journal for the Semiotics of Law*, Vol. 21, No. 3, 2008, p. 223 ff.

of a sign, which are for him also a triadic and not a dual occurrence. The latter development fits precisely into the thoughts of sociologists and social philosophers who defended a "symbolic interactionism", which in its turn has close relations to the psychological and psychiatric notions of Lacan, not to mention US psychologists such as Sullivan, Mead or philosophers like Gurwitsch or Blumer.

Peirce's Philosophical Texts

The unfolding influence of the Peircean corpus of *philosophical* texts (he did not write *legal* texts) is important, and the electronic edition of the Collected Papers facilitates the spreading of his ideas. There are, however, debates about the quality and implications of that edition, which will undoubtedly lead to newly corrected editions and progressing clarifications[5]. In his Foreword to the Electronic Edition, John Deely mentions a number of reasons to have a critical mind alerted when reading Peirce's texts. He criticizes the order of fragments, the dispersion and misrepresentation of themes, the biased interpretation of thematic connections in disordered text fragments. His Introduction: "*Membra Ficta Disjecta* (A Disordered Array of Severed Limbs)" goes mainly to the *editing* of texts; the *essence*, Deely remarks[6],

> is a question at bottom of the principal optic through which Peirce early and ever-after came to view the problems of philosophy, the optic of "semiotic", as he called it after Locke, or the doctrina signorum, as both Locke and Peirce called it. . . . through the Peirce Edition Project at IUPUI, Fisch had shown the new generation not only the importance of the unpublished Peirce manuscripts, but, equally importantly, how to read them with semiotic eyes. . . those of us alive today and interested in Peirce would like to have access to as much of his work as possible as soon as possible. At present, as far as published writings go, that still means the CP [short for "Collected Papers"].
>
> The story of the Harvard edition titled CP, . . . is a story fairly well known, and a sad one. Hartshorne and Weiss, along with Burks later, deserve our thanks for getting the volumes out, but we must at the same time regret the manner of their editing, which was to construct a topical scheme of their own devising under which to sort and dissect the papers left whole to Harvard through the good intentions of Josiah Royce. How Harvard abused that trust! The story, at least, is now out with the bursting upon the scene of the newly worked (after more than thirty years of repression) biographical dissertation of Joseph Brent in the form of the book, *Charles Sanders Peirce. A Life*. (Bloomington. Indiana UP 1993). This publication is a tribute in equal parts to the writing skill and historical tenacity of its author, to the editorial genius (to say nothing of the detective skills) of Thomas A. Sebeok, and to the publishing genius of John Gallman, the Director of the Indiana University Press. . . . Using the electronic CP, a reader can reconstruct this whole and print it out as such for scholarly or classroom use. Thus the "bodily parts" of the Peircean corpus, so far as they are included in the CP, may be easily re-arrayed in proper order so as to appear in something closer to the light under which Peirce left them.

[5] The CP edition volumes I–VI of Charles Hartshorne & Paul Weiss was published between 1931 and 1935, and the Arthur W. Burks edited volumes VII & VIII followed 1958. There was, and still is, however, no undisputed and entirely complete text edition.

[6] Deely, John: "Membra Ficte Disjecta (A Disordered Array of Severed Limbs)" Editorial Introduction to the Electronic Edition of *The Collected Papers of Charles Sanders Peirce*, 1994.

The explanations of Deely provoke the mention of at least three general issues:

a. *Interest in the work of Peirce is even in the beginnings of the twenty-first century growing on a worldwide scale.* Peirce will be acknowledged as one of the major American philosophers of the ninetieth and twentieth century, not only in the US but globally. He was recognized as logician, as the philosopher who coined the concept of pragmatism and who developed a phenomenology based on a philosophy of the sign. All those themes are outstanding in his philosophical work.
b. *Peirce's semiotics is encapsulated in philosophy.* Legal scholars, who exposed the relations between law and semiotics after the period of the Critical Legal Studies movement in the US or structuralism, structural linguistics and deconstructivism in Europe, studied Peirce mostly to place some of his insights in legal context—like they did with Kant, Hegel or Derrida. There does not exist a central essay or an encompassing Peirce text on legal theory or on legal semiotics in particular. Lawyers who are fascinated by the opportunities semiotics deliver must read non-legal texts of mainly logical and philosophical character, when they want to include Peirce in their intellectual baggage. The problems with text editing, as indicated before, belong to the history of philosophical texts and do not directly relate to jurisprudence.
c. *Peirce's work on semiotics is not explicitly designed for law and legal theory.* Legal semiotics tries to bridge the gap between the two, and needs therefore the accompaniment of legal practitioners. Lawyers read and study Peirce on a personal initiative and do not pursue aims dictated by the requirements of legal practice. The problem of applicability of semiotics in law and legal discourse remains an issue that is absent from Peirce's works, although it fascinates lawyers and philosophers alike and is a touchstone for legal semiotics.

From Philosophy to Semiotics to Law

The unfolding of semiotics in Peirce's thoughts is in the first place a matter of philosophy. One of its pillars is the dialogue, the fundamentally inter-subjective character of his thoughts—at certain points in flagrant contrast to Western law, because the latter is deeply individualistic in practical attitude and theory. This has its expression in the style of his philosophical considerations—which in contrast to the analytical and henceforth predominantly monologue character of many contemporary philosophers—invite the reader to think dialogic and have a virtual conversation with its author. The texts written in daily reflections upon events of everyday life are an *environment* in which the reader lives, thinks and concludes with Peirce as a guide. *Signs* are culminating in the stream of textual utterances and considerations—they peak in quotidian events. This is precisely food for lawyers, since it is their profession to qualify outstanding events and their meaning in terms of law and legal discourse. Peirce considers:

> Two things here are all-important to assure oneself of and to remember. The first is that a person is not absolutely an individual. His thoughts are what he is "saying to himself," that is, is saying to that other self that is just coming into life in the flow of time. When one reasons, it is that critical self that one is trying to persuade; and all thought whatsoever is a sign, and is mostly of the nature of language. The second thing to remember is that the man's circle of society (however widely or narrowly this phrase may be understood), is a sort of loosely compacted person, in some respects of higher rank than the person of an individual organism. It is these two things alone that render it possible for you ... to distinguish between absolute truth and what you do not doubt. (Peirce CP 5. 421)

There is an important issue involved in these lines. It pertains to one of the major considerations that characterize Peirce's backgrounds when reflecting upon man's language and his circle or context in a society, which he calls pragmatism. That pragmatism—new in philosophy during the final years of the nineteenth century—is the exclusive foundation for, and privileged method to develop a theory of signs called semiotics, which is for instance in the eyes of Roberta Kevelson a viable means of diagnosing and hence solving international conflicts[7]. Peirce's pragmatist maxim formulates:

> Consider what effects, that might conceivably have practical bearings, you conceive the objects of your conception to have. Then, your conception of those effects is the whole of your conception of the object.

An important role is fulfilled in this broadening of conception, which extends from the spoken word by an individual to the textual environment in which words and discourses unfold and speakers participate rather than take a subject-bound initiative. Essential is here, how Peirce re-interprets our thoughts, saying

> There is no reason why "thought," (...) should be taken in that narrow sense in which silence and darkness are favorable to thought. It should rather be understood as covering all rational life, so that an experiment shall be an operation of thought. Of course, that ultimate state of habit to which the action of self-control ultimately tends, where no room is left for further self-control, is, in the case of thought, the state of fixed belief, or perfect knowledge. (Peirce CP 5. p. 438, 420)

Peirce changed the classical problem of how thought and action relate (H. von Wright, H. Castaneda). He states that all thoughts are actions, not solely a matter of consciousness or of a state of mind but a disposition to action, which would be unthinkable without inter-subjectivity and the support of a community. This is the point where Karl Otto Apel unfolds his sympathy for Peirce on the basis of his theory of the *a priori* character of a community, which always pursues acts of *interpreting* language, reality, human relations and social order in a semiotic manner.He refers to this community in Peirce's spirit as "a supra-individual unity of interpretation on the basis of experimental experience in the long run"[8]. Peirce suggested:

---

[7] Roberta Kevelson: "Crisis in International Law: Signs and Symptoms" in: *Peirce, Science, Signs*. Lang, Paris/New York 1996, p. 147.

[8] K.-O.Apel: *Transformation der Philosophie*, Band II: *Das Apriori der Kommunikationsgemeinschaft*. Frankfurt a. M. 1973.

> ...The real, then, is that which, sooner or later, information and reasoning would finally result in, and which is therefore independent of the vagaries of 'me' and 'you'. Thus, the very origin of the conception of reality shows that this conception essentially involves the notion of a Community, without definite limits, and capable of a definite increase of knowledge. (Peirce CP 5. 311)

Community is essential because it demonstrates semiotic relevance through its unity of interpretation and experience. *Who speaks about Words, speaks about 'Together'*: the word 'community' points on the one hand to *semiotics* because of its social practice to engender consistency in interpretation of signs and meanings, and on the other to *logic* because of the structure of its experiences. In so far as legal awareness depends on language and the understanding of one self, Peirce has really something to say to lawyers!

As a consequence, Roberta Kevelson dedicated most of her life to make lawyers understand the importance of semiotics for their specific vocation. We want to highlight four themes of Peirce's philosophy which are related to this goal:

a. The philosophy of a sign has to be transformed into a full theory of semiosis, which implies the unfolding of semiotics.
b. The distinction between formal logic and the logic of discourse (in particular legal discourse) must be re-engineered and its rigidity put into perspective. Peirce confronted traditional logic with the logic of inference, abduction and with pragmatism.
c. The further differentiation of what Peirce called "pragmatism" or later "pragmaticism" challenges legal pragmatism as understood by American lawyers in particular. Lawyers generally focus on the question how to achieve the best results in cases and related, often purely contextual legal issues. They consider a discussion about the path to that goal and its inherent principles, strategies, values and norms as pragmatism, which is often a fierce instrumentalism, which is often also called legal realism. Llewellyn remarks: "Realism is not a philosophy, but a technology"[9].
d. Peirce focuses not on that technology but on its foundations and shows how a lawyers' move is not a matter of psychology but of genuine philosophy. His maxim suggests that the meaning of a concept or sign is rooted in the habits it would establish in a mind that rightly and correctly interprets it. That semiotic conception of a lawyer's mind is of vital importance for legal discourse.

Peirce offers a new set of concepts to replace the traditional Kantian categories, but in doing so he systematizes reality anew in accordance to reality being approached in terms of modes of being described by Peirce as *firstness, secondness* or *thirdness*. *Firstness* can be manifested by unmoored sense of self, understood as the quality of "being" in itself without referents; something like the Biblical expression, "I am that I am" without reference to an "I" other than "I." *Secondness* sounds in action and reaction relations, that is in the situateness of objects; this is "I" understood in

[9] K. Llewellyn: *The Common Law Tradition*. Boston 1960, p. 510.

relation to other "Is" that are distinct and in distinction bound "I" to a particular objectification. *Thirdness* sounds in interpretation of the context in which objects exist. Thirdness is manifested connectedness and systemicity; "I" now acquires meaning beyond an acknowledgement of the simple facticity (Faktizität) of you and I. Together they provide the foundation for systematic unity among distinctions according to a universe of means that produce a coherent system of relations/reality—it is the way that a world is "made".

These concepts are different, yet coherent, attitudes of the human mind and a lawyer would profit from them with a simple exercise to find out in which attitude he finds himself when issuing a judgment, exploring or investigating a legally relevant reality, writing a brief or interpreting statutes. The allocation in especially the second and third attitude highlights the semiotic dimension of his real, virtual or future activity: "They are the being of actual fact, and the being of law that will govern facts in the future"[10]. It seems a lawyer's business to constantly change from the one to the other—but is she aware of that modification and its qualities? "... the mind is a sign developing according to the laws of inference"—an insight of pragmatic nature inherent to the "law-job", Llewellyn would say in his 1941 *My Philosophy of Law*.

Peirce thus forwarded the view that 'man is a sign'—an observation immediately relevant in law and legal discourse as long as one considers carefully the precious coherence of the three human categories *vis à vis* his relation to what he calls reality. This intriguing issue was for him an element of 'evolutionary cosmology' in which law is almost naturally incorporated. It supports Peirce's idea that all knowledge results from a process of inference, from presumptions, deductions and conclusions, so that signs are continuously involved in questions pertaining to knowledge, which is also in issues of legal theory. A basic concern in that philosophy is in plying *chance* together with *continuity*. The togetherness of these two is omnipresent in his thoughts. We cannot live, think and know without continuity, he says, which means that past ideas must be present in every movement of our mind, although in often totally different forms. However, novelty exists by the grace of chance rather than of continuity!

The tension between these two took almost the philosopher's entire lifetime, when he writes as early as in 1891:

> The next step in the study of cosmology must be to examine the general law of mental action. In doing this, I shall for the time drop my tychism out of view, in order to allow a free and independent expansion to another conception... I mean the idea of continuity. (...) there is but one law of mind, namely, that ideas tend to spread continuously and to affect certain others which stand to them in a peculiar relation of affectability. In this spreading they lose intensity, and especially the power of affecting others, but gain generality and become welded with other ideas. (Tychism is named after Tyche, the Ancient Greek Deity that governed prosperity and fortune of individual and city/polis. See: Peirce, CP 6, pp. 103, 104)

---

[10] Peirce, CP 1. 27. See also: Carl R. Hausman: *Peirce's Evolutionary Philosophy*, Cambridge UP 1997.

A further path forms the expression 'word', 'community' or 'discourse'. The majority of philosophers, linguists, social scientists, and anthropologists on both sides of the Atlantic use and explore those words and their consequences. He thus wrote already around 1903

> ... it is sufficient to say that there is no element whatever of man's consciousness which has not something corresponding to it in the word... the word or sign, which man uses, *is* the man himself. For, as the fact that every thought is a sign, taken in conjunction with the fact that life is a train of thought, proves that man is a sign (...) All communication from mind to mind is through continuity of being. A man is capable of having assigned to him a *rôle* in the drama of creation, and so far as he loses himself in that *rôle*... (1892). (Peirce: CP 5, p. 314; CP 6, 572)

This role only unfolds in a community:

> A man has consciousness; a word has not, ... our thought is an index for itself of itself on the ground of a complete identity with itself. But so is any word or indeed any thing, so that this constitutes no difference between the word and the man.

Word and man depend on their community in which they find support for their articulation:

> (...) reality depends on the ultimate decision of the community; so thought is what it is, only by virtue of its addressing a future thought which is in its value as thought identical with it ... so that it has only a potential existence, dependent on the future thought of the community. (Peirce: CP 6, 585, CP 5, 311)

Word and community, both understood as signs of man's essence, lead to the contemporary uses of the concept "discourse." A discourse is, as Morris explained already in the 1930s of the twentieth century[11] on the one hand a coherent series of articulations through the use of a natural, and on the other through the use of an artificial, language. Legal articulations are a unique case. Legal discourse is an artificial language discourse made through the management of natural language components. This combination of artificiality and naturalness forms a philosophical challenge for semiotics as well as philosophers of law.

Reading Peirce

To read Peirce is not an incidental occurrence. Reading his texts (despite all discussions, doubts and polemics pertaining to editorial questions) means choosing a guide. How often and how intensely does one discuss with his guide about meaning and sense of a project at hand? That is a good question for a busy lawyer who has to pay attention to more than one case at the time and is involved in thorny matters of interpretation. In the middle of the road, such disputes seem dangerous. The answer is clear: a reflection on their practices is for lawyers already a difficult theoretical

[11] Ch. Morris: *Signs, Language and Behavior*, New York 1955[2], p. 130, and: *Signification and Significance*, Cambridge MIT, 1964, p. 60 f.

job to perform, which has virtually nothing to do with law-philosophical questions about the legal system, its norms, values or social impact.

Peirce texts are read as open-minded conversations, so that it is as if one does not need any knowledge of philosophical theories and viewpoints at all. A conversation with one's guide is not a matter of polemics: the lawyer will become informed—in particular about how to approach reality and its semiotic dimensions—so that the conversation has always great legal relevance. Are not lawyers constantly too busy to approach reality? Well then, Peirce shows hitherto unknown deep layers of a lawman's subject of interest.

One can always learn from Peirce's examples. The most outstanding example, or metaphor he uses is exactly *the hand of the sheriff.* Pencak's rich and sensitive essay on Peirce in his Pennsylvania estate called "Arisbe" describes Peirce's proximity to the law because of his enduring financial difficulties[12]. In a letter to Lady Welby, May 7, 1904, he writes:

> A court may issue injunctions and judgments against me and I not care a snap of my finger for them. I may think them idle vapor. But when I feel the sheriff's hand on my shoulder, I shall begin to have a sense of actuality. Actuality is something brute.
> The law of gravitation is the judge upon the bench who may pronounce the law till doomsday, but unless the strong-arm of the law, the brutal sheriff, gives effect to the law, it amounts to nothing.

One cannot dismiss the gesture of the sheriff as incidental or inadequate but *the sheriff's gesture makes meaning for me: I am a bearer of rights and duties!* The rupture in decent human relations, realized in the brute gesture of the sheriff's hand, makes me instantaneously into an actual legal subject. This meaning is new and this meaning is legal: the sheriff is a meaning maker, not unlike all our lawyers today. Change is the keyword here: shock and struggle, constraint and compulsion are its constitutive elements. Yet the sheriff is both symbol and object; she is the other and oneself, object symbol and interpretant in action. The hand of the sheriff can be abstracted as well to social expectation or communal responses; the old punishment of sunning provides a communal expression of the hand of the sheriff in a law system with an internal logic a little distinct from that of early twenty-first century states, but for all that still potent. But both law and the sheriff's hand can be further abstracted. At the limit, and as Foucault suggests as the condition of modernity in panoptic states, one can internalize the sheriff—my own hand can serve as a sign of the other (the sheriff) even as it constitutes me a legal subject. This internalization of sign, and interpretation exists autonomously of but in the shadow of the sheriff (in the form of the police power of the state, who also stands in the shadow of the law, which also stands itself in the shadow of the apparatus of law making/interpreting). What Peirce describes as a singularity, Kevelson sees as pieces of a system.

Moreover, there is the process character of semiosis. Signs are by no means fixated forever; they are temporary meanings in contextual situations, fluid and multi-interpretable—especially in law! Legal practitioners should acknowledge how their job establishes webs of (legal) meaning through the creation and maintenance of

[12] W.A.Pencak: "Peirce and Arisbe" in: *History, Signing In*. New York/Paris. Lang, 1993, p. 17 ff.

references. It contains the description of a rhetorical task. Rhetoric, in a universal sense, is according to Peirce the study of general conditions under which a problem presents itself for solution, and then under which one question leads to another. The latter remark articulates the process character in its entirety. Here is one of the invitational features of Peircean texts: the jurist will immediately experience the relevance for her own performances and conclude for herself that there is never an end to the process of meaning making, and never a moment of meaning fixation for good and forever—even not in the judgments of a Supreme Court! Our insights in Peirce's texts and their relation to the performances of lawyers contain an answer to the question why lawyers should read Peirce.

Why Lawyers Read Peirce

As was said before, reading Peirce is a fit task for lawyers. Peirce invites lawyers to rethink their own metaphors, everyday-life examples and steps of a legal profession. Those are encapsulated in the logic of discourse, in the techniques of pursuit of legal meaning, the growing awareness of the importance of language and communication. One does not need to read long strains of texts or to follow complex reasoning with abstract conclusions when reading Peirce's texts. Peirce as a philosopher is a master of short formulations as if he embraces the attitude of Wittgenstein in sentences like: "The philosopher's treatment of a question is like the treatment of an illness" or "obeying a rule is a practice", or "is what we call 'obeying a rule' something that it would be possible for only *one* man to do, and to do only *once* in his life?[13]" "Peircean thoughts in Wittgensteinean phrases", *or vice versa*—who would not read and contemplate them in the daily practices of law and life? Peirce's philosophy is on its way to become one of the most famous of American philosophy tout court. His work unfolds its importance for all who came to put analytical philosophy in perspective, for all who read Derrida and were fascinated by the vogue of deconstructionism, for all who were seduced by positivism in law and the sciences, for all who had difficulties to choose between principles, rules or original constitutions. His philosophy has a bright future.

Think of the post-Kantian categorization of reality, so that one learns to better understand how to change from one level of orientation to another or how to make a sound distinction between habits, rules, viewpoints, ideologies, beliefs, fixations and the like. These are altogether manifestations of the human mind involved in different regions of reality. Lawyers should keep differences between *firstness* and *secondness* in mind and to appreciate *thirdness* as a power of mediation—as if Peirce gave us a new compass to learn to know where we are! The categories first, second and third inspire practitioners and theoreticians of law as expressing (1) chance, (2) reaction, and (3) regularity or habit-formation. Important is also his differentiation of the various types of logic that guide us even where we do not precisely follow with scientific

[13] L. Wittgenstein: *Philosophical Investigations*. Blackwell, Oxford 1958 Nr. 255, 202, 199.

precision. Peirce's fascination by the logic of discourse towers above opinion battles among lawyers such as rule following, principle ridding, rule abiding, textual interpreting, literal meaning or narration adhering of lawyers. His philosophical fame is beyond most of our –isms, especially in as far as the founding of semiotics is concerned, which is a fact that can be an inspiration for lawyers and support their meaning making role in a globalizing society.

One should not forget, that Peirce's theory of signs forms the basis for a metaphysically relevant description of a universe in process. Everything that exists can be seen as a cosmic, an evolutionary process that embraces all humans alike. Peirce writes:

> (...) the entire universe, not merely the universe of existents, but all that wider universe, embracing the universe of existents as a part, the universe which we are all accustomed to refer to as "the truth"—that all this universe is perfused with signs, if it is not composed exclusively of signs. (Peirce CP 5. 448, note 300)

As a consequence, signs do not form a single factor of the semiotic approach, they are only functioning in a context of understanding the world in a pragmatist sense, that is as an ensemble of signs entering in and belonging to the flow of human activity. Signs join signs and their patterns form a universe that one can interpret like Aristotle already did: as The Universe.

> The universe is a vast representamen, a great symbol of God's purpose, working out its conclusions in living realities. ... In the little bit that you or I can make out of this huge demonstration, our perceptual judgments are the premises for us. The Universe as an argument is necessarily a great work of art, a great poem—for every fine argument is a poem and a symphony—just as every true poem is a sound argument. But let us compare it rather with a painting—with an impressionist seashore piece—then every Quality in a Premise is one of the elementary colored particles of the Painting; they are all meant to go together to make up the intended Quality that belongs to the whole as whole. That total effect is beyond our ken; but we can appreciate in some measure the resultant Quality of parts of the whole—which Qualities result from the combinations of elementary Qualities that belong to the premises. (Peirce CP. 5, 119)

Let us summarize the substantial arguments for a lawyer that may convince him to read Peirce, if his time budget allows or the structure of his meaning making forces her to do.

1. There is *no direct mention* of law, legal theory or legal practice in Peirce's oeuvre. As a lawyer, one should *not* attempt to organize a search for fragments or formulations that are immediately directive or otherwise relevant for law and legal practice. Who studies Peirce's texts is confronted with philosophical ideas, analyses and often bewildering conclusions from observations of everyday life. This gives the lawyer as it were *a passport for interpretations* that may highlight her own legal view on reality—never direct but always in balanced prose, rich in symbols of life in a semiotic process.
2. Any *quotation from the works of Peirce* in legal context is, despite the difficulties of editorial nature, a reliable quote. It will never be a quote simply because one sympathizes with a certain literary fashion, as was often the case with jurists citing for example Derrida and other deconstructionists in their legal theoretical considerations, briefs or decisions. Peirce's work receives increasingly global

respect and in particular interdisciplinary power of persuasion. An interdisciplinary approach is important for the entire legal profession. It is worthwhile to underline that the semiotic dimension of the Peirce texts makes his philosophy accessible to scientists and lawyers alike. Law will be more and more confronted with *binary* thought patterns, sign systems and semiotic processes, which are already dominating the world of e-communication and e-sciences together with the conceptualization of virtual reality.

3. The idea to understand *legal discourse as constituted by signs* is extremely fruitful for legal sciences, jurisprudence and the practice of law. It leads to an understanding of one's own sign interpretations, names (for instance of cases) becoming signs, references which signs necessarily unfold and other issues that Peirce offers for maintaining a logic of discourse. It furthermore clarifies how a lawyer's own activity is embedded in those uses of signs, symbols and reference patterns as well as other linguistic elements. Law and legal discourse are understandable and interpretable as a language on the basis of Peirce's intuitions, so that a renewed self-understanding can result from reading his texts.
4. A lawyer should not solely think about applications, but begin to understand how she is by definition in a privileged position in the process of semiotics. Lawyers are involved in the activity to conduct, understand, participate and create involvements in specific modifications of signs and meanings. This newly conceived view on reality and the jurist's own position enables him to adept a great variety of attitudes and signifying complexities within hitherto undiscovered horizons.
5. Jurists reading Peirce transcend today's battle of opinions and philosophies in legal philosophy and legal theory as well as global jurisprudence. They do not need to position themselves in legal positivism, legal realism, instrumentalism, natural law, interactionism, institution theory, systems theory, autopoiesis or legal pragmatism. Peirce's pragmatism does not initiate a new fashion in jurisprudence, but strives for a realistic and semiotically well-grounded view on reality as expressed in laws, statutes, decisions and other legal activities. It truly concerns "the lawyers' job" and creates distance to traditional syllogistic approaches in legal decision-making (A is, and B is, so C must be. . .). Peirce's philosophy is by no means a subject-centered and individualistic project. It could stimulate a lawyer to embrace a dialogic attitude and to reconsider the position of *self* and *other* in discourse. That contains a plea to perceive *affects* rather than to achieve *effects* when the legal job has to be performed—a truly new chapter opens when lawyers read Peirce!

Peirce Foundational for Law

Lawyers have to thank Peirce for encouraging them to adapt to the attitude and skill, which perceives the world as a sign. The legal mind can be liberated from traditional word-related views and habits (sign v. word). This is in effect when confronted with questions of interpretation debated on a scale reaching from literal interpretation towards originalism. *Otherness* permeates all forms of legal discourse, and concerns an opposite, a negation, a ground, a contrast, a shadow, an unexpected, a clown, a trickster, an absence, the true and the false and many more that normally bewilders jurists. Peirce laid the groundwork for the principle of *continuity* (logical as well as ontological), which includes a (re)-presentation of O/otherness. In so doing, he unfolded many features that are relevant for the foundations of a philosophy of law and legal discourse[14].

As biographer Joseph Brent highlights, there is an essay as early as 1867, which Peirce considers as being a part of "the substance of my central achievement." That is *not* his *pragmatism*[15]—the publicity given to *pragmatism* overlaid Peirce's deep and lasting concern about *the unity of things and ideas*. To unravel the connectedness of thingsappeared for him to be the truly philosophical task to complete. So, his philosophy deals with the *inter*connectedness of things. Legal language/discourse articulates these connections via the activities of the legal mind, accompanied with and most often created by *signs*, which are neither a reproduction of reality nor a copy of what they signify, but *constructions,* like maps, icons, or plans of action, and therefore do not limit their function to linguistic articulation. He focuses on the emergence of *novelty* as a principle upon which our conceptualizations are based—conceptualizations, which erroneously tend to bring reality to the fore as if 'words for things' exist. Under the heading of the concept 'continuum', Pierce contemplates the requirement that we bring novelty in harmony with already existing identities[16].

He thus unfolds his doctrine of Pure Chance as a factor in the context of *becoming*, and thus, as Kevelson notices, establishes *semiotics as a process of growth of thought.*[17] A sign is the fulfillment of the capacity to master inconsistency by connecting it with consistency; signs can thus (as was suggested a few lines above) be an opposite, an injunction in the surface of our text, speech or action. That conceptual appearance of "*a sign including its own very opposite*" brings the sign as just a phenomenon under the innumerable phenomena with which we are confronted. A sign makes us understand its conceptual representation, and not the thing it represents. Lawyers instinctively understand this—an aggregation of individuals can be signed "corporation" or it can be signed "partnership" or something else, yet the object, the group of people has not changed, even as its sign and the position of the interpretant has changed. Yet lawyers also have a difficult time consciously digesting this because it pertains only to knowledge, which can be approximated: the real is precisely *not* what is immediately before us, nor what seems predestined and ordered through laws. *The real is what emerges in new relational patterns*. As a result, one of the vibrantly

[14] Charles Sanders Peirce: *A New List of Categories* in: Proceedings of the American Academy of Arts and Sciences, Vol. VII, 287–298; Joseph Brent: *Charles Sanders Peirce. A Life.* Indiana UP, 1993, p. 69, and: -Id.-: "Pursuing Peirce" at members.door.net/arisbe/menu/library/aboutcsp/brent/pursuing.htm.

[15] For which Peirce is still known as a companion of William James, and which constitutes an elaborately discussed theme in legal philosophy.

[16] Kelly A. Parker: *The Continuity of Peirce's Thought,* Vanderbilt UP 1998. Ch. 4 & 8.

[17] Peirce, CP 6, p. 47 f.

modern features of Peirce's insights is a *pattern philosophy*![18] When lawyers apply these insights instinctively they are said to have absorbed the essence of common law lawyering; when they can through the semiosis develop their instincts into consciousness, they become more astute makers of meaning, because they may direct what their instincts once could only suggest.

What we think we know as legal realty and perhaps also reality tout court is always a reality represented by means of linguistic articulation. Reality is at every given time incomplete and inaccurate, even when interpreted with a logic that is capable of prediction. Kevelson comments: "only an inductive mode of inference can advance our knowledge of the world as it is becoming".[19] When we conceptualize a sign we enter an *unlimited* process of semiotics, as not only Peirce himself but later also Eco and Colapietro concluded[20]. This characterization has a far-reaching conclusion for the presence of reality as a concept in our discourses and the role of chance therein. Since there *are* no signs, Peirce suggests, and nothing *is* a sign, everything *can become* a sign such that there are ultimately solely sign functions, and those are only temporarily exercising such a function. Conceiving the very origin of reality involves a community, without limits and capable of a never-ending increase of knowledge.

> The real, then, is that which, sooner or later, information and reasoning would finally result in, and which is therefore independent of the vagaries of me and you". Hence Peirce: "There is nothing, then, to prevent our knowing outward things as they really are, and it is most likely that we do thus know them in numberless cases, although we can never be absolutely certain of doing so in any special case, Peirce writes. (Peirce CP 5, 315 f)
> We cannot remain steadfast with any doctrine of necessity or of determinacy. The combination of steadiness and chance is a major theme. Any moment she may interfere, spurring change, growth, twist and turn, or unforeseen development.
> Everywhere the main fact is growth and increasing complexity. (...) By thus admitting pure spontaneity of life as a character of the universe (...) I account for all the variety and diversity of the universe, in the only sense in which the really sui generis and new can be said to be accounted for. The ordinary view has to admit (...) that variety can spring only from spontaneity, or else shoves it back to the beginning of time and supposes it dead ever since. (Peirce CP 6, 58)

And he completes on the very same page "Yet chance is explanatory of change, which is a fact". This insight leads Peirce to his *evolutionary semiotics*. This viewpoint appears in the understanding of the sign: *signs are only possible in an open-ended, non-finite, complex and evolving process with chance as one of its major components*:

> I start by defining what I mean with a sign. It is something determined by something else its object and itself influencing some person in such a way that that person becomes thereby mediately influenced or determined in some respect by that Object.

[18] William Gibson: *Pattern Recognition*. Berkley/Penguin 2005; Daniel C. Dennett: "Real Patterns", in: *The Journal of Philosophy*, Vol. 88, 1. p. 21 f., Leonard Uhr: *Pattern Recognition,* New York Wiley & Sons 1966.

[19] Roberta Kevelson: *Peirce, Paradox, Praxis*. Mouton de Gruyter 1990, p. 310.

[20] Umberto Eco: *A Theory of Semiotics*. Bloomington. Indiana UP. 1979, p. 69, 120 ff. See also: Vincent M. Colapietro, *Peirce's Approach to the Self. A Semiotic Perspective on Human Subjectivity*. New York, 1989, p. 35 f.

Peirce could do so after already describing in 1901 how anything which determines something else must refer to an object to which itself refers to something else in the same way; that the 'something else' must become in turn a sign, and so on.

Emphasis is on the last three words: the '*and so on*'. This statement suggests that it is questionable whether consciousness can ever be seen as the sole condition to understand a sign. There is always a determination of a sign of the same object at work of which it is itself a sign! As a consequence, there is virtually an endless series of signs when a sign is understood, and a sign never understood cannot be said to be a sign. Not consciousness, but the virtually endless series of signs in which consciousness is involved is essential for understanding a sign. Signs are the outcome of evolutionary processes. If we do not accept chance, we cannot understand signs! Thus, there exists for Peirce a remarkable tension between chance and design, between novelty and habitual patterning. What is essential in the concept of a sign is also of essence in the entire project of semiotics—law and legal discourse included.

The General and the Particular

Peirce focused not on law and its practices. His fascination concerned nature, history and mankind in general. But he shows clearly that our understanding of the law depends on the relation between propositions of universal and/or of particular character. This is a *semiotic* issue, which has its foundations in many of his philosophical insights. *Legal* laws are *particular* (even when they seem to be general within their own discourse) and make Peirce's plea for 'coherence *together with* chance' important. Kevelson calls that plea a "'hotbed' of possibility" of greatest importance for modern law.[21] She thus characterizes "the attempt to transform the idea of law from a universal proposition which is indefinite and vague to a particular proposition which is definite and resolved of vagueness" as a stumbling block[22] that Austin and others met when discussing legal positivism and determinism. That voice changes our view on the relationship between universality and particularity from *deterministic* to *chance-related*. Peirce has shown this in most of his works.[23]

His thoughts concern a hitherto unwritten study on law. Fisch underlined a huge relevance for the foundations of law and legal discourse:

> I argue that Peirce had a much greater and lifelong interest in law and in social philosophy than has hitherto been recognized.

---

[21] Roberta Kevelson: *The Law as a System of Signs*, N.York 1988;—id.: *Peirce and the Mark of the Gryphon*, N.York 1999;—id.: *Peirce, Paradox, Praxis*, N.York/Berlin 1990.—id.: *Inlaws/Outlaws*, Peter de Lang, Lisse 1977;—id.: *Peirce, Science, Signs*, N.York/Bern 1996.

[22] Kevelson, *Peirce, Paradox, Praxis*, see (18), p. 173.

[23] Peirce, CP 5, Ch 5, and CP 6, 32, 51 f, 63 f, 200f, 204, 270, 336.

He placed Peirce's concern with law and legal thinking in a biographical perspective, and writes:

> Philosophers of law (. . .) have often remarked that there were several distinguished lawyers in the Metaphysical Club in which pragmatism was born, and have traced connections between pragmatism and 'legal realism'; but more recently Roberta Kevelson and others have found relevance to legal reasoning in a much wider range of Peirce's work on logic.[24]

Legal semiotics, as prepared in Peirce's logic, metaphysics and pragmatism, takes the spirit and the form of such a philosophical endeavor. His inspiration profiles a legal philosophy in at least the fields of meaning and argument, chance, and the open character of discourse.

We are not used to a life based on the idea that every discourse must be perceived as a place where meanings are made, ideas grow and novelty occurs. Where is room for chance, fate and fortune?[25] Certainly, legal-doctrinal features are in essence *rhetorical.* They fortify the narrative that keeps *law as an institution* alive and appreciate habit formation. One does this very effectively with regard to legal argumentation.[26]

The *semiotics of argument* in law and legal practice demonstrate how contentions are offered as if they were facts, but once we are clear about how inconsistency creates consistency, incoherence causes coherence, and incompleteness functions as an element of completeness, Greimas would suggest. We understand how arguments are *made* (and not simply represented) within the boundaries of discourse[27].

The days Peirce participated in Harvard's Metaphysical Club in 1872, Sir Frederick Pollock had just written several lines which were clearly ahead of their time, stating: "Law in the widest sense is a condition or assemblage of conditions under which the evolution of things proceeds. . . ".[28] Yet he could also have been echoing Aristotle; "for the people do not easily change, but love their own ancient customs; and it is by small degrees only that one thing tales the place of another; so that the ancient laws will remain, while the power will be in the hands of those who have brought about revolution in the state."[29] That emphasis on evolution is explored where James Boyd White offers an example that reflects upon how a text named "The Constitution" inspired modern US society to create *a culture of argument.* He

[24] Fisch, Op. Cit., p. 13, 438. The *Metaphysical Club* is a philosophical club with the future Justice O.W.Holmes Jr, the psychologist William James and with Charles Sanders Peirce, established in January 1872 in Cambridge, Mss and dissolved in December 1872. When Peirce arrived at Johns Hopkins University in 1879, he founded a new Club there, which existed six more years.

[25] John H. Merryman: *The Civil Law Tradition,* Stanford UP 1985 (2nd Ed.) Ch 2; Ch 5.

[26] I. A. Richards: *The Philosophy of Rhetoric,* Oxford UP 1936, Ch. 2.

[27] Algirdas J. Greimas & François Rastier: "The Interaction of Semiotic Constraints", *Yale French Studies,* Vol. 41, 1968.

[28] F. Pollock: "Law and Command", in: *Law Magazine and Review*, 1872,1. p. 189 f.

[29] Aristotle, *A Treatise on Government*, Book IV; Ch. V, at 117/(William Ellis, trans., London: JM Dent 1912).

concludes how "this is thus in a literal sense a rhetorical constitution: it constitutes a rhetorical community, working by rhetorical processes that it has established but can no longer control. *It establishes a new conversation on a permanent basis.*"[30]

Arguments establish law and legal discourse during the process of meaning making that unfolds whilst determining a truth in an incidental case.[31] Is this meaning making a process beyond discursive coercion? "One should beware of believing that the inventive mind operates according to chance." That sentence of the French Enlightenment philosopher Destutt de Tracy provides Greimas with a motto for his groundbreaking 1968 essay. A major problem is, how an *order of things* emerges, and encounters us with vision, feeling and spontaneity where human creativity unfolds. Peirce understood his own personal fate as well as the development of his ideas about an evolutionary cosmology, which colored his lifelong interest in philosophy and logic, in this light. In *Evolutionary Love,* written in 1893 he suggests that all forms of evolution reign over a person in his or her social context.[32] Thus, the development of a human character shows how *any self is a sign for itself.*

> Every thought, or cognitive representation, is of the nature of a sign. 'Representation' and 'sign' are synonyms. The whole purpose of a sign is that it shall be interpreted in another sign; and its whole purport lies in the special character, which it imparts to that interpretation. When a sign determines an interpretation of itself in another sign, it produces an effect external to itself (...) not in this or that metaphysical sense, but in an indisputable *(read: argumentative, rhetorical)* sense. (...) Thinking is a kind of action, and reasoning is a kind of deliberate action; and to call an argument illogical, or a proposition false, is a special kind of moral judgment, and as such is inapplicable to what we cannot help. This does not deny that what cannot be conceived today may be conceivable tomorrow. But just as long as we cannot help adopting a mode of thought, so long it must be thoroughly accepted as true. Any doubt of it is idle make-believe and irredeemable paper. (Peirce CP 8, p. 191)

---

[30] James Boyd White: *When Words Lose Their Meaning,* Chicago UP 1984, p. 246; also Ch. Perelman: *The idea of Justice and the Problem of Argument*, London/New York 1963, and Perelman/Olbrechts-Tyteca, *The New Rhetoric: A Treatise on Argumentation*, Notre Dame UP 1969. Notice the proximity to I. Prigogine & I. Stenger: *Order Out Of Chaos,* Glasgow 1984.

[31] Jan M. Broekman & William A. Pencak: *Lawyers Making Meaning. The Roberta Kevelson Seminar on Law and Semiotics at Penn State University's Dickinson School of Law,* IJSL Vol. 22, Nr. 1, 2009. See there D.J.Brion: "Trial Argumentation: The Creation of Meaning" p. 23 ff. See also: Paul Van Fleet: "Tarski, Peirce and Truth-Correspondences in Law", in: *The Semiotics of Law in Legal Education*, Jan M. Broekman & Francis J. Mootz III [Eds], Springer 2011, Chap. 3.

[32] Ch. S Peirce: *The Essential Peirce*, N.Houser & Chr. Kloesel (Eds), Vol. 1. Indiana UP 1992, p. 362.

Chapter 4
Greimas, Law, Discourse and Interpretative Squares: The Precursor De Saussure

The Precursor: De Saussure

The Swiss linguist Ferdinand M. de Saussure (1857–1913) gave his first Course on General Linguistics in 1906, his second 1908 and his third 1910 in Geneva. The texts were published 1961 in Paris, after they had already confirmed his fame during the last years of his life. His name remains acknowledged in realms of linguistics, structuralism and semiotics, as the many quotations from his Course prove. It is therefore almost natural that also Greimas' linguistics and semiotics shows traces of insights originated by De Saussure. Three of them are of importance in the context of legal semiotics: (a) the cultural and linguistic circuit that is in operation when we speak, (b) the arbitrary character of a sign, and (c) linguistic terms must become studied in view of their differences and similar relations.

The Language Circuit in Operation

Components at various levels, which are reaching from physiology to social relations, are at stake in a 'language circuit in operation' when we speak. The individual speech act reveals the circuit of the word, which depends on at least two individuals and a context. Each act in the language circuit represents an embryonic linguistic circuit that approaches a social fact, De Saussure remarks. One should notice a series of distinctions that determine this circuit.

a. There is an exterior part, made by the sounds that travel from mouth to ear, and an interior part, in which unfolds all this psycho-physiologically.
b. So there is, more generally spoken, a mental part to distinguish from a non-mental part, which relates to specific organs as well as to the mental properties of the individual as such.
c. Furthermore, there is an active and a passive part, the first pertains to what goes from the center of association in one subject to the ear of the other; the second what goes from that ear to the other's association center.

J. M. Broekman, L. Catà Backer, *Lawyers Making Meaning*,
DOI 10.1007/978-94-007-5458-4_4, © Springer Science+Business Media Dordrecht 2013

d. Finally, one has to account what is situated in the brain, where is executive what seems active, and receptive what seems passive.

The greatest role in the organization of language as a system is for the associative and coordinative function, which manifests itself as soon as non-isolated signs are in play. The latter function leads to the *social* importance of language, which is supported by the insight into its *structural* properties. This leads De Saussure to two important conclusions in view of legal semiotics.

Firstly, individuals are bound by language in that they tend to reproduce same (types of) signs united with same (types of) concepts. This is called "social crystallization". Secondly, the inherent division between the social and the individual as well as the necessary and the accidental dimension causes De Saussure to distinguish famously between *langue* and *parole,* between language as a pattern or structure and word as a component. It interests, that the mental part of the circuit may always be individual, and this individual always masters that part—here is the reason to relate this to a word and to distinguish this word from the language, which is never a solely individual occurrence. When a judge asks a defendant to say a word, he appeals to what he has in common with the defendant when the latter performs the mental act of uttering a word. Is a judge ever able to relate to this mental component of the defendant? De Saussure would formulate his doubts[1]. The second conclusion, discussed more fully below, touches on the arbitrariness of signs.

The Arbitrary Character of a Sign

A famous observation concerns the *arbitrariness* of meaning and function of a linguistic sign. De Saussure considers this an essential fact for any type of semiology, because he defines that as the science, which studies "signs at/as the basis of social life". Language is only one specific system within the totality of semiological events. The answer in most of our everyday life situations is that language is a nomenclature, which we all use and thus do not challenge to perform further research about its true nature. We are, however, surprised by the fact that *a sign always seems to escape an individual or a social power of determination!* De Saussure underlines that a linguistic sign does *not*, like our general opinion holds, bring a name and a thing together, but only a *concept* and an *acoustic image*. The image is not a physical sound but a mental imprint of the sound, the sensorial representation that gives us the impression of a sense. It follows, that defining a linguistic sign (and a sign in linguistics) is *a mental entity with a double face*: the face of the *signified* and the face of the *signifier*—which is an observation not far from Peirce's considerations. The expression "sign" thus designates the totality of signified and signifier. But, one should add, that totality is in itself an issue to review. Derrida and Barthes have suggested that this totality is identical with a 'humanist' worldview at the center of

[1] F. de Saussure: *Cours de Linguistique Générale.* New Edition, Paris 1972, p. 27–35. English transl: *Course in General Linguistics,* (Roy Harris, Ed.) Open Court, Chicago/La Salle, 1983.

which a European image of men functions. It is exactly this totality that should be conceived of as a dissipating historical fact, so that the signifier-signified system breaks down. A link between De Saussure and Peirce would be this: that a linguist and a philosopher view that dissipation concordantly. In that view, they suggest expanding the signifier-signified relationship; they understand it not only as a linguistic but also at as a global political issue that ultimately touches our understanding of human nature[2].

However, De Saussure does (in contrast to Peirce) not give signifier and signified a full and independent position, so that his vision on relations in the sign context remains in essence *dualistic,* as his focus on signifier and signified shows. Here is a vital difference with modern semiotics, phenomenology and linguistics. De Saussure tries to illustrate how the speaker-hearer relation functions at the basis of each speech act, which covers all elements of the linguistic circuit as described earlier in this paragraph. He creates, in other words, a straight line from brain, ear and mouth or tongue of person A to the same in person B, vice versa. There is no trace of any more complex or context based consciousness in the performance of a speech act.

The sign in De Saussure's linguistics combines concept and acoustic image, but the performance of a sign seems designed according to the acoustic image alone: signified and signifier are equivalently taking their role in that one performance act. Moreover, languages have their own concepts and sound images. Languages have a relational conception of their elements; words and their meanings are defined by contrasting comparison of one to another. For instance, the sound images for and the conception of a book differ from those of a tree.

Linguistic signs are arbitrary because of the nature of their elements—if one comes to this conclusion, then they must be defined in terms of function rather than in terms of inherent qualities, as De Saussure shows. Moreover, they are arbitrary because nothing justifies a priori an order of phonemes that leads to a particular association, which delivers in its turn an idea of the signified. The arbitrariness, one must conclude philosophically, results from the subtle dualism, which De Saussure keeps intact when analyzing the basic linguistic act: the speech act: in his own words the "parole" rather than the "langue". It means, that he perceives language (formally) as a system of differential elements, which is a look at language and linguistics that differs from earlier scientific approaches, which consider the inherent qualities of language elements rather then their position and function.

Differences and Other Relations

The theme is already included in the earlier paragraph, which tell us that words and their meaning are in De Saussure's view understood through contrast and comparison. The linguistic *sign* is an outstanding example for how the unity of signifier and signified plays an outstanding role in the system of linguistic elements and how they

---

[2] T. Hawkes: *Structuralism and Semiotics,* California UP, 1977, Ch. 4.

are different in place and function within that system. To perceive those differences as being essential elements for sense and meaning of the signs, words or expressions includes the acceptance of *language as a system* (not as some naturally grown organism) and as a composite of different sounds combined with different ideas. The formal account of this plurality does not delete the qualities at stake, but this account produces a new light on linguistics and semiotics. A language does not contain ideas and sounds, which existed *before* the linguistic system, but only conceptually and phonically different elements *in* that system. The proof is, according to De Saussure, that a linguistic term can be changed without one even touches its sense or sound but only because a neighboring term in the system changed or acquired another place. Two general and parallel conclusions come up: first, "in language are only differences" and secondly, "language is a form and not a substance"[3].

This type of ideas is very near to what became *structuralism*, together with *phenomenology* and *existentialism*—all being well-known philosophical mainstreams in the decades before and after the Second World War[4]. In particular the Prague School in structuralism, with R. Jakobson and N. Trubetzkoy, underlined that language was a lively hierarchy of markedly distinctive features. That idea appeared to be concordant with American authors from Bloomfield to Chomsky, who in their turn underlined what De Saussure had observed, namely that linguistic studies concentrating on speech, on the coordination of sound and sense, were equally valid in their observations of textual structures. The writing seems often more clear in this regard then the speech activity: understanding differences as distinctive seems extremely important for text analysis and for understanding discourses (the latter as a unity of speech and writing). De Saussure has confirmed this in a formulation in which he notices that all language is like a piece of paper. There exists always a recto side and a verso side of language, he writes, and this combination is also valid for linguistic sound/thought on one side and linguistic form on the other. No wonder, that the textual dimensions, which are revealed here, as well as the combination of arbitrary and differential features in language—two qualities that are correlative forms in themselves—are fulfilling a decisive role in founding semiotics, as is the case in the work of Greimas.

---

[3] F. de Saussure, *Cours*, p. 166, 169 (see note 69).

[4] Jan M. Broekman: *Structuralism. Moscow, Prague, Paris*. German Ed. Freiburg 1971; English Ed. Dordrecht 1974.

Chapter 5
Greimas, Law, Discourse and Interpretative Squares: An Author, his Squares and Legal Discourse Analysis

Squares and Discourse Analysis

The are at least two themes of particular interest for legal semiotics in the oeuvre of the French linguist Algirdas Julien Greimas (1917–1992), who is with his close friend Roland Barthes considered the most important semiotician in modern French culture. The first is his construction of so-called semiotic squares, an instrument to analyze semiotic dimensions of concepts in daily but also importantly for scientific discourses such as law. The second is an exemplary analysis of a legal discourse, in particular pertaining to commercial law and groups of commercial companies. The squares are proposed in his 1966 *Structural Semantics* and in a 1968 article with François Rastier on *The Interaction of Semiotic Constrains*. The legal discourse analysis is a chapter of his 1976 book: *The Social Sciences. A Semiotic View*.

Law and Greimas Squares

Greimas' semiotic square is characterized as "a discovery instrument" focusing the construction of meaning in terms of language, including all various semantic topics[1]. No wonder, that this instrument became so important for legal practice. His famous deployment of semiotic squares illustrates the full complexity of any sign or other semantic term within a system of signification—including law as a system of signs, as Kevelson noticed. The semiotic square posits a set of reverberations from a core binary opposition from which a semiotic universe of contingent symbol and interpretation may be adduced. For example: start with a primary opposition: black (S_1)–white (S_2). Each then generates its own contradiction; $<$ black (S_1)–not black ($\sim S_1$) $>$, and $<$ white (S_2)–not white ($\sim S_2$) $>$. But it also generates its own complementary set as well: $<$ black (S_1)–not white ($\sim S_2$) $>$, and $<$ white (S_2)–not black ($\sim S_1$) $>$ and its inversion: $<$ black (S_1) AND white (S_2) $>$ (for example grey);

[1] See the exemplary uses and construction of squares in: Michelle L. Wirth: "Semiotics of Parenthood in Legal Perspective" in: *The Semiotics of Law in Legal Education*, Jan M. Broekman & Francis J. Mootz III (Eds), Op. Cit., p. 157 ff.

J. M. Broekman, L. Catà Backer, *Lawyers Making Meaning*,
DOI 10.1007/978-94-007-5458-4_5, © Springer Science+Business Media Dordrecht 2013

and < not black ($\sim S_1$) AND not white ($\sim S_2$) > (for example, red). The complexity becomes systemic when individual semiotic squares are themselves layered; the object is to map all logical possibilities of interpretation within a given set of objects-signs.

Greimas points at the importance of oppositions in semantics like De Saussure did, because we have to be attentive to the fact that any given *seme* entails its opposite or "contrary." "Life" is for example understood in relation to its contrary "death"; the same is the case for all gender issues, ultimately for all articulated issues of human life and its cultures. Yet, one should notice that the square is meant to be a heuristic instrument because it combines structure and flexibility in an unusual way. Squares can in that regard become determined as "post-structural" or as issues developed "after structuralism"[2]. The axes of the square define its structure and the formal relationships they express. But the terms that compose the axes are not static at all; they interact dynamically with all present actors and factors, and these interactions bring new terms to the fore. This leads to a formal representation of social dynamics inherent to the semiotic discipline.

Semiotic Constraints

The beginning of the groundbreaking article on the implied method and philosophy, published 1968 in *Yale French Studies* under the title "The Interaction of semiotic constraints", has a motto of the French writer Destutt de Tracy that formulates in an astonishing proximity to Peirce: "One should beware of believing that the inventive mind operates according to chance". The Ancient Greek Goddess of chance, providence or fate, *Tyche*—which we encountered in Peirce's expression 'tychism'—determines how an *order of things* emerges. It will fascinate lawyers that she was understood as *the constellation virgo*, the *Dike* who took care of Justice. She encounters us with vision, feeling and spontaneity in the case of human creativity, and exactly that type of creativity is the focus of Greimas' analyses. A central issue is the recognition of Tyche as a force that reigns over a person in his or her social context, thus influencing and often even determining the development of a human character: the self itself is for itself a *sign*. This structural self-understanding is based on insight in *order* tout court, an order that expands itself in the form of *accelerating reasonableness*[3]. This theory of identity focuses on the cosmic dimensions of human life. The analysis of human creativity is indicated with a non-scientific expression that could irritate the reader even today: with the expression *the play* and the analysis in its entirety as *a journey*[4]. Greimas and Rastier write:

---

[2] This distinction is missing in the standard publication about Greimas and legal semiotics: Bernard Jackson: *Semiotics and Legal Theory,* Kegan Paul London 1985, Reprint Deborah Charles 1997, p. 31 ff.

[3] Peirce, CP 5, 3.

[4] Peirce has already 1897, under the influence of the German philosopher Fr. Schiller's idea on "Spieltrieb", used the expression "the play of musement" for a scientific attitude in a new key. The

> The play in question here is not to be understood as a free activity productive of literary objects, but as a long journey punctuated with compelling choices that leads, through a series of exclusions and of options, manifesting personal and social phobias and euphorias, to the constitution of an original and unique work. Instead of analyzing a completed text, the authors have tried to see how, starting from kernels of meaning, from categories of meaning which are at once simple and basic, the creative faculty operates, a faculty which, proceeding from the simple to the complex, from the general to the particular, makes its way, through a number of determinisms, toward an exaltation of liberty.

From the viewpoint of legal semiotics one could ask whether those approaches and methods are apt to lead to understanding anything of law and legal discourse. *Law and the exaltation of liberty*—are they compatible at all? And can one find traces of the play of the creative mind in the construction and management of legal discourse, not to mention law as a social institution? Yet, the aim of the authors who wish to introduce their analytical project of analyzing human creativity, especially in their textual expressions, would by no means exclude legal discourse.

> It is obvious that, in the first part of its journey, there is nothing specifically literary in the play of the creative mind, obvious that it draws from the same sources as the whole of meaningful human activity: the theoretical aim of this study is thus largely anthropological, in open opposition to the suspect tradition of occidental humanism which sets forth literature as a basic datum. Thus the text to be read, while illustrating a possible semiotic approach to literary objects, is at the same time a calling into question of the literary phenomenon.

Then they take a commonplace methodology in proposing a line of development, which reaches from textual depth structures to manifest surface structures:

> Perhaps out of a desire for intelligibility, we can imagine that the human mind, in order to achieve the construction of cultural object (literary, mythical, pictorial, etc.) starts with simple elements and follows a complex course, encountering on its way constraints to which it must submit, as well as choices which it can make.

Our aim is to give a rough idea of this course. It may be considered to move from immanence to manifestation, in three principal stages:

- *deep structures*, which define the fundamental mode of existence of an individual or a society, and subsequently the conditions of existence of semiotic objects. As far as we know, the elementary constituents of deep structures have a definable logical status.
- *superficial structures* constitute a semiotic grammar system which arranges into discursive forms the contents susceptible of manifestation. The products of this grammar system are independent of the expression, which reveals them, in as far as they can theoretically appear in any substance, and, in the case of linguistic objects, in any language.
- *the structures of manifestation* produce and organize the significances. Although they can include quasi-universals, they remain particular to any given language (or more precisely they define the particular characteristics of languages), or to

---

scientist should then be a "Dandy", an expression of what later was described by Walter Benjamin as "flaneur". See also: Jack M. Balkin & B.S.Noveck (Eds): *The State of Play. Law, Games, and Virtual Worlds* New York UP 2006.

any given material. They are studied by the superficial stylistics of morphemes, shapes, colors, etc.[5]

To introduce the backgrounds of legal semiotics in the sense of Greimas' analyses and the construction of Greimasian squares as a consequence, we focus here only on two introducing paragraphs in the path-breaking article, which deal with the elementary structure of meaning, and the author's view on the construction of semiotic systems. Additional and more extensive information is in the reading of the entire text—an exercise, which by the way is seldom performed by legal semioticians that practice a Greimasian analysis in the case of law and legal discourse, and highlight meaning making.

The Structure of Semiotic Systems

This title in the Greimas article is somewhat misleading. Semiotic systems do not have one fixed structure, so that there is not one structure of semiotic systems, but semiotic systems have as their particular property that they are continuously in a process of structuring and thus also of re-structuring. Once a structure is established, one could perceive how other structures incorporate that structure and form superior structures, transforming the former into signs that function in the latter. This is the point of departure for the next paragraph on semiotic systems, which relates closely to the first on meaning making. Greimas writes:

> If deductive considerations thus encounter inductive descriptions, it is because the elementary structure of meaning forms into systems the semantic universes taken as a whole. Indeed, each of the contents, which it defines, can, as a semantic axis, include others, which are in turn organized into a structure isomorphic to the superior hierarchic structure. Thus, the elementary structure articulates in the same way the semes and the constituent systematic instances of semiotic systems. For example, the contents Life and Death embrace the whole semantic universe of Bernanos: that is S_1 vs S_2. Each one articulates in two systematic instances (negative and positive definitions) which are written respectively: s_1 vs s_2; s_2 vs s_1. They are articulated in their turn into semic systems.
> The *terms* of the model, using each of the four terms as point of departure, one can obtain the three others by the two operations: by taking the contradictory and by taking the contrary. Their definition is formal, and anterior to any investment.

The *relations*:

a. hierarchical: a hyponymic relation is established between sj and s2, and S; another between$^{-g}{}_2$ and S.
b. categorical: —a relation of contradiction is established between S and S; and at the hierarchically inferior level, between s_1 and and $-s_2$—a relation of "contraries"

[5] See a parallel/precursor text in: Noam Chomsky: *Topics in the Theory of Generative Grammar*, Lectures Indiana 1964 re-published in the *Janua Linguarum*, Series Minor No. 56, Mouton, The Hague, Paris 1969, p. 37 f. And also: Julia Kristeva: "L'engendrement de la formule" in: *SEMEIOTIKÉ Recherches pour une Sémanalyse*, Paris 1969, p. 278

articulates s_1 and s_2 on the one hand, and "g_2 on the other. In the terms of Hjelmslev, it may be identified as solidarity, or double presupposition.

Note: The two operations: that of taking the contradictory and that of taking the opposite, are involutive: the opposite of the opposite of s is s; the contradictory of the contradictory of s is s.

The two axes, formed by relation of contraries, are themselves in a relation of contradiction.The two schemas, defined by relations of contradiction, are themselves in a relation of opposition.

We propose calling the double presupposition of the two schemas *semiosis*. We reserve for later study the question of whether this double presupposition corresponds to that of linguistic content and expression, considered as the two schemas of a single model.

Series of Squares

A semiotic square might in turn be tied to other binary oppositions in the narrative. As Greimas explains, nothing permits us to assert that a semiotic manifestation is dependent on only one system at a time. And so far as it is dependent on several systems, its closure can be attributed to the interaction of the different systems that produce it. In other words, one can construct a series of, say, three semiotic squares that explore various levels of a story, each semiotic square related to the next. The entire mechanism is capable of generating at least ten conceivable positions out of a rudimentary binary opposition (which may originally have been no more than a single term, e.g., 'white,' which proves to be internally defined by a hidden opposition we articulate by promoting the concealed pole 'black' to visibility)". The importance for legal discourse is understandable as a semiotic instrument to cope with legal texts. All sorts of phenomena are organized by this semiotic logic of narratives.

A good nonliterary and only peripheral legal example is the logic of European traffic lights. In Europe, the yellow light has two functions: when a yellow light follows green, you are expected to slow down and prepare to stop (as in the United States and Canada); when a yellow light follows a red light, you are warned to get ready to move forward. The story of the yellow light differs, however, from the story of red and green. The yellow is of a later date, after red and green had been functioning for a long time. Particularly in the US is its full meaning not always evident to the road users. The green light is in clear contrast to the red light but the relation of green and red to the yellow is less clear. The green light represents "prescription" or a "positive injunction" (cross!); the red light represents an "interdiction" or a "negative injunction" (don't cross!). In the European system of lights, there are also given both contradictory pairs: when the yellow light follows green, the sign is a non-*prescription* (get ready to stop!); when the yellow light follows red, the sign is a non-*interdiction* (get ready to go!). If the yellow light stands alone without changing, it assumes a neutral position: both a nonprescription and a non-interdiction (get ready to stop if you see someone crossing but be ready to go if you see no one!). The point is that we are all constrained by the finite series of possibilities opened up by such semiotic oppositions.

An author, a producer of any semiotic object, operates within a fragmented system of knowledge, which is the result of his individuality and the society in which he is inscribed. At this point, an expansion of the example is interesting. In the inverse situation in which a EU person has to decipher US traffic signs, other problems arise. The majority of US signs are written, in contrast to the pictorial signs and symbols in the EU. Some of them are clear commands in words: "Do not enter", "Do not pass" or even "Stop Here on Red". Others are directives regarding driving situations, such as "Don't Tailgate", "Watch for Ice". But many are neither commands nor signs, although thy look like traffic signs and mean to order traffic and traffic behavior, such as: "D.U.I. You Can't Afford It"—those are moral prescriptions rather than traffic signs. The general conclusion from such examples is, that only within a specific culture and a society it is possible to make a limited number of choices. They result from the investment of organized contents, that is, contents endowed with values /valorizations (possibilities of relations). What is possible in Europe is impossible in the United States, and vice versa; each world of meaning has been made differently. It is at this point that one turns again to communication when systems interact—for example when France and the United States develop programs for mutual recognition of drivers' licenses.

With this example in mind it seems evident that Greimas distinguishes (later followed by Kristeva) between "deep structure" and "surface structure" of narratives. The first has a definable logical structure, whereas the second transforms semiotic materials into discourse forms. Especially deep structures are explained and analyzed by means of the semiotic square. The self-reference of legal discourse is manifest in its deep structures, but the series of legal signifiers forms also a self-referential whole so that there should be pictured a twofold self-referential feature in law and legal discourse.

A Legal Discourse Semiotically Analyzed

In his chapter about a semiotic analysis of a legal discourse—one of the pillars of his 1976 publication on semiotics and the social sciences—are many important legal issues to withhold and understand. We select two observations,one that focuses on the *definition of a legal discourse*, and another on *law as a text*.

Discussing the definition of law and legal discourse has always been an interesting but rather useless effort. Yet, the theme has for centuries fascinated the minds of lawyers and philosophers. If one adheres to a rather loose understanding of the business of defining, and accepts actions such as describing, changing terminology or metaphors, explaining or redirecting the narrative, one finds such mental moves all over the Greimas text.

That is no surprise, because any semiotic discourse analysis requires a notion of the discourse's specificity and insight in questions about the character involved.

Greimas speaks in this context about a dominant *myth* in social sciences as the main context for a specific discourse analysis. One of the most persistent myths is the *multidisciplinary* approach—a semiotic analysis of legal discourse performed by sociologists, political scientists, linguists, philosophers and lawyers would seem to be its perfect realization. This, however, does not fulfill the requirements of the mythical dream, since a semiotic analysis is not served by a plurality of viewpoints and approaches but rather by a commonly designed knowledge resulting in a unique methodology. A first manifestation of such a methodology is the acceptance of the insight, that a legal text can only be understood as a *legal* text if one is in agreement about what legal discourse in its totality means.

Greimas offers three considerations to determine any agreement about what a legal discourse is or should be given that name. The first, almost certainly subject of consideration in many regards, is the fact that any legal discourse is always subordinated to more encompassing discourses in a society, and that legal discourses manifest themselves in broader natural languages. Secondly, legal discourse is in a true sense of the word a discourse, which means a linguistic organization comprising such elements as lexemes, syntagms, enunciations (which he calls 'phrastic') as well as elements like paragraphs or chapters (which he calls 'paraphrastic'). Finally, *the qualification of legal discourse as legal implies the discursive organization of specific elements, in particular of acknowledged and institutionalized legal speech acts*.

Is there any specific difference between a natural language discourse and a legal discourse? Greimas acknowledges the problematic relation between them, between a *natural language* discourse and a *legal* discourse, although the latter seems to be a manifestation of the first. He observes that a legal discourse unfolds in a most remarkable double sense: it is a *legislative* as well as a *referential* discourse. Judgments and performative acts create things to be, rules to follow and behaviors to qualify. References are implied in every discursive move; everything once said or laid down is given a second or a third life within the boundaries of legal discourse. Its referential power is amazing: relations between words and things are in the hand of legal discourse participants and their major speakers (such as judges). Are these relations between words and things compatible with those created in a natural language discourse? Their relations to a natural language are linguistically and for semiotics in particular, very important. The legislative level of meaning of legal discourse cannot exist nor be effective without reference to its inherent referential level. How everyday-life reality relates to legal reality remains the semiotic issue par excellence. The character of that relation appears circular: there is no legislative expressiveness without reference, but also no reference without a view on legislative meanings. As a conclusion, one should formulate that a natural language is a semiotic complex system; it supports special discourses as a sub-discourse in the realm of natural languages. In legal issues or in striving for justice in everyday life, the manifestation of a sub-system remains a function of the natural language, Greimas formulates, as a connotation to the daily facts of life.

Law as a Text

When studying law, one encounters a specific *grammar* at work in legal discourse. This legal grammar differs from the grammar of the natural language in which law wants to be effective. Each student of law has to learn that grammar, and each lawyer must practice law along the lines of that grammar. All this leads to the presupposition of the existence of a more or less autonomous legal dictionary. Grammar and dictionary are in that light the major manifestations of legal semiotics. Each text in law shows therefore the necessity to *combine* legal grammar and legal dictionary and *is limited in meaning and expressiveness by those two*. However, the system character of legal discourse is very weak: a legal grammar shows a small and finite numbers of definitions and prescriptions without a conceptual hierarchy or a coherent series of rules. The main task of a legal grammar is solely to form correct enunciations and discursive unities, which sustain legal discourse in its totality and above all its effects through the natural language of everyday.

De Saussure's attention for the combination of sound and sense in language developed in the studies of Greimas towards more abstract concepts, with grammar and dictionary as symbols for a formal grip on language. Yet, the speech act in law serves him as a prevailing activity although a reading/writing faculty is more important for legal practice in daily life. Two features, which determine the semiotic appreciation of a text in law and legal discourse, are of outstanding importance: one is that legal speech activity is inherently a creative act, and not just a fact-description. *Saying is doing in law*—there is no way around! Secondly, writing or reading a legal text is always a double semiotic activity: all textual activity concerns a surface structure on the basis of a deep structure. The relation of those two levels determines nearly all dimensions of legal practice.

Greimas and Peirce

The contrast as well as the close relationships between semiotics in the sense of Greimas and Peirce is important in legal semiotics. The difference in content of their theories is visible in the two approaches. Major issues are in this context:

1. There exist in their semiotic project a very different type of logic: Greimas' logic can be characterized as narrative and holistic, whereas Peirce's logic is mathematical, logical and atomistic, even in explanations of the social in the terminology of thirdness. The preference of legal semiotics is in part created by their interpretations of law: law being understood either in holistic (inclusive) or in atomistic/individualistic terms.
2. Semioticians who prefer to operate with Greimas' tools use two powerful analytical instruments. The first is in the dynamics of deep versus surface structures of texts, and the second in the analytical power of the semiotic square. Both fit in legal discourse appropriately. Peirce's semiotics will, through the wealth of implied analytical tools, operate often in complete conformity with the traditional atomistic approaches in law and legal discourse.

3. There are two different cultural traditions incorporated in the two semiotic approaches and theories:
   a. *Greimas* develops his theory in the context of cultural anthropology and comparative linguistics, a climate that was favorable for developing structuralism, already in vogue in Moscow and Prague decades before it came to Paris. The legal discourse he referred to was at the point to develop from a nation-bound system towards a multinational system, which was the system of EU Law. Most basic concepts, such as 'legal subject', 'legal causality', 'justice', 'individuality" or 'citizenship' were at the edge of fundamental change. Greimas' semiotics prepared for discourses that belonged to a "post-modern" period in European culture, if not even a "post-postmodernism".
   b. *Peirce* lived and worked in a society that characterized the beginning of a century, which came to a close with Greimas' theory. But it was a century in North America characterized by an intellectual response to industrialization and immigration into a legal society deeply imbued with notions of custom and tradition but increasingly exposed to the scientific methods of late 19th century Germany. This produced a strong tendency toward optimism, functionality and pragmatism that distinguishes North American from other societies to this day.

This difference is important in a semiotic sense as well. Both Peirce and Greimas made a world from out of the quite distinct worlds in which they were formed. It means that in Peirce one does not find a cultural or metaphysical vision that had anything to do with "post-modernism". Pragmatism was Peirce's basic philosophy, and mathematics the ultimate science, whereas in Greimas, structuralism (and relativism as its metaphysical constituent) was a dominant philosophical approach, and anthropology with psychoanalysis the lead scientific code. No wonder, that what is well documented for Peirce, is missing and no longer appropriate in the case of Greimas. One is reminded how considerable interest is being taken in Peirce's ideas from outside the arena of academic philosophy, from industry, business, technology, and the military.

That has resulted in the existence of a number of agencies, institutes, and laboratories in which ongoing research into and development of Peircean concepts was undertaken. It is clear, however, that the initial question why Peirce and Greimas are the two most influential semiotic thinkers in legal semiotics cannot be answered by a simple reference to the content or the essence of their theories. The question is rather a matter of cultural history, in which developments of features of a legal system are embedded as well as philosophical and metaphysical principles in action within the engineering of semiotic theories. Contextual theories of language or even sociological analyses should be surpassed in order to establish insight in the question. One of the eye-catching features is, that both do not operate via the simple scheme of semiotic criteria (such as sign characteristics can create) to become applied to fact-situations. This is the more remarkable since many judges practice law by means of that syllogistic scheme, and although they deny performing any other intellectual move than of a legal pragmatic nature, their pragmatics remain within the limits of the semantics of legal discourse.

Chapter 6
Lacan: The Semiotics of Law's Voices

The 'délire à deux': a Challenge to Lawyers

The French psychiatrist and psychoanalyst Jacques M.E. Lacan (1901–1981) is neither a lawyer nor a semiotician. The relevance of his work for law and legal thinking is, however, immense. He was trained as a medical doctor and defended a PhD thesis in Paris in 1932 on the relation between psychosis and personality—not a theme that is welcome in legal thought patterns or jurisprudence. His initial research focused an issue that would irritate any lawyer: the '*délire à deux*', which is a clinical picture that describes the inability to develop an established identity and create the awareness of a single individual. One should remember that a "*dèlire* à deux" befalls one person, whereas a "*folie* à deux" affects two persons. The first pertains to an individual, whereas the second concerns a social pattern that governs relations between two separate individuals who are unable to be called an "individual". The structure of the answers to the question "who are you" that are given in those two clinical pictures differs in a manner which is deeply related to language as a social means to identify and bear social consequences of that identification.

An Appeal to Language

Lacan developed his research *before* genetics, *before* the predominance of psychopharmacology in medicine, *before* modern neurology and *before* electronically sustained medical imagining. He sought to broaden psychiatry and psychoanalysis through philosophical, linguistic and even mathematical considerations, which he intertwined with existentialism, structuralism and semiotic viewpoints. The delirium he studied shows how individuals can be unable to experience themselves as an *entity in se* because these individuals are dominated by a specific quality of relations/engagements to others or other things that impede them from living and speaking as a single voice. Today, we would look for neurological research or try to find a specific genetic predisposition to initiate our understanding and exploration.

J. M. Broekman, L. Catà Backer, *Lawyers Making Meaning*,
DOI 10.1007/978-94-007-5458-4_6, © Springer Science+Business Media Dordrecht 2013

But Lacan focused on language, observing how speech activity in cases of this delirium is always governed by an unseen but omnipotent o/Other (a bodily present *other* person) or an inner voice representing an *Other* as a symbolic identity (contemplate the proximity of Peirce's "interpretant" in the process of understanding a sign)—and that seems for lawyers beyond legal imagination.

Why? The reason is at first sight very simple: what can a lawyer do or think without a fixated identity and the ability to focus a subject in law? His or her 'who is who' and 'what to do' case/conflict/problem-directed reaction depends on the ability to detect a subject appropriately. If there is no determinable subject, there is no legal activity! So, what to do if that identity is doubled and none of those two able to carry the weight of law's reference? A second thought concerns deeper layers of the problem. A 'délire' can be seen as an indication of severe personality disorders caused by a history of familial conflicts such as disturbing behavior of the subject's parents or of other socio-pathological aspects that deviate or block one's growth as an individual identity. Awareness of these issues destroys the general expectation of a lawyer that a subject in law is always there and accessible for any sort of legal understanding. Lacan's approach thus confirmed that a human identity (so natural and self-evident to lawyers) is a matter of all ups and downs of a culture that cause an individual's growth and development, and not a purely natural issue. Because social (in particular parental) relations play a key role in the emergence of an individual entity, law—a social discourse itself—does not encounter human identities that exist already before and outside law. On the contrary, law emerges *via* the *formation* of identities—the latter becoming most important elements of a lawyer's discourse! In other words: *engenderment of an identity is in itself a component of law* because there exists no identity *before* any type of legal discourse emerges within which a human mind can unfold!

Narcissus' Ego and Me

Lacan's analysis of the development of a child's sense of *life* and *self* in the context of *language* has great relevance for legal discourse. His understanding of the "mirror stage" in a child's development during the first years of life is not a play with images but rather an insight of important semiotic relevance. The central issue is that a child's emergent sense of a self is always formed *in reference to* some 'other'—as the 'délire' showed in a precarious life situation. Lacan's thoughts evolved with *the concept of reference* in a most central place. *Reference to an o/Other*is already the semiotic implication of Freud's concept of identification—a fragment without which no human life unfolds. This mirror stage, the mirroring of one's own image accompanied by words of the mother, which confirm 'this is you', is the hinge of an identity in occidental culture. Its consequences are disturbing for legal ideology, as are most theories of identity engendered in modern social and psychological sciences. How?

The mirror stage constitutes a critical phase in the development of the ego. Human infants pass through a stage in which an external image of the body (reflected in a mirror, or otherwise presented to the infant through the mother or primary caregiver) initiates a psychic response that gives rise to the mental representation of an "I". Infants identify with the image, but because their image does not correspond with the underdeveloped infant's physical vulnerability and weakness, this image is established as 'ideal ego' or 'ideal-I' throughout his or her life. Because one enters into social relations through language, this image will resurface in social and linguistic frameworks of each subject's personality. The importance of this mirror-stage theory, first laid out for his colleagues in 1936, is enormous. Lacan writes:

> The mirror stage is a phenomenon to which I assign a twofold value. In the first place, it has historical value as it marks a decisive turning point in the mental development of the child. In the second place, it typifies an essential libidinal relationship with the body image. (J. Lacan: *Some reflections on the Ego* 1953)

We encounter here an element of Lacan's theory that we will also meet elsewhere in the book: the mirror stage is, in contrast to Freud's psychoanalytic insights, *not* a priori a scene of harmony! The idea that an *ego* unfolds its life as a harmony, is embedded in more than one phase of our Occidental culture. This presupposition is polemically contradicted in Lacan's thoughts: the *ego,* he claims, is rather a process of contrast, of conflict, of adversarial attitude and alienation. That observation goes, as was suggested, against a general belief. Lawyers, philosophers and psychologists cherish the opinion that the cradle of the ego is a harmonious one. Adversarial attitudes and conflicts are at distance from that original harmony and they do *not* belong to the original engenderment of a human identity, is said. This belief, one could encounter after Lacan, stems perhaps from a predominant biological understanding of the functioning mother's womb and her relations with the unborn/born child, so that physiological harmony leads straightforwardly into psychological harmony.

So Lacan opposes the myth of an *ego* naturally born as harmony, and suggests that an *ego* emerges from a fundamental alienation, which masters an individual's unfolding sense of self. Read the strong words in one of his *Écrits*[1]:

> One understands that to prop up so obviously precarious a conception, certain individuals on the other side of the Atlantic should have felt the need to introduce into it some stable values, some standard of the measure of the real: this turns out to be the autonomous ego. This is the supposedly organized ensemble of the most disparate functions that lend their support to the subject's feeling of innateness. It is regarded as autonomous because it appears to be sheltered from the conflicts of the person.

This observation goes into two directions: (a) the *ego* and (b) *psychoanalysis* itself. The *ego* appears (at distance from a misleading ideological conception) to be no more than an illusory conceptual understanding of a self. To 'cure' problems related to the ego, as some make us believe to be the task of *psychoanalysis*, is then a misbegotten adventure. Lacan notices that a mirror-stage experience, the stage in which an infant is confronted with its own mirror image, is only a fragment of an

[1] J. Lacan: *Écrits. A Selection.* London, Tavistock 1977, p. 230 f.

entire and all-embracing process of reference to the o/Other. The latter is primarily dominated by rivalry to- and within the self: an ego bears *hostility* towards all possible identifications with an o/Other within it before it can unfold any *stability* in a self. The human *Self* is the result of a search, a battle, a risk and reaches out to a stability which in itself is continuously endangered.

A human *Self* is the outcome of social processes in which hostility and alienation may and can lead to stability and harmony, he concludes. In that process, the object of reference: the referent (an o/Other)—the semiotic issue *par excellence*—shows that we should understand *reference as growth, as an unfolding of a self* whereby reference always creates relations in which one object designates by linking to another. Since the creation of relations appears to be of central importance for every human individual, psychoanalysis should not be understood as a science but rather as a relationship between analyst and psychoanalyst in which the two interpret the language of the unconscious together. That language must be analyzed in terms of semiotics (as suggested by Greimas, Kristeva and others) as a *surface* phenomenon in constant relation to its *deep* structures. This change of perspective opens through semiotics a hitherto impassable highway *to legal talk and language in law about a human unconscious.*

Das Ich muß entwickelt werden

Jurists are surprised once they fully understand how these words of Freud and Lacan form a central theme of their own discourse. *"The ego has to be developed"* means for them, that each judgmental act pertaining to a legal subject is an incision in a life process of a human individual and not a conclusion about any type of objective fact. His or her judgment is an intimate part of that process, so that *judging* a subject equals *developing* that very subject in one way or another. There are many implications to register, which all have their semiotic consequences. Freud and Lacan initiate medical and psychological observations, which are indeed remarkably parallel to an outstanding (mainly German) philosophical tradition with thinkers such as Kant, Hegel, Schelling and also contemporaries like Nietzsche, Pierce or Husserl. All of them underline how a human "I" or *ego* is not a unity from its very beginning, but an *ego* divided into pieces, parts or elements. Kant used the word *Ichspaltung* when dealing with the constitutive power of the *ego* or *Ich*. A human "I" is split, divided, and existing in pieces. Human striving for secure knowledge is always confronted with a *split ego*. Personal identity and psychological harmony seem to be contrasts, even antagonists in a human life. It makes clear, that identity cannot be understood as a fixed property but rather as a process in which one is involved. That process is a search. Identity does not search for a self that is the same, as if it were a copy resulting from the mirror, but the search for "the appropriate otherness of my self", an extension of my self that is one of the many braids that form the "I am" composition.

Freud discovered the situation of the *split ego* whilst studying the dynamics of psychological development. He thus reaches far beyond what so-called "ego psychologists" had in mind. The development of a human *ego* is as such a mirror portrait of life in all its phases. To correctly achieve this picture, one has to engage into a process framework, he discovered. Lacan followed him. Freudian phrases such as "A unity comparable to the ego cannot exist in the individual from start; the ego has to be developed"—"the ego is based on relations between others and its own body" and "the body of an amoeba is related to the pseudopodia which it puts out" should remain engraved in a lawyer's mind. They articulate *a pertinent dynamism with process character* where lawyers think to encounter psychic stability that has to be honored by means of legal judgmentand discourse of law. This contrast should inspire students of law! Not only lawyers do not know about this contrast—also each individual in process does not know. Freud writes: "Each individual lives a double existence: as its own goal in itself and as link of a chain, which it serves against or without its own will.[2]" The power to deny the double character is very strong indeed. Freud cites as an example that a human individual tends to understand its proper sexuality as one of its very own controllable and manageable forces, whereas this sexuality is a supra-individual force of all life in our universe.

All this relates to the function of the mirror stage in every infant's life. An infant discovers its *ego* or "I" by being confronted with its mirror image. Two issues mark that confrontation: first, *someone else* (father, mother, caretaker) has to *tell* the infant (here is already the *linguistic* component), that what he or she perceived is himself or herself. Words and views need each other in a foundational statement; life unfolds in the course of time as anchored in that verbal statement. Mind those words: *life unfolds* (at least in occidental cultures) *on the basis of words, speech acts and other utterances of others*! Secondly, the *image* is central here—the image has a key function, because recognition of that image is necessarily mediated by what it is *not* itself: by words, and not by another image. The other is therefore not solely an external datum but an already internalized condition of identity. Identity processes are flowing from image to language, and in this flow from narcissism to socialization, which ends the reign of imaginary identifications primarily experienced with the mother.

A riddle is concealed in the necessary development. Like everything in nature, an ego should always be perceived as being in a phase in a larger and encompassing development. *Panta rei*—'everything flows' was Plato's popularization of Herakleitos' philosophical impetus. Can we develop ourselves into an "I" without someone having pointed to us and uttered "you" in our direction, and talked to us and used that word, "I" whilst talking to us about them? Could this conversation be useful in the absence of a context within which "I" and "you" acquire a meaning that is meaningful for both "I" and "You"? Most probably not: we should acknowledge that our most private and unique ego relates one way or another to the words of a language someone else uses when communicating with me; but it is a language that we also use ourselves—or we train someone in that language. That describes both the linguistic socialization of the

---

[2] S. Freud: "Zur Einführung des Narzissmus" in: *Gesammelte Werke, Werke aus den Jahren 1913–1917*, Imago London 1960 p. 142 f.

infant, and the training of the student in the language of the law. Lacan's explications about the difference in the words of the mother and of the father seem no more than a psychoanalytic construction within this more general and linguistic framework of understanding how a personality emerges.

A conclusion of major importance is indeed, that *the riddle is in language*: not in language as fixated in grammars or vocabularies, but in language in use, in speech. The flow of words and other linguistic expressions befits the reality of an "I" better than any fragment of grammar or syntax. Indeed: life unfolds on the basis of words, on speech in the first place. Speech provides us a place in mind and society, allows us to be someone, and challenges us to unfold an identity: "I said to myself..." equals in that regard "I am who I am". A danger is, however, in the misreading by one ego-component of an other component. Understand in the many times a person tells another person that ..., how through performing that speech act, she told herself that ...! Such talk is exactly founded in the fact that there was no clear, evident, harmonious relation between Self and I: the split of ego-components creates disharmony rather than its opposite. Disharmony and misreading belong to the flow-character of the *ego* itself, because a 'self' is never identical to what it was and will be. "I" and "self" are verbal expressions, which are only a one-to-one indicator within the exact moment of speech. And what I am in view of my self is also true for what I am in view of other(s).

Rimbaud's famous "Je est un autre" is in this regard ambiguous: there are too many voices incorporated in the "Je" for an unambiguous understanding of his adage. The 'other' of the 'I' is either my self or somebody else—if it is somebody else, the other of the 'I' that is meant to be by myself is already an "other" within that very act of speech! Indeed, a riddle remains concealed in the flow that is "my self". The alienation in the innermost *ego* is in the otherness of the other that I am for my self, Rimbaud suggested. However, the same alienation is in the other person in view of me, which perceives me as a component of the flow of identity on the basis of which social relations are possible. Rimbaud's adage upholds nevertheless the major structure of the occidental theatre of metaphysics; it does not convert any essential feature on that stage: subjects emerge as a subject within harmonious and disharmonious relations in the scene of an "I" involved in speaking to a "Self". If that scene had a title, it would be called "The 'I' for an 'I'" or "The Interiority of 'Becoming'" or "My Self as You".

Today, we hardly have a stage for such scenes anymore. Deconstructionism, based on insights of twentieth century structuralism, helped destroy Plato's vision of the world as an extension of an inner dialogue between ego-components. New roles unfolded, new egos claimed recognition on the stage. They tell us that they are *an ego not stemming from words exchanged between other egos but from a different exteriority*: from social structures creating their awareness. This requires a different relationship between what Peirce might understand as firstness and secondness—between "I" and a differentiated "I". That difference is bound up in the abstraction of the contextualized "I" within aggregations that are themselves bundles of "I" reconstituted as society, corporation, religion, etc. Such institutional structures gave a command, like States did, to *adept*—yes, *to be*—an identity given by them *as if* it were the word of another individual: citizen, consumer, bearer of rights, performer of duties, proprietor, criminal, shareholder. And "the o/Other" bears names such as "the State", "the Rule of Law", "the Corporation" and the like. Those words became *names* in the course of modern occidental history; they were not simply *roles* to play as a fulfillment of the omnipotent role of the subject anymore. Metaphors changed accordingly: freedom had suddenly a different content; justice was obliged to change décor. With those new metaphors came new meanings stemming from new actors and authors. Lawyers used 'human' in contexts they never articulated before: human rights were read in legal textbooks, criminals were given a human face, DNA and other domains of virtual reality created social justice. Judges changed the interpretive structures of aggregations and incarnated abstractions—the state could now function like a corporation; a corporation could exercise the attribute of personality; religion could be both object of law, body of law and external to law. The surface structure of that new vocabulary had the change of theatre as its deep structure, and with those new names came new feelings of the post-subjects on stage. Did they not enter a dark podium for walking unknown steps? These are themes that will be taken up again in Chap. 9.

We may always walk unknown steps, notwithstanding our idea that we know where and how to go! That knowledge and trust does apparently not stem from some innate natural source we inherited physically but from our life amidst others with whom we speak, act and live together. Social dimensions of our existence make us qualify well-know phenomena as 'natural'—that counts also for the *self* we impute to ourselves. This becomes clear in considering a psychiatric case of "loss of natural evidence" also called "self-evidence" as expressed in a German psychiatrist's 1971 study on what he calls *The Loss of Natural Evidence*[3]. That psychiatric problem highlights the question: *How can one lose what one does not possess?* The answer appears to be: *only if the world of words possessed by others is the only criterion for the self to hold on*. This is Anne's problem, as her case study clarifies. Her case represents important categories of psychiatric illnesses. But it should in the first place be underlined, that the expression "a natural evidence" was coined by Anne *long before* the psychiatrist met her. It was apparently her life-theme, perhaps the sole fruit of her life-tree, and she kept using that expression in all her conversations. Essential fragments of a phenomenology of her case are in the notes of her psychiatrist and author of the publication of her case, such as: ". . . she spoke of thoughts imposed on me. Everything was powerless against them". But, as Blankenburg further states, it was not apparent that she experienced an imposition or any hypnotic compulsions. Most striking, and never observed before, were facial behaviors, nearly grimaces, and a strong excitement she experienced, which articulated beyond doubt how she was threatened by the dangerous nature of life in general. As far as could be clarified, these were behaviors or reactions—even fragments of complete scenes—belonging to others, which she felt compelled to imitate.

[3] W. Blankenburg: *Der Verlust der natürlichen Selbstverständlichkeit*, F.Enke Verlag, Stuttgart 1971, p. 98 ff.

Characteristic of Anne's conversation was how much remained un*said* by her. Language became less, and bodily gestures on the other hand more used in her communication. Also her facial expressions helped her, especially when she clearly touched the boundaries of the unutterable. "... 'What am I missing? Something very small, it's funny, something important without which one cannot live. At home, with my mother, I was not there as a human being. I had not grown, was not developed. I was simply there, just there, but not with them. I need a bond, which guides me so that not everything is artificial ... now I have always to see that I do not lose everything ... I simply feel that I still need a hold ... that might be a natural evidence, which I miss'... 'To find boundaries and experience limits is becoming an adult ... I take things always like others do, and could never take an opposite position—I could never trust my own judgment'" she told her psychiatrist, who reports about many years with an important variety of therapies and continuous residence in the clinic, until in an unattended moment she committed suicide.

There are a number of issues to underline in remembrance of Peirce's concept of *Firstness*; we highlight four of them:

1. In the majority of cases, any pre-existing natural evidence is taken as self-evident. The use of the concept "nature" in this expression serves our understanding of human reality by means of this important anthropomorphism. It plays a major role at the level of human experience—the management of meaning in each individual's life—rather than at the level of positive facts. This also functions as a basic observation for semiotics and its power to enhance experience and knowledge and does not solve ontological questions.
2. The importance of a 'natural' evidence helps differentiate the often rigid debate of a 'to be' or 'not to be'. To suppose that there is any natural evidence *beyond* cultural and anthropological differences is not feasible. Peirce's interest pertained to semiotics as a general theory of signs, was not natural-ontological but cultural.
3. Any confrontation with a primordial function of natural evidence underpins the social dimensions and fundamental social needs in human life. Life is definitively a life with others—this insight is implied in the sign, which Peirce characterized as an index. The indexical quality of a sign leads to others, as in the footprint that Robinson Crusoe found in the sand, an index for some creature existing on the island. However, *life with others is only possible as a self*—an insight confirmed in the case of Anne. To be your 'self' is not the result of a dearly obtained autonomy in isolation but a mode of being (in conversation) with others.
4. Anne's loss was not a loss and could never be understood as a loss, because she had not developed a self. Natural evidence, as well as a natural self-evidence, has a self as precondition. Her loss was solely a loss in so far as others (who were in contrast to Anne successful in developing a self) articulated her situation as a loss. It was the language and its meaning of others she had missed and would never possess and made her articulate her complaints or bewilderment. Her psychological handicap could only be articulated and experienced in the language of others, as much as her psychiatric anamnesis could never be in her own words, because she did not have such words at her disposal. Together with

> this lack, she was psychically ill because she did not have what others told her is a possession, a self.

Anne complained about her loss of a natural evidence to articulate this loss as a missing. She showed in her situation of psychiatric patient how natural evidence is an issue of semiotic nature, which requires a language of others and a well-developed self. Peirce's *indexical* aspect of *Firstness* confirms how *the language of "self related to others"* is the foundation for 'natural' evidence, which is thus not there '*by nature*'.

The mirror conditioning as described changed unnoticed because the ground patterns of social life of others changed. Subjects became post-subjects who could no longer unfold their identity via the speech of other subjects, so that they became aware how they were puppets on unknown strings moving at that stage. The new names (proprietor, bearer of rights, free citizen) were not theirs, so that they felt a need for de-possession to be somebody with a say on that metaphysical scene. A drive towards de-possession was caused by the silent change of earthquake dimensions called 'global'. The outcry audible all over the world was born: 'occupy'. There is no-thing to occupy other than meaning—an immensely important semiotic insight. Indeed, it's the mirror again: faces not solely mirror, identities not solely grow through mirroring, but also words and meanings whilst changing their language do. New worlds originate, the metaphysical theatre empties. Even legal discourse must adept to new expressions and perform its acts elsewhere in different metaphysical dimensions. Awareness of post-subjects being puppets on the strings of institutions, corporations and a world economy without identities occupies the place of its grammar formerly called 'category subject'.

Yet the conversation about the global takes the work of the previous century to an entirely new level, one anticipated by Lacan, Peirce, Kevelson, and the American Critical Legal Studies. The nineteenth and twentieth century was the culmination of the age of the individual. The focus of philosophy was to move from the individual outward; the individual was the center of the universe, even the semiotic universe. But what happens when the more intimate focus of semiotics—on triadic relations among individuals, on an "I" moored or unmoored, on semiotic squares moves from the level of the individual to that of the aggregation. A semiotic revolution is possible—one that starts with the symbolic consequences of abstracting individuals in the construction of aggregates, but not of obliterating the individual within the construct. Triadic relations become three dimensional and hyper-contingent. Conventionally expressed in the language of lawyers and politicians, these are issues about the personality of states, or corporations, of religious organizations, and of the relations between them and within them between the entity (now incarnated) and their aggregates (shareholders, citizens, adherents, etc.). Semiotics offers a way of disentangling and of rigor in analysis of multidimensional relations between objects, signs and interpretant, who occupy multiple positions. And here one encounters the current frontier of semiotics—applying Kevelson's notions of systemicity to Lacan's intuition about the self, where the self consists of a set of stacked sub-selves (shareholders, citizens, etc.) and this aggregated self operates within borders and between them. Yet this is precisely the context within which lawyers, economists, regulators and others now must discuss globalization and its consequences. The mirror has been repositioned and it reflects something different and layered; the regulatory effects of de-centering the state as the principal source of regulation, the regulatory effects of corporate activity, the legislative authority of religious organizations all pose problems of meaning, of structure and of governance that frame the new operational territory of semiotics.

Lawyers are now remaking the world, but one that is porous, multi-leveled and reflected in mirrors that faceted and sometimes fractured, and that at its core is abstracted with intangible objects and symbols built on symbols. "As far as we can estimate now, the capital of twenty-first century is not found on Earth; it is located on the Internet.... Globalisation, then, is, among other things, the hypertrophy of the inner Other".[4] Lacan's emphasis on language is now moved to a central place in analysis in a world that is de-natured and that shows itself through text and the representations contained on the Internet. The world of lawyers has embraced this as well—from electronic filings to the excavation of facts from the world the Internet built for the basic work of lawyers (litigation, property organization, and contract). *Das Ich muß entwickelt werden* now acquires a new basis—grounded in the old order of the semiosis of the person, to that of the aggregate and system. But which "I"? An "I" detached from the individual, an aggregated "I" produces multiple planes of meaning that operate staked and intertwined in the meaning-orders of modern global society. The turn toward polycentricity in transnational governance, the character of global corporate social responsibility and the like provide the new frontier for semiosis in a terrain in which the "I" has been liberated from the "I" and recast not as "We" but as a collective abstracted corporate "I". The semiotic insights of delirium are especially useful here. These are subjects taken up again below in "*Master Signifiers, Master Discourses*" and in Chap. 9.

The Ethics of Signifying

Lacan's major merit is in emphasizing the importance of language. This unifies Freud's psychoanalysis and De Saussure's linguistic structuralism: *the unconscious is structured like a language*—if that were not the case, the transition from narcissism to language would never be possible. Julia Kristeva once made a challenging remark, which should in this context be taken by lawyers. She agrees with Lacan about the infant entering into language and social relations whilst becoming a speaking subject, and that in doing so a human individual constitutes history and society. Her conclusion is, however, different from Lacan, and important:

> ...if language is the articulation of a heterogeneous process, with the speaking subject leaving its imprint on the dialectic between the articulation and its process, then the linguist

[4] Göran Sonesson, "The Globalisation of Ego and Alter. An essay in Cultural Semiotics," *Semiotica* 148:153–73, 168, 169 (2004).

> and the semiotician should study *the ethics of each signifying process*. (J. Kristeva: *Desire in Language. A Semiotic Approach to Literature and Art*, Columbia UP, 1980, p. 23, 34)

A coordination of *law and ethics* is embedded in this issue; the harmony between the two is grounded in their shared structure of language. Ethics of law are decidedly *not*—as many lawyers today believe and practice—a matter of judging rules or rule application ethically, but rather a matter of judging the linguistically structured process of being a human individual in a specific cultural context. If a speaking subject is supposed to constitute history and society, then it constitutes its proper identity in the form of language and society. The Ancient Greek understood their *nomoi* as an achievement of linguistic nature! No wonder, that Kristeva coined the term 'subject-in-process' and understood that term as an articulation of a 'subject-on-trial':

> ... we recognize, on the one hand, the unity of the subject who submits to the law—the law of communication, among others; yet who, on the other hand, does not entirely submit, cannot entirely submit, does not want to submit entirely... always in a state of contesting the law.... (Ross M. Guberman (Ed.): *Julia Kristeva Interviews*. Columbia UP, 1996, p. 26)

It is exactly due to the subject-in-process that assigning values to elements of (social) reality is deemed important in occidental culture and in particular essential for any process of meaning making—for *legal* meaning in particular.

English majors exposed relations between love and meaning in the 1980s, as Eugenides described in his novel. As we see now in the light of semiotics, both are sensations to which values are assigned in discourses that create the factual character of love and meaning linguistically, Kristeva suggests. Such assignments of value to meaning are essential for language as a social instrument *par excellence*. In speech performance we experience how each activity of speaking creates its own authority within the multiple constrains of social and cultural patterns. This authority shows us how not only speech but also literature is a matter of signifiers referring to signifiers who refer to signifiers, as Peirce often underlined—a type of reference that shows how meaning making is performed and varies with cultural conventions. The same applies to law. An excellent example is the reference in contract law to common conventions in business to interpret the text of a contract between individuals, a text that was made in the shadow of those conventions but that may also seek to vary from or oppose them. Yet the meaning is extracted from the signification of objects (text and intent) digested through an interpretant (the judge's mindset) who is a stranger to convention and text but bound by them.[5] An ethics of signifying enveloped in language is truly a *social* ethics.

Language - Identity - Reference

Emphasis on language characterizes all dimensions of Lacan's project. The first speech acts to account for as a psychotherapist, are of course the dialogues in a therapeutic situation—an issue very different from legal practice, where speech occurs

[5] E.g., Rainy Sky S.A. and others v Kookmin Bank [2011] UKSC 50 (U.K. Supreme Court held that courts were to resolve issues of textual ambiguity in contracts by adopting the meaning which is consistent with commercial common sense is to be preferred).

mainly at various levels of data exchanges. Lacan *shortens* and often *disrupts* sessions with his patient to avoid any identification with the analyst so that the necessary reality-character in the relation with a patient remains intact. A punctuation or fragmentation of speech and an emphasis on the dialectical features of the curative talk in the doctor-patient relationship contributes to patient stabilization. It is remarkable how the latter seems to be based upon the reinforcement of a differentiation between, on the one hand, the "I" that speaks and, on the other hand, the inner images of and ideal ego projected onto the o/Other—images that sustain an existential reference.

Speech is of issue also where the emergence of an identity is concerned. Speech has its foothold in a reference to the o/Other; its continuity is a basic requirement for the creation of meaning. What something (a fact, an event, an occurrence, a situation) means for me in contrast to what it means for you has the positioning of myself in reference to you as a crucial component, most needed when individuals entangle in social patterns. Growth in speech confirms how an o/Other is needed for an evolving identity to become an "I". Only on that basis can an "I" become related to a 'you', a 'we' and an 'us'. An individual emerges only in reference to o/Others. In other words, *socialization occurs always in the shadow of an o/Other*. It means that there is no dialogue (neither in psychoanalysis nor in everyday life) without in-depth reference to the period of emergence of an individual, which is in itself a language-determined situation.

In the world of Lacan's observations and conclusions, language is first a means of personal development and identity formation and only on that basis a communication instrument. Research of Hart and Risley would fit into this context[6]. Those researchers sampled during more than three years the actual numbers of words spoken to young children from forty-two families at three socio-economic levels: welfare homes, working-class homes, and homes of professionals. *The being-spoken-to appears more important than the speaking-of-someone.* Children in professionals' homes were exposed to an average of more than fifteen hundred more spoken words per hour than children in welfare homes. Over one year, that amounted to a gap of approximately 32 million words—differences in tone and complexity not considered. These factors relate to the qualities of verbal experiences in life, and—more importantly—to a fundamental understanding of the growth of a human identity within the boundaries of language, as we encountered in observations of Lacan and Freud.

Those observations are not far away from impressions of Peirce. Fisch documented "that there are no more pervasive themes in Peirce's work . . . than that *all thought is in signs and is dialogic in nature*". This fascination for dialogic dimensions (dialogues between fragments of a split *ego* in the first place) includes Freud's and Lacan's research pertaining to the engenderment of such dialogic possibilities from infant to adult life in a human individual. Fisch underlines

[6] Betty Hart & Todd R. Risley: *Meaningful Differences in the Everyday Experience of Young American Children*. Brooks Publ. Co, 1995, and: *The Social World of Children Learning to Talk*, Brooks Publ. Co, 1999.

> ... that even at its most private and silent it is non the less dialogue between the self of one moment and the oncoming self of the next. And he (Peirce) found relevance from the beginning, not only in the vernacular 'I says to myself, says I', and in Socrates's arguments in the *Theaetetus* and the Stranger's in the *Sophist*, but also in the fact that one major philosopher had put so nearly his entire thought-life into the written *form* of dialogues. (Max H. Fisch: *Peirce, Semeiotic, and Pragmatism*, Indiana UP 1986)

The "split, dissociated ego" enriches life, because it accesses to a unique form of language, called 'dialogue'—dialogue with itself, and with o/Other(s). That observation fascinated Peirce: "the entire thought-life of any person is a sign", he claims, and that sign-feature exists thanks to the possibility of dialogue, which is engrained in the development, growth, and life process of a human individual. Peirce reads around 1898 on Plato's Socrates defining thought at *Theaetetus* as "a conversation of the soul with itself" and writes in the margin: "This is, I think, Plato's greatest contribution to thought" [7]. And what is more: the necessity of this conversational and dialogue structure manifests itself not as a constraint but as freedom in the deepest sense of the word.

An o/Other in our life forms for each of us individually a body of '*nomoi*'. Lawyers describe those *nomoi* as a 'system of norms and values'. The child observes how this body of '*nomoi*' moves the mother and gives the father a force to completely identify his saying and doing, so that his word becomes the act and is set free from its purely descriptive nature. The child will understand these important occurrences only later in life, and sometimes exclusively in retrospect during a psychoanalytic process. That 'cure' is, as Lacan emphasizes, *an intensified (self-)understanding*, and that linked with the concept of dialogue. If each "I" needs an "o/Other", then the world of others (referring on their turn to their o/Other) makes the realization of my existence possible. Signs bring a form of mediation unknown to law or legal discourse: words of law withstand the centuries, but they have a meaning in each specific historical and cultural occurrence. Battles about legal words are battles about *momentary* meanings. They exclude the unique coincidence of historic processes of growth and individual, specific meanings.

The *language* of law *as language* is thus a medium to establish (what Lacan and Freud called) a 'symbolic identification' with the normative body of culture: the language patterns, the grammars and their words, the norms and directives of a cultural collective. Language and law parallel when they reprove for not following the rules of communication: 'I do not understand you'; 'you are not clear in your expressiveness'; 'I can no longer talk to you'. Lacan remarks: "identification is always identification with a normatively circumscribed way of organizing the socio/intersubjective space within which the subject can take on its most lasting imaginary identifications". The legal and semiotic relevance of this remark speaks for itself.

That is the more so, because our social space is loaded with real and imaginary identifications, which find their effects in language. An important example is the vividly debated and age-old *contract theory* of law and society (which affects law in particular), which forwards social relations as contractual relations, as relations

---

[7] Fisch Op. Cit, p. 442.

between owners (ultimately owners of a 'self'). The Roman proverb 'do ut des' (give and receive) is central in this context. There are two components to notice: *first* that language is structured and practiced as a social pact/contract. Everyone knows that others will remain inaccessible to the constraints of reason if a rule of debate does not come into force to bring agreement. A *second* consideration is that in general one should be aware of the fact that any speech act awakens a concealed body of conventions within which I am obliged to speak.

Lawyers know this, and are convinced that the true meaning of what they wish to convey will ultimately always emerge and be registered in some place. Even if an immediate auditor doesn't 'get it', there is the universal auditorium that rhetorically guarantees necessary reception (Perelman). This auditorium, a "big 'other'", is the place (as a collectivity or as a single person), which will, we presuppose, register the truth of what we say when we speak. Speech is thus a process in which the subjects get their meanings back from the o/Other in the form of linguistically articulated patterns of social relations. Precisely this deeply anchored 'feed back' mechanism seems to support our idea of 'contract'. In the innermost center of my speech I presuppose (mostly symbolic) an 'Other' which knows the truth of my communicative acts, 'slips' (Freud) and symptomatic behaviors. That basic trust is anchored in the fact that one understands the world in terms of the natural language of one's community. This language forms an essential part of an individual's identity. Any reordering of signifiers takes place through mediation of meanings engendered by the communicative act in it self. Do *legal* signifiers solely re-order preconceived meanings?

Master Signifiers, Master Discourses

Lacan's thoughts became famous for these expressions: *master signifiers* most intimately bind a subject's identity and *master discourses* function as important ensembles of speech acts that guide, restrain and lead linguistic communication. The power of these masters is in the importance those signifiers give to a subject's identification with them, so that orderings of all other signifiers appear in their perspective and meaning context.

Take expressions such as 'freedom' or 'liberal', 'diversity' or 'tolerance'. They can mean totally different social practices, some of them clearly hidden in the deep structures of explorative social practices embedded in capitalism and its liberal ideology. Guess how many implications a politician's speech on 'democracy' includes, or what 'equality' in his perspective means. There is an urgent need to elevate new 'master signifiers' to enable the subject to reorder a sense of a self and relations to others. That is an ongoing process of great importance for law and legal practice.

To know the influences of the master signifiers in a lawyer's practice and speech and to be aware of the all-embracing influence of the master discourse within which judges consider cases means a heightened semantic awareness when managing legal discourse. If a Supreme Court speaks with one voice, even with a dissenting opinion, the legal master signifiers utter a unique *voice*. If a legal case is engraved in decades of a culture, the master signifiers determine legal and political considerations by means of a *text* that carries a name, as one can observe in Common Law practices that create a *voice*. Master signifiers order and reorder opinions, prejudices and notions of a self that indulges in fragments of cultural history. This is bound up with the ethics of language and the historicity of master expressions.[8]

Repressed prejudices become integrated in social, legal or political values once they are reordered. The masters of signification prescribe, coerce, narrow down and limit freedom of articulation of the subjects' discourse in society, but they also debar access to what is deeply engraved in them. The power of reordering meanings in a master discourse is legally, socially and politically one of the most important sources for an individual subject in society. It is, however, a feature of human finiteness that there is, on the one hand, no subject without language but that there is, on the other hand—to rephrase the terminology of structuralism—no constitutively fixated secure and central place for the subject in language.

When I perform a speech act, I put myself at risk because of uncertainty about the position of the o/Other, which I apparently need but cannot bridle. It is Lacan's insight that a master discourse diminishes that existential risk through reordering the subject's catalogue of meaning. These dynamics are an essential element in any social relation. Are those semiotics of "meaning re-ordering" also of importance for a lawyer's task in modern society?

[8] Cf. Larry Catá Backer, "Chroniclers in the Field of Cultural Production: Interpretive Conversations Between Courts and Culture", 20 *Boston College Third World Law Journal* 291 (2000); and: Larry Catá Backer, "Retaining Judicial Authority: A Preliminary Inquiry on the Dominion of Judges," 12 *William & Mary Bill of Rights Journal* 117 (2003).

Chapter 7
Those Three Godfathers, After All

Godfathers and the Law

The three godfathers have at least two features in common within perspectives of modern thought: they are not lawyers, have an only peripheral knowledge of law and legal discourse, and take part in one of the most important changes in modern philosophical insight, generally called 'the linguistic turn'.

The first remark does not surprise: initiating and promoting semiotics in modern thought is by no means a lawyer's affair. Peirce's contacts with the law and with lawyers were limited. He writes about an experience of the hand of a sheriff on his shoulder in the case of delayed payments, but it did not come to a deeper account of the sheriff's motion as an important signifier in social life. "... When I feel the sheriff's hand on my shoulder, I shall have a sense of actuality ... ", he wrote.[1] Such a sense of actuality may have dominated other contacts between Peirce and legal scholars such as Holmes, Pollock and others who regularly met in the two Metaphysical Clubs in Cambridge, 1872 and Baltimore 1879. Yet, Fisch notices in this context "that Peirce had a much greater and lifelong interest in law and in social philosophy that has hitherto been recognized, by myself or anybody else."[2]

Things are somewhat different with Greimas, who was interested in law because law-as-text could serve as an object for his discourse analysis. His desire was to produce a *grammar of narratives* and find in that context a finite number of functional themes, which could be placed in binary opposition and can be noted by means of systematically placing and replacing squares that represent those themes. These oppositions should then be juxtaposed with roles played in the narratives, such as subject/object, sender/receiver etc, who altogether would generate the superstructure we call 'story'. One should notice how all elements are defined syntactically, in other words: by their place and not by their incidental function in the narrative structure.

It all implies a very different understanding of a subject (also a subject in law, for that matter) at important distance to classical philosophical approaches of the concept: not substantial but rather formal, not exclusively human but also open for

---

[1] Peirce, CP 1, 24.

[2] Fisch, Op. cit., p. 13.

J. M. Broekman, L. Catà Backer, *Lawyers Making Meaning*,
DOI 10.1007/978-94-007-5458-4_7, © Springer Science+Business Media Dordrecht 2013

non-human subjects. Subjects are furthermore determined by their position in the all-embracing narrative; they are occupying a position in that narrative which Greimas calls 'the journey'. Their positions result from their 'play'. All this should show that law (and particular legal discourse as a narrative and as a play) is a rich field for testing the value of this new semiotic approach and for experiencing whether lawyers gain a larger and more differentiated insight and knowledge of law through this view.

Latour and Akrich reformulated on the basis of Greimas' explorations the concept of semiotics. Transference of semiotics into functionalism would alienate the semiotic enterprise from the linguistic and textual approaches and eventually loosen ties with the sign-concept. We mention their opinion because it shows the distance from Greimas (as a godfather of semiotics) to modernity. But it shows also a vital interest in law from an unexpected perspective. Law can easily be understood and researched as a narrative, and its functionaries are in the sense of a semiotic analysis (legal) subjects with- and within a narrative. To perceive the work of godfathers in the light of those developments leading to modernity is a privilege that can inspire. What remains today of their visions on semiotics, what residues should we keep in mind? A possible answer is the Latour /Akrich proposal in their "Vocabulary" that states:

> Semiotics: the study of how meaning is built, but the word 'meaning' is taken in its original non-textual and non-linguistic interpretation; how one privileged trajectory is built out of an indefinite number of possibilities; in that sense, *semiotics is the study of order building or path building* and may be applied to settings, machines, bodies, and programming language as well as texts . . . (M. Akrich & B. Latour: "A Summary of Convenient Vocabulary for the Semiotics of Human and Nonhuman Assemblies" in: W. Bijker & J. Law (Eds): *Shaping Technology/Building Society: Studies in Sociotechnical Change*, Cambridge MIT Press 1992, p. 259.)

Law's Order, Semiotic Path

Semiotics is the study of *order* as a major component of meaning making: the formula would have been attractive to Peirce, Greimas and Lacan—in particular the latter who embraced from the very beginning Freud's insight in the linguistic structure of the conscious, which brings him to the understanding of all mental phenomena as "structured like a language". And this formulation represents in its turn a view on modernity, which philosophers articulated as "the linguistic turn". The interest for patterns of language and linguistic structures underlines how language is a central issue in human sciences—not solely as an instrument for understanding and communication. The three godfathers share this platform when they face both human and nonhuman reality. Peirce's sign-concept carries those elements as an essence of the world and the human individual that inhabits this world and unfolds what he called his 'glassy existence'.

Those steppingstones are also paved for Lacan, who excelled in understanding the metaphoric essence of the concept of law in human affairs. Keystone is the observation that the word, or better: the speech acts, of the father in his relation with the infant find their most appropriate metaphor in 'law'. From this metaphorical core, a parallel engenderment of two concepts unfolds: '*nomoi*' parallel the o/Other, and the location of that parallel is (again a metaphor!) the mirror. That story is incomplete when one does not consider how language plays its epistemological role, the role of creator of knowledge. Only years after the mirror stage, language completed the experiences of the infant and begun to confer a personal identity its power of expression. Greimas' new analysis of narratives appears productive at this point, because a human subject can in language, and particularly in narratives, transcend the boundaries between human- and non-human subjectivity. Human brains that co-evolve today with computers show us consequences of what the godfathers of semiotics wanted to actively unfold with language as their privileged medium. Common to them and these contemporary developments is the insight that each speech activity should be understood as a process of meaning making. Our conversations do not make use of language particles that are available for ordering and re-ordering. They are much more creative, if one understands the process character of language itself.

Meaning Making

The process of meaning making has priority in all situations, and that observation includes many elements:

(a) There is (what Peirce often underlined) the commonness of the community, which is needed to create the simplest utterance. To talk—to realize a linguistic and a language activity—presupposes the real as well as the virtual presence of others.
(b) One of the issues who most neighbor legal discourse is the coercive character of the speech acts of others, the 'nomoi' they lay around me when I want to articulate an opinion, an experience or a feeling.
(c) Furthermore, lawyers profit from the performative character of their speech. They know little about the powerful and characteristic features of their own speech activity, as they study them no more than in the form of a legal rhetoric.
(d) There are the defining political decisions that shape each legal speech act. The apparent dominance of perceiving speech as communication cause lawyers to neglect this political implication, as becomes particularly clear in their l meaning making processes in legal doctrine.
(e) The significance of legal speech, once formulated in a broader perspective, is a product of selection, choice, sentiment, group ethics, professional responsibility, preference and evaluation of precedent and many more issues that remain mostly in the dark.

(f) Greimas and Kristeva point at the deep structures that create the surface of speech, but only Greimas aimed at examples in legal discourse, whereas poetry, literature, novels, drama and other literary phenomena are less clear in this regard.
(g) Language seems a total (or at least an all-embracing) metaphor but this metaphor takes only seldom a front seat in semiotic literature.

We suggested that lawyers should try to understand the saying that "human consciousness is structured like a language" and practice it in their opinion. Linguistics has a power that transcends language itself, and the potency to provide knowledge of its own structures, which in their turn leads to knowledge of reality as such. Here is the abyss with which the three godfathers of semiotics once stood eye in eye.

Part III
Jurisprudence and Legal Semiotics

Chapter 8
Legal Theory and Semiotics: On The Origins of Legal Semiotics

Questions about the origins of *legal* semiotics are never posed. They are not an issue when studying the godfathers of semiotics or the later relations between legal semiotics and jurisprudence. References to the Ancient Greek understanding of signs in medicine—as formulated in the introducing chapters—are no more than a simple transposition from medicine into legal discourse. That is clearly insufficient in view of the context and content of any specific *legal* branch of semiotics; its specialized Journal remains silent on the issue from the first to the last pages[1]. Why? Some mention a biographical event in the career of Roberta Kevelson during the early eighties of the twentieth century. It tells us how Thomas Sebeok should have suggested that law is an interesting area to study the constitutive powers of signs in law. However, her 1988 publication "The Law as a System of Signs" cannot solely be seen as an answer to that suggestion. Where are the first attempts to formulate *legal* semiotic insights: who took initiatives; what were the themes of legal interest and importance, what its cultural context? Those considerations underline how insight in the origins of legal semiotics could accomplish the self-understanding of a lawyers' meaning-making capacity.

Semiotics and Significs

The centenary of the death of Lady Victoria Welby (1837–1912) reminded the world of a peculiar constellation, which was hitherto insufficiently researched[2]. *"Semiotics" was never the only term in use for the study of signs and of meaning!* Lady Welby promoted—in parallel and whilst corresponding with Peirce—her term "significs" for the same discipline. And as if wrestling with the importance of the pragmatic dimensions of sign-uses and meanings like Peirce, she highlighted that there is no study of meanings without interpretative power occupying a core position

[1] See the *International Journal for the Semiotics of Law,* since 1988 comprising until March 2012 a total of 25 Volumes.

[2] John E. Joseph: "Meaning in the Margins. Victoria Lady Welby and significs" in: *Times Literary Supplement,* March 23, 2012, p. 14/15.

J. M. Broekman, L. Catà Backer, *Lawyers Making Meaning,*
DOI 10.1007/978-94-007-5458-4_8, © Springer Science+Business Media Dordrecht 2013

in life. She appears—not unlike Peirce—entangled in pragmatism, because it shows how her position between skepticism and philosophical naivety urges for decisions, actions and social commitment rather than for scientific endeavors such as linguistics or theories of knowledge. When reconsidering this, and opening related perspectives of the problem, we already assess a profile of the constellation at hand. It tells us that in view of the origins of *legal* semiotics (a) *terminological uncertainty* (choices between *significs* and *semiotics*) reigns as well as (b) *language issues* (not all contributions are written or translated in English) and (c) *personality issues* (who came originally forward with legal semiotic viewpoints). These three components of the profile should be outlined in a sketchy manner in order to inform the reader without disturbing the main lines of research and representation of this book.

First we suggest that there is no real choice or any agonizing discrepancy between the two terms for the newly developing discipline: significs and semiotics. Both have their own variations that highlight different aspects, such as Lady Welby's *sense, sensifics, meaning, signification, significance* or *ideal worth,* and Peirce's *semiotics, semeiotic, semeiosis* or *synechism.* Lady Welby clearly juxtaposed 'significs' to 'semeiotics' in a Peircean sense[3]. Such variations show a close togetherness and exchangeability between the two major concepts[4]. For Lady Welby as well as for Peirce truly counts what Max Fisch formulated in his study on "Peirce's General Theory of Signs", that "most needed (is)... a lexicon that quotes Peirce's best definitions or explanations of the terms he uses and that gives references to other passages in his writings...". In the absence of such a lexicon, one has to refer to the correspondence between Peirce and Lady Welby published 1953 and 1977. The letters show a mutual understanding and close commonness of purpose, so that we can to a high degree equalize *significs* and *semiotics* the way we understand these concepts today. Lady Welby writes 1908 to Peirce: "You have always been kindly interested in the work to which my life is devoted" and Peirce writes her: "... when I have myself been entirely absorbed in the very same subject since 1863, without meeting, before I made your acquaintance, a single mind to whom it did not seem very like bosh"[5]. *Legal* semiotics and *legal* significs can consequently be regarded as identical so that a first suggestion about *legal* semiotics can as well originate within a *significs* context[6].

---

[3] See the foundational study of Susan Petrilli: *Signifying and Understanding. Reading the Works of Victoria Welby and the Signific Movement.* De Gruyter Mouton, Berlin 2009, p. 288 "Significs and Semiotics: Giovanni Vailati and Charles S. Peirce" and p. 748: "The Signific Movement in The Netherlands".

[4] Irwin C. Lieb (Ed.): *Charles S. Peirce's letters to Lady Welby*, New Haven, Conn. 1953. Charles S. Hardwick/James Cook (Ed.): *Semiotic and Significs. The Correspondence between Charles S. Peirce and Victoria Lady Welby.* Indiana UP 1977. See also: Max Fisch, *Peirce,* Op. cit., p. 142.; and: G. Deledalle: Vistoria Lady Welby and Charles Sanders Peirce: Meaning and Signification" in: H. Walter Schmitz (Ed.): *Essays on Significs*, J. Benjamins, Amsterdam 1990, p. 134.

[5] M. Fisch: *Peirce, Semeiotic, and Pragmatism*, Indiana UP 1986, Ch. 17, p. 321, 342.

[6] Subtle differences can be found in representations of signific viewpoints, in particular in the Dutch movements, for instance about the communicative component in speech act research, the system character and the reference to logic (as in Peirce's philosophy) admitted in analyzing understanding

Second, there is the language issue. Roughly spoken, semiotics has thanks to Peirce's philosophical project developed in English during the second half of the nineteenth and the first of the twentieth century, whereas French linguistic and psychological contributions (Greimas, Lacan) are until now only fragmentarily translated. Semiotics under the name '*significs*' was written in English in so far as the work of Lady Welby and some of her followers/correspondents were concerned, however, important works were conceived in Dutch during the first half of the twentieth century in Amsterdam and its *signific* movements: 1917 the "Internationaal Instituut voor Wijsbegeerte", established in four (!) languages, Dutch, English, French and German, and 1922 (at distance from Lady Welby's work) the Dutch "*Signifische Kring*" to support *signific* language-studies and philosophy, in particular studies on mutual understanding, speech acts and related linguistic utterances)[7]. The latter contacted incidentally German philosophers and psychologists, but there were no major *signific* works in German conceived.

Close encounters between the Dutch poet, novelist, psychologist and cultural icon Frederik van Eeden and Lady Welby during the London "International Congress of Experimental Psychology" in August 1892 lead to a uniquely deepened interest among Dutch scientists and literary figures. Lady Welby's 1893 and 1903 publications in the Journal *Mind* supported that interest. The Dutch mathematicians L. E. I. Brouwer and G. Mannoury, the sinologist Henri Borel, the author/psychologist Frederik van Eeden, the linguist J. van Ginneken and the writer, poet and jurist Jakob I. de Haan formed the first generation to support, explore, criticize and publish from diverse *significs circles* in The Netherlands. They felt a common urge to examine the effect of language on thought, feeling and behavior, investigate means and structures of human communication ('verstandhouding') and concentrated on the constitution of meaning of words in linguistic connectivity. Would it surprise that *legal* semiotics could become profiled in this intellectual and political climate—and yet remain globally unknown because of the isolation caused by its native language?

---

or in the communicative orientation of Peirce's semiotics. See H. Walter Schmitz: *De Hollandse Significa. Een reconstructie van de geschiedenis van 1892 tot 1926.* Assen 1990, p. 356 f., which is a Dutch translantion of his originally German "Habilitationsschrift", 1985: *Verständigungshandlungen-eine wissenschaftshistorische Rekonstruktion der Anfänge der signifischen Bewegung in den Niederlanden (1892–1926).* Petrilli writes in two contexts that "In contrast to... 'semiotics', 'significs' was free from technical associations, thus making it suitable to signal the connection between meanings and value in all its aspects": in: P. Cobley (Ed.): *The Routledge Companion to Semiotics and Linguistics",* London/New York 2001, p. 264 and Petrilli: *Signifying and Understanding,* Op. Cit., p. 255 without precisely determining those "technical associations".

[7] Studies in Dutch and English on Significs in The Netherlands written in Dutch language are scarce, see the outstanding publications of H. Walter Schmitz: *De Hollandse Significa.* Op. Cit., and H. Walter Schmitz: "Frederik van Eeden and the Introduction of Significs into the Netherlands: From Lady Welby to Mannoury" in: H. Walter Schmitz (Ed.): *Essays on Significs*, Op. Cit., p. 219 f. as well as Susan Petrilli: *Signifying and Understanding*, Op. Cit. p. 829–885 with short texts of van Eeden, Mannoury, Brouwer and Vuysje, giving an English language impression of the issues discussed in Dutch language in The Netherlands from 1892–1951. The section concludes with a special "Significs in the Netherlands. A General Survey" by David Vuysje, pp 883 f. See also H. Walter Schmitz & E. Heijerman (Ed.): *Significs, Mathematics and Semiotics. The Signific Movement in the Netherlands.* Münster 1986.

Third there is to consider a personality involved, the originator of a semiotics of law who has never been acknowledged as such, not even in circles of *significs* or semiotics[8]: Jacob Israel de Haan (1881–1924), *the first legal semiotician*, was one of the members of the first generation in the Amsterdam *Significs Circle*. De Haan was an untimely personality: a writer and precursor of Amnesty International with his work on the prisoner rights and life conditions in Russian prisons 1912/1913, one of the first openly gay authors of literary works in The Netherlands (Pijpelijntjes 1904; Pathologieën 1908), a widely appreciated poet (Collected Poetry 1952), and a politically active Zionist murdered in Jeruzalem in 1924 by a member of the secular Zionist organization Hagana. He had gradually become an anti-zionist, spying for the British secret service, a contact person to the father of King Hussein, Emir Abdallah, and ultimately a victim of the first political murder in Palestine.

Jacob Israel de Haan

De Haan's scientific work as jurist and law professor at the Universities of Amsterdam (1916–1918) and Jerusalem (1920–1924) focused exclusively on "*Legal Significs*", the theme of his PhD dissertation in Amsterdam 1916, in relation to basic jurisprudential concepts (liability, responsibility, accountability) and areas of law (criminal law, civil law, contract law, rights positions). That focus was prepared from 1912 on, as Petrilli mentions: "From 1912 onwards De Haan developed legal *significs*, that is, the analysis of legal problems from a *significal* perspective, writing forty articles and two books on the subject."[9] Three issues should be exposed in this short oversight: (1) De Haan's concept of legal *significs*/semiotics; (2) his appreciation of 'language' and (3) of the 'jurisprudence -language' relationship.

Legal Significs

Legal Significs is the concept that covers the understanding of mutually grasped meanings and inherent appreciations among human individuals in a cultural pattern. Without ever having studied Peirce, the discipline includes most of the elements the latter has mentioned for his semiotic project, which clearly focuses on sign, interpretation and meaning. *Legal* semiotics is as a consequence the ensemble of

---

[8] The Dutch legal historian Govaert C. J. J. van den Bergh wrote the only English article on De Haan in a semiotic context, the *International Journal for the Semiotics of Law*, Vol. IX, 25 (1996) entitled: "Jacob Israel de Haan's Legal Significs", and motivated his text exclusively with the remark: "I believe that this work, with all its flaws, is still of interest today" (p. 81); the same is the case for his: G.C.J.J. van den Bergh (Ed.): *De taal zegt meer dan zij verantwoorden kan,* Ars Aequi Libri, Nijmegen 1994. Both publications do *not* position De Haan as the first *legal* semiotician. See also: G.C.J.J. van den Bergh & Jan M. Broekman: *Recht en Taal*, Kluwer/Deventer 1979. p. 55 f.

[9] Susan Petrilli, *Signifying and Understanding,*Op. Cit., p. 757.

descriptive, explanatory, critical and active *significs*/semiotics of law—three levels and contexts of approaching law's meaning making power. That insight leads to the concepts 'sign' and 'signification/meaning' and their relevance in legal discourse by means of a new understanding and appraisal of legal language. *Significs*/semiotics (no fundamental difference found) of law was presented by De Haan to his legal colleagues between 1910 and 1920 in more than ten essay-titles, all of them focusing on various legal areas and in the first place on the language lawyers use in those contexts. The ultimate goal of this approach is a more precise, a better understanding of language. Poets know this from their innermost experiences, de Haan argues, which means that the distance between immediate experience and reflection, between science and wisdom, leads to the insight that experience is what not is experienced but to what is grasped as experience through reflection. In that same sense, legal semiotics/*significs* does not focus *legal science* in the first place but the *concept of law* itself, as it does not relate to linguistics but to the concept of language itself.

The essence of legal semiotics/*significs* culminates in a philosophical reflection upon the power of legal language upon the law. A legal semiotician does not analyze the multiple meanings of words and expressions in legal language in each case and in each application individually. A word does not 'possess' a meaning but 'is' the (temporarily and culturally determined) unification of a number of meanings. Words are mutual and thus in equal relations, and therefore differences (Mannoury 1915). Were De Haan's considerations to explain legal *significs*/semiotics at first more or less identical with semantics as an integral part of linguistics, they grew in the course of the later years. They became a systematic study of expression, of understanding, of self-preservation, of symbols and other means of communication. All can play a role in legal discourse, as do sound, images, signs, movements—but legal *significs*/semiotics should focus on words in the first place. In an extremely relevant and modern manner, De Haan formulates 1916: "The word penetrates my mind and my mind penetrates the word". This penetration forms the foundation of *significs*/semiotics for the lawyer, who works with words and gives words a meaning. It has irritated and offended many legal colleagues and it has given legal semiotics a bad name among jurists from its very (and mostly unknown) beginning. Schmitz' remark interests, that the "recently expressed view of *significs* as a uniquely Dutch form of scientific endeavor dealing primarily with fundamental problems of mathematics and social sciences, is not exactly false, but it is one-sided.... The Dutch *significians* cared about more than the treatment of special problems involved in knowing mediated by symbols. They also addressed themselves to the analysis of interaction by means of signs, namely communication ..."[10]

---

[10] H. Walter Schmitz: "Frederik van Eeden and the introduction of significs...." In: *Essays on Significs*,Op. Cit., p. 225

Language

Language is at issue in all regards. Legal semiotics concerns all meanings in legal language[11]. A semantic analysis of all major legal concepts is the ultimate task of legal *significs*/semiotics. This implies a critique of the current legal language and its general expressiveness: that language is often incomprehensible for the citizen and full of misconceptions created by the lawyers. And it implies an idea about legal discourse in general, which is close to the Vienna Circle and its positivism, and close to Wittgenstein's Tractatus: legal language should allow law to become a reliable element of scientific argumentation—that would lead to a better law! De Haan's purpose is in a slogan of his PhD dissertation: "Betere taal is beter denken. En beter denken is beter recht" [Better language is better thinking. And better thinking is better law].[12] *Significs*/semiotics is, expressed with a variation on Wittgenstein, about language-games and not about word-games. The words that are subject of his dissertation: liability, responsibility and accountability, are elements of legal language: they are only in that quality 'words', and as words are they constitutive elements of law.

These concepts are analyzed as building blocks of criminal law, which represent the entire structure (a *dogmatic* structure in the wording of Civil Law) of legal science. That is one side of the coin. These words, belonging to criminal and penal law, belong to a firm legal practice, which is interwoven with a specific form of (legal) politics. This interests, because we meet a question, which is also posed in the context of the Critical Legal Studies movement of the seventies and eighties of the twentieth century in the US. The reference shows an unexpected coherence between semiotics and CLS in law. The common experience is, that jurists always meet language: as law, as statute, as practice and as a means of action. De Haan formulates therefore in his PhD dissertation: "The insight that that legal language has to improve, is in particular dear to those who take legal science not as a dogmatic issue but apply law as a factual social science."[13] The idea that an improved language, better, clearer defined and more effectively applied, can result in more just social relations is foundational for legal semioticians who described themselves as '*significians*'. Do not forget that the critique on language in the Vienna Circle, in parallel to the Amsterdam *Significs Circle*, shared the ethics of these principles: a liberation of conventional language patterns and the release of the creative expressivity of the individual were important for a new and just society.[14] All criticism inherent to *significs of law* focuses in the first place on the words that are used in jurisprudence and laws. In several publications De Haan rewrote existing texts of laws, and attacked the formulations

---

[11] J.I. de Haan: *Wezen en taak der rechtskundige significa*, Amsterdam, Van Kampen 1916, p. 5.

[12] J.I. de Haan: *Rechtskundige Significa en hare toepassing op de begrippen: "aansprakelijk, verantwoordelijk, toerekeningsvatbaar"* [Legal Siginifics and her application on the concepts liable, responsible, accountable] Amsterdam, Versluys 1916. See also: Jan M. Broekman: "Betere taal is beter recht" in *Wijsgerig Perspectief op maatschappij en wetenschap,* Vol. 20, No. 2. 1979/80, p. 49.

[13] De Haan: *Rechtskundige Significa,* Op. Cit. p. 69.

[14] A. Janik & St. E. Toulmin: *Wittgenstein's Vienna*, Chicago 1996.

of parliamentarians designing new laws. They can be written *clearer* and *better*: two requirements that diminish the distance between legal- and everyday language uses. Lawyers, he says, do not invest in focusing upon their expressiveness—they do in the first place not understand how to obtain a 'living harmony' between their expressions and the expressive dynamics of citizenship. Not only dots and dashes, but also important words or concepts in our jurisprudence should be chosen with much more care and precision. Examples of such neglect are discussed in the case of terms as: liability, responsibility; accuser, petitioner; void, remission; fact; interest; damage; guilt; creditor, to have a right, and the like. Does insight in the problems pertaining to correct words in legal language indeed lead lawyers to deeper understanding of the essential connections between law and language? Many contemporaries of De Haan expressed their skepticism and doubt.

Discourse Levels

"Let us finally know what we do when we speak!" was an outcry of Frederik van Eeden, the famous Dutch poet, psychologist and most influential participant in all *significs* circles of his time in 1921. Can we know what we do when we speak the language of law and legal discourse by means of analyzing its standardized words and fixated terms? The question is essential for any attempt to initiate and exercise legal semiotics, De Haan's legal *significs* has shown. Speaking legal discourse, performing speech acts in law, is in the eyes of De Haan and his comrade *significiants not* a matter of using words in a uniform discourse. They never concluded as we can do today, that legal discourse is an artificial discourse constructed with linguistic material of everyday (native) language. But Mannoury, Brouwer, De Haan and others were very near to this thesis when they agreed upon one important step before that rather radical conclusion. They distinguished five levels of discourse with each having their specific properties[15]. That idea shows how a *differentiation of discourse is needed to understand law's language activity*—although none of these levels could specifically become assigned to law despite the fact that they have each their particular communicative property.

Mannoury, Brouwer, Borel and Van Eeden *first* distinguish a "foundational language level"—a sort of mother-tongue in which each word on itself relates directly to one's particular imagination and understanding. Examples are children's language, the language of deep and passionate emotions, or the hypothetical primitive language.

Second, there is the "tempered language level" in which words are seldom coupled and mostly become effective through a direct relation with other words in a human mind, as is the case with recollections and memories. Personal experiences

[15] "Signifisch Taalonderzoek", published in *Mededeelingen van het Internationaal Instituut voor Wijsbegeerte te Amsterdam,* No. 2, Amsterdam Maart 1919, p. 5 f. p. 30 f., signed by Mannoury, Brouwer, Borel and Frederik van Eeden. See H. Walter Schmitz: *De Hollandse Significa,* Op. Cit., p. 415.

or moods are already constructed in subject-predicate constructions, as is perceivable in popular, poetic, and some Eastern languages embracing written image-signs.

Third is the "everyday language level" in which word coupling became most important and each deviation of fixated coupling norms becomes problematic. It regards the language of commerce, traffic, Western written languages. It should be underlined that word-couplings are understood as associative connections, psychic events related with auditory or visual word-images.

Fourth is the level of "scientific languages" whereby word couplings are a matter of conventions, agreements or prescripts. The languages of laws, regulations, financial relations and technical issues are structured likewise.

Fifth is the level of "symbolic language", which includes logical systems, levels of axiomatic, postulate and in general mathematic meanings.

It fascinates modern legal semiotics how these language levels are understood as an analytical as well as a descriptive tool to approach the meanings of key expressions in different discourses. The author of the unique PhD dissertation on what he called in 1916: "rechtskundige significa"—honoring his colleagues in the Amsterdam Circle and University milieu—would have placed legal discourse in a mixture of the third and the fourth language level, with a heavy accent on the third. That viewpoint is still an interesting point of departure for any recent semiotics of law.

Significs and Jurisprudence

Read Hugo von Hofmannsthal's "Brief des Lord Chandos an Francis Bacon" and experience the deep mistrust towards *the word* that characterized the poet's period of European culture. Silence is to prefer to expression. Tales, he writes, are "like shepherd games tumbling under the abundance of their words", and he reports how "I wanted to unveil the fairytales and mythical stories we inherited from our ancestors, and read them as hieroglyphs of a secret, immense wisdom, whose touch I often was aware of, but as if behind a veil". He wishes, in this famous letter, "to know the language whose words are not known to me, a language in which the silent things speak to me..."[16]. When this characterizes the attitude towards the word as the major component of language of West-European intellectuals during the years shortly before and during World War I, we should not be surprised that legal semiotics/*significs* approaches legal discourse and jurisprudence through criticizing the reliability of the word. Is jurisprudence, taken uncritically, not like the shepherd games; do judges and lawmakers not tumble under the abundance of their words? Be aware, that these questions did not and do not today pertain to the *style* of legal reasoning and representation, but in a deeper sense, to the *truth* in words—as Wittgenstein's Tractatus suggested so precisely and eloquently. What truth is in words of law? What truth in

[16] Hugo von Hofmannsthal: *Erfundene Gespräche und Briefe,* in:, B. Schoeller & R. Hirsch (Ed.) *Gesammelte Werke, Bd VII,* Fischer Verlag 1979 p. 461.

the diverse tumbling levels of legal language, what truth in the meaning of a word that law confined to solitariness, to one specific powerful and authoritarian discourse?

De Haan and colleagues posed all these questions about the character and major features of jurisprudence. Jurisprudence condemns words and concepts to solitary confinement and forgets how meanings of a word are always determined by the complex system of meanings to which it belongs. Jurisprudence manipulates its own unity and neglects how law as a discourse, is a particular semantic field. In his 1919 *Rechtskundige Significa,* de Haan analyses the results of this solitary confinement of terms and words when pointing to the words "appropriate" in the criminal code, and "lost" and "stolen" in the civil code of the Civil Law system. The need for a semiotic analysis of legal language cries out when jurists speak or write. It was the first legal semiotician in Amsterdam in the twenties like other philosophers in the thirties of the twentieth century (Tarski, Carnap) who came to that conclusion: *legal language cannot be measured with criteria of truth*, although there seems no other therapy for jurisprudence than the pursuit of a logical analysis of speech, uses of words or professional expressivity. Is there only a logical analysis possible, or has legal rhetoric its own analytical power to answer questions and critiques of semiotic nature?

Chapter 9
Legal Theory and Semiotics: Semiotics, Theory and Practice of Law

Semiotics and Legal Theory

"Jurisprudence" is a concept with many meanings, traditions, cultural- and linguistic roots. There are some interesting differences in the various languages and their legal vocabulary. German and the Anglo-American understandings of jurisprudence refer to theory, philosophy and foundations of law. French lawyers understand jurisprudence as a totality of legal cases, or in Anglo-Saxon words, as case law—but strictly within the limits of their particular understanding of a case in law. Spanish, Italian or Dutch uses of the expression refer to predominantly theoretical notions, which include the idea, that the total body of law must understood as a theory in law schools and as a practice in court. That hierarchy turns often upside down, so that practice comes first and theory or philosophy is regarded to be naturally included.

All this seems to be reinforced by the fact that the Anglo-American use of the term "Law" as used without much differentiation next to "jurisprudence", unfolds at distance to what is pertinent in for instance German legal thought: in "Law" is no dominant notion of law in general, law as an entity in itself, and as an entity that is at stake in every single judgment or legal meaning making. Positivism in English jurisprudence relates to legal acts or the enactment of rights—not to Law as a most valuable discourse in society in its entirety, and in abstraction from individual acts or enactments. The German understanding and appreciation of Law as a specific unity or wholeness articulates itself in individual legal acts—a linguistic issue of semiotic relevance in itself. Don't forget, that an argument in a Civil Law Court can be: "This argument affects or damages the Law" whereas in a Common Law Court mainly legal interests are affected. An example is in the jurisprudential concept of "Rechtsbewußtsein". "Legal consciousness" is by no means an appropriate translation because the concept of "Law/Recht" differs. In the English expression is not "Law" the issue that relates to consciousness, but "Rights". And so is in "Natural Law" also "Rights" (often 'individual rights') a major criterion in the Anglo-Saxon use, a meaning that supports legal pragmatism and can lead to forms of legal positivism. "Rights" are easier and more practically subject for positivist approaches than "Law" in its general sense!

J. M. Broekman, L. Catà Backer, *Lawyers Making Meaning*,
DOI 10.1007/978-94-007-5458-4_9, © Springer Science+Business Media Dordrecht 2013

That is an example of how law could be understood in terms of semiotics as *a field with different referents*. To repeat this in a simplified manner: cases of common- or civil law provenience *are law* and have law as its sole referent, whereas legal philosophy or legal theory *are not law*; they are discourses *about* law, and have not law but philosophy or (social, linguistic, psychological, sociological) theory as their major referent. It means that jurisprudence is predominantly understood as a theory of law and as a legal philosophy. Legal theoreticians introduced the study of coherence between semiotics and legal theory[1] and legal practitioners kept considerable distance in that same regard.

Even the idea of a legal practice is often considered as a *theoretical* notion. The virtue of practice in law is, that it is *done*, not *reflected* on anything beyond the boundaries of action-in-discourse. In recent (2011, 2012) *New York Times* articles,[2] US law Schools are criticized for not educating students to perform legal practical activities appropriately. The suggestion is, that legal education fails to include the practice of law. In the light of a semiotic insight about the theoretical character of practice one could ask whether that is ever possible. What are the boundaries of legal discourse—are they in the doing or in the thinking? David Segal writes with the title "What They Don't Teach Law Students: Lawyering"[3]:

> The lesson today—the ins and outs of closing a deal—seems lifted from Corporate Lawyering 101. "How do you get a merger done?" asks Scott B. Connolly, an attorney.
> There is silence from three well-dressed people in their early 1920s, sitting at a conference table in a downtown building here last month.
> "What steps would you need to take to accomplish a merger?" Mr. Connolly prods.
> After a pause, a participant gives it a shot: "You buy all the stock of one company. Is that what you need?"
> "That's a stock acquisition," Mr. Connolly says. "The question is, when you close a merger, how does that deal get done?"
> The answer—draft a certificate of merger and file it with the secretary of state—is part of a crash course in legal training. But the three people taking notes are not students. They are associates at a law firm called Drinker Biddle & Reath, hired to handle corporate transactions. And they have each spent three years and as much as $150,000 for a legal degree.
> What they did not get, for all that time and money, was much practical training. Law schools have long emphasized the theoretical over the useful, with classes that are often overstuffed with antiquated distinctions, like the variety of property law in post-feudal England. Professors are rewarded for chin-stroking scholarship, like law review articles with titles like "A Future Foretold: Neo-Aristotelian Praise of Postmodern Legal Theory."
> While most of law schools' professoriate still happily dwell in the uppermost floors of the ivory tower, the view from the ground for new graduates is growing uglier. (...) The nature

[1] Bernard S. Jackson: *Semiotics and Legal Theory,* 1985. (1997 reprint).

[2] See, e.g., David Segal, "What They Don't Teach Law Students: Lawyering", The New York Times, Nov. 19, 2011, available http://www.nytimes.com/2011/11/20/business/after-law-school-associates-learn-to-be-lawyers.html?adxnnl=1&adxnnlx=1339261374-/OtUnhILMMMBOThHaF+1kQ; Editorial: "Legal Education Reform", The New York Times, Nov. 25, 2011, available http://www.nytimes.com/2011/11/26/opinion/legal-education-reform.html; David Segal, "For Law Schools, a Price to Play the ABAs Way", The New York Times, Dec. 17, 2011; David Segal, "For 2nd Year, a Sharp Drop in Law School Entrance Tests," The New York Times, March 19, 2012.

[3] David Segal: "What They Don't Teach Law Students: Lawyering" see note 133.

> of legal work itself is evolving, and the days when corporations buy billable hours, instead of results, are numbered.

Segal suggests as a conclusion:

> To succeed in this environment, graduates will need entrepreneurial skills, management ability and some expertise in landing clients. They will need to know less about Contracts and more about contracts.

Two more remarks are overdue:

First, practical social purposes are predominant in all situations in which the expressions 'legal theory' and 'jurisprudence' are used. There is the *public* interest, often exemplified by the penal model of law, and the *private* interest, which functions for example in cases of contract, taxation and many others. The two fortify each other, they are often intermingled and they are also often unclear about the precise determination of their referent.

Second, both types of expressiveness touch the problem whether there exists a real *unity* of the legal system—even where Kevelson speaks of "Law as a System of Signs" is this unity at stake! Most *Law* derives from or relates to a particular State or Nation and the State-concept (although diminishing in our days) remains constitutive for law. Legal theoreticians would therefore venture the thesis that there is always a minimum of positivism operational in law.[4]

This can be observed from the very beginnings of (European) jurisprudence in the eighteenth century on, where *natural law* was predominant and its principles discussed with ardor. In any case, referents were diverse and reference was problematic: problems *in* law and legal systems were from the very beginning separated from problems *of* law as a social institution, including its politics and socio-economic conditions. Apart from Natural Law were Legal Positivism and Legal Realism mainstream trends of legal philosophy and legal theory: close to jurisprudence, but their closeness varied in time, language and place/nation. The Critical Legal Studies movement is the most recent theory of jurisprudence developed since the 1970s, claiming that law is largely contradictory since it expresses the policy goals of dominant social groups. The conclusion about its contradictory character was drawn and defended by means of semiotics of law and legal discourse.

Semiotics and Legal Interpretation

Jackson[5] underlined the importance of such considerations. Before describing "a semiotic model of law"—an expression that will be met by practicing lawyers with skepticism, because they question how a non-legal discourse such as semiotics can ever *model* law—he researches presuppositions in the work of legal theoreticians that

---

[4] Jan M. Broekman: "The Minimum Content Of Positivism" In: *Rechtstheorie*, XVI, 4, 1985, p. 349.

[5] Bernard S. Jackson: *Semiotics and Legal Theory*, 1985, 1997 p. 283 ff.

show semiotic features. They pertain in particular to (a) legal *rules* (Hart), (b) legal *institutions* (McCormick), (c) legal *argument* (Dworkin) and (d) legal *acts* (Kelsen). Each of them represents a vital aspect of contemporary law and legal theory, as the following short outlines demonstrate.

H.L.A. Hart. Hart's exposé on legal rules exploits the famous distinction between a *core* of undisputed meaning in law and a *penumbra* of uncertainty about legal meaning; both of which are determinative for opinions of courts and judges. In essence is this a semiotic distinction, because it *shows the tendency to identify the 'core' with 'meaning' and the 'penumbra' with 'interpretation'*—an operation often embraced by practitioners of law in all institutional contexts, such as courts, law firms or legal politics. Those operations show, how legal meanings influence law's communicative power and structures. The dominant model for that power is articulated in Hart's widely known expression 'the open texture' of law, so that he argues:

> In any large group, general rules, standards, and principles must be the main instrument of social control, and not particular directions given to each individual separately. If it were not possible to communicate general standards of conduct, which multitudes of individuals could understand, without further direction, as requiring from them certain conduct when occasion arose, nothing that we now recognize as law could exist.... (Herbert L.A. Hart: The Concept of Law. Oxford 1994, 2nd Edition p. 124.)

All components of legal discourse, from meaning to case and from rule to conduct, seem to finally focus an underlying model of *communicative* activity. It appears that in the heart of legal practice and legal discourse the overwhelming importance of communication is shared with non-doctrinal discourses such as legal semiotics.

There is, however, an important restriction pertaining to the range and quality of social communication effected by law in Hart's analysis: he provides the *user* of law and language a prevailing position, so that his theories are philosophically speaking strongly subject-centered. This constitutes an important difference between Hart and McCormick.

D.N. McCormick. A subject-centered understanding of law forms a contrast to an institutional approach, which displays necessarily *narrative* features. The latter was originally outlined in John Searle's philosophy of language,[6] which highlighted the constitutive power of expressiveness engendered by social institutions in the Western world. Weinberger & McCormick observed how legal institutions not only form a framework for legal practice but also determine legal expressiveness in general. This pertains in particular to the rules for expressing oneself as a lawyer, which is an activity in all cases determined by institutions and institutionally framed language. Following the lifeline of an institution, McCormick distinguishes between *institutive, consequential* and *terminative* sets of rules that make the legal system coherent.

Jackson signals a clear coherence between the Weinberger/MacCormick institutional theory of law and the semiotic approach to institutionally constituted narratives as initiated by Greimas Op. cit., p. 169:

---

[6] J. R. Searle: *Expression and Meaning*, 1979 Cambridge UP; -Id: *Speech Acts. An Essay in the Philosophy of Language,* Cambridge UP 1969.

> Narrative is there [in Greimasian narrative grammar] conceived as a genre, which represents life in terms of a sequence of states and transformations. There exist semiotic constraints upon the range of possible states, and the manner in which they may be transformed, these constraints themselves representing the construction of human culture out of nature. So too, within the particular universe of law, legal subjects may be conceived as proceeding through a life history represented by different legal states and the transformations between them. The 'states' are the various sets of consequential rules, the 'transformations' are the institutive/terminative sets of rules which apply to those states. Each legal institution may be compared to a single 'narrative syntagma', these various narrative syntagmas being linked in an overall narrative algorithm. McCormick sees a similar process of interlocking of institutions in complex chains. He gives as an example the case of a right of ownership of a piece of land.

Following Searle's distinction between *institutional* and *brute* facts, McCormick's legal theory concentrates on *legal facts,* which are *institutional facts*. The same consideration comes to the fore as on the first page of this chapter: it is unclear, and changes with the language articulation, whether law itself *as a discourse in its entirety* is either understood as 'institutional fact' or as 'a discourse made of institutional facts called "law"'. This is the reformulation of discussions that reduce law to fact and neglect how law and its facts are *meanings* given to human behaviors in the first place. McCormick's intuition approximates semiotics: behavioral meanings are not solely products of a rule-following attitude (as in precedent cases) but rather the product of communication as an encompassing process. That focuses the important gap between legal practice and legal theory.

Does not legal theory require legal writing texts as well as interpreting texts in the context of law and legal discourse, in order to function socially? Practitioners may not be interested in such broad perspectives because they tend to use only one particular fragment of law and neglect general legal literature and discussions about law in its entirety. The latter play anyway a more important role in the Civil Law than in their companion Common Law. It is, however, clear that law's globalization forms the recent new framework for the speedily growing convergence of both systems of law and legal practices, which are more and more influenced by the new economic tactics of global companies. In the light of that development, any semiotic understanding of law reaches today beyond the gap between theory and practice of law.

R. Dworkin. Dworkin's interest is dominated by his analyses and descriptions of lawyers' *interpretative* practices, so that he often considers law as a narration or as literature in a larger sense.[7] He thus unfolds an argumentative and rhetoric understanding of legal discourse, in which literary criticism and legal interpretation come close to a semiotic identity. Ties between those two appear to be strong and important. Consider for instance how Dworkin's often disputed remark about the question whether there is or there is not a 'no-right-answer' in case law enhances the strength of that identity. One should understand that there is in law, like in literary criticism, no absolute (or absolutely objective and truthful) argument in interpretation or argumentation; legal arguments are not an exception to the rule that all arguments are constructed—and not encountered as if they were an immovable

[7] R. Dworkin: *A Matter of Principle*, Harvard UP 1985, p. 146.

and unchangeable entity in any nature or culture. And, what is more, legal arguments can come from everywhere; they are not necessarily limited to matters at hand, and are not restricted to, deduced or concluded from specific texts, as the large majority of Court decisions display.

In other words, *criteria for legal interpretation and application are not a matter of objective realities but of appropriateness*, of constructions that 'fit'. One can hardly underestimate the importance of this conclusion, since this goes even beyond an analysis of law's interpretative practices. This argument leads us beyond what lawyers have in hand and even beyond the boundaries of legal discourse in its entirety, and directs us towards the realm of semiotics. One should perceive how lawyers engineer meaning when they "recognize" signs, symbols and meanings in texts! In other words, Dworkin's 'best solution' is not a matter of finding the law in a legal/doctrinal space, but of *constructing the discourse so that it all fits*—which is a truly semiotic issue.

Jackson has two truly surprising remarks in this direction, when he states that "the choice of rationale of a particular statute or precedent is to be judged on criteria of 'fit' with other aspects of the (legal) system", and that "Dworkinian semiotics may be regarded as the application of a form of structural semantics at the discursive level".[8] An important consideration is, however, whether legal practice 'fits' the idea of application at all—an issue to be highlighted in the context of a semiotic understanding of legal practice in general. Is the expression "semiotics of legal argument" *pleonastic,* because legal reasoning is not a matter of law, but of semiotics in law?

There are two consequences of Jackson's observation: (a) that the choice of criteria appears to put the internal logic of legal decision making in perspective, and (b) that, as a consequence, legal judgments are based on semiotic rather than legal activities. If one agrees with this observation, there is food for thoughts about the status of legal semiotics! Jackson gave this theme considerable attention, when saying:

> Legal semiotics is hardly a discipline, since it does not follow a common set of methods... To many, it functions inter alia as a meta-discipline, providing a language within which to study the traditional methods of "legal science". ... It is, perhaps, the absence of a common approach to the status of legal semiotics that makes the field at one and the same time puzzling yet vibrant. (Bernard S. Jackson : "Legal Semiotics and Semiotic Aspects of Jurisprudence" in: Wagner & Broekman [Eds] *Prospects of Legal Semiotics,* Op. Cit. p. 29.)

One of the ways to safeguard this vibrancy is to discuss whether in cases of semiotics such criteria as the commonness of methods and with it the commonness of reference to other disciplines remains decisive. Referring to disciplines seems necessary but those disciplines are referred to as specific discourses. The latter denomination could very well be based upon other criteria and features than the first—a semiotic issue of interest.

H. Kelsen. Kelsen's emphasis on legal acts and norms does not solve that question. However, his approximation to semiotics is clear. Jackson formulates

[8] Bernard S. Jackson: *Semiotics and Legal Theory,* 1985, 1997 (reprint), p. 223.

> Kelsen's conception of the norm is intimately bound up with the relationship between facts and the different kinds of meaning, which may be attributed to them. Semiotic relationships are therefore involved in Kelsen's conception of the norm; the legal norm belongs to a particular semiotic universe—that of 'objective meaning' (of a particular type). But his statements on the nature of the norm show traces of an internal conflict between the use of two different semiotic models, a 'communicational' model on the one hand, and something resembling a 'speech act' model on the other. (Jackson, Op. cit., p. 227.)

The latter could equally well be understood in terms of the tension between a 'hierarchy of norms' and what he conceives as the 'meanings of an act or will'. The latter, 'subject-centered' concept of norm-following on one hand, and (free) will on the other is a broad semiotic spectrum in its own right, since semiotics guarantee that meanings of an act and of an interpretation could be understood as identical. That identity is important for a correct view on the semiotic dimensions of legal practice, especially as far as the interpretation of a norm as the heart of the process of applying the law is concerned.

All dimensions of a legal norm are at stake when a legal judgment is required, and which of them find their location with*in* the law and legal discourse or are *out*side, is a matter of creating the fitting legal arguments. Kelsen distinguishes therefore between legal-scientific interpretations (which are cognitive and show their semiotic dimensions) and legal-practical interpretations (which are in need of authentic or institutionally authenticated interpretations that tend to hide their semiotic dimensions). Doctrinal authority excludes occasional arguments of semiotic nature. So the semiotics of facts and arguments depends in Kelsen's positivist theory upon the *institutional* definition of law, in other words: the line between law and non-law is a constructive decision and not an objective datum.

This list of legal theoreticians could be importantly extended, but all of them would show the same pattern: a pattern of close ties between law and legal practice on the one hand and semiotic positions on the other. A rigid line between legal scientists and theoreticians and legal practitioners does not alter that picture.

Two Legal Semiotic Traditions

Without being dogmatic in this approach, one could venture the idea that there are two traditions within the legal semiotics movement, which embrace different techniques, goals, philosophical and cultural roots and languages.

One is the *North American* approach, in the main based on the philosophy of Charles Sanders Peirce and the fruitful expansion of his ideas for law and legal discourse by Roberta Kevelson. That approach focuses on the sign concept, a focus being the core technique for understanding meaning in law—an approach which is predominantly monolingual: all studies, enrollments, texts, analyses are in the English language. It is worth noticing that apart from various semiotic approaches of law, American legal scholarship contributed importantly to the legal exploration of semiotics parallel to the development of rhetoric as a closely connected field of legal interest.[9] An exemplary character of those scholarly exposés is, however, its inward looking character and obsessed with the peculiar and temporally fashionable issues that interest the US legal academic establishment. Semiotically, one might be tempted to suggest that semiotic studies in the United States is itself systemically symbolic, and focused on academic status relationships within a small closed circle. As a consequence, North American semiotics is sometimes difficult to grasp for non-Anglo-American legal scholars, since they almost naturally refer to the US Common Law, without mentioning the simple fact that this legal system is not the only legal system in the world. That produces a danger of irrelevance; fortunately one dissipated by some level of European and Asian interest in the U.S. sources of legal semiotics.[10]

The other is the *West European* approach, based on philosophical mainstreams such as structuralism and phenomenology, many times referring to the analytical work of Greimas and the technicalities of meaning-elucidation through outlining semiotic squares. The goal of that approach is predominantly linguistic/analytic, and unfolds within the boundaries of legal theory, decidedly at distance to legal practices. The approach is, moreover, entirely multilingual, with English, French and German as the main players, not to mention Spanish and Italian. Be aware that not all contributions to the field are in English, and being not translated from, let us say Italian, into English is not a sign of depreciation. They furthermore refer most generally to the Civil Law and do not mention issues related to, or exemplified by studies pertaining to the US or other Common Law systems. Milovanovic provides various orientation points in our Western post-modern culture.[11] We quote:

> The American tradition is more rooted in *Pragmatism*, (which favors the contextual and situated nature of meaning); *Referentiality*, and *the triadic nature of meaning*: the sign (or the word), the interpretant (or referant), and the object.
>
> Exemplary in the development of this American style of semiotics are the works of Charles S. Peirce and C. W. Morris. The key theorist who has pioneered a Peircian approach to law is Roberta Kevelson.
>
> It should be noted that some variations of the Peircian approach have recently developed in the American tradition, such as those of "speech act theory." This variation looks at the intentions of the users of a discourse. Here, "'to mean something' is grammatically equivalent to the expression 'to intend something', and this intention 'imparts a purpose or point to language use"' (Jackson, 1985, p. 15 and Brown, 1974, p. 118). So "referring" is equated with goal-oriented behavior; put in another way, "'action' in this tradition is firmly identified with 'intensionality"'. (Jackson 1985, p. 15)
>
> In the European tradition, some variations have developed that focus on unconscious motivations and forces as a basis of social action (e.g., Lacan, Kristeva, Foucault, Derrida). Eco, for example, tells us, that "the subject is spoken by language" (1984, p. 45; Kennedy 1997, p. 134). Lacan defines the subject as a *parlêtre*, or *l'être parlant* (the "speaking," or

[9] Francis J. Mootz III: *Rhetorical Knowledge in Legal Practice and Critical Legal Theory*, Alabama UP 2006.

[10] E.g., Grupo de Estudiuos Percianos at the Universidad de Navarra (Spain); available (in English and Spanish) at http://www.unav.es/gep/index-en.html.

[11] D. Milovanovic: *An Introduction to the Sociology of Law*, 2003 New York, 187–190.

> the speaking-being). Peirce, himself, is opposed to the Cartesian notion of a centered ego in control and has been identified with arguing for a subject, immersed in sign usages, a "sign-using self" or "semiotic self" (Corrington 1993, p. 76–115). Perhaps the most enigmatic of the definitions of "signifier " has been offered by Lacan: "a signifier is that which represents the subject for another signifier" (1977, p. 316; for some similarities between Peirce and Lacan, see Milovanovic 1998). Here the subject disappears in the signifier, which then comes to represent it for other signifiers within the unconscious realm. Again, meaning is non-referential; here it refers to a psychic (unconscious) reality, which has a semi-autonomous existence.

It is interesting how the European and American traditions differ; they do not in their interpretation of signs and symbols, but in their philosophical roots that shape semiotic understandings.

> A Legal Semiotics will find itself based on one of two main directions of semiotic thought: European or American. The European tradition is more concerned with:
> * *Structural and semantic analysis*: some "deep" structural level is said to exist which is coordinated by the paradigmatic and syntagmatic axes. Paradigm stands for the totality of dictionary meanings of words; syntagm the proper method of arranging them in linear form in order to make sense. In law, for example, a legal concept which is chosen must be placed in a particular linear narrative; in cross-examination and in deductive logic, there is a very particular way of choosing only relevant legal terms and arranging them in particular sequences in narratives (consider also, for example: the allowable form in the introduction of testimony or expert witness information; the injunction against "leading the witness"; or consider the allowable "scope" for a particular line of questioning that constitutes the boundaries of discursive exchanges during the trial court proceedings).
> * *The binary nature of the sign*: A sign, that is: a word, is composed of two parts, the *signifier* and the *signified*. The former stands for the acoustic-image, the psychic imprint; the latter, to what it refers (e.g., the concept, or mental image).
> Say the word "tree," for example, and the image of a tree appears. In law, signifiers such as "person," "life," "liberty" and "property" have specific meanings, specific signifieds attached to them; and
> * *Non-referentiality*: meaning is internal to some linguistic system, such as legal discourse. One word refers for it's meaning to another, which, in turn, refers to another, etc. Consider, for example, looking up a word in a standard dictionary. In law, one does not make use of the everyday dictionary, but *Black's Law Dictionary*, which provides very particular meanings of signifiers in law.

This overview shows how indeed two authors dominate and inspire linguistic, philosophical and sociological research focusing the semiotics-law relationship in US and European context. Their prevalence overwhelms and could be understood as an original constellation, which determines the field. The theme became later more articulated and also more differentiated under the influence of authors such as Sebeok, Kevelson, Jackson, Landowski, Goodrich and others.

They did, however, not clarify *why* especially legal discourse has opened up to semiotic interpretations and analyses, so that "legal semiotics" was established. This is even more fascinating since legal discourse has always been characterized as closed, non-reflexive and hardly able to connect to other discourses at an equal level. Furthermore, any attempt to deal with the idea of a *legal* semiotics will meet critical questions pertaining to the status of legal practice. Perhaps only theoreticians debate the status of legal practice and what particular knowledge is produced by legal discourse.

Semiotics and Legal Practices

Law focuses on human relations—that is the most general expression, which the two legal semiotic traditions have in common. There is no doubt that this is also the most important issue in all types and variations of legal scholarship. It means that legal semiotics needs to shed a special light on the patterning and emergence of human relations. Despite this need, not many semiotic studies are undertaken to further research in the semiotics of human relations within law and legal discourse. There are two issues in law that determine its importance, *autonomy* and *abstraction*. First, autonomy goes to the fact that *legal practice* is in fact a specific articulation of human relations which happens to differ from non-legal relations because of the difference between legal- and non-legal language. Second, abstraction goes to the fact that basic human relations, such as *face-to-face relations*, do not seem to be of primordial importance in the legal patterning of relations between individuals.

Legal practitioners often show an attitude they call *pragmatic*. A challenging question is whether semiotics ever meets such a pragmatic legal mind-set and what exactly the semiotics of legal pragmatism should mean in this context. The question is not far away from structuralism, as one remembers how human history might be a matter of graphs, spurs and inscriptions, of acts and deeds that leave marks behind as were they inscriptions in the stones of the ages. The Latin expression ‘pragmaticus’ refers to the ‘jurisconsult’, the legal advisor who grounds his advice in experience with and knowledge of the history of facts. His pragmatic knowledge does justice to the facts and in doing so creates an equilibrium that can be appreciated as ‘just’, or even ‘right’. It thus becomes clear that a pragmatic attitude embraces more than an incidental appropriateness of applying norms to facts, or principles to bewildering forms of disequilibrium and conflict. In accordance with semiotics, structuralism claims the renewal of attitudes that makes the multicultural prevail. In doing so, it engenders *a view beyond the surface* of our perception. It always provides a view at reality behind the scenes of appearances: a truly semiotic move and a privileged code in a deconstruction mode. The latter is only useful if *structures* are recognizable in non-apparent layers of reality—even in the often-mysterious depth of virtual realities. It imports that those are perhaps solely accessible by means of linguistic articulations and (re-)constructions.

Language is our most important mental construct—and the ‘our’ is the riddle: we do, and we do not construct language ourselves, Husserl explained and Derrida, Foucault, Lacan, Piaget successively reformulated. Language sets man apart from other organisms, and functions as the basic tool of thought and reason—even in processes where humans transcend their biological limits. Consider, how the view behind appearances, which is decisive in this transcending, is not an *optical* but a *linguistic* metaphor, suggesting how perception becomes language! Remember Nietzsche’s mistrust of language, which reverberates in structuralism and its challenging options. Pragmatism has always been either a validation or a subversion of constraining standards. Peirce knew the tension between objective and subjective dimensions of pragmatism, whereby the latter precluded deconstruction efforts, which were for him in his days idiosyncratic and negativistic. Today, we appreciate deconstructionist efforts rather as an attempt to make the human mind reach beyond the appearances of daily life whilst underlining the wealth of possibilities to deal with reality. This is in any case today's cultural and spiritual background for lawyers who just want to practice law! How do they manage the many meanings of their expression: "to practice law"? And, as was suggested before: is that idea in itself not definitively theoretical, so that there are no words or meanings of a practitioner to be shared with legal educators, doctrinal experts or semioticians?

Yes, lawyers *manage* meanings, because meanings are not beyond any human power of using or inventing words, signs, symbols and special meanings. Consider how legal practice incorporates a specific body of knowledge, which at law's core issue: *making law fit to multiple contexts of society*. The 'fit' is essential here, since the process of making fit is hitherto only understood as a matter of human acts so that lawyers are not prepared to even consider a 'fit' created by as computers and eventually other machines. That issue is important, because the question "What is law" does not primarily have as a focus point what lawyers *think*, but what they *do*! And what they *do* cannot be characterized by theoretical considerations, which are by definition external to a judge's legal activity. A judgment can in a jurist's mind only unfold from within their competence and thus remain an issue that is internal to law and legal discourse. In other words: what practitioners do, does not relate to abstract criteria maintained by others. The Romans already had an adage for that attitude, when they stated that *law is what jurists say that law is*. In other words: professionals tell non-professionals that they are not able to determine the qualities of law because they are positioned outside the profession and its discourse. We already noticed how legal practitioners tend to say that concept and interpretation of legal *'practice'* is theoretical in itself. The word 'theoretical' means precisely this 'outside the discourse'. What then is the task of semiotics, and how does the need for determining a referent for the diverse discourses play its role?

If law as a discourse is dominated by actions and thought patterns of its practitioners, how then should semiotics be understood? Does semiotics have to focus practices of law because these practices express all dimensions of doctrinal nature, which constitute the legal discourse in its entirety? Peirce might suggest a distinction between pragmatism in semiotics and a descriptive project grounded solely in practice, which sometimes passes for doctrinal analysis.[12] (1) A *first* possible understanding is in *opposing* semiotic analyses on the one hand and legal practice on the

[12] "It appears, then, that the rule for attaining (...) clearness of apprehension is as follows: Consider what effects, that might conceivably have practical bearings, we conceive the object of our conception to have. Then, our conception of these effects is the whole of our conception of the object." C.S. Peirce, "How to Make Our Ideas Clear", *Popular Science Monthly*, v. 12, pp. 286–302, 293; reprinted in *Collected Papers of Charles Sanders Peirce* (CP 5,388–410). This is semiotic pragmatism grounded in the context of meaning. Again Peirce: "The entire intellectual purport of any symbol consists in the total of all general modes of rational conduct which, conditionally upon all the possible different circumstances and desires, would ensue upon the acceptance of the symbol." C.S. Peirce, "Issues of Pragmaticism" in *The Monist* v. XV, n. 4, pp 481–499, see p. 481 (1905, CP 5, 438).

other, thereby couching that idea in the generally accepted form of a "theory-praxis contrast"—a typical European cultural context and Civil Law approach, which seems an unsolvable problem. (2) A *second* is to *mirror* semiotic and legal practices and treat legal semiotics in parallel to, for instance, literature or religion. Hermeneutics as well as narrative theories of law and a 'law and literature' movement justify that approach. (3) A *third* understanding would treat semiotics as a *non-legal* discipline, which has no influence on legal discourse and the practice of law. Those three approaches evolve parallel in that they do *not* solve the question how to mold the 'law and semiotics' relation, nor the question how humans create relations among them. The two forge together, although lawyers tend to deny this and keep the specificity of legal discourse in their own hands. An argument not to follow them is in the enormous importance of *the human face* as a component of law.

Faces in Legal Relations

How does a semiotics of human relations work out in face-to-face relations such as in legal consult, Court sessions or penal law decisions?[13] Language is again the encompassing context in which we orientate others and ourselves. Hence the core question: how do you define yourself and the subject we speak about in law and particularly in legal discourse? That definition is way beyond rationality or logic; it includes emotional and social issues and forms the basic context of all representation. Indeed: an "I" represents itself in a "You" through speech rather than by means of individual words. A context is thus engendered that ultimately uses the "us" as its final expression. On the basis of such an act of trust, questions about the dimensions of this trust come to the fore, such as: who are you, what do you mean, where and when do we begin, what do you mean, how would you define what you're talking about. All such questions are basic not only for understanding but rather for acquiring linguistic knowledge before any understanding can occur. Basics of relationships have to be settled *before* speech and discourse unfold. Most of the work to be done in order to guarantee that these basics are appropriately functioning, unfolds in speech without yet being spoken. Faces play a key role in this context.

This observation refers again to our earlier remark that language *precedes* analysis and consensus, two concepts of language and mind that are continuously in danger of denying the constitutive power of the social. Language proficiency is a prime condition for action—hence the importance of the major brain processes pertaining to language, which are becoming profiled in modern research. Language capacity is not solely a means or just an instrument for human communication, language is the *milieu* in which the capacity unfolds to speak and make oneself clear. Do not forget, that a language has to function in order to make the unfolding of a new human life possible: a consideration, which is equally important on the neurological level

[13] See Broekman: "Faces Face to Face" in: Jan M. Broekman & Francis J. Mootz III: *The Semiotics of Law in Legal Education",* Springer 2011 p. 20 ff.

as at the social level of every newborn individual. A *social structure* is therefore much more than a sole conversion of speech acts. Speakers and hearers, senders and receivers depend on contents and structures of that *milieu*.

Names

Names and faces characterize the presence of an individual. Not we ourselves, but others have given us a name and taught us its language in accordance with the requirements of law and legal discourse. Names profiled us and set us free from an unidentified life under the condition that we embrace a legally valid identity. We are indeed seldom aware of law's presence in the same appearances when we see a face, look at a passport picture or hear a name. Names bridge the gap between nature and culture, but also, very powerfully, between the observable and the understandable. Names contribute to make the observable understandable and, in doing so, represent an order of the world. So do *legal cases*: they bear a name created by codes of court activities and law books and their names identify their place in the discursive order of jurisprudence—an order that sustains the meaning-making task of lawyers. And so does *language*: names are a medium to make meaning in social life, and in doing so they determine the essence of human relations. Its culmination is in the definition of "face" as suggested by Levinas: "the way in which the Other presents itself, transcending the image of the Other in myself, is called "face".[14] That definition is an important issue in legal semiotics. *Names show us where and why we live with our own images.* Names are the faces that populate our imagination as well as our daily encounters whilst representing images of our selves.

Levinas underlined how one cannot understand a person without speaking with him.[15] What occurs with language when it transcends the everyday meaning of the term 'understanding'? I cannot encounter a human being without articulating the modalities of this encounter itself, an act that decidedly differs from other forms of understanding and knowledge. Any judge or other representative of legal discourse tends to neglect this fact, and reduces such encounters to series of bits of knowledge. That is a semiotic loss: *judges look into empty faces and perceive senseless bodies because their professional discourse leads them to approach others without semiotically and linguistically connecting with him.* This does not become compensated when lawyers prepare their clients in practice for such disturbing experiences, or juries are criticized in that very same context. Both situations became subject of serious, mostly sociological, criticism. What is true for *names* is equally true for *faces*, occasional 'face to face' situations included.

Names are, moreover, important in the context of memory: complaints about a failing memory concentrate often on names: lost or forgotten names of places,

---

[14] E. Levinas: *Totalite et Infini. Essai sur L'extériorité*. Phaenomenologica Bd 8, M. Nijhoff, Den Haag 1961, p. 21.

[15] E. Levinas: *Difficile Liberté,* Ed. Michel, Paris 1963,– Id.—*Humanisme de l'Autre Homme,* Paris 1972.

persons, circumstances, dates and data show the dynamics of a consciousness. "I cannot remember this anymore" is an articulation tied with modern neurological brain theories. Memory is relevant for the brain mechanisms influencing consciousness, so that different memory theories have different explanatory effects on human behavior in its entirety.[16] But the main issue for memory is that names are embedded in language and the brain relates to linguistic components with their consciousness base. So the question arises: 'Linguistically connecting to others'—what does it mean?

Faces Function Linguistically

Faces fulfill a semiotic key role through their function in the social process of "linguistically connecting to others", shaping the essentials of inter-subjectivity. Signs are never alone; they are always entangled in patterns and networks of human relations. They are meaningful because they are *given* a meaning, like names! The latter is important in all regards, in particular where the process of language acquisition is at stake. The understandable becomes understood and interpreted when the constitutive forces of signs are set free in an acquired linguistic competence.

Faces are an artifice because of three philosophically important reasons. *First* is the *mental* component, which undoubtedly shapes and influences the effect of faces in life. *Second* is the fact that faces are not understandable and even not perceivable without an *abstract* dimension. This relates to the generalizing power of everyone who perceives a face, because the comprehension of a face needs forms of abstraction in order to try to understand the very essence of the facial features at hand. *Third* is the existential dimension, which is embedded in the fact that *faces always need to be interpreted.* The making of and encounter with a "blank face" does not form an exception in this regard.

If ever faces are meaningful, than the bearer of that face is not the only one that creates meaning! The meaning of a face is also a result of an interpretation of the Other who participates in that encounter. There exists no natural and solipsistic expressive autonomy. Faces relate to the bearer as well the observer who is at the same time interpreter—both activities determine the sign quality of the face in a process of interactivity[17]

Each particularity of a face forms a series, or a set of series, that possess a more general character in social life. Pure presence (Peirce speaks of 'presentness') is left behind in that process of articulation, and the idea relates to more abstract categories that one finds concretely in individual images and symbols. The power of articulation is one of the most fascinating properties of a human face. Changing faces are thus differing articulations—and that is what makes them human and society social!

---

[16] Gerald M. Edelman & G. Tononi: *A Universe of Consciousness. How Matter becomes Imagination.* Basic Books 2000, p. 93.

[17] For details on the specifics of "interactivity" see Jan M. Broekman: *Binding Words, Unfolding Selves,* New York 2008, p. 25 ff.

Signs of law are everywhere. Pierce noticed how literally everything could become a sign for us. As a consequence, signs unfold amidst *all there is*—not pertaining to the way *it is* but rather as a *potential* for *whatever there is*. That observation manifests the power of change. The dynamics from potentiality to reality of becoming a sign is in essence the basis for what he called *Firstness*. It also includes, that *signs can only become signs in an already signified world*. The major signifier is language. A world without language would not be able to develop signs and be significant. All problems with identity formation show that if anything is not fit for becoming a sign, it is not fit for human society and the lives lived in it. This requirement of 'fit' has its importance for Roberta Kevelson's attempt to understand—in the context of what she calls 'historic semiotics'—how changes in the system of transitivity and intransitivity in the English language show that language changes because people do. Here is an important and encompassing aspect of Peirce's philosophical view on life, which is the crux of his philosophy: there is no life that is not embedded in what we notice as being potentially significant. That potentiality unfolds first and foremost by understanding how we are *a being as a possible sign* so that we, humans, understand ourselves as living in a field of transformational energy. One cannot underline strongly enough in what regard the dynamics of this energy form the basis for Peirce's philosophy, a philosophy that always includes semiotics as its essential approach.

If we understand that signs of law are everywhere in social life, we must accept how those signs are not there by nature, but are created by lawyers driven by this encompassing energy of transformation. If law is a system of signs, then that system is the dynamic context for any creation of legal meaning. There 'are' no signs and there 'is' no meaning beyond this ever-emerging primal energy of transformation, Peirce would conclude. It would be great to investigate the concept of 'system' in his texts, not because of an interest in any form of systems-theory, but rather to find every possible aspect of this dynamism at the basis of semiotics concealed in his idea of a system. Do not forget how semiotics as a science is in Peirce's view a method to approach the flow of dynamics in life, which continuously regenerates the most essential signifying processes.

The idea of man as *'animal symbolicum'* (Aristotle) remains the foundation for our life in law. Law is a *symbolic* discourse and legal effects are channeled through processes of appropriate semantic transposition. This is how law is language: its symbolic dimensions do not disappear, but remain in action whilst even the subtlest layers of meaning are articulated. Lawyers confirm that this conversion is essentially a legal technique. No matter whether lawyers are right about their option, semiotics demonstrates the importance of that social process before a jurist's eyes. Do lawyers perform their task whilst denying its foundation in symbolic dimensions when they are face-to-face with a human individual that they determine as a legal subject or a bearer of rights and duties? When they are not aware of law's semiotics and thus exercise only specific and strictly defined forms of interaction, a face-to-face situation is senseless and does not have the quality of a truly *human* relationship.

Faces of Justice

A semiotic study of justice is most prominent on the list of all who are interested in a wider unfolding and a broadening specter of legal semiotics. *Mimesis* is beyond doubt one of its central motives, not only because equilibrium might be a concealed drive for every qualification of justice,[18] but also because the semiotic importance of mirror-scenes fascinates in all fragments of daily as well as social life. And finally, mimetic forces are in effect when justice is concerned. In all those cases, a plain understanding of *mimesis* as 'mirroring', 'repeating' or 'reproducing' will suffice for a fresh look at the issue. It is equally present in view of more complicated structures that are inherent to the concept, for instance in the case of constituting an *identity* as for instance Freud stated and also Lacan suggested. Insights of those two show that the human face is involved in a semiotic approach to justice.

It is interesting to consider how Perelman sums up examples of analyzing justice and of the concept of justice in the proximity of his theories of legal argumentation.[19] His first example bears the weight of *mimesis* meaning "to each the same thing", which goes to argumentation schemes which take the diversification between Courts of Law and Courts of Equity in English Law into account. In US practice, the distinction between law and equity is the set of remedies each offers. The most common civil remedy a court of law can award is monetary damages. Equity, however, enters injunctions or decrees directing someone either to act or to forbear from acting. *Barron's Law Dictionary*[20] mentions how equity develops as a separate body of law in England because of the inability of the common law courts to entertain or provide remedy for every injury. Perelman quotes the ironic remark, which can be heard in the street, that finally death is the most radical example of the most radical justice. This idea does, however, neither solve nor disclose the secret of *mimesis*. What does sameness mean in this context, what game of identity is at stake here, what forces condition justice as a total equilibrium, one could ask. We touch here apparently one of the most basic and at the same time most hidden thoughts that govern law and legal thinking.

One has to consider in this context the character of a pronouncement, not unlike as it fulfils a role in religious discourse. Every pronouncement cumulates the self-determination of an identity. The basic pronouncement in religious discourse as well as in the unfolding of any personality in education, the "I" in a secular form of the "I am who I am" exemplifies this supreme mimetic character. Modern philosophy and recent political self-understanding underline the many dimensions in this pronouncement. In a semiotic context, one should underline how the "I am" is in essence static, conservative and parochial, in particular because the stasis of the pronouncement does not allow for any involvement of the o/Other or liability for the inherent

[18] Jan M. Broekman: "Justice as Equilibrium" in: *Law and Philosophy,* 1984 Vol. 5, pp. 369–391.

[19] Ch. Perelman: *De la Justice*, Brussels 1945, (Eng. Transl. 1963), reprinted in his *Ethique et Droit,* Brussels 1990, p. 19 f.

[20] Steven H. Gifis: *Law Dictionary*, Barron's Educational Series, 1991, p. 162.

quality of an "I am". That is a challenge to the inherently mimetic dimension of the statement. The truth in the expression is that a relationship between the "I" and the "I" is concealed. No doctrine can unfold or open up to this concealment, other than an "I" that is able and willing to be a "Self". Let us not forget that the diversification in the mention of the two "I"'s remains a spoken word, a token of ability to articulate, a power of performance as well as a mastership of the relation between the multiple "I"'s and the Self. The pronouncement unveils precisely its meaning as speech act. In the step from mimesis to rapture becomes clear how a more radical split of the ego than in Kant's "Ichspaltung" is present: the Kantian "higher and judgmental Reason" does not only judge, and through judging creates justice and peace, but also seems to show the burden of liability. The "I am" is not only a matter of what I am, or of the "I am" as an indication of an anthropological and psychological structure, but also a matter of *how* I am what I am—all legal consequences included.[21]

Zoon logon: the Aristotelian expression implies representation in the Unity of the One and the dispersion of the Multitudinous. The intentional dimension of *mimesis* expresses itself in the speech act as *Name*, which is the Identity itself, and which is an Identity in itself. That dimension regards the attempt to determine the discourses within which mimetic forces can occur. Aristotle does not characterize all the arts as mimetic, precisely because of this extensional dimension. Logos, harmony and rhythm are the means to achieve artistic *mimesis*, and this is fundamentally a musical consideration, i.e. only a representational understanding of *mimesis*. But *mimesis* also regards representation in view of modern epistemology, which plays a major role in art, society and cultural anthropology. No form of representation is ever without the connotation of a certain self-representation. Representation is not a description, nor a representation of a human relation with reality: representation *is* this relationship itself![22]

Any study of the dynamics of *mimesis*, which are so close to the problem of identity, leads to the poetic methodology of German Romantic theory of Art.[23] The mimetic relationship of two centers of identity is according to Fr. Schlegel the generative matrix for all great works of art. Here is a constitutive duplicity which functions mimetically with regard to pure reflection, which in itself is a constant play of two poles that are separated and One at the same time. Great literary works have therefore a meta-function: they are, as a *work* of art, also a *theory* of art—like precedent cases in law are/represent a legal judgment on the one hand and an element of legal doctrine on the other. Both types of work *reflect*, and in doing so, they produce the essence and appearance of what they are, namely a work of art, of law. This identity is never static; it is dynamic, generative, and emergent. So there is a double task at hand: in their representation of reality (multi-layered) they bring about the order of law, in particular of justice, being a standard in legal discourse. This dynamic play of

---

[21] See also Chap. 9 of this book.

[22] Jan M. Broekman: "Holism, Law, and the Principle of Expressibility" in: *Rechtstheorie,* Vol. 28, No. 4, 1990, p. 424 f.

[23] W. Menninghaus: *Unendliche Verdoppelung. Die frühromantische Grundlegung der Kunsttheorie im Begriff absoluter Selbstreflexion*, Frankfurt/M., 1987.

multiple dualities is concealed in *the idea of a legal fiction*. Fiction is an interactive process between the two identities for which we use the words 'fiction' and 'reality'. There exists a continuous pulsation between the two. Merrell analyses how[24]

> ... this pulsating back and forth occurs so quickly that like the discontinuous frames of the film which pass through the projector at such a rapid rate that they appear to be a continuum, we are not aware *that* our conceptual/perceptual-imaginary focus constantly undergoes alteration. Consequently, what is tacitly experienced as a continuum is in reality a discontinuity between complementary frames. Hence simultaneity of frames is only apparent. (...) All fictions, then, entail the (ordinarily tacit) establishment of a continuum between two wholes, which would otherwise be at least partly incompatible.

Identity is concealed, and its unfolding is presented in the pronouncement, the sublime speech act itself: a Name, a Word, a Verb or a Substantive—all functioning as the *speech act with a Face*. A specific lack of possible differentiation disperses as soon as the face belonging to the speech performance becomes visible. A trace of enunciations is created in that dispersion—a process in clear contrast to the dual character of a rule. In the case of a rule is a ruler, a rule-giver or a process of rule-formulation, which is not focusing on other faces, as they have no face themselves. As a consequence, the spur of rule-pronouncements has no place for a word of justice because it presupposes solely rule-followers. The function of a human face is not unlike a pronouncement in the performance of justice. The identity of the pronouncement is mirrored in the dynamics of distribution and redistribution of reward and punishment as well as in the sympathy with the good and the antipathy with the bad. That identity is appreciated as author who distributes and directs sympathy, and rather not as an authority. No wonder that 'justice' has long been interpreted as a concealed power of law. Justice remains, however, an element of further semiotic consideration, because it discloses some of the most important secrets of identity, which set mimetic forces free. In that regard, an old question comes again to the fore: how is identity compatible with rules, since identity relies upon unity, and rules upon dispersion. Can law unite the One and the Dispersed?

Application, Analysis/Assemblage, Engineering

We keep those approaches and attitudes in mind when focusing three dimensions in the 'law & semiotics' complexity: (1) the concept of *'application'*, (2) the concept of *'analysis,'* with Deleuze & Guattari's expression '*assemblage*' as a borderline concept that leads to (3) the concept of *'engineering'* meaning—three essential concepts for the semiotics of jurisprudence.

(1) The lawyer's concept of *application* represents, as a social form, a *limited* reach of knowledge and interest. It also expresses an application of the pragmatism that is at the heart of the Anglo-American legal reflex. Semiotics is in that case the application

[24] Floyd Merrell: *Pararealities. The Nature of our Fictions and how we know them.* Philadelphia 1983, p. 24, 60.

of signs and symbols, and law the application of rules, norms and laws. The thought model named 'application' is generally operating *atomistic* patterns. That is clearly visible where legal practices perceive language as a composite of linguistic elements and where semiotics perceives meaning as a composite of individual signs or related semantic units. This view brings a positivist, a naturalist and a realist interpretation of reality together. Semiotics applied to law is *positivist* in so far as the semiotic object is taken as a fixed datum, a definable and empirical object. The same applications are *naturalist* in so far the existence of universal systems of meaning need to be embraced for that particular application, and *realist* because a semiotic analysis reads the message that is codified in the object. The inherent epistemology of semiotics thus combines three major philosophical approaches, whereby the positivistic perspective is the most proximate to law.

But that is not enough. Any application procedure itself is based on atomistic presumptions: meanings are composed of single elements such as signs and symbols, which are there before they enter specific discourses such as the law. Understanding the law-semiotics relation requires an epistemology beyond those atomistic presumptions—ask Mr Jourdain: he profited from the philosopher's suggestion that he spoke prose, and with that knowledge could write his letter as eloquently as he desired. But he also failed to consider the limits on expression that the philosopher suggested as an expression of the limits applicable to the reality that was Mr. Jourdain. The same is true for lawyers: providing them the awareness that they operate in a semiotic manner without consciously knowing that is the issue. This awareness makes them understand that the law-semiotics relation is not a matter of application but of intensifying and heightening a particular quality of oneself. If one does not accept this thesis, one concludes mistakenly that law and semiotics are two congruent discourses. This relates to a widespread idea about the law and semiotics relation, which suggests that the semiotic view applied to law leads to a more appropriate and reliable *analysis* of law. Before such an analysis can take place, a particular awareness must be developed. This is the background of many legal semiotic studies and of a host of publications. In that very perspective citizens would be more clearly informed about their place and function in the legal system and about the possibilities to develop an emancipated life. To study the signs and symbols, as well as their operative forces in legal discourse, makes clearer than the doctrinal explanations of lawyers how and what legal discourse does and wants to achieve in law's institutions and in society.

This semiotic attitude neglects the fine line between law and non-law and risks to be judged irrelevant by law practitioners. One can read in Kevelson's publications how she attempts to avoid that risk through paying attention to the dialectics between two types of legal system: on the one hand as a *complete*- and on the other as a *fragmented* discourse that fulfills a constitutive role in understanding law in terms of lawyers. She underlines how

> ... a semiotics perspective on law ... is not to be confused with some recent structuralist approaches to law, which sometimes are confused with what is called here legal semiotics. Although, from a historical point of view, the emergence of structuralism and semiotics in this country coincided in the early 1960s totally different philosophical assumptions underlie

> each of these approaches despite certain surface similarities. Furthermore, although there are important correlations between a semiotic approach to legal interpretation and the popular Continental movement in hermeneutics, the relationship between the latter and a Peirce-grounded semiotics and its methods of interpretation and inquiry is not so much superficial as reflective of a divergence between the objectives of these two distinct modes of sign interpretation. (Roberta Kevelson: *Law as a System of Signs,* Op. Cit., p. 274.)

Her historical balance touches many issues as exposed in the above lines. Yet, all would become appreciated differently in the light of contemporary technical developments and knowledge in the light of today's new economic and political keys. One of the issues of importance among them is the strong tendency of *approximation* and *convergence* between Civil Law and Common Law, especially in Civil Law's construction of EU Law. This issue in recent legal history emerged together with the expanding dimensions of *global* law. Common Law and semiotics are indeed closely related through the dynamics of (legal) pragmatism. That pragmatism unfolds many new forms: legal systems, their harmonization and incorporation in other orders as well as their globalization are today importantly coordinated with domestic legal orders, which become silently less important because of their socio-political incorporation. Non-state actors and principles focus on *contract as a new and democratic form of command* as a legitimate successor of traditional law and state activity.

Even where Kevelson establishes considerations about the essence of a sign, or a semiotic interpretation of complex legal meaning in legal reasoning, the idea of pragmatics in the form of analysis prevails, though perhaps it prevails as itself a sign of systemic constraints. But there is a distinction that can be made between pragmatism—as a direction and structural symbolic element of semiotic analysis, and practicability or praxis, which suggests application. Analyses through semiotic understanding of the flow of meanings in law binds legal theory and legal practice, because on that level of understanding

> the lawyer, no less than the legal philosopher, would be engaged in the same acts of law—where act is both on the level of ideas and their development in thought and in the courts with respect to practical legal procedure ... (Kevelson, Op. Cit., p. 276)

But semiotic analysis on its own does not bridge the gap between legal theory and praxis? A widened awareness of lawyering is necessary. Practicability remains the often theoretically misunderstood or underestimated force of law. Praxis is managed and translated in terms of theory, but remains in essence practice in the heart of social relationships, which are denominated by 'law'! Hence Kevelson:

> ... a semiotics of law should be able to show how constituents in any given system ideally called the law are really a network of competing legal systems which, as Friedman has shown, are social subsystems in semiotic interaction.
> Furthermore, a semiotics of law should also be capable of accounting for intersystemic communication between system the origins of which are culturally, historically, and ideologically different from the various branches and outgrows of common law... (Kevelson, Op. Cit., p. 277)

Do semiotic analyses lead to a "one law, one world" view, the law being folded in a 'globally mixed legal system'? Linguistic approaches, often roots for semiotic analyses of legal discourse, do indeed need emphasis on a general denomination, on principles, on common coherence or on disambiguated terminologies. This relates to the fact that, as was said, the concept of 'law' itself changed meaning in a global perspective. There are no uniform legal systems anymore, sustained by uniform concepts and/or practices of a State, and 'mixed' legal systems do indeed prevail, mixing for instance Civil- and Common Law features. It is apparently not sufficient when semiotics informs us about how legal acts and judgments are made and managed. One always needs to develop an insight in related politics as well as sciences to understand the actual intertwining of discourses. A relevant speech act within a semiotic analysis of legal discourse would be like: "this is what we used to do now formulated in other words, via other thought patterns and formulated in other discourses". When observing such developments, one asks whether legal semiotics as a fresh and new analysis of law can ever lead to opening the closeness of law's discourse so that it allows another look than at its surface.

(2) "*Assemblage*" is Deleuze and Guattari's surprising term[25]—surprising because one would not expect such a challenging translation in the context of lawyers' activities. What does their expression mean in the context of the law-semiotics relationship and what does it express about law and its discourse? Is it possible to gain any further insight into the specificity of law through semiotics? Emphasis is here on semiotic aspects of the problem. A first remark aims at the fact that a variety of viewpoints exists to make us understand law. Extremes of that range are (a) a complete autonomous and self-referential determination what law is and how law should be practiced, and (b) the understanding of law as one of the many discourses of- and about society, with power and importance that varies from one socio-political structure to another. The concept of 'assemblage' in view of lawyers' practices approximates the latter. Deleuze indicates that contemporary law should be perceived as "oedipal law", which seems inappropriate for our post-modern age.[26] Law does for that reason not provide us lawyers who are producers of *new* forms of life—they do not exhibit any desire to initiate or further new ways of life and do not educate us in new dimensions of a non-oedipal socio-political situations. In order to do so, law should not remain focused on restriction but rather on expansion of our life-forms. Unger criticizes in this context what he calls "the cult of state law" which forms the background for the (often concealed) desire of many citizens and lawyers to remain nursed in oedipal types of law.

> In its place we should put a vision of the great constructive forces *legal analysis as institutional imagination* should serve. One such force is practical experimentalism embraced to heighten our powers: of insight The association of the quest for latent moral order with the cult of the state and its law had its progressive aspect in its corroding effect upon the belief in a natural, prepolitical system of social life. As the great lever of transformation, the state links social change with social will. The price of this appeal to the state, however, is high. It has been steadily increasing: We recognize only part of the cost of pietism about power. (...)

---

[25] Assemblages or agencement is "simultaneously a machinic assemblage and an assemblage of enunciation" Gilles Deleuze and Félix Guattari. *A Thousand Plateaus*, (Brian Massumi, trans. London and New York: Continuum, 2004 (original 1980), p. 504).

[26] Gilles Deleuze, and Félix Guattari. 1972. *Anti-Œdipus*. (Robert Hurley, Mark Seem and Helen R. Lane, trans. London and New York: Continuum, 2004 (1972)

> To avoid paying this price, it is not enough to cool the fervor of our statolatry by dissolving the bond between the cult of the state and its law and the search for latent moral order. We must go further and rid ourselves of the residue of the idea of latent order itself into our circumstances, and of emancipation from drudgery, infirmity, and insecurity. At the heart of practical progress lies the relation between cooperation and innovation. (. . .) The other great constructive force is the demand for personal freedom and self-assertion. (. . .) Moreover, we must live in a way recognizing the truth that there is more in us, individually as persons or collectively as mankind, than there is in the institutional and discursive worlds we make and inhabit. (Roberto M. Unger: *What Would Legal Analysis Become?* Verso London 1996, p. 182. See also Chaps. 8 and 9 of this book.)

The catchword for this appeal is in Deleuze's quest for perceiving law as *emergent*, and to embrace *semiotics* to teach us the dimensions of that emergence. This attitude is very different from conceiving semiotics as an exquisite instrument for a more perfect analysis of law! Once we accept for instance the Civil Law metaphor to perceive law as a body that expresses law's coherence, consistency and continuity, then we are also able to understand how *emergent law is constituted by information.* That is a type of information, which transcends fixed linguistic categories, a transcendence, which also influences the qualities of semiotics.

'Law is emergent' means primarily that law is constituted by information, not from a non-law region outside any standardized legal discourse, but from a within that remains exterior to doctrinal rule following. This contradicts any organic philosophical approach towards law: thinking along the lines of organism in the case of law requires painstakingly precisely drawn lines between law and non-law. Legal practitioners consider their legal activity in that context as 'art' more than as 'science' because they are trained to walk such thin lines and manipulate them accordingly! But the power of today's information—example 'social networks' and their various forms/techniques of e-communication—might strongly influence our imagination of what law is. What law is in a future society (combining the virtual and the real reality) puts each attempt to delineate between law and non-law in perspective. It thus justifies the idea that understanding semiotics in relation with law depends heavily on our understanding of law as a discourse in a constantly evolving society!

A position called *emergent law* should be the type of law in use by the average lawyer. Only a radical reformulation of what law is supposed to be can clarify this formula: *law is emergent law because law is there*! Emergent law exists without detectable origin, without unambiguous source, without a first law-word ever written or spoken by an omnipotent authority (the 'command'-idea), without a first law or legal experience instigated as its solid foundation.

(3) "Engineering" implies that lawyers accept the idea that they *manage meanings*. Their management is a form of engineering society through meanings. That is a truly semiotic issue! A question comes up as soon as one is aware how lawyers master two languages: the *language of everyday* delivers them meanings of life in a directness that does not exist in law, and the *language of law* delivers them meanings to operate in a jargon that does not exist in daily life. The two, of course, intertwine but the legal- and state institutions wish to have the citizen's interests be translated in legal language so that the latter type of language dominates their lives. An irony is how

lawyers and institutions force us to "forget" the scope and dominating force of those translation efforts, which are vital for state and citizen alike.[27]

Multiple dimensions of 'engineering' are at stake. They form a counterbalance against concepts as "application" or even "analysis" in the law-semiotics relationship. One should bear in mind, how *legal hermeneutics* is indeed accepted by a well-considered focus on the two, but is missing a semiotic context. Twentieth century hermeneutics in philosophy (Gadamer) and in legal theory (Esser) did *not* pay attention to legal semiotics. No wonder, that "application" and "analysis" were taken by lawyers as the pillars of their activity whilst operating with meanings, which they called their legal "practice".

To mention the concept of *engineering* in the context of law and the legal sciences is not aberrant. "The Acropolis and the Parthenon in Greece, the Roman aqueducts, the Hanging Gardens of Babylon, the Pharos of Alexandria, the pyramids in Egypt, Teotihuacán and the cities and pyramids of the Mayan, Inca and Aztec Empires, the Great Wall of China, among many others, stand as a testament to the ingenuity and skill of ancient engineers", the Wikipedia suggests. And, one can add, so does the Justinian Code, an essentially Roman Code conceived in a Greek-speaking country, the Bologna studies of that very same Code, the Napoleonic Code—not to mention the Treaties of the European Union. Those are mega-constructions of legal texts aiming at an ever effective and just order of a globalizing society. But micro-constructions for daily life situations bear the same characteristics, produced in equally conceived discourses. However, to understand the engineering aspects of legal discourse, one needs to overcome the limits of application or analysis, and value the semiotic dimensions of law as an engineered discourse.

Of particular interest is the concept of *re-engineering*. Originally used for business processes, the concept enjoys nowadays a wider interest. Two elaborations of re-engineering law and legal discourse are in the linguistic formulation of the 're-': re-engineering emphasizes the *re* used in *re*peated, but also as the *re* of *re*constructed. It is clear that both differ fundamentally, and also have a different epistemological status. The most surprising and renewing use is in the concept of re-engineering as a dynamic reconstruction. A major problem is, that re-engineering legal discourse means in the first place tackling the structures of law's institutional hierarchy. Why are we trained to refer to *higher* cases, *higher* courts, or *higher* judges? 'What is up, must go down' could be a slogan for re-engineering, who rather would inverse hierarchical levels. Re-engineering might become a far more important mode of operation to acquire knowledge of all sorts of processes, among them the question of our references to *higher* levels of authority. One could ask: 'do higher levels of authority, expressed in cases or court decisions, fit the concept of emergent law'? They do not, is the answer—and that challenges the semiotics-law relationships. If one accepts that lawyers manage meanings through semiotic operations, then the

[27] It reminds us of the constant tension, as well, between state and law, jurisdictio and gobernaculum. See Larry Catá Backer, Symposium: Law and the State in the Transnational Legal Order: "Reifying Law: Understanding Law Beyond the State," 26(3) *Penn State International Law Review* 521 (2008).

meanings themselves are to be understood as signs, symbols and other semiotic entities.

De Saussure and other linguists have taught us how the meaning of a sign does not exclusively determine semiotic operations: all linguistic studies confirm this insight. To shuffle signs and symbols has not a meaning in and of itself, we learn. One should discuss this with lawyers or judges high and low in legal hierarchy. Law and semiotics is not a theme that focuses exclusively on broadening a lawyer's awareness. Meaning and understanding in terms of legal discourse is an *emergent* property of its complex patterns of activity. Emergent patterns have the same role in non-biological systems as they do in biological systems. Re-engineering is a major epistemological operation. Legal semiotics would challenge legal theoreticians to accept re-engineering in order to acquire knowledge about law as a set of emergent patterns.

Two conclusions are important for the law-semiotics relationship in the context of the emergence of human relations:

a. The opinion that an understanding of law is the privilege of legal practitioners only, fits the idea that legal knowledge is the outcome of *application*. The power of that thought pattern is dominant. Semioticians who share that opinion limit the contribution of semiotics in legal discourse, and become blind for the creation of meanings in law and legal practice.
b. An insight is required into the fact that semiotics combines identity and togetherness even beyond knowledge of language, words or linguistic components. We know each other *before* words or linguistic performances become functional. Verbal expressiveness serves solely as a means to secure the emergence of social patterns.

All in all, one has to underline that the question how law shapes forms of public life seems strongly related to the specificities of the main features of legal practice. The semiotics of human relations depends greatly on the specifics of lived legal practices—lived by lawyers as well as by citizens.

The Critical Approach

Apart from structuralism, deconstruction theories, literary criticism and other denominations of a philosophy in a critical mood during the second half of the twentieth century the *Critical Legal Studies* movement could in hindsight be regarded as a precursor of all critical and ideological components, which come up when studying and/or practicing legal semiotics. Semiotics awakened a renewed interest for *critical* dimensions in legal scholarship, but bend to the particular ideological and political objectives of the CLS movement itself before it fractured into a number of sub-movements in the 1990s.

In 1983, Harvard Law Professor Roberto M. Unger wrote a concise overview of the CLS movement in a booklet with the same title. He claims: "themes of leftist legal thought and practice have now been reformulated while being drawn into a larger body of ideas. The results offer new insight into the struggle over power and right, within and beyond law..."[28]. The CLS movement has not produced a single, monolithic body of knowledge and texts, and the same can be said for the Legal Semiotics. The movement was also short lived. It's most influential successors include critical race theory, queercrit theory, critical feminist theory, latino critical studies (LatCrit) and class crits. None of these, however, carried forward the exuberance and universal aspirations of the first flowering of critical legal studies.

Outlines of critical studies with particular semiotic relevance lead us to the phenomenon of law's social power and the position of the subject in that field of power. But first, we should consider the major themes of Critical Legal Thinking as they manifested themselves at the end of the twentieth century and still function in law and legal scholarship—perhaps not on the surface of their texts but in any case in their politically relevant engenderment.

The CLS themes

CLS themes include the presumption that law is not completely autonomous and self-referential, that law is politics, that law serves power (however defined), that law embodies contradiction, and that the goal of perfection is illusory. We highlight:

a. The claim that, contrary to the common perception, legal materials (such as statutes and case law) and their inherent reasoning do not *completely* determine the outcome of legal disputes. In other words, law may impose many significant constraints on adjudicators in the form of substantive rules, but, in the end, this may often not be enough for a particular decision in a given case. This claim has, quite predictably, triggered many debates among jurists and legal philosophers, some of which continue to this day.
b. The claim that, at the end of the day, "all law is politics." Many modern-day commentators have suggested that in the eyes of the CLS scholars all "legal decisions" are just like "political decisions" in the sense that it is impossible to separate judicial from legislative acts. This is plausible if one considers both law and politics as acts based on generally adopted and fixated norms. Also legal pluralism claims that the concept of lawmaking does not have to be limited to states or legislatures. The "law is politics"-thesis is really about the character of the arguments used in the legal and political decision-making processes, not the nature of the practical activities (much less the institutions) involved. These arguments sometimes also tended at times to mirror Marxist-Leninist approaches to the law-politics-economic troika, which tended to privilege the political agenda of CLS over its philosophical and jurisprudential mission. Denied is here the notion that in the modern Western society discourses of law can be meaningfully separated from discourses of politics: every type of argument normally made

[28] R.M. Unger: *The Critical Legal Studies Movement,* Harvard UP 1983.

in the course of a legislative-deliberative process, they claimed, could be, and in practice usually is, also made in court. This includes arguments about social welfare, rights, morality, distributive justice, economic efficiency, as well as institutional arguments.

c. The claim that far more often than is usually expected the law tends to serve the interests of the wealthy and the powerful by protecting them against the demands of the poor and the subaltern (women, ethnic minorities, the working class, indigenous peoples, the disabled, homosexuals etc.) for greater justice. That claim is most of the times sustained by globalizing economic constraints, and the latter function more and more as a legal motivation in favor of judgmental arguments. This claim is often coupled with the legal realist argument that what the law says it does and what it actually tends to do are two different things—an observation that is particularly relevant if one considers the growing distance between meanings of legal- and of everyday language. That issue is a semiotic component of legal discourse in its own right. Many laws claim to have the aim of protecting the interests of the poor and the subaltern. In reality, they serve the interests of the power elites. This, however, does not have to be the case necessarily, as it does not belong to the "nature" of law and legal discourse, claim the CLS scholars. There is nothing intrinsic to the idea of law that should make it into a vehicle of social injustice. It is just that the scale of the reform that needs to be undertaken to realize this objective, is significantly greater than the mainstream legal discourse is ready to acknowledge.
d. The claim that legal materials are inherently contradictory, i.e. the structure of the positive legal order is based on a series of binary oppositions such as, for instance, the opposition between individualism and altruism or formal preference for strict rules and equitable flexibility, articulated as a preference for broad standards. yet it fails to consider the mediating role of law or that the oppositions exist outside of law and are managed within them.
e. The claim that a belief in the one, coherent and only correct judicial deduction is in essence a *religious* belief: compare judicial reasoning with shamanic practices (a typical postmodern consideration). But it was also a belief that gave character of the culture of the judiciary—permitting constant reconsideration by multiple courts which served as a means of seeking perfection and as a cover for shifting results to suit the needs of the hierarchically arranged parties to the litigation, and adjusting the results to the political needs of the state. This claim was weakened, to some extent, by the willingness of American courts to fracture law to mirror the multi-systemic character of the U.S. legal system.[29]

These issues are most certainly not beyond the horizon of contemporary legal semiotics. They have influenced the reception and application of the Greimas squares and their critical power, also the analyses of Kevelson and those of discourse-oriented

[29] Larry Catá Backer, "The Mechanics of Perfection: Philosophy, Theology and the Foundations of American Law," in *On Philosophy In American Law* 44–52 (Francis J. Mootz, Jr., ed., Cambridge UP, 2009)

linguistic and semiotic researchers. The major point of critique is still the formalism and objectivism of legal thought formation and its practices. A fundamental question is, whether all types of social organization in modern Western life show an unchallengeable built-in legal structure, which is sustained by legal theory and the formation of legal doctrine. One should highlight that this consideration is in essence a semiotic issue: *is the meaning of our social organizations at least in conformity, if not identical, with law?* That focus is encountered in CLS as well as in modern legal semiotics. We remember for the understanding of this critical question three essays written by legal scholars in the heart of US legal scholarship: Jeremy Paul, Jack M. Balkin and Duncan Kennedy.

To take the language of law in one's own mouth is a dubious gesture, as history has demonstrated clearly, Unger suggest in his CLS text, Op. cit.:

> (...) by choosing to speak in the language of law, powerful people and interests can sometimes be called to account because they try to legitimate what they are doing in those terms. The people they take advantage of can argue that this is a misuse of law, an illegitimate attempt at mystifying rhetoric. They can appeal to the values that law seeks to protect to promote better, more just, and more humane practices and forms of human association. Important theoretical debates among critical scholars in the 1970s and 1980s period revolved around which conception of law was the best one. Some critical scholars adopted a largely pejorative conception, focusing primarily on law's defects. They argued that the rule of law was enmeshed in irreconcilable contradictions; they denounced rights talk as sterile, useless and counterproductive. Others, especially feminist and critical race theory scholars, pointed out that rights discourse and rule of law values were among the few resources that disempowered people had. Rule of law and rights talk were potentially emancipatory discourses. They held a limited but important potential for liberation and for contesting the arbitrary and unjust use of power.

This observation shows that there is no closure as far as the virtues of critical approaches to law and legal discourse are concerned. It has become clear, however, that legal semiotics has an important critical potential also at distance to the ideas and ideals of the CLS:

> (....) The ideals of human association embedded in the concept of the rule of law—like the ideals of liberty and equality—are well worth fighting for and realizing in our legal institutions, even (and especially) if we realize that all efforts to instantiate them in law are always subject to evasion, capture, and manipulation. In the world of the 1970s, critical theory noted how law failed when it was not supported by a robust politics; in doing so it deemphasized and marginalized the positive elements of law and legal culture that were always implicit in an ambivalent conception. But in a world of executive arrogance, authoritarian posturing, and blatant disregard for rule of law values, those elements must necessarily come to the fore in any critical account. Critical scholars have prided themselves on their deconstructive acumen—their ability to elucidate the hidden and marginalized values and assumptions that bodies of legal doctrine deemphasized but on which they secretly depended. We should apply those same deconstructive techniques to critical legal theory itself. The focus of a critical approach to law—and its ambivalent conception—will inevitably shift as we introduce it into new contexts of judgment. Deemphasized aspects will emerge. Sometimes a critical approach to law will focus on how rule of law norms, legal institutions, and legal culture serve important political values; but not because law is independent from politics, or because law does not apologize for and legitimate injustices. Rather, legal culture and institutions are valuable to critical theories of law because they are a way of doing politics, in the sense of shaping, restraining and challenging power.

Chapter 10
Legal Theory and Semiotics: The Legal Semiotics Critical Approach

The Critical Approach and Semiotic Perspectives

Critical legal theory is not solely a matter of ideology, it says, of questions pertaining to justice, of problems of motivation and legitimacy, but rather of law's power to shape forms of life in modern society. Law includes the self-understanding of its subjects as well as its citizens and social institutions. It is important to conclude that this point of departure is in essence semiotic, since critical questions pertain to the meanings law installs in our lives. In reference to Foucault, Balkin states:

> Law proliferates power by making itself true in the world. It generates new institutions, new conventions, and new social realities, and it generates new forms of professional knowledge about all of them. It shapes the imagination of those who live under it around the categories and institutions that it produces. Law does not simply distort the world—or even merely represent it correctly; rather it makes a world, one in which and through which we live, act, imagine, desire and believe.

Understand how critical legal theory can, by means of its own critique, perceive semiotics as a constituting force of everyday life. It means that we do no longer speak about the force of law in social life abstractly; we have through semiotics an instrument in our hands to experience how law creates life in society. It also means, that we are able by means of perceiving and understanding law,

> how that discourse offers an unjust and unwieldy system for apprehending, incarcerating, and destroying human beings. It may also offer important elements of procedural fairness, equality and human dignity. It does both of these things simultaneously, and it may be difficult to fully separate its harmful and beneficial aspects in practice. Justice and injustice, responsiveness to the world and mystification, are often inextricably bound together.[1]

[1] J.M. Balkin: "The Hohfeldian Approach To Law And Semiotics" In: *44 Miami L. Rev*. 1990, 5. pp. 1119 ff; J.M. Balkin: "The Promise of Legal Semiotics" In: 69 *Texas L. Rev* 1990/91. pp 1831 ff., Jack M. Balkin: *Critical Legal Theory Today* In: *Philosophy In American Law*, Francis J. Mootz III (ed.) Op. Cit.; Jeremy Paul: "The Politics of Legal Semiotics" In: *69 Tex. L. Rev* 1990–1991, pp. 1779 ff., Duncan Kennedy: "Semiotics of Critique" In: *22 Cardozo L. Rev*. 2000–2002, p. 1151 ff.

J. M. Broekman, L. Catà Backer, *Lawyers Making Meaning*,
DOI 10.1007/978-94-007-5458-4_10, © Springer Science+Business Media Dordrecht 2013

When considering this aspect of law's influence in society, we immediately focus new meanings that are engraved in an old question: "is law politics"? Balkin suggests in the tradition of the most far-sighted authors in the CLS context:

> When people speak of the relationship between law and "politics," they mean law's relationship to the many different forms of power—economic, social, cultural, political, military and technological—that law might constrain, enable, or propagate. They also mean the ideals, ideologies and arguments that people use to justify these forms of power. "Politics" refers to people's contrasting visions and to the values that they want to realize or recognize in public life. But it also refers to the power to realize or recognize those values and visions. So when we consider the relationship between "law and politics" we are also interested in the question of law and power—how people justify and legitimate power—directly or indirectly—through law. And we must also account for law's own methods of proliferating its own power, whether it be through legal concepts, legal institutions, legal culture, legal education, legal officers, or the legal profession. In any case, law is not simply politics; rather it is a surprisingly plastic medium of discourse about power and for the exercise of power.

The relation between law and politics, and certainly the question whether law *is* politics, is not definitively clarified with these reformulations about law as a social power. Law is in semiotic perspective *a discourse of power*, and that formula opens new dimensions. Once citizens become aware of the fact that they are speakers of a specific discourse, they are indeed empowered *to speak differently*—to each other as well as to their respective social institutions. This different type of speech could be seen as the result of *legal semiotics as criticism*. This is far more than a harmonious image of society speaking a newly transformed language. The relation between politics and semiotics of law transforms the meaning of *politics* in as far as that meaning is brought in a closest possible relation to the subject in law and society: "In any case, law is not simply politics; rather it is a surprisingly plastic medium of discourse about power and for the exercise of power", as Balkin formulated, and thus shows *discourse* as the main field of that socially constitutive subjectivity. CSL considerations contain an important view on new understandings of the concept of politics in semiotic context, which could even be extended after so many years CSL ideas entered legal scholarship.

We mention in that context two ground lines: *first*, there are the many embranchments of critical theories in today's law and legal scholarship, which focus on law's power in society and the position of the subject therein. These lead in a new and most interesting manner to understand what traditionally was called 'anarchism' as a social movement—a concept that also deals with law as power, and attempts to reformulate the concept of culture in the twenty-first century as a basis for law and society.

If the first strain could be described in the framework of CLS consequences, the *second* is by nature philosophical and focuses on new attempts to reformulate a core theory of knowledge. That leads on the one hand to reconsider the *concept of a subject* in philosophical traditions, and on the other to determinations of *human knowledge* resulting from new insights in astrophysics, quantum mechanics, nano-techniques and economic models. Yet this is a challenge that Critical theory in the American academy rarely took up in a conceptually coherent manner. Its foundations were strong nonetheless: "What CLS brings to our attention, however, is that 'correct' and 'right' are not the only terms of criticism we can apply to judicial decisions."[2]

Politics and the Semiotic Approach

The question whether law *is* politics was a core issue in Balkin's considerations, first and foremost brought to attention in the context of the CLS movement by Jeremy Paul's essay. He introduces the semiotic approach in a 1990 article, a year of great publication activity of Roberta Kevelson and entirely in the perspectives of the CLS movement:

> Although Kennedy's initial emphasis on argument pairs grew largely from systematic study of legal materials, both he and Balkin have recently noted important similarities between their analyses of legal argument and the strand of linguistic theory known as semiotics (...) Kennedy and Balkin refer us to semiotics because each scholar has emphasized the ways in which legal concepts draw meaning from their place within broader legal argument, just as semioticians have stressed the ways in which words take meaning from their place within a larger linguistic system. The semiotic flavor of Kennedy's work, then, constitutes my first method of distinguishing it from other attempts to systematize legal reasoning. Following Kennedy and Balkin, I have adopted the characterization "legal semiotics" as shorthand for this approach.[3]

The question about the intellectual and theoretical value of legal semiotics is interestingly enough coupled with questions after the CLS influence faded away. It does not seem that this coupling, as highlighted by Paul, has ever been subject of a specific study in the context of legal semiotics. Yet, the importance of the semiotic perspective remains intact:

> We have now reached the heart of the matter, for the juxtaposition of progressive politics and the more arcane topic of legal semiotics raises an obvious question. What intellectual connections, if any, are there between these two seemingly diverse phenomena? Why, in other words, have scholars prominently identified with a progressive political agenda devoted a great deal of time and energy to the systematic study of legal reasoning?
> (...) First, I will argue that despite the fancy label, legal semiotics holds significant potential for bringing together people of diverse training and background in ways that will foster a true sense of intellectual community. Second, and equally important, I will explain why legal semiotics can help challenge traditional notions of meritocracy, notions that in my judgment form the most sincere and powerful response to the brand of progressive politics I described.

One possibility to further any critical legal analysis is in the opinion, that there is little or no connection between progressive politics and legal semiotics. To use semiotics for a better understanding of one's law and legal system is a scientific and legal

---

[2] Paul J. Gudel, The Skepticism Of Critical Legal Studies And The Function Of Moral Discourse, Oct. 2010, p. 75; available http://works.bepress.com/paul_gudel/6.

[3] It surprises that Kevelson did not notice Paul's text, which was central in legal scholarship, and that Paul did not mention any of Kevelson's contributions to the same theme so shortly after she published her famous book "Law as a System of Signs" at the end of 1988. That omission in legal- and philosophical scholarship is still problematic.

theoretical goal in itself, which remains at distance from law as politics. Another is to accept how semiotics creates new perspectives on law, so that formalism and objectivism are understood as a manipulation of legal discourse—a discourse that is in itself indeterminate but is made determinate by means of political maneuvers. To enhance this critical question, Paul argues that

> any effort to divorce legal semiotics from the progressive goals of its proponents belies the kick semiotics gives to first-year law classes and depends on an unlikely coincidence drawing CLS members to semiotic study. At the same time, there is only marginal progressive bite in the idea that systematic study reveals legal argument to be indeterminate or artificial. The problem is not that the law is relatively determinate. Indeed, I wish to avoid any effort here to address the more general problem of legal indeterminacy. Rather, the central difficulty with attributing a progressive character to demonstrations of legal indeterminacy (or artificiality, for that matter) is the implicit reliance on the existence of alternate forms of moral discourse that are somehow more determinate or authentic. (Jeremy Paul : "The Politics Of Legal Semiotics" In: 69 Tex. L. Rev 1990–1991, pp. 1779 ff)

It fascinates how the form and substance of legal education enters the debate on the critical influence of semiotics in law. Legal education shapes law in society by means of extension and underlining the responsibility of students for maintaining their ideology, and is—according to Paul—not just a machinery to convey positions and techniques:

> . . . the importance of legal semiotics becomes apparent. The classroom challenge is to convey to the student some sense of connection between legal decision-making and political ideology that escapes the trap of trying to explain one in terms of the other. This is precisely the contribution to legal education of Kennedy's "Form and Substance in Private Law Adjudication" and ensuing efforts to blend its message with classroom technique.
> The crucial point is to show students that the play of arguments often invoked in legal controversy resembles in crucial ways the play of arguments invoked in political debate. Thus, a seemingly technical case about expanding the doctrine of mistake in contract formation mirrors and thus is partly about a contest of political visions. This is not because a liberal will always favor expanding the doctrine of mistake, or because class analysis indicates which outcome will favor the ruling class. No, the case is about political visions because the advocates invoke principles and counter-principles that transcend the context of the dispute and lie at the heart of a wide range of debate. It may be a coincidence that the attorney seeking a flexible doctrine seems to be invoking altruist themes.
> Or it may be that there is a deep-seated connection between altruism and flexible standards. The important point is that in some very important contexts there is such a connection. Students alerted to it may recover confidence that their legal education is relevant to the broader themes they entered school caring about.
> (. . .)perhaps legal semiotics' relentless emphasis on the structure of opposing arguments will lead students to question the naturalness of any legal outcome. For if traditional positions are justified largely in terms of legal arguments that are the subject of semiotic study, students will be well armed with contradictory arguments that may lead to unconventional results. Thus, legal semioticians may create arguments that the Constitution requires socialism or invent hypotheticals in which workers keep manufactured products and pay capitalists rent for providing materials and management. In this sense, legal semiotics in its very essence is oppositional to the status quo.

He thus adds:

> Thus, if conservatism is defined, albeit unfairly, as unreflective acceptance of things as they are, semiotics will be anti-conservative if only in its ability to create reflection. To deny

> this aspect of the legal semiotics project is to ignore the extent to which students may find their improved argumentative skills liberating and, in any event, will find the semiotics classroom exciting. Indeed, from the perspective of the teacher-student hierarchy, there is a distinctly progressive flavor to legal semiotics' contribution in empowering students to question authority.
> (. . .) legal semiotics teaches that the meaning (and thus the merit) of any legal argument cannot be determined without understanding the context in which the argument is made. Indeed, legal semiotics demonstrates the extent to which the identified alternatives are in fact often necessary to give content to our most familiar argumentative moves. Legal semiotics shows that the strength of an argument depends as much on the consciousness of the listener as it does on the skill of the advocate. Accordingly, the student who grasps the structure of arguments encapsulated in the Pierson v. Post grid will come to appreciate that choosing which arguments to advance in a given situation involves tactical judgments and questions regarding the values of the decision maker much more than a quest for a so-called "best" argument.

It is beyond doubt that legal education is schooling in rhetoric, in particular in the management of arguments within the strict confines of jurisprudential discourse. Semiotics inform about the why's and how's of that type of management. One of the core issues concerns a systematic but often also personal set of preferences to give rule A preference over rule B. A Greimasian square can make clear how this comes always down to a system of opposites, just as De Saussure mentioned for language opposites and meaning formation in linguistic communication.

Balkin revised in his "The Promise of Legal Semiotics" his considerations about the question whether this opposition driven attitude justifies the conclusion that 'law is politics'. He concludes in the spirit of Derrida's deconstructionism how such binary oppositions should be undermined because the suggestion to be mutually exclusive shows in fact their strong dependency on one another:

> The arguments rejected in the choice between A and B, become the arguments used to justify the choice of rule D over rule C. I have called this phenomenon the "crystalline structure" of legal discourse—the basic structure of moral and political choice is reprised at each level of discourse, so that large-scale structure resembles small-scale structure, as is the case with some types of crystals. In hindsight, it would probably have been better to call this phenomenon the "fractal structure" of legal thought, since fractals, which also display self-resemblance at micro and macro levels, are more basic and pervasive than crystalline formations.
> The crystalline structure of legal thought suggests that one can go through the various compartments of the law and discover many doctrinal choices that are in tension with each other, because the policy justifications that support them (over alternative doctrines) are themselves in tension.
> An earlier generation of Critical Legal Studies scholars might have described this as "contradiction," but I prefer the word "tension" because we deal here not with a contradiction in the logical sense, but rather with a conflict of values that does not appear, at least on its face, to be resolved by existing legal materials or the justifications offered for them. Now tension, either in moral or legal thought, is not in itself a bad thing. It reflects the fact that we live in a complicated world in which values are often in conflict.
> Nevertheless, the discovery of moral tensions within the law-justifications which point in opposite directions in different areas of the law-suggests that we should rethink our policy choices in those different areas, or that we must re-describe them under an alternative or more general theory in which they can be understood as consistent. Thus, Professor Paul rightly ascribes to me the position that legal semiotics is useful because it will allow us to clarify hidden tensions in the law and assist us in the continuing refinement of our moral and legal intuitions.

A more general conclusion about the political implications of a semiotic attitude is imminent as soon as one considers these viewpoints. Balkin offers a preliminary conclusion:

> The legal semiotician asks questions about the materials of doctrinal argument and factual characterization that the practicing lawyer is not likely to ask or even need to ask. These questions concern why the choices of argument and characterization occur in the way that they do with respect to different rights and different factual situations. The legal semiotician is interested in legal ideology, and she sees the way that people argue for moral and legal positions as central to this study. Rather than viewing ideology as a smokescreen for illicit motivation, the legal semiotician takes the language of the law very seriously indeed. For her, ideology is constituted in part by the very patterns of argument and factual characterization that persons within the legal culture adopt.

This goal may or may not have progressive political implications,[4] but this approach opens many perspectives. We read the text in a certain period of legal and cultural developments: the end of the CLS movement, which unfolded a new criticism and new goals in trying to understand law and legal practice. The 'promise' of his article is therefore pertaining to *semiotics as a follower from CLS,* including a specific re-orientation in the achievements of critical thinking about law[5].

We have to raise the question whether this position is still valid. Much of the argument is no more than transplanting fundamental questions about law and society into student perspectives, such as: determine the critical context beyond political criticism (difficult to perform!), emphasis on rights-dimensions (gay rights etc). This must be combined with the promise-dimension: to better understand legal meanings and to see how law is created: do law schools do that[6]?

There would be a broader perspective regarding the promise, if one asks: "Consider when studying law, HOW *law is and is made:* PERCEIVE *law as 'made'.*" That change in perception is critical.Peirce's way in which signs are studied (signs are not signs if they are not constantly understood as made in the broader context of signs, resp. a sign-culture) is an excellent example here – law cannot be thought if one does not think 'law as made'.

That consideration changes perspective and leads directly from 'promise' to 'responsibility': a move towards politics in a broader and wider sense than 'law as politics'. *That responsibility is not growing "by nature" but has to be taught.* The importance of this insight grows in the year of the worldwide acclaim for the "Occupy Wall Street" movement and the problematic relations between law and economy—at large distance to the former Chicago "law and economics movement" insights.

---

[4] J.M. Balkin: "The Promise Of Legal Semiotics" In: 69 *Texas L. Rev 1990/91*. p. 1831 ff.

[5] See: Anne Wagner & Jan M. Broekman (Eds.): *Prospects of Legal Semiotics,* Op. Cit., 2010, *Introduction,* p. V ff.

[6] See Broekman/Mootz: *The Semiotics of Law in Legal Education,* Op. Cit., 2011.

A Lawyer's Words and their Meaning

Are the words of lawyers, especially those used in the exposition of their arguments, meaningful beforehand, or are they making words having a particular meaning during the creation of their argumentative speech, their rhetoric? It is clear that this question is in close proximity to the critical question about law being politics, but not identical with it. So the critical potential of semiotics is not only a matter of experience and appropriate education, but also an issue of linguistic technique, in other words: of mastering the semiotic instrumentation as a matter of analysis and to better understand what a lawyer does and how she performs particular speech acts. Greimas' suggestion, that each word and bit of meaning has a counterpart, so that meaning is a matter of knowing the one's and the other's meaning is fruitful in this regard. It also confirms the insights of the French linguist F. de Saussure, who underlined that there is always a set of distinctions, which makes a structural analysis of language utterances possible. The relations between the elements of language are determinative for the meanings of the utterances. The latter form strings of words/elements in accordance with the grammar/syntax of that language. That also enriches the predominating attitude of Kennedy in his often-quoted 2000/2002 essay entitled "Semiotics of Critique", which focuses less on the preceding critiques of the CLS movement than on the more precisely semiotic approaches to law and legal discourse.

First we notice the *theoretical platform*, which is derived from structural linguistics:

> The particular utterance called a legal argument can be analyzed using the language within a language idea. There is a set of necessary elements—a rule, facts, and an application—at least one of which must be in question. When the rule is in question, we can identify the "argument bites," such as, for example, "no liability without fault" or "your rule would be too difficult to administer," that legal arguers select, arrange, modify, and supplement in order to produce an argument for the choice of a rule, an argument recognizably spoken in the legal langue just because it uses the bites that compose this part of it.

Then comes the *application* for legal semiotics:

> What makes all this the rationalist side of semiotics is that we are looking to establish the lexicon, or collection of signs, and the rules for their combination and transformation to produce a meaning, on the assumption that the "speaker" in the system in question has something in mind, and the "speech" straightforwardly does or does not "represent" what he has in mind. If the something is an inner state, it preexists its expression; if it is an image of the external world, the speech represents that image as well. If it is an "ought," why then it represents the "ought".[7]

It thus does not surprise that unexpected questions come up within the broader goal of an economic analysis, which uses insights of legal semiotics and structural linguistics. One of them might shock the reader and in particular the law student: "Can you ever say what you mean or mean what you say?" With that question, we are engaged not only in critique in a political or epistemological sense, but rather confronted with fundamentals of speech in law and life that were hitherto taken for granted. This is

[7] Duncan Kennedy: "Semiotics Of Critique" In: *22 Cardozo L. Rev*. 2000–2002, p. 1151 ff.

semiotics as critique at its highest level! One related idea is Kennedy's phrase that our sign production, which takes place in our speech activity, is a matter of human action in an equally human world.

There are various aspects to distinguish here: one aspect is John Searle's philosophy of language and in particular his *theory of speech acts*:

> (. . .) when we say things, we may be doing something other than expressing a true or false meaning. We often intend not to speak true or false, but to change things in the world. Some classic examples: words like "I promise" or "I thee wed" or "I resign," spoken in the context of ceremony, are neither true nor false (though they might be fraudulent or void) but rather intended to change the speaker's relationship to another.

A further aspect is the conclusion that no human being ever speaks or produces language utterances beyond a given *vocabulary or lexicon of signs*. It thus does not matter

> (. . .) whether we are talking about words, clothes, or architectural elements, or about a production in a language within a language, like legal argument-may do (and be intended to do) more than express a meaning. For example, utterance may function to persuade its audience that particular things do or do not exist, although the utterance is not in any way "about" the existence or nonexistence of the thing in question.

So Kennedy's conclusion is radical, but also *a directive for the emerging self-understanding of a law student*, highlighting that there is no *extra-textual domain* available for lawyers. That insight may be characterized as one of the strongest critical forces of legal semiotics. If there is an 'economy' in legal speech and legal argument, then that economy has to cope with the limits of expressibility:

> The rhetorical, pre-rational argument built into langue itself, the a-rational perlocutionary force of utterance, is a claim roughly analogous to the claim that we are all gendered beings. Implicit in the posture of representation is the claim that representation is possible, that is: the denial of the "inevitable" suppression or effacement in the representation of all the aspects that can't be grasped within the linguistic (langue/parole) "logic" of representation. The practical meaning of this insight is that living as the objects of utterance, and spending our lives sucking up utterance, closes us down to the inexpressible. The final irrationalist twist is that both love and justice, "if they exist," belong to the inexpressible.

Chapter 11
Politics, Semiotics and Law: Self and State

Self and State, State and Self

We encountered a US philosopher, a Swiss linguist and a French psychiatrist/psychoanalyst: Charles S. Peirce, Ferdinand de Saussure and Jacques Lacan. The first has opened a new understanding of the *sign* in philosophy and sciences. The second has importantly clarified how words and texts are never a clear and self-sufficient, completed entity but rather a *surface* that results from semiotic labor, and the third that the human *Self* is never a harmonious entity in itself, as given by nature, but the result of social forces—language and education in the first place. Those three are truly Godfathers of semiotics in the sense that they opened perspectives hitherto closed by ideologically fixated viewpoints about man and reality, nature and culture, the suppressing character of our reading and dualistic views on world and self. Peirce was, as Fisch tells us, lifelong impressed by the fact that Plato had written the main part of his philosophical oeuvre in the form of dialogues, and suggests in the Theaetetus:

Socrates	I mean the conversation, which the soul holds with herself in considering of anything. I speak of what I scarcely understand; but the soul when thinking appears to me to be just talking—asking questions of herself and answering them, affirming and denying. And when she has arrived at a decision, either gradually or by a sudden impulse, and has at last agreed, and does not doubt, this is called her opinion. I say, then, that to form an opinion is to speak, and opinion is a word spoken,—I mean, to oneself and in silence, not aloud or to another: What think you?
Theaetetus	I agree.

Self and Harmony

Those words made a lifelong impression on many philosophers in the course of the two millennia after they were written. Remarkably enough, they also form the starting point for understanding some of the *political* implications of a *semiotic* approach to

J. M. Broekman, L. Catà Backer, *Lawyers Making Meaning*,

DOI 10.1007/978-94-007-5458-4_11, © Springer Science+Business Media Dordrecht 2013

law and legal discourse[1]. If lawyers manage and make meaning, then their politics ignites their *management* and their *making* of meaning at a very same point: the dialogic structure of the innermost self that characterizes a human individual. That insight is of essence. Political discourses (such as legal discourse) begin with the clarification of often-unknown dynamics, which constitute the human self. Political discourses also begin with the clarification of dynamics, which constitute the human self. And political discourse itself arises from a cultural context that gives structure to the Self situated within a particular environment—the self in Riyadh and the Self in Berlin or Beijing start from different places (literally and figuratively) that gives form to distinct political implications of a semiotic approach to law and legal discourse. Is the Self a Self (fixated, unified, integrated) or just (dis)associated bundles of disparate particles?

We already encountered those very same dynamics, and how they inspired and transcended considerations of the CLS and other mainstream legal theories to discuss whether law "is" politics. These eagerly underlined how "legal decisions" are like "political decisions" in the sense that it is impossible to separate judicial from legislative acts. This is plausible if one considers both law and politics as acts based on generally adopted and fixated norms. The "law is politics"-thesis is really about the character of the *arguments* and not of *significations* used in the legal and political decision-making processes, not of the nature of the practical activities (let alone institutions) involved. Every type of argument normally made in the course of a legislative-deliberative process, CLS authors claimed, could be, and in practice usually is also made in court. This includes arguments about social welfare, rights, morality, distributive justice, economic efficiency, as well as institutional arguments.

The "is" question could rather be an effective concealment of most aspects in semiotic insights. The question of those days (phrased as: "'is' law politics") remembers us how in those same years Habermas formulated worries about the widening gap between democracy emerging at the level of nation-states and democracy emerging in supra-national economic integration[2]. Law was only included in the first, he thought. Today, our supra-national economy and our national identity both practice democracy. They do so, however, in very different circumstances at unclear distance to large intercultural varieties of legal branches. New forms of an 'economy on the basis of non-identity' are a real change in the 'economy-law-society' relationship. Max Weber mentioned in the twenties of the past century how *to think difference is to think the validity of one's own (legal) order*: today, anonymity and (above all) loss of identity caused by an emerging virtual/global order makes his "thinking difference" irrelevant if not socially impossible—one of the recent weaknesses of the so-called multicultural approach in European politics.

The "is" question could rather be an effective concealment of most aspects in semiotic insights, a repetition of the classical unanswerable question "what law *is*" in contrast to "what law *does*". The slogan: 'law is man-made', does also not transform

[1] In how far a semiotic of politics is a matter of (American) identity, see N. Wiley: *The Semiotic Self*, Op. Cit, Ch. 1, 5 and 9.

[2] Jan M. Broekman: "Signs, Diversity and Tolerance" in: *The Journal of Comparative Law*, 2011.

society. That is visible in all manifestations with which the year 2011 begun, from the so-called Arab Spring to the *indignados* in Barcelona, Madrid, Los Angeles, London, Berlin and the later *Occupy* movements all over the globe. Some call it a new anarchism, but such a neo-anarchism has its complex semiotic implications, which we should analyze. "Consider, how law is, how law is made and how to perceive law as man-made" may be a sound academic advise, but it does not create a political theory for the next decades. So there are various issues to consider. Some are a matter of policy-making of meanings and others bear more rigid philosophical features. The problem is, that all seem to be intertwined, so that there is no possibility to deal with a solid list of items, one after the other. *A first cluster is, however, in the semiotics of the 'Self'*. Indeed, the slogan: 'law is man-made', does not transform society. The theme connects with many aspects, in particular of Lacan who is remembered, quoted and re-interpreted intensively in our days, but also with Kant's ideas on the substance and the qualities of the *ego* as the source of human reason and knowledge. The essence of the semiotics of the Self and its view on society is in the awareness of its own structure: is the self by nature (genetic predisposition or neurological order) an integrated harmonious entity—or a process, a lifelong search for integration by means of meaning making and the creation of sense and sensibility? It appears to be a highly relevant political question. The key to any semiotic understanding of politics may well be in an understanding of the self. The challenge connected with this observation is that Socrates' description of a human inner dialogue, constituting a self, shows a peaceful and harmonious world. Does modern politics not sustain that image? Four possibilities arise: peaceful and harmonious world (S_1); world of conflict and disharmony (S_2); not peaceful ($\sim S_1$); and not conflicted ($\sim S_2$); peaceful and conflicted (S_1 and S_2; the world of globalization) and neither peaceful nor conflicted (neither S_1 nor S_2; the world of self contained states). Here are the beginnings of a semiotic square to the fundamental problem of the semiosis of politics and the self in law! To understand the disquieting compulsion of this problem and this framework one must start (again) with Kant.

Kant and the Semiotics of the Self

Kant was shocked. He had been writing for months and years in the early morning hours of every day to accomplish a theory of knowledge. It should all be based on a reliable insight into the innermost structure of human knowledge and form the culmination point of his *Kritik der reinen Vernunft* (Critique of pure reason) (1781, Ed. 'A', and 1787 Ed. 'B'), a point to resound in 1787 in his *Kritik der praktischen Vernunft* (Critique of practical reason) and in 1790 in the *Kritik der Urteilskraft* (Critique of Judgment). The three books never mirrored the content of his academic lectures, although they became later an epistemological centerpiece of occidental culture. But he was shocked. Why?

Kant was deeply engaged in what was called the Enlightenment, an intellectual and philosophical movement with outspoken political and social implications flourishing in his days. Our history books take Descartes and his *Discourse on Method* in 1637 as a starting date of that period. When he wrote his three Critiques some hundred fifty years later, he strived to perfect this Enlightenment idea in finding secure truths within geometrical or mathematical thought patterns of reasoning. His deductive method focused on mental processes rather than on sensory experience or social and linguistic practices. That approach should deliver a truly *transcendental* philosophy. And, what is most important: human individuals strive for their identity in accepting the form of *a thinking subject* as their master image—an image predominant in the entire Enlightenment period. Kant's embarrassment unfolds in the center of that cultural determination and rational reasoning, when he becomes confronted with *breaches and divisions* in the ego that forms the center of the concept of human reason. He thus describes how

> ... reason, in the midst of her highest anticipations, finds herself hemmed in by a press of opposite and contradictory conclusions, from which neither her honor nor her safety will permit her to draw back—

and formulates as if he had Socrates' phrase in mind:

> ... the soul when thinking appears to me to be just talking—asking questions of herself and answering them, affirming and denying ... I say, then, that to form an opinion is to speak, and opinion is a word spoken.

But his concern was not so much pertaining to inner speech and conversation, or the priority given to language and speech. His attention was on the *speaker*, who can only be a part, an element, a particle, a composite of the total ego. A more general linguistic understanding of this insight came only in the early twentieth century with the so-called 'linguistic turn' in philosophy. Kant's concern with the *split ego* and his problem with the multitude of ego particles is a philosophical and cultural issue developed *before* that turn, whereas semiotic consequences of this ego-architecture affecting language and speech stem from the days *after* that turn. Yet, his insight in the *fractured* structure of the ego remains fundamental for us today. Where is Socrates' harmony?

With focus on the split ego and the speaker only as a component, we approach the inner motivation for Kant's shock: he lived in an age, which considered each infant that emerges from a mother womb as a supreme token of harmony, peace and integration. That infant was considered gifted with 'human reason' as an innate faculty. Now the *ego* shows to be split in parts and particles—what Kant calls *Ichspaltung*. So the center of the human spirit is not a stable and harmonious entity. Particles that compose the human ego, he concludes, exist in continuous disagreement among each other, so that the first task for any reasonable individual is to reflect upon its inner disagreement and the weight of opposing and contradictory conclusions: "there is no other course left open to her, than *to reflect with herself* upon the origin of this disunion in reason ..."[3].

[3] Immanuel Kant: *Kritik der reinen Vernunft* (*Critique of pure reason*, Meiklejohn, Ed., Amherst 1990) B 492, and Jan M. Broekman: *Phänomenologie und Egologie*, M. Nijhoff, Den Haag 1963, p. 138 f.

A harmonious reason, so dear to his culture, is nowhere anchored in human reality; that culture's last resort is a matter of skirmish, contradictions and entanglement in opposite conclusions, each defending its proper position. Kant concludes, that human reason is formed by this multitude of composites, so that there is "a natural and unavoidable dialectics in pure reason . . . ". Self knowledge in a person is thus the outcome of positions and counter positions, of weighing interests and arguments and of becoming a *partisan* at one side or another—Plato, his Socrates and Theaetetus could not agree more, and Lacan struggled two millennia later with the same consequences for an important part of his life as psychoanalyst in Paris! The major struggle of mankind appears to be the struggle with every human individual being divided against his or her self. Does not already Luke's gospel tell us, how threatening this divide is, because "every kingdom divided against itself is brought to desolation; and a house divided against itself falleth"? It is already any tragedy's hidden theme (in particular those of the fourth century BC) and it remains the center of each plot, which unfolds in an individual's life.

Kant cannot propose to his readers the disunion in human reason as if it were a fact of nature beyond reasonable insight. That would be against the founding principles of his culture and in particular against his own definition of Enlightenment as the spiritual movement that challenges man's emergence from his self-imposed immaturity. The 'self' of this 'self-imposed' process seems threatened! This insight would ruin his academic position, his inner circle of friends and his good relations with the Prussian Court. So he had to find a way to transcend this apparently negative insight pertaining to the split, broken and irreconcilable features of human reason. How? Two observations are important here. The *first* is, that he articulated his position against all disparages of human reason by means of a particular *metaphor*. That prevalent exploration of a metaphor in itself is exceptional in his days and forms a semiotic step hitherto unnoticed. The *second* is in his attention to *law* as the metaphor that answers the vital question at issue and thus has all antinomies of reason in grip. Reason is like a Court Judgment. In the 'talk-to-yourself' occurrence, who is the speaker and has the power to speak, and to whom does he speak; who populates the stories told? It becomes visible, that the metaphor is the articulation of power positions in the innermost *self* of a human being. A major task of human reason is to install self-knowledge as if it took the arrangement of a court of justice, concludes the metaphor -at-work. Not *the philosopher* Immanuel Kant, but *human reason itself* is Judge in this Court. Pure reason is always related to the highest tribunal, which is the name for the essence of itself—always in appearance before a High Judge, *vor einer höheren und richterlichen Vernunft*:

> The very existence of reason depends upon this freedom; for the voice of reason is not that of a dictatorial and despotic power, it is rather like the voice of the citizen of a free state, every member of which must have the privilege of giving free expression to his doubts, and possess even the right of *veto*, . . . although it is a melancholy reflection that reason, in its highest exercise, falls into antithetic; and that the supreme tribunal for the settlement of differences should not be at union with itself. (I. Kant: *Kritik der reinen Vernunft*, Ed. B. 767, 772, 513, 492.)

The overarching greatness of law and legal procedure seems to compensate the lack of harmonious unity in the innermost regions and processes in a self. Harmony within reason, so threatened by the experience of a split ego, is brilliantly determined by means of philosophical analysis and at the same time saved by the power of law as metaphor. Composure of reason results from the harmony of law and legally balanced situations of peace thus exist, and so does all internal coherence of human reason. Kant's impressive semiotic use of the concept of law has clarified what Plato already mentioned in Socrates' Sophist: that all human thought is dialogic in form: "I told myself the other day, but now I am telling myself quite differently . . .". This dialogic feature has *political* implications—a consequence of the semiotic metaphor move—so that his three Critiques, completed in 1790, forecasted the 1795 manifesto *On Perpetual Peace*.

This text encourages us to strive for *harmony in reason* by means of *activity* and not by *passively* accepting what we think that nature once decided about the essence of human beings. He suggests that we have to become a *partisan* in the numerous and dynamic positions within our own ego/reason and that the State is the ultimate terrain of that partisan struggle. In other, more contemporary words, 'to be' is 'to be a partisan' rather than 'to be a submissive spectator'. No wonder that Kant refers to the judge in court who achieves a situation of peace with his verdict (that is ultimately: by means of legal speech acts). The contrast between activity and passivity as constitutive dynamics of the subject seems essential in this language—a point Michel Foucault missed in his famous essay on Enlightenment and his lectures on subjectivity[4].

The Kantian appropriation of the metaphor 'law' seems to be deeply intertwined with politics—as becomes apparent from the essay on perpetual peace. His idea that there is no law without political dimension is also important for us contemporaries. As a consequence, the movements of all ego particles mirror movements within political entities, the Nation State being one of the most evident for Kant. Peace is thus the result of (narrative, declarative) communications in- and between States. If a *semiotics of the self* can be performed, it can on the basis of Kantian insights only occur within the State as society's ultimate form of socialization. Law and politics flow together at precisely this point. It's centuries old symbol is the human body: State and Law are perceived as a body; both have bodily properties such as health, harmony, peace, coordination of organ functions, expressiveness of freedom and indeterminacy as well as the flow of mutual respect. Self and State possess parallel qualities within the semantics of this body-metaphor; they are each other's explanatory patterns. *In other words: the logic of the State is understandable through the logic of the Self and vice versa*. The coherence of those two logics is the foundation for semiotics of Self and State. The Kantian law-metaphor provides us access to the realm of semiotic insights in politics.

---

[4] M. Foucault: *Qu'est-ce que les lumières?* 1978, [*What is Enlightenment?* In: P. Rabinow (Ed.) *The Foucault Reader*, 1984], -Id.-: *The Government of Self and Others: Lectures at the College de France, 1982–1983*. Picador 2011. See also: Martin, Gutman & Hulton (Eds): *Technologies of the Self: A Seminar with M. Foucault.* Massachusetts UP 1988.

The crux of this issue is, that *an appropriate understanding of the State and its political structures results from insights in how we understand our Self.* The Kantian use of the law-metaphor appears to be a culmination point in the history of self and state—an issue already envisaged by Plato and connected with images of the human figure, of which Hobbes' Magnus Homo is most known, and which the 48.000+ participants celebrate in the yearly Burning Man experience in Nevada's Black Rock Desert as a state of happiness, euphoria and freedom after one has conformed to "normal" life in the Magnus Homo for too long. Or one remembers the architects Choi & Shine who received the 2010 Award of the "Boston Society of Architects Unbuilt Architecture" with their design that transforms mundane electrical pylons into statues in the Icelandic landscape by making human form alterations to existing pylon designs[5]. But Kant does not yet confront the global order. From Kant to globalization there is a perhaps deep chasm. Can Kant's insights be used as a first step in the construction of a bridge?

The Semiotics of the Magnus Homo I: Figures, Images

No wonder that modern semiotics vehemently emphasizes questions of identity. Semiotics relates identity with images and the visual as well as with language and the structure of its articulations. Image and expression have political relevance in a wider sense than lawyers ever would consider, Hobbes taught us already with the frontispiece of his famous book. Instead of being impressed by modern images, we read the front page of his Magnus Homo again, as Kant did nearly one and a half century after Hobbes and many more recent generations before us[6].

The upper part of the famous frontispiece is by far the most striking. A gigantic crowned figure emerges from the landscape, clutching a sword and a pastoral staff beneath a quote from Job: "*Non est potestas Super Terram quae Comparetur ei*"—linking the figure to the monster of that book. Heavy words: 'nothing is comparable to you'. Most important in the context of our considerations is the fact that the torso and arms of the figure are composed of over three hundred persons facing the giant with just his head having visible features. The image is normally quoted as the "Magnus Homo", and the figure fascinates thinkers on law, politics and society until our days. It is a mysterious and impressive emblematic challenge to any philosopher. Numerous individuals who enter into its Body and form a 'machina machinarum', the machine of all machines, compose the Giant: the State. One should understand the essence of this image, which most probably was suggested by Hobbes himself and executed by Abraham Bosse around 1650, a famous artist in his days who worked in a style preferred by Louis XIV. The metaphor is clear: a state is on the

[5] Thus creating a "Land of Giants" that speaks to the modern Self. See: choishine.com/port_projects/landsnet/landsnet.html

[6] See an extensive representation of the frontispiece and its history on en.wikipedia.org/wiki/Leviathan_(book)

one hand an organization that acts like a machine, and is on the other a composite or a combination of persons acting together for a common end under the leadership of a boss or a clique—which is exactly what the Latin 'machina' originally suggests. The frontispiece shows the landscape unpopulated and the town completely deserted. The buildings are empty, the fields, churches and houses left. The walls of the town protect empty streets. All individuals retired from their daily lives and just glance at and move towards the Crown. They turned their back to their own land, town and region, which they called 'homeland' moments ago. They gave up this reality of everyday life for another, more protected life in the Magnus Homo.

That new life took possession of everything, even of history: in the empty town, statues stand meaningless in streets and at crossings, the arms of past heroes reach with desperate gestures in a history that now seems abolished. A new contract named the *pactum unionis* reigns; the name indicates the fiction that legitimates the silence and emptiness of society. Notice how emblems of worldly and spiritual authority are fragmented and represented in a diversity of individual scenes in the lower part of the emblem. One cannot find a unity of the two anymore in town and landscape and neither in the book's frontispiece. Crown and Authority, Emptiness and Abolished History in Homeland, Dominance of Written Text and Silence replacing Speech are the components of Crown and its authority! The fragmentation of emblems represents the social and legal situation after the appearance of the Magnus Homo. Two patterns of thought reinforce the legal ideology one reads in the etching: on the one hand the well-known and for centuries widely appreciated *more geometrico* theory of science, and on the other the dominance of what is 'before our eyes' and is evident, an evidence that denies further questioning as always.

That ideology should remain concealed, because its representation is determined to be evidence in itself. What is formulated, written, spoken, structured and organized in the images of law and state has to be consumed as such. No wonder, that deconstructionism, semiotics and other modern theories about speech and text become characterized as a blasphemy in the eyes of the Magnus Homo, because questioning the legitimacy of the Crown has the potential to destroy the *machina machinarum*. It interests how all those considerations have also in our days their consequences for law and state. A major consequence is that the *burden of interpretation* might become too heavy for lawyers if semiotics, deconstructionism or other theories become practiced in the face of the sovereign. The large production of legal texts would lose its coherence and change into contrasting political discourses and decisions. Complexity threatens and must be reduced towards one powerful Sovereign who represents Law and the State. Texts in law serve the centralized power of the state and the omnipresence of one and the same legal rationality. Power and rationality shall continue silently, as Hobbes suggests: "... the greatest liberty of subjects, dependeth on the silence of the Law ...". That silence of the Law is the presence of the Sovereign, as well as the absence of (multiform) text theories in legal practice. The judge is the 'mouth of the law' (bouche de la loi), as Montesquieu formulated famously and as Art. 4 of the 1804 Napoleonic Code restates with precision. He is destined to produce the necessary silence in the *machina machinarum*, since nothing but a *pluralis maiestatis* can be pronounced—the single voice of plural authority. No wonder, that each *Cour de Cassation* in Civil Law or Supreme Court in Common Law is the Royal Household of legal discourse. That Household is well figured in the Leviathan.

Yet the image is outdated to the extent it stops with the construction of the state. Ernst Jünger, a grand old man of nationalism conceded toward the end of his life: "What does a nation mean when you can fly across it in ten minutes?"[7] New machinae machinarum have emerged—international organizations, non-governmental actors, the multinational corporation. Each also in its own way emerges crowned with sword and staff in hand.' And with it there has emerged a new contest for the evolution of an ideology compatible with the realities of the new world orders—polycentric, functionally differentiated, and jurisdictionally diverse. The question for this century is similar to that of the seventeenth century—can the symbolic frameworks and structures of power be transposed from old to new orders; what is the new face of Leviathan and how shall we recognize her in her many forms? For that, the language of law is essential; it is to the lawyers and courts that the globalized world will be remade.[8]

The Semiotics of the Magnus Homo II: Legal Language

Law's ruling is not the only issue at stake in the Magnus Homo: if there is a ruling, than it is based on a seizure of the minds of those who are ruled. Rules are not rules when those who are ruled do not recognize them. *Words of law are* no longer the words of a free and everyday-life subject but rather of the authority, which the subject articulates by means of *words loaded with (legal) meanings after transition into the Leviathan.* Beyond that articulation is no legal speech. Utterances of a judge are utterances of an *Other* and the life of legal subjects is the life of *someone else,* of the Leviathan. Speech acts of those who live in the Magnus Homo change into a new speech, the language of the *machina machinarum,* after the transition from Land and Town into the Crown and its Authority. Hobbes remarks how 'Of Persons Artificiall, some have their words and actions *owned* by those whom they represent. And then the Person is the *Actor*; and he that owneth his words and actions, is the *Author*; in which case the Actor acteth by Authority'. Hobbes' frontispiece speaks that language and shows a direct relation between the fundamental values of the social contract and the linguistic structures of western European languages.

Subject-centeredness is primordial in this context and central in the process of meaning making. Owner and speaker of words are subjects in different stadiums of appropriation and seizure; the individual as subject is the foundational concept of everyday life on the basis of social contract. That contract is primordially a product of a widely spread thought pattern in Western Europe from Hobbes to the waning of the twentieth century, Enlightenment and Idealism included. An individual appears in the

---

[7] Jones, Nigel: *Hitler's Heralds: The Story of the Freikorps 1918–1923* New York 1987.

[8] Hirschl, Ran: Toward Juristocracy *The Origins and Consequences of the New Constitutionalism.* Harvard UP, 2004.

guise of a legal subject and/or a legal person in all phrases, sentences or statements of legal discourse; individuality mirrors the enjoyment of rights in the format of legal discourse, which needs in its turn phrases conceived on the basis of a subject belonging to the grammar of legal language. These transitions and reformulations find their ultimate destination in an individual's legal power or legal act. Subject, act and fact are the triple hinge of articulations in legal language—legal acts are together with legal subject and legal fact the foundation of expressiveness in law as laid down in legal doctrine—especially Civil Law traditions underline.

A *more geometrico* thought pattern solely accepts what results from composites of autonomous individual entities. A legal *subject* is in this light the founding unity in a center position amidst multiple legal relations; a legal *person* represents a conceptual unity called legal act. Any *enjoyment of rights* is based on the free human will, so that a legal act can consequently be understood as a composite of *subject* and *fact* in law. The Magnus Homo thus elucidates how law is in essence based on the willful mastering of a language, in particular of mastering a syntax, which is the sentence-formation of legal activity. *Whoever masters this linguistic performance, masters the State* . The perfection of mastership pertaining to law and the grammar of legal discourse creates precisely the idea of legal competence, which is predominant in the Leviathan. In the perfection of this competence unfolds the absolute anthropomorphism of individual and society in language and form of the Magnus Homo: "(. . .) the multitude so united in one Person, is called a Common-Wealth, in latine Civitas. This is the generation of that great Leviathan, or rather (to speak more reverently) of that Mortall God, to which we owee under the Immortall God, our peace and defence", Hobbes annotates and, in doing so, confirms the semiotic analyses of legal language in the Leviathan.

We should not cherish the though that all this is only a historical picture, and that modern law does no longer confirm that structure of the discourse and its sentence constructions. The issue of *interpretation in law*, a theme of importance in Common Law as well as in Civil Law, shows us differently. Transparency in social and legal determinations has been a forefront ideal since Hobbes or Rousseau and Habermas in our days. The latter embraced even the idea of communicative structures, which are *not* dominated by social power—a 'herrschaftsfreie Kommunikation'. However, communication can only be free from power within the framework of the ultimate power-machine: represented and sublimated as 'the State'. Transparence is not only in theories of communication but also found in the legal expression on interpretation: 'interpretatio cessat in claris'—one needs no interpretation where things are clear. The expression is nonsensical beyond the boundaries of law and legal discourse; clarity and unequivocal meaning make *only within that discourse* freedom to interpret no longer necessary. A clear text is like a clear social structure; both do not require or allow any further questioning, which is hardly a Utopia. The transition from everyday life into the life created by the Leviathan exists not in vein. Its Latin expression is the perfect formula of mechanistic thought patterns. In the Leviathan is no place for free interpretation, tells us its emblem. On the contrary, such freedom does not exist! All individuals, transposed into the Magnus Homo, received all possible meanings from their cultural context in which they are educated and unfold their lives. They do hardly know or experienced the scope of their seizure. There exists no meaning outside of the Leviathan, as there is no meaning outside of what law and legal discourse permit—debates on pornography in Western cultures are an excellent example in this context.

Hobbes' frontispiece, the subject of semiotic analysis, shows how a *text* acquires a literally *royal* position in law, the position of a monarch in legal doctrine and legal discourse. Crown and staff confirm that a concise legalistic reading of law in society is the only appropriate read[9]. There is no law beyond or outside law, Luhmann once suggested. There is no meaning or sense outside the Leviathan—its streets are empty and its statues without meaning or sense. *There is no meaning outside the modern State*. That is the essence of the semiotics of State and the Self: the latter is the cultural product of the first, without any power to reach beyond. Hence we should consider how Lacan's reference to the word of the Father in the education and enculturation of the infant is confined to the State creating the ultimate limits for all his and our education pronouncements. In other words: the father's spoken *word* (an issue of cultural transference) *reproduces* (in a process called education) *conditions* (in the freedom of unfolding) of what in a State perception is categorized as *norm*. Understand the "yourself and himself"—language as a basis for global talk, which tries to escape those limitations and bounds but tragically fails in its multiple attempts. Expressions such as "The US and the world", "Argentina and its friends", or "Europe going global"—all of them, as much as concepts of the individual or the self, lose identity in what we call 'memberships' like cards in our wallets; states lose identity in the smog of the global and the dust surrounding the laws of corporations without names that decide about our daily life.

Four features of legal speech and legal writing (still in a mechanistic *more geometrico* framework functioning in modern law) show the character of legal discourse made at its maximum effective in doctrinal and other legal writing:

1. One single idea should be represented in texts by one and the same term/meaning.
2. Compositions of single terms should represent single meanings only.
3. Grammatical constructions of sentences or texts should never result in multiple and unequivocal meanings.
4. All textual activity should be directed towards (legal) rationality, and thus focus a rational individual in law and society.

The four demonstrate the multiple effects of Staff and Crown in their rigorous character. However: the real secret of the semiotics of Leviathan and its frontispiece is in the *revolutionary character* that Hobbes and our contemporary semiotic approaches share: he or she who is truly able to read those images and their meaning, *knows* about all this—even in a fragmentary manner—and does *not* live completely passively and consumptively in the Magnus Homo as the multitude of man called citizen after their transition into the Body, do! But how many of those who left homeland and birthplace know why they did leave and what it means that they engaged in a transition towards the Leviathan? How many of those, who knowingly engage in the

[9] Cf. Judith Shklar: *Legalism* Op. Cit., 1964

transition, understood that this is their sole way to create meaning? In other, more politically relevant words, will they ever experience that this involvement is their only way to be creative and to think positively? Answers to these questions—which are by no means purely rhetoric—are in such popular sentences as: "what is good for you is good for your country" or in the inverse: "what is good for your country is good for you". Some remember the perverse inversion in nazist slogans as "Du bist nichts, Dein Volk ist Alles" [you are nothing, your people is everything]. Individualism (represented in these expressions with "you") is by no means innate, as many political conservatives believe, but the result of a powerful process of enculturation, which has often the effect of a powerful seizure. The above explanations should make clear that meaning making has its boundaries and restrictions in the State, *beyond which there is no-thing*.

The Semiotics of the State

'So Self, so State'—as well as the inverse—would be the appropriate slogan to recapitulate the above considerations of the Leviathan. The togetherness of law and politics focuses on the understanding and management of meaning delimitated by a State. This is clear in Kant's introductory remark to his pamphlet on *Perpetual Peace*, an idea he found painted on a Dutch innkeeper's signboard, on which a burial ground represents perpetual peace. His introduction says:

> Whether this satirical inscription on a Dutch innkeeper's sign upon which a burial ground was painted had for its object mankind in general, or the rulers of states in particular, who are insatiable of war, or merely the philosophers who dream this sweet dream, it is not for us to decide. But one condition the author of this essay wishes to lay down. The practical politician assumes the attitude of looking down with great self-satisfaction on the political theorist as a pedant whose empty ideas in no way threaten the security of the state, inasmuch as the state must proceed on empirical principles; so the theorist is allowed to play his game without interference from the worldly-wise statesman. Such being his attitude, the practical politician–and this is the condition I make–should at least act consistently in the case of a conflict and not suspect some danger to the state in the political theorist's opinions, which are ventured and publicly expressed without any ulterior purpose. (I. Kant: *Zum Ewigen Frieden. Ein Philosophischer Entwurf.* 1795; Ed. J.H. von Kirchmann, Berlin 1870, Vol 6.)

The idea of a State is related in Kant's essay with activities of a variety of subjects, such as: (a) mankind in general, (b) rulers of states as characterized by the wars they make, (c) philosophers who dream about the contrast of what characterizes the ruler, namely peace, (d) the practical politician, (e) the political theorist and (f) the roles to play in conflict relations between states. But *how* are they related to the encompassing idea of a State and what does this pattern of relations tell us about the State beyond its history, administration and comparable themes? One answer is in the *political* quality of their connections, another in the architecture of *meanings*, which provide the foundations of the State. In other words, one is a *political/legal* and the other a *semiotic* view.

Kant focuses only on political/legal dimensions, and that makes him concentrate on thought patterns, which indeed have the State as their ultimate boundary. He describes those components as if State relations parallel those of an individual's *ego*: particles form the State (in all their positions and counter-positions, arguments pro and contra, striving for different goals and in need of a final verdict) in order to acquire an identity. *So Self, so State*. This parallel is strongly and safely maintained by the metaphor of law. The Self parallels the stability of the State in the heart of the legal metaphor. Both depend on deliberation, self-awareness, agreement and institutional power as well as external cultural and economic conditions.

The general consequence, in particular when one focuses on commonness as the result of a continuous exchange of members in society, is again semiotic: the *meaning* of all components is determined by what the total composite determines. *So Self, so State* is a *semiotic hinge,* which seems to be in effect beyond thought patterns of Kant and Enlightenment. That hinge is in his days essential in the case of the idea of a perpetual peace, just like in the days of Grotius approximately two centuries earlier. Grotius created in 1609 international law by applying the same structure and thought patterns. His *The Free Sea* formulated the principle that a sea was international territory, patterned like Nation States who were free to use for seafaring trade among them. States like Persons/Selves: he thus provided an ideological justification for the breaking up of existing trade monopoly practices to establish his own monopoly. Meanings always depend on references to their context, a totality without which they cannot exist—persons or selves are since Roman Law a major legal-semiotic component, as later, in 1786/1789, also Jeremy Bentham explained in his *A Plan for an Universal and Perpetual Peace*, part IV of his *Principles of International Law*.

In how far are these remarks a step in the direction of a "semiotics of the State"? How should our concept of the State be analyzed in terms of semiotics, which means: in the light of signs and significations? A semiotic approach highlights what *sign* a State is and what *meaning* the State concept has for us who must live in a State. General studies of the State, in particular those that originate in social or political sciences, do not mention the inherent sign dimensions of the idea and its economic, sociological and legal sign-politics in occidental culture. Do not States fulfill the super-determining role of *Speaker* as the "Grammatical First-Person Singular, for short: Subject, of a Language named State"? That language unfolds for instance when States declare and make war in the name of their representatives, when they order and protect social life and create optimal life conditions for their citizens, when they educate their subordinates, when they allow governments to issue legal measures and to represent them, when they order administrations to prescribe behaviors in daily life, balance rights and duties for persons and society. The breach with our general imagination is that *we, the people*, do not *possess* any of these properties or powers before the State *ascribes* them to us as citizens or other individualized components. And we, citizens, do *not* possess the State or a Rule of law, nor a democracy, although we are educated to say so and to think that way. The idea that we *possess* them or are the responsible owner of the rule of law is exactly the ultimate and most necessary *meaning* created by the State in order to make the State function.

Marx once called this "a powerful ideology". Any semiotic approach of the State is confronted with that ideology, which seems to be rooted in the act of inversion of what *we are* into what *we say that we are*. That inversion is perhaps the central issue in the unfolding of a semiotics of the State. Our most intriguing question is thus of linguistic and semiotic nature, an issue that fascinated Kant as well as Lacan centuries later. So, we ask in other words how such a strong discrepancy between what we are, and our language expressing our self-awareness can exist? Two issues come to the fore: (1) the *semiotics of a self* plays a major role in understanding social life and its form called State, and (2) the fact that a *human ego* is not a singular and harmonious entity but composed by elements that contradict each other—"*contradict*" means here: ego particles say different things and speak different languages. We encountered already the idea that an *ego* is divided into pieces, parts or elements. A human "I" is split, his striving for knowledge and behavior is always resulting from a *split ego*, Kant suggested. Identity cannot be understood as a fixed property but rather as a process in which one is involved. Identity does not search for a self that is the same, as if it were a copy resulting from the mirror, but the search for "the appropriate otherness of my self". It is about an extension of my self that is one of the many braids, which form the "I am".

See how new roles unfold and new egos claim recognition on the stage. *They are not an ego stemming* from words exchanged between egos, *but rather from a* different exteriority: from social structures enforcing awareness. Such institutional structures gave a command, like States did, to *adept*—yes, *to be*—an identity given by them *as if* it pertains to another individual: a citizen, consumer, bearer of rights, tax-payer, performer of duties, proprietor, criminal, shareholder. What we say that we are, even when using words like 'citizen', 'tax-payer' or 'bearer of rights', belongs definitively to the language of the State, taught in order to unfold our life in the State in accordance with the categories we received in our education. To be 'a responsible citizen' is one of them. *Names* are more crucial then we ever think of: 'tax-payer' is a name given; we only bear the name 'citizen' as a given name. These were the new names given to the numerous individuals who changed into individuals that create the Magnus Homo. A modern example is article 8 of the EU Maastricht Treaty declaring "Art. 8, 1. Citizenship of the Union is hereby established. Every person holding the nationality of a Member State shall be a citizen of the Union". The new *name* "EU Citizen" was given and this name giving had enormous consequences for those who lived in the Leviathan called "European Union" and those who would follow since 1992, date of the Treaty. *Governance takes places via names,* we learn: *the State is the Supreme name in the name of which persons and issues are called by their names.* Those names are chosen because of their consequential meanings designed in law, articulated in legal discourse and adapted in everyday discourse of each one who entered the Magnus Homo. *So State, so Self, so Law*: the unison is staggering and it does not wonder, that also lawyers operate via names given to names.

That is not a cool interpretation or a scientific conclusion. In all of this is *a turning point,* a point in which human consciousness becomes aware of the insight that it is involved, even encapsulated in a rapid transition towards a new state-of-mind, a new intensity that manifests itself as different: a realization of time, space and self. One has, in semiotic perspective, to begin with the self—a lesson to learn from the Godfathers of semiotics. What is more: that transition is nowhere else than on its way—it is, in other words, a process! It is not a future of things that are to become discovered: it is there, it is in our life, in our selves, in our world and it only becomes increasingly evident, underlining what Nietzsche called a fare more and hitherto unknown *will* of humankind, the will to ignorance, to the uncertain, to the untrue, to the free course of the trickster. Today, the *indignados* wait to experience the power of that will and to fulfill the moment, a moment in which the change of consciousness is no longer chained by psychiatric, economic or scientific categories or legal names to act upon because there are consequences concealed in names that determine mankind's history. But the multinational corporation and the global non-governmental organization may already have reached escape velocity from the state![10]

It is a moment in the history of mankind that was never planned to happen because it stretches far beyond any boundary of human self-imagination. It shows the importance of the self as subject of imagining and understanding social structures. Ozone holes, fundamentalist perceptions, identities washed out by banks and corporations do change dimensions of being human forever. The planet is not the same home anymore and we even do not know whether it will remain a home at all.

The mirror of self and state precludes in the first place how human consciousness—this riddle of a never-unified unification of man's essence in mind and matter—is at the center of meaning. An inner development, which is inaudible in the conversation within the mind, seems to have found a hitherto unobserved exteriority, which manifests itself in crises of cultural, economic or social and even philosophical dimensions. Times change and words change with them, but meanings stay relatively stable and alive. Culture was the catchword of the eighties of the past century; it was combined but not integrated within philosophy. Semiotics' role in academics diminished quickly, as the Eugenides novel shows. Social dimensions took the stage when creating other large-scale forms of institutionalized togetherness. Today, we focus on economy, its global dimensions and its destruction of identity. What challenges do we have to envisage when our Self (in forms of consciousness) is challenged and has to enter unknown realms of change again.

Individual, State, and the Semiotics of Anarchy

What happens after discovering that the State is no longer the State we knew and that he is no more the ultimate boundary of our meaning making activity? Nevertheless, we are forged not to forget the name: 'State' is the Name I need in order to

---

[10] Larry Catá Backer, "Governance Without Government: An Overview", in *Beyond Territoriality: Transnational Legal Authority in an Age of Globalization* (Günther Handl, Joachim Zekoll, Peer Zumbansen, (Eds), Brill AP, 2012

articulate my proper Self! State is the name I live in, the one that makes me a citizen, an individual, a bearer of rights, the ruler of my representations. Just a Name . . . no more—nobody knows any more? Speech and language are preferred processes of articulation in cultures, so that not only what is being articulated but also the possibility of articulation and speech is at stake when the word "State" is considered[11]. It is not easy to understand that speech and language are cultural values, which determine the total axiological structure of society. Words and utterances are part and parcel of these values. Language articulation in words and speech is a value in its own right. This value is exposed and thus at risk in each articulation. A speech act is therefore not instrumental, a means to communicate between individuals, but a highly sophisticated form of protection of social values. The silence in the Leviathan and its language of law and State are meaningful and constitute an important sign in this context. Silent citizens expose themselves in the Magnus Homo but are not prepared to acknowledge that they represent any basic value. Such understanding shows the limitations of the discourses concerned, which should remain concealed—hence the vigorous reduction to instrumental and institutional speech as well as a language of submission to the Crown.

The figure of the Crown, visible as Leviathan or Code, always seizes the figure of the Speaker. The speaking individual acquired its natural ability to perform speech acts in order to *individualize*, as the emphasis on subject-centered speech in law, state and politics demonstrates. That linguistic form dominates in order to *not* unveil its essence. If this unveiling would happen, the axiology of thought formation in the Magnus Homo, Civil Code, Common Law Precedent would at best become subject of a critical philosophical analysis or subject of social revolt. A new rationality would unfold and different forms of speech in law and politics become audible. That situation, which is a delusion and a dangerous phantom in the mind of today's rulers, lawyers and politicians, became qualified as *an-archy*.

There exist various politically interesting connotations pertaining to the expression 'anarchy' in this context. They all have semiotic relevance. The first and most powerful is, that 'anarchy' is understood and experienced as an assault on the foundations of law and society. The word itself seems to interrupt the flow of speech, particularly in law and rationality, which is necessarily presented as possessing an untouchable foundation and as supporting a socially stable Self in social action and self-expression. There is no law or legal science without security about those foundations. A legal theory may debate and even tone down the profiles and content of law and legal rationality, but not the foundations of the two. That silence is the concealed truth in each legal thought pattern—no matter whether Common Law, Civil Law, religious-or indigenous Law or any other legal form one encounters on the globe. A discussion of the foundations of law and legal rationality is a blasphemy. The discussion in legal philosophy pertaining to Hans Kelsen's 'Grundnorm' [founding norm] in law has for that reason always been encapsulated in the larger context of the debate how to appreciate legal positivism. The most radical interpretation was,

---

[11] Jan M. Broekman: *Individual, State and the Semiotics of Anarchy,* in: Law at the End of the Day, Larry Backer's blog, Nov 12, 2011.

that this Kelsen norm should be understood as a foundational *fiction* in legal thought patterns[12]—no matter how 'foundation' and 'fiction' fit together.

Language and speech serve the conservation of thought patterns on which the Leviathan is grounded. Both support the close ties between doctrinal structures of law and the notions on which society is based—their words, grammar and rules included. It is a bewildering experience that all words about our words, all language about language and its articulations is a language that encounters its limits in our understanding of the world. The issue is, remarkably enough, not whether language is limited by occidental metaphysics (Heidegger) or there is yet a language able to design discourses beyond metaphysical borderlines. The issue touches apparently deeper levels in which the word 'anarchy' plays a surprising role—evidently differing from a social attitude or a political expression. One should consider that in our times of change, protest, revolt and anxiety.

The issue is complex and difficult to grasp, so that we outline a few characteristics in the context of semiotic approaches to law and politics. When we reflect upon a word or a concept there is much more at stake than language or linguistics. Even Heidegger's differentiation between 'Being' and 'being(s)' or 'what is' (Sein v Seiendem) presupposes language as an object that one can approach from different perspectives. One is language as directly representing Being (Sein), the other as a form of being(s), a something that is (Seiendes), an object. His focus is, however, on Being *before* this split—on Being, which is in our occidental culture 'forgotten' (Seinsvergessenheit) because we only perceive and think of its phenomena and do not seem to be able to think Being itself. Being is original, and as such (a) the foundation and (b) the goal of all thought formation: the *topological ground of all that is*—and therefore the ultimate goal of all philosophy or metaphysics. This Being, forgotten and not (yet) perceived, is in essence a first discovered Being, or —Peirce formulated—Firstness[13]. Heidegger's 'ontological difference' stimulates the use of a surprising legal metaphor—a metaphor, which is immediately relevant for explaining *anarchy*.

That explanation interests the more when no language is left anymore to fully articulate the meaning of a State, in particular when States diminish in public life. Yet all expressions that I use are embedded in one meaning that expanded as if it were a language in its own right. Together with the State, I lost reference, lost meanings. I used to live in the space of occidental metaphysics, delineated between arche and telos—how can I ever understand myself beyond that master dimension? How does one deny one's own arche? Does it suffice to be an anarchist?

[12] Ali Benmakhlouf: *L'identité. Une fable philosophique.* Presses Universitaires de France, Paris 2011, p. 127.

[13] See Jan M. Broekman: "Firstness and Phenomenology" in: Wagner/Broekman (Eds): *Prospects of Legal Semiotics,* Op. Cit., p. 37 f.

Individual, State, and Personhood

As a consequence, we have to conclude that the expression "Personhood"—in particular used as a political item in the US—is given to us by the State in order to let the State function. Individuals have to appropriate that concept and use it as an indication of their own identity. The State thus tells me the myth of my identity, which should be the cradle of my social life. Lacan reminds us how the word of the father is the voice of the law. But without the State in which we unfold our selves, there would never be a word of that myth or of the father therein. Anarchists reject those words; *they are not against the State but against the tyranny of the word that makes us a citizen as its individual*. The slogan 'Occupy Wall Street' is semiotic by nature: it wants to indicate that the meaning making processes should take place elsewhere and have a different outcome. Those who understood, practiced or even criticized 'occupy' in terms of possession, did not grasp the deep semiotic revolve at hand.

A central thesis of this book is, that the "semiotics of subjectivity" belongs to the most neglected issues in law and legal theory. Yet, the position of a subject remains indeed important in law, as is shown every day in court decisions, legal advise, criminal law or contract law all over the Western world. Any understanding of law as a narration presupposes that this narrative has a subject: that what it is all about, and a subject: one of the personae of the story, judge, lawyer and defendant. This subject in the exemplary narrative called "law" is in a process of disappearance: the subject is divided in itself, a division, which can be judged positively as well as negatively. Kant's 'Ichspaltung', Freud's 'narcissism', Lacan's 'growth of the ego' are altogether ideas that fit to a fundamental disorientation of the I about itself. But they remain within the traditional boundaries of philosophy and culture.

Can an acting subject act, one could ask. Can a split subject act, in particular politically? Political implications of the position of the acting subject in legal semiotics are more complicated than many observations of Foucault or Lacan suggested. The subject acting in society is not identical to the subject in semiotics, although legal-theoretical and even philosophical studies seem to suggest such an identity. Both subjects—the subject of socio-legal operations and the subject of semiotic action—are capable to constantly change from one level of attitude to another, and back again! Contemporary philosophers underlined that an important difference between a subject in everyday and a semiotic subject cannot be abolished. They say, that the latter is unable to act socially, so that the power of meaning making always needs the transposition from semiotics into everyday life.

Peirce as well as Husserl related this critique to the possibility of each ego to achieve an *attitude change*. One should consider how De Saussure underlined what Peirce also noticed, namely that a sign is not a fixed semiotic entity but rather the meeting ground for independent entities. There *are* no signs, nothing *is* a sign, everything *can become* a sign, so that there are ultimately only sign-functions, and these are only temporary exercising such a function. "Finally, . . . reality depends on the ultimate decision of the community" Peirce once noticed.

Legal cases are signs that fulfill a role in this decision process. They are names for sign functions and thus limited by their temporary character and by the limited discourse in which its subjects operate. The limits and definitions of law are defined by lawyers and by what society considers as legal, which includes that the defining procedure happens in a changing society and historical context. Those changes are overwhelmingly mirrored in the pace of today's changing e-technology.

Moore's Law is generally accepted as a first radical attempt to understand this. Gordon Moore, with Robert Noyce the founder of Intel and in the mid-seventies its chairman, had accomplished a series of inventions pertaining to integrated electronic circuits. His law—which he never called a law himself—expressed the observation that every twenty-four month twice as many transistors can be loaded onto an integrated circuit as in the period before. His law laid down the foundations of insight pertaining to our culture's character and pace, and is therefore also important for our legal future, its discourses and institutions included, the more where his law holds in nano-dimensions. Legal semiotics attempts to coordinate the unlimited and the limited acceleration of history for reasons of better understanding the dimensions of society's major discourse. No wonder that the future of the law seems extremely precarious. Law is deeply intertwined with a multitude of cultural developments, so that legal discourse and Court practices are often perceived to be based on uncertain premises and unwarranted assumptions. It is true that most legal articulations do by no means include essential knowledge about the powers that shape future cases and legal case materials. And, moreover, they do not include clues about the true character and the pace of technology and culture that are developing in the first decades of this century.

Hence the suggestion of a forthcoming *semiotization*—an acceleration of understanding social processes as sign processes—of law and legal discourse, which is in itself a process of a new understanding of politics on hitherto unimagined scales. Moore's law has largely held the test of time to date, challenging limits for the number of transistors in the most complex chips. This issue becomes gradually interpreted as a sign for historical processes within which law has to function. Is the Self a comparably complex chip? All particles of the cohesion between *firstness* and phenomenology seem to concentrate on their respective subjects and their actions[14]. That is essential for our theme: those subjects are, no matter in what attitude level involved, at a certain moment of their life time communicating subjects, and their communication processes function thanks to overarching systems of meaning. Peirce explains:

> Consistency belongs to every sign, so far as it is a sign; and therefore every sign, since it signifies primarily that it is a sign, signifies its own consistency. The man-sign acquires information, and comes to mean more than he did before. But so do words.... But since man can think only by means of words or other external symbols, these might turn round and say: You mean nothing which we have not taught you, and then only so far as you address some word as the interpretant of your thought.

---

[14] Jan M. Broekman: "Firstness and Phenomenology—Peirce and Husserl on Attitude Change" in Wagner & Broekman (Eds.): *Prospects of Legal Semiotics*, Op. Cit. p. 37 ff

Men and words reciprocally educate each other; each increase of a man's information involves and is involved by a corresponding increase of a word's information. Our thesis is, that this process of annihilation of the subject (inherent to the progressing semiotization of the subject) is not longer an extension of a philosophy, its literature and ongoing thought processes. It became an un-identifiable, anonymous half real/half virtual, non-nation-bound or state-bound issue, reinforced by global economics and a progressing power and importance of corporations, which in fact annihilate also the forms of state, which hitherto were the cradle of subject-conceiving. This is the contact point of semiotics of law and semiotics of subjectivity. The culmination of all of this is in a new understanding of the concept of anarchism.

Chapter 12
Politics, Semiotics and Law: Person and Thing

Identities evaporate or concentrate in the intertwinements of Self and State all along the lines of changing depressions or other atmospheric conditions. Today more than in earlier times, those same identities—experiencing the innermost tensions between Self and State, which are driven by an unperceived dynamics like clouds at the blue sky—display the need to incarnate, or in many cases to be incarnated in order to be kept alive.

Persons and Things

The attraction of the Magnus Homo, which made us "citizen" (and—in more perverse articulations—a "responsible citizen") is still felt in the Occident and unfolds at a global scale. Semiotics, as the most encompassing search for meaning and meaning-making, unveils the subtle fabric of this Leviathan-like attraction. Its origins seem to be Roman, where Civil Law was said to be concentrating on Persons (personae) and Things (res) as major legal concepts. Violent discussions and other behaviors pertaining to anarchism show how important these motives are in modern times. Self and State, Archè and Telos still hold their grip on us. Jesus of Nazareth was said to say, "I am alpha and omega."[1] Usually understood as the beginning and the end, it might be easier to understand as indications of dominion and purpose, of origins and ends—of *archè* and *telos*. These are words of description, of fact and of relation between the persons of speaker and hearer; yet these words also stand in for, and in a sense establish, the self-conception of each in light of the character of the other; they establish an order to things and a purpose. These words are signs. "A sign, and its representamen, is something which stands to somebody for something

[1] Revelation 22:13 (KJV). More fully, "I am Alpha and Omega, the beginning and the end, the first and the last." Id. The notion of first and last in its more nuanced form follows from the first testament: "Thus saith the LORD the King of Israel, and his redeemer the LORD of hosts; I am the first, and I am the last; and beside me there is no God. And who, as I, shall call, and shall declare it, and set it in order for me, since I appointed the ancient people? and the things that are coming, and shall come, let them shew unto them." Isaiah 44:6–7 (KJV).

J. M. Broekman, L. Catà Backer, *Lawyers Making Meaning*,

DOI 10.1007/978-94-007-5458-4_12, © Springer Science+Business Media Dordrecht 2013

in some respect or capacity. It addresses somebody, that is, creates in the mind of that person an equivalent sign, or perhaps a more developed sign. The sign stands for something, its object."[2] Contrast the sympathetic rephrasing by Umberto Eco: "I propose to define as a sign *everything* that, on grounds of a previously established social convention, can be taken as *something standing for something else*."[3]

Beyond these there is nothing, for the description itself delineates the framework within which things can be understood. That is, there is nothing that would fall within the parameters of recognition presumed by the system of meaning attached to sign, symbol signification established within the interpretive community. But of course, the world beyond is rich, just opaque to the self-referencing community producing meaning from sign. Consider Nietzsche on this point: "Nihilism as a psychological state has yet a third and last form. Given these two insights, that becoming has no goal and that underneath all becoming there is a no grand unity in which the individual could immerse himself completely as in an element of supreme value, an escape remains: to pass sentence on this whole world of becoming as a deception and to invent a world beyond it, a true world".[4] These words suggest as well the techniques through which the relationship between speaker and hearer will be elaborated—by words that themselves are signifiers and symbols of authority, and when consumed (interpreted) produce reaction and direction to action. Thus, the simple statement—alpha and omega—opens windows on meaning and relations between speaker, hearer and the object that is embedded in the speaking. Those meanings define and bind in ways that then have enormous effect on the way in which speaker and hearer relate to each other and to the object that is the subject of the speaking. Speaker, hearer and object together produce order and purpose, as well as the recognition of places where disorder and no purpose can also exist. This is the essence of semiosis. "All communication is a process of exchange of meaningful signs, and sign systems, such as natural language, mediate between communicating personal and those objects in the phenomenal, physical world of experience to which they refer." It is that process of exchange centering around the corporation as object, sign and interpretant, that is the object around which the examination of politics, semiosis and the state will be centered. [5]

The semiosis of the person of Jesus has, in modern times, been adapted to the transfiguration of the state. It also has been understood as the alpha and omega of the political and social order.[6] We rethink the semiotics of the state, moving us away from ideology to the more fertile plane of referential interpretation, as the above cited words of a blog recapitulate: "What happens after discovering that the State is

---

[2] Charles S. Peirce: "Pragmatism and Pragmaticism," in CP 5, 636

[3] Umberto Eco: *A Theory of Semiotics* Indiana UP, 1976, p. 16

[4] F. Nietzsche, *The Will to Power* 12–13 (Walter Kaufmann and R.J. Hollingdale, trans. W.Kaufmann, (Ed.) New York 1968) But Nietzsche was careful to suggest that this world outside is itself untrue. "One simply lacks any reason for convincing oneself that there is a *true* world."

[5] Paul Bains: *The Primacy of Semiosis: An Ontology of Relations* Toronto UP, 2006. Roberta Kevelson: *The Law as a System of Signs*, New York: Plenum Press, 1988.

[6] Cf. Stephen D. Kramer: *Sovereignty: Organized Hypocrisy*, Princeton UP, 1999.

no longer a State, as we knew him? But we do not lose or forget the name: 'State' is the Name I need in order to articulate my proper Self! State is the name I live in, the one that makes me a citizen, an individual, a bearer of rights, the ruler of my representations. Just a Name . . . no more—nobody knows any more? There is no language anymore to express the meaning of a State, yet all expressions that I use are embedded in that one meaning that expanded as if it were a language in its own right. Together with the State, I lost reference, lost meanings. I used to live in the space of occidental metaphysics, delineated between *archè* and *telos*—how can I ever understand myself beyond that master dimension? How does one deny one's own *archè*? Does it suffice to be an anarchist?"[7]

The corporation, like the state from which it preceded and to some extent superseded, can be understood in terms of Peirce and its triadic sense—as sign, interpretant and object. Like the state, corporations serve as an incarnation, an object, the sign and interpretant which shimmers with meanings that from a distance appear solid and yet which, on closer inspection, dissolve into a dynamic complex of interlocking and interacting signification. The corporation produces meaning within its organization. It projects meaning from the organization outward with respect to itself and its activities. But meaning is projected onto it from the state, from consumers, investors and others who form relationships with the organization directly or indirectly. The object itself is a moving target—the producer of goods to some, the instrument of social interactions with property, the origin of desire, the instrument of state power, the source of employment. It is constituted as an infinite variation of itself—its own *archè* and *telos* —the source and object of meaning reflected in itself and reflected through its interpretants.[8] Its mechanics introduces *technè*, the mechanics of the production of meaning, the lubricant and transportation system between *archè* and *telos*, that is, between beginning and end or dominion and purpose. But it is also as the negation of both—the corporation produces anarchy and nihilism, the domination of nothing and the imposition of an object order founded on a positive rejection of purpose. "Nothing has any meaning"[9]—a phrase more precisely understood when the emphasis is placed on the first word, suggests the idea. For some, anarchy and nihilism (at the center of which stands the sign-symbol of the corporation) is the essence of the market. For others, the corporation as sign and object within the emerging system of economic globalization suggest the practical interpretant of this

[7] Jan M. Broekman, "Individual, State and the Semiotics of Anarchy," Law at the End of the Day, Nov. 12, 2011.

[8] The corporation, in this sense, understands its construction as object and sign through a corporate semiosis that replaces corporate communication, as itself both instrument and shield. For a particularly instructive example in the context of brand communication, see the slide show produced by KMB|Konzept Management Beratung für Unternehmenskommunikation in conjunction with a paper presented to the 10th IASS/AIS World Congress, Klaus M. Bernsau, "Corporate Semiosis Instead of Corporate Communication: How to Apply Semiotics Pragmatically in the Field of Entrepreneurship and Management." Corua Sept. 2009. Available http://www.slideshare.net/KMB/corporate-semiosis-iass-world-congress.

[9] F. Nietzsche, *The Will to Power*, op. cit., p. 660: "this melancholy sentence means 'All meaning lies in intention, and if intention is altogether lacking, then meaning is altogether lacking, too.'"

understanding. The corporation, like the state before it, can be itself and its opposite. This idea is nicely embedded in the idea of the embedding of the concept of the state, first in the person of the King.[10] In contemporary times the semiosis of kingship has itself become more complex as the physical body of the King has been replaced by a statistics that have incarnated the masses as the embodiment of the abstraction—state.[11]

Thus, the above challenge[12] encounters its own inverted *doppelgänger;*[13] the challenge itself provides its answer in the very formulation of the challenge itself. That challenge reformulated, can lead to the following understanding, and thus to the thesis of this chapter: When we discover that the corporation is no longer a corporation as we knew it, we do not yet lose or forget the name—"corporation": "embodiment". Indeed, the opposite is more likely, the corporation becomes a larger space within which meaning is extracted and imposed. Corporation (like State) remains the name needed (by those who are constituted in relation to it—the consumer, investor, employee, citizen, etc.) to articulate the self—as the self (investor, consumer, citizen) is necessary to articulate the corporation (and the State). The corporation is both the name individuals ("I") live in and also one that is itself an aggregation of this "I." But it is an unstable and dynamic object and sign: not just a name, but also and simultaneously the name of its opposite. We already mentioned how States fulfill the super-determining role of *Speaker* as the "Grammatical First-Person Singular", for short: "Subject"—of a Language named "State". That language unfolds for instance when States prescribe behaviors in daily life, balance rights and duties for persons and society. Our treacherous imagination is that *we, the people*, do *possess* any of these properties or powers before the State *ascribes* them to us as citizens or other individualized components. But we, citizens, do *not* possess the State or a Rule of law, nor a democracy, although we are educated to say so and to think that way. The idea that we *possess* them or are the responsible owner of the rule of law is exactly the ultimate and most necessary *meaning* created by the State in order to make the State function. Corporations tend to suggest that a multiple embodiment can belong to one and the same identity. States as well as corporations want us to speak to them as an "original subject", as an "I" they did not enforce nor incorporate. They want us, once called citizens, to be incorporated in them by means of the belief that we performed that incorporation as an original "we", "I" "persona" or "subject". This

---

[10] See Ernst H. Kantorowicz, *The King's Two Bodies: A Study in Medieval Political Theology* Princeton UP, 1997.

[11] See: Michel Foucault: "Security, Territory, Population" in: *Lectures at the Collège de France 1977–1978*. New York 2007, p. 104–110.

[12] Jan Broekman, "Individual, State and the Semiotics of Anarchy," Op. Cit., 2011.

[13] There are echoes here, as well, of Fyodor Dostoyevsky: *The Double: A Petersburg Poem*. 1846 (Constance Garnett, Tr.), available http://ebooks.adelaide.edu.au/d/dostoyevsky/d72d/. The government clerk who goes mad in the face of his double, an incarnation present, absent and opposite, one with apparent effect but no trace, suggests the solidity and porosity of the problem of the meaning of an object, like the state, or the corporation, at once in and outside of itself, at once represented by itself and constructed by and through others.

semiotic analysis surpasses even Marx' analysis of the ideological components of each State, Democracy, Economy or Corporation.

Consequently one *can* understand the inadequacy of language that describes this corporation. There is no language anymore to express the meaning of a corporation, in part, because language must describe an object that is also not itself. As such, meaning is not lost; it is instead simultaneously situated. The corporation is object (the corporate entity), sign (aggregation of economic activity), and interpretation (systematization of the forces of production, active agent of social, political, cultural and economic power). But it can also be object (property held by an owner in the form of shares or debt), sign (diversification of individual economic power) and interpretation (an extension of shareholder power manifested in its activities).

And this dynamic context provides the foundation for all expressions that an "I" can use embedded in one meaning expanded as a language in its own right. As such, there is not so much a loss of reference or meaning but a proliferation of both. *Technè* (as the object, law) mediates between *archè* and *telos*, embedding an-*archè* and nihilism as additional referents, the *technè* (now understood more in its sense as the craft, especially of law) of which is inter-subjective.[14] Roberta Kevelson understood the fundamental intersubjectivity of law in its aspect as justice. She noted that the principles of justice are "linked by means of itself as inter-subjective action, the changing context of institutions and values in an appropriately dynamic and not static manner."[15] Broekman substitutes the more nuanced notion of inter-activity for inter-subjectivity.[16] But it also suggests the construction of a semiotic square: start with a primary opposition: archè (S_1)—telos (S_2). Each then generates its own contradiction; < archè (S_1)—an-archè ($\sim S_1$) >, and < telos (S_2)—technè ($\sim S_2$) >. But it also generates its own complementary set as well: < archè (S_1)—technè ($\sim S_2$) >, and < telos (S_2)—an-archè ($\sim S_1$) > and its inversion: < archè (S_1) AND telos (S_2) > (for example the state); and < an-archè ($\sim S_1$) AND technè ($\sim S_2$) > (for example, the corporation).

The semiosis of the corporation is thus revealed, one that is grounded in symbolic and interpretive *poly-centricity*, which characterizes the subject involved as well as the functionality of each citizen in state-like and legally sustained economic constructs.[17] This poly-centricity, functionally crafted through law, was at the center

---

[14] On inter-subjectivity, see, e.g., Alex Gillespie: "The Intersubjective Nature of Symbols", in *Symbolic Transformation: The Mind In Movement Through Culture And Society* (Brady Wagoner (ed.), London: Routledge, 2009 p. 28: "words, or signals, often have different meanings depending upon who hears them, and which assumes that communication begins with impression rather than expression.").

[15] Roberta Kevelson: *Peirce, Science, Signs*. Op. Cit. p. 87.

[16] Jan M. Broekman, "Faces Face to Face", in: Broekman/Mootz III, (Eds) *The Semiotics of Law in Legal Education*. Op. Cit. 21, 51–53.

[17] Pushpanathan v. Canada (Minister of Citizenship and Immigration), [1998] 1 S.C.R. 982, ("a polycentric issue is one which involves a large number of interlocking and interacting interests and considerations." § 36).

of a recent U.S. Supreme Court case, Citizens United v. Federal Election Commission.[18] We consider the legal construction of the corporation as object, symbol and interpretation within multiple frameworks through a close examination of *Citizens United* , now understood as an expression of a complex polycentric semiosis. After this introduction, the next paragraph examines the case closely. We then draw together Citizen United's semiotic elements. The incarnation of the corporation, and its representation as simultaneously political person and property, that is, as *person and instrument*, signifies both the entity and the person it now simultaneously signifies in ways that suppress and transform both. *Citizens United* illuminates the object of the corporation as a site of primacy and purpose and also as the place without place or meaning. Within this space of simmering meaning, law assumes as "fictive" or as a necessary and constructive "legal fiction", a solidity as the enterprise it means to capture through its own craft. What is left is primacy (of the corporation) and purpose within disorder and the absence of meaning, a state of affairs well illustrated in the aftermath of the decision.

Citizens United Unveiled

On January 21, 2010, the US Supreme Court closely and bitterly divided on fundamental issues of constitutional political theory decided Citizens United v. Federal Elections Commission. Justice Kennedy authored the majority opinion in which all justices but Justice Thomas joined as to the issue of the constitutionality of the disclaimer and disclosure provisions. Justices Alito, Scalia and Thomas, and the Chief Justice joined that portion of the opinion dealing with the constitutionality of Section 441b. Justice Stevens, joined by Justices Ginsburg, Breyer and Sotomayor, filed an opinion concurring in part and dissenting from that portion dealing with the constitutionality of Section 441b and overruling *Austin*. Over several hundred pages of majority, concurring and dissenting opinions, the case raised and sought to resolve a number of complex and important issues of constitutional law. These include the constitutional contours of stare decisis, the scope of the First Amendment, the extent of a government's powers to regulate the processes of its elections, the proper scope and use of original sources in constitutional interpretation, and the prudential rules guiding the proper circumstances when issues raised in a case may be "constitutionalized," that is when a court may reach constitutional issue embedded in a case where resolution may be possible on non constitutional grounds. These issues impact the understanding of the American constitutional order and the political theories on which that order is grounded. *For this reason, the case is an important marker (in legal semiotic context) in the evolution of the construction of the political forms of the American Republic.* It is unlikely that the settlement of these issues as represented by the opinions of the justices in the majority will remain intact for long. These are

[18] Citizens United v. Federal Election Commission, 558 U.S. 08–205, (2010), 558 U.S. ——, 130 S.Ct. 876 (January 21, 2010)

extremely dynamic areas of law and there is no emerging consensus with respect to any of these issues. Yet they merely suggest rather than center on the *semiotics of the corporate form*. The treatment of each of these important issues suggest, in their own way, the playing out of the basic symbolic and interpretive assumptions that derive from the encounter with the object—corporation.

To a considerable extent, then, *Citizens United* is also a case touching on basic issues of corporate law. Central to the decision was a fundamental disagreement among the members of the Court as to political consequences of activity undertaken in corporate form. This rift reflects a deeper set of disagreements relating to the appropriate conceptualization of the corporation in political society and the regulatory consequences of that conceptualization. Central to the determinations of both majority and dissenting opinions are fundamentally distinct views of the nature of the corporation, and consequently, of the relationship between the state and the corporation as institution, property or a manifestation of state power.

In its modern form since the beginning of the twentieth century, the issue of corporate personality, the character and nature of a corporation that permits it to be constituted autonomously from shareholders, directors, employees or the state, has been hotly contested from time to time. By the end of the twentieth century, it could be argued with some confidence that three distinct views of the character of the corporation had emerged.[19]

1. *The corporation as autonomous institution*. Under this view, the corporation is understood to be an autonomous entity. This means more than that it is recognized as distinct, in law, from shareholders, creditors, directors and the like. Rather, it suggests that the corporation is as autonomous and independent of its stakeholders as the government of a state is distinct form its citizens. As a consequence, the corporation, as institution, can be understood as a distinct "person" in the sense that it must act (through its board of directors) to maximize its own welfare and interests distinct from those of its shareholders, officers and directors. That mandatory distinctness can be enforced through the mechanisms of corporate governance—fiduciary duty, derivative actions, control transactions and the like (we do not suggest the functional success of this view, merely its elaboration here). An *institutional* view of the corporation can be understood in shorthand as vesting the corporation with "personhood". The consequence, for law and policy, is a concentration on the powers and independence of the board of directors, and the preservation of the legitimacy of the board and its actions. The corporation, as a result, may acquire rights under public law in its own right, and (in the United States today) may participate even in the political life of the state. What about the responsible citizens?

2. *The corporation as property in the hands of its shareholders*. Under this view, the corporation is understood as an amalgamation of economic interest, as a convenience to the shareholders who come together to engage in profit oriented economic

[19] See, e.g., Katsuhito Iwai, "The Nature of the Business Corporation: Its Legal Structure and Economic Functions" in: *The Japanese Economic Review*, 53(3): 243–273 (2002)), discussed in: Larry Catá Backer: "Corporate Institutionalism and Fiduciary Duty: On Professor Katsuhito Iwai's Nominalistic and Realistic Corporations Model", *Law at the End of the Day*, July 10, 2006.

activity. Whether understood in its popular variant as a "nexus of contract" or by the shorthand reference to the aggregation of rights to income, assets and control represented by an equity interest in the corporation, this view understands the corporation as nothing more than an aggregation of these contractual-or property interests. As a consequence, the corporation cannot "speak" other than to express the views of those shareholders who control the corporate machinery. The corporation cannot exist autonomously of its stakeholders. The segregation of corporate assets and the governance mechanisms for communal ownership of enterprises does not produce a new and separate organism; rather it produces only a collective expression of individual will. The focus here is not on the entity but on the stakeholder (and usually principally the equity holder). The consequence, for law and policy, is to focus legal management of the firm on issues of shareholder power–shareholder democracy and participation in corporate governance. The public law rights of this understanding of the corporation is grounded firmly in the rights of stakeholders–corporations may have rights to property because its owners are accorded those rights and the corporation itself is the sort of property the ownership of which is accorded constitutional protection to its holders (the shareholders). What about the responsible citizens who happen to *not* be a stakeholder or shareholder?

3. *The corporation as a nexus of privileges and obligations* derived from and subject to the control of the state. The oldest conception of corporate personality, and one derived from the ancient notions of corporate concession from the superior feudatory lord to inferior vassal, now constituted in the abstract (as bodies corporate, with the supreme body corporate understood as bound up in the "person" of the state) is that the corporation is merely a vassal that represents a bundle of rights, privileges and obligations derived from the state. Corporations, in this variant, are understood as creatures of the states that have created and now regulate them. The principal obligation of these entities is to the state, and the state's interest. Chinese corporate law, for example, and some variants of corporate law in Europe, can be understood as grounded in this view. The interests of shareholders follow in importance that of the state. The regulatory and policy consequences of this view are to focus on the interests of the state and its management of the entity.[20] Again, one has to ask about the position and qualities of the responsible citizen in this context.

These fundamental differences in conception were neither accidental nor evidence of confusion. They are ancient and well considered positions on the nature of the corporation that are to some extent irreconcilable and give rise to substantially different constitutional and regulatory consequences.[21] *Citizens United* has effectively recast them anew. The effect of *Citizens United* is thus not merely confined to issues touching on the constitutional protections of speech rights, and the form of legitimate of constitutional jurisprudence. Rather, it will have potentially significant effects on

---

[20] See, e.g., Niemietz v. Germany, ECHR, Series A, No. 25-B, 16 E.H.R.R. 97 (1972).

[21] The differences, in modern form, were first well-exposed in First National Bank of Boston v. Bellotti, 435 U.S. 765 (1978), and contested in Austin v. Michigan Chamber of Commerce, 494 U. S. 652 (1990).

approaches to the regulation of corporations far beyond the constitutional framework in which the case was decided.

Facts in/of Citizens United

Law students as well as practicing lawyers are used to neglect the specific text-character of cases presented to them. Cases are legal texts, and are thus to be treated in semiotics as texts, loaded with their problematic reference to a reality they suggest to represent. One of the features of legal texts is, that they focus indistinctively between two different text layers, determined by Greimas and Kristeva as *phenotext* and *genotext*. The *phenotext* is the text surface as offered to the reader, and functioning as preferred subject for politicians to act accordingly. Buy two morning papers, which represent a different political viewpoint, and read the presentation of the same fact. It becomes clear how a surface text is the result of emphasis, choice, wording and policies meant to influence the reader in his or her political option. Watch two different TV stations when reporting the same occurrences, and the like conclusion will be made.

The *genotext* is a deep structure of each text, the engenderment of formulations, a process often within one or a limited group of authors. During the unfolding of this engenderment, a surface is created—often partially unintentional. If the phenotext is a production, often a mixture of reality and pretext, a façade, then the genotext is on the other hand an often concealed process, a search for expressiveness under influence of social and psychological forces.

The phenotext functions politically in society, the genotext emerges under the influence of dark powers and as individual decision-making. It is clear that both text types are influential in legal discourse: the texts of court decisions function as political orientation and reference material, the opinions of judges even before they are classified and published for instance as dissenting opinions, are an example of the genotext. It is extremely difficult to make a clear distinction between those two and to draw semiotic conclusions accordingly. We must make reference to facts[22] when analyzing Citizens United, but cannot offer two distinct text-fields in this complex reference.

The Case

1. The case arose from a challenge to certain provisions of federal law prohibiting entities from making expenditures for speech that advocated the election or defeat of political candidates.

[22] See Jan M. Broekman: "Legal Discourse and Legal Facts", Op. Cit., Milano, 1994 p. 181–201.

1a. Federal law prohibited corporations and unions from using their general treasury funds to make independent expenditures for speech defined as "electioneering communications" or for speech expressly advocating the election or defeat of a candidate for public office.[23] "Electioneering communications" were defined as "any broadcast, cable, or satellite communication" that "refers to a clearly identified candidate for Federal office" and is made within 30 days of a primary election,[24] and that is "publicly distributed."[25]
1b. However, corporations and unions may establish political action committees (PACs) for the purpose of engaging in such otherwise prohibited speech activity, as long as they complied with the substantial operational, monitoring and disclosure rules relating to PACs. The statutory prohibitions applied to for profit and not for profit corporations in equal measure. These regulations had been unsuccessfully challenged in some respects,[26] and earlier with respect to corporate expenditures,[27] and non-profit corporations.[28]
1c. With respect to disclaimer and disclosure, federal law also imposed requirements. "Under BCRA § 201, any person who spends more than $10,000 on electioneering communications within a calendar year must file a disclosure statement with the FEC. 2 U. S. C. § 434(f)(1). That statement must identify the person making the expenditure, the amount of the expenditure, the election to which the communication was directed, and the names of certain contributors. § 434(f)(2)."[29] BRCA Section 311 required that televised electioneering communications contain a disclaimer identifying the person or entity responsible for the communication.[30]

2. The plaintiff, *Citizens United* is a non-profit corporation supporting conservative causes and candidates.[31] It is a nonprofit corporation organized under the laws of

[23] 2 U.S.C. Section 441b (as amended by the Bipartisan Campaign Reform Act of 2002 Section 203).

[24] § 434(f)(3)(A).

[25] 11 CFR § 100.29(a)(2).

[26] McConnell v. Federal Election Commission, 540 U.S. 93 (2003).

[27] Austin v. Michigan Chamber of Commerce, 494 U. S. 652 (1990).

[28] Federal Election Commission v. Massachusetts Citizens for Life, Inc., 479 U. S. 238 (1986) (MCFL) (where the Court found unconstitutional only that portion of Section 441b that applied to nonprofit corporations that were formed for the sole purpose of promoting political ideas, did not engage in business activities, and did not accept contributions from for-profit corporations or labor unions. Id., at 263–264).

[29] Citizens United, supra, slip op., at 51.

[30] Id., at 50–51.

[31] According to the civil society organization Source Watch, information available http://www.-sourcewatch.org/index.php?title=Citizens_United, the civil society organization Citizens United was created in November 1988 by conservative activist Floyd G. Brown, who served as its founding president until 2000 and was associated with aggressive media campaigns against political candidates deemed to be liberal. See Floyd G. Brown, Source Watch, available http://www.sourcewatch.org/index.php?title = Floyd_G._Brown.

Virginia and tax-exempt under section 501(c)(4) of the Internal Revenue Code.[32] It has a budget of $12 million, received mostly as donations form individuals.[33] It accepts a small amount of funds from for profit corporations.

2a. Ironically, before filing its case, it had participated in an effort to use the provisions it challenged in this case to stop distribution of Michael Moore's *Fahrenheit 9/11* in a complaint to the Federal Election Commission.[34] In January 2008, *Citizens United* released a film entitled *Hillary: The Movie*. We refer to the film as 'Hillary'. It is a 90-minute documentary about then-Senator Hillary Clinton, who was a candidate in the Democratic Party's 2008 Presidential primary elections. Hillary mentions Senator Clinton by name and depicts interviews with political commentators and other persons, most of them quite critical of Senator Clinton.[35]

Citizens United released this cinematic effort in theaters and on DVD. Eventually it sought to arrange additional distribution through a video-on-demand service. *Citizens United* intended to make this service, and a series of advertisements publicizing the film, available within 30 days of the 2008 primary elections.[36] Fearing that these efforts would run afoul of Section 441b, *Citizens United* sought declaratory and injunctive relief against the Federal Selection Commission. Specifically, it sought to have both Section 441b and the disclosure provisions in Sections 201 and 311 of the BCRA declared unconstitutional as applied to Hillary. "The District Court denied *Citizens United*'s motion for a preliminary injunction, and then granted the FEC's motion for summary judgment.[37] The Supreme Court noted probable jurisdiction[38] and then compelled reargument to consider whether the Court should overrule "either or both Austin and the part of McConnell which addresses the facial validity of 2 U. S. C. § 441b."[39]

---

[32] Citizens United is affiliated with The Presidential Coalition, a 501(c)(4), and the 2007 Conservative Victory Committee, a Section 527 political action committee. Previously, it was affiliated with the National Security Political Action Committee (National Security PAC), Presidential Victory Committee and Americans for Bush. Citizens United is led by David Bossie, who has served as president since 2000. Its offices are on Pennsylvania Avenue in the Capitol hill area of Washington, D.C. SourceWatch, Citizens United, available at http://www.sourcewatch.org/index.php?title=Citizens_United. These organization have all been identified as self styled conservative organizations.

[33] Citizens United, supra, slip op. at 2.

[34] Susan Jones, "Michael Moore Film Violates Campaign Finance Law, Group Alleges," (formerly *Conservative News Service; now Cybercast News Service*), June 23, 2004).

[35] Citizens United, supra, slip op. at 2.

[36] Id., at 4.

[37] 530 F. Supp. 2d 274 (DC 2008) (per curiam).

[38] Citizens United, 555 U.S.—(2008)."

[39] Id., at 5.

2b. In a lengthy discussion,[40] the Supreme Court determined that it could not avoid the constitutional issue. It overruled Austin with respect to both its limitations on non-profit and for-profit corporate political expenditures, and that part of McConnell that extended Section 441b's restrictions on independent corporate expenditures as inconsistent with the protections of the First Amendment. Lastly, it upheld the disclaimer and disclosure requirements of BRCA Sections 201 and 311. The discussion that follows looks at the opinion solely from a very limited perspective. It considers the way in which different conceptions of the corporation contributed to the arguments deployed by majority and dissenting opinions.

Privileging the Corporation as Autonomous Entity

The majority opinion suggests the consequential power of a conception of corporation as autonomous entity in the context of constitutional rights adjudication. Justice Kennedy is able to frame his argument—focused on the prohibition of speech limitations applied to corporations—only by developing a set of premises that together constitute a corporation as an entity capable of independent action. If corporations are not autonomous, then the rights they claim, and especially the constitutional protections extended to them, would have to derive from those for whom corporations act. If, on the other hand, corporations are understood as entities separate from others, then it may be extended protection ion its own right. This distinction is crucial for the elaboration of the majority's argument. It suggests that Section 441b constitutes an outright ban on speech, backed by criminal sanctions. It is a ban that is a function of the identity of the speaker (a corporation) though not a function of the nature of the origin of the speech (in collective speech). Thus PACs are permitted speech rights where corporations are denied them. On the other hand, PACs were understood as being burdensome because of the nature of the rules for their operation.

Of course, this would make no difference if corporations were assumed to be no more than the sum of statutory privilege or the creature of the state. In either case, all corporate attributes would be understood as privileges rather than rights. Moreover if corporations were understood as property, then the fact that they could not "speak" for themselves would be of little moment—their real voices could be heard when shareholders chose each to speak as they liked. Corporate speech, in this sense, would merely duplicate shareholder speech, and thus would not have an independent value. "We find no basis for the proposition that, in the context of political speech, the Government may impose restrictions on certain disfavored speakers. Both history and logic lead us to this conclusion." The issue, then, reduces itself to a simple one: do corporations (or other aggregations) constitute rights bearing "speakers" for purposes of constitutional analysis. The Court determined that they were. To get there they necessarily embraced a particular understanding of the nature of the

[40] Id., at 5–57.

corporation. We add five essential points halfway between geno-and phenotext in Justice Kennedy's analysis for the majority opinion:

1. He starts with the general proposition that the "Court has recognized that First Amendment protection extends to corporations."[41] He cites among a slew of cases. This is noteworthy, if only because Bellotti was among the first cases where the majority opinion explicitly relied on an institutional conception of the corporation—as an independent and autonomous entity distinct from its stakeholders and capable of independent expression—in reaching their holding that a state could not ban corporate expenditures relating to referenda put to voters. Justice Kennedy builds on this by suggesting that this proposition has been extended to political speech in general.
2. Against this judicial movement toward protection of corporate political speech, Justice Kennedy identified a legislative movement toward restriction of corporate speech in political campaigns. These courts increasingly found distasteful to its own views of the scope of political speech holders. It is in this context that Austin is considered, and characterized as an aberrational judicial moment. Its aberration was precisely in its privileging of a view of the corporation that suggested both its power to corrupt through aggregations of power and its in authenticity as a legitimate autonomous speaker. Justice Kennedy constructs a notion of the corporation as an entity substantially different from that on which both the statute, and Justice Stevens' dissent, is based.
3. He furthermore grounds his rejection of the anti-distortion rationale on an acceptance of a parity among individual and corporate speakers. Each is treated as independent, autonomous and a co-equal contributor to political discussion. But that parity requires acceptance of another premise—that corporations contribute in their own right rather than serve as amplification of the views of individuals who have a stake in the enterprise. He notes: "If the First Amendment has any force, it prohibits Congress from fining or jailing citizens, or associations of citizens, for simply engaging in political speech. If the anti-distortion rationale were to be accepted, however, it would permit Government to ban political speech simply because the speaker is an association that has taken on the corporate form."[42] Because there is a parity between individual and corporate speech, there is no basis for distinguishing between speech on issues (permitted in Bellotti) and speech advocating the election of a candidate (prohibited in Austin). For this purpose, Justice Kennedy specifically rejected the idea of corporations as a nexus of privilege or as a construct of the state—and therefore subject to whatever limitations the state might choose to attach to that existence.
4. For those who have been arguing that there is little difference between political parties—as special purpose political corporations in the business of securing political power for their followers—and corporations in the business of making money or fomenting some sort of social, cultural or other objectives, his argument

[41] Id., at 25–32.

[42] Id., at 33.

suggests that corporations thus re-imagined might well be burdened with political obligations. Yet this is something that has been rejected by the very people who have embraced the notion of corporate institutionalism for the purpose of freeing these entities from the limitations of participation in the political process. At some point the contradictions inherent in that position—that corporations are purely private enterprises that cannot have political obligations without interfering with the democratic organization of the state while simultaneously holding that corporations have a protected constitutional right to participate in the political process—will have to be confronted. To some extent that process is already occurring at the international level.[43] The position of Justice Kennedy here will make those efforts much more difficult to resist.

5. Lastly, and perhaps most importantly from the perspective of the corporate law perspective of the case, Justice Kennedy rejected the argument that the provisions were valid as a basis for the protection of shareholders form their managers. Rejected, in this way, was the idea that corporations are passive shells that reflect the views of their managers, and that any use of corporate funds for purposes other than to make money might well misuse corporate funds to the detriment of shareholders. This conception, grounded in the idea of corporation as property in the hands of shareholders, was rejected in favor of the view of corporation as autonomous institution with the principal obligation to preserve itself rather than the interests of its shareholders. "There is, furthermore, little evidence of abuse that cannot be corrected by shareholders "through the procedures of corporate democracy." (quoting Bellotti, 435 U. S., at 794) Those reasons are sufficient to reject this shareholder protection interest; and, moreover, the statute is both under-inclusive and over-inclusive."[44]

Left unexplored is a consequence of the decision—the ability of foreign individuals and states to participate in the American democratic process by acquiring "citizenship" and speech rights through ownership of American corporations. Justice Kennedy is at the end of his conceptual rope on this point. He merely points to 2 U.S.C: Section 441e (forbidding political contributions by foreign nationals), suggesting, that this fear is not cured by retaining Section 441b. Yet this is hardly satisfying as a matter of corporate law. And the ideals of the nature of the corporation as autonomous entity actually suggest that it will be exceeding hard to prevent

[43] See, e.g., Special Representative of the Secretary-General on the issue of human rights and transnational corporations and other business enterprises. Business and human rights: Towards operationalizing the "protect, respect and remedy" framework, at 15, U.N. Doc. A/HRC/11/13 (April 22, 2009).

[44] Citizens United, supra, at 46. He elaborates: "As to the first, if Congress had been seeking to protect dissenting shareholders, it would not have banned corporate speech in only certain media within 30 or 60 days before an election. A dissenting shareholder's interests would be implicated by speech in any media at any time. As to the second, the statute is over-inclusive because it covers all corporations, including nonprofit corporations and for-profit corporations with only single shareholders. As to other corporations, the remedy is not to restrict speech but to consider and explore other regulatory mechanisms. The regulatory mechanism here, based on speech, contravenes the First Amendment."

foreign participation in the political process on the basis of the corporate conception at the heart of the decision. Corporations are deemed to be citizens of the state of their incorporation. The citizenship of their shareholders is not deemed to affect that citizenship, or the rights of the entity to assert those citizenship rights. There are exceptions, with respect to ownership of sensitive industries. But even there, it is usually the case that the implementation of approaches safeguards is usually enough to satisfy most limitations.[45] Yet, though corporations are deemed to speak independently of their owners, their views would necessarily be shaped by the preferences of those owners, especially if they own a sizeable stake in the enterprise. This issue will become much more pressing when, for example, it is determined that an American corporation, with substantial expenditures in a political campaign, is a wholly owned subsidiary of a Chinese or Norwegian sovereign wealth fund, which has announced its intention to be an active shareholder (something applauded as a matter of American corporate policy) to induce the corporation to further its own political and policy objectives.

Privileging the Shareholder

It fascinates in this context, how Justice Stevens' dissent offers a conceptual basis of corporate organization substantially different from that on which Justice Kennedy's majority opinion was grounded. The dissent suggests the consequential power of a conception of corporation as property in the hands of its shareholders in the context of constitutional rights adjudication. Understood on the basis of this foundation, the focus of Justice Stevens' dissent becomes both clear and inevitable. Justice Stevens understands the case as one of reasonable management of corporate speech in the context of the election of natural persons to office.[46] While Justice Kennedy privileges the corporation as entity, Justice Stevens privileges the shareholder. For him the corporation is less entity than the nexus of shareholder interests, regularized and managed through law. The conceptual foundations of corporations at the heart of this dissent could not be more distinct from that of the majority opinion.

More relevant for the corporate law implications of the opinion are Justice Stevens efforts to attack three of the bases of the majority's argument. "First, the Court claims that Austin and McConnell have "banned" corporate speech. Second, it claims that the First Amendment precludes regulatory distinctions based on speaker identity, including the speaker's identity as a corporation. Third, it claims that Austin and McConnell were radical outliers in our First Amendment tradition and our campaign finance jurisprudence. Each of these claims is wrong."[47] But that effort is grounded on

---

[45] See Eben Kaplan, Foreign Ownership of U.S. Infrastructure, Council on Foreign Relations, Feb. 13, 2007, available: http://www.cfr.org/publication/10092/foreign_ownership_of_us_infrastructure.html.

[46] Citizens United: Stevens, J., concurring in part and dissenting.

[47] Id., at 23.

a vastly different understanding of the corporate form. Justice Stevens first suggests that the idea that Austin and McConnell ban corporate speech is wrong because corporate shareholders and executives remain free to aggregate their resources to assert speech rights. Central to this argument is the idea that there is an identity of interest between corporations and their principal stakeholders, or better put, that corporations do not speak for themselves, they serve to amplify the speech of the individuals who control them. That conflation, that idea that corporations, as property in the hands of shareholders is incapable of autonomous activity is further refined by Justice Stevens in this context.

Justice Stevens offers a similar argument against the "second pillar of the Court's opinion is its assertion that "the Government cannot restrict political speech based on the speaker's . . . identity."[48] The crux of that effort is the suggestion that Justice Kennedy misread Bellotti. "Like its paeans to unfettered discourse, the Court's denunciation of identity-based distinctions may have rhetorical appeal but it obscures reality." First, Justice Stevens reminds us that the Supreme Court has approved identity-based restrictions on speech rights in a number of contexts. "When such restrictions are justified by a legitimate governmental interest, they do not necessarily raise constitutional problems."[49] This applies even in the election context. Here, the idea that corporations are not distinguishable from the individuals that control them drives the difference in conceptual approach.

Notice the importance of the embrace of a particular understanding of corporate nature to the force of this argument. Rejected here is the idea of corporate existence as an autonomous institution embraced by Justice Kennedy. *Corporations are derivative entities. They speak only as the individuals who control them desire*. As such, there is no such thing as corporate speech per se. There is only speech by individuals through the corporations they control. "Under the majority's view, I suppose it may be a First Amendment problem that corporations are not permitted to vote, given that voting is, among other things, a form of speech."[50]

Justice Stevens devotes a substantial portion of his dissent to the idea that Austin and McConnell are not outliers. Central to this argument is a discussion of the original understanding of the role of corporations in American political life. There is substantial irony here and a bit of role reversal. It is Justice Stevens, rather than Justice Scalia, who is the champion of arguments from original understanding in this context. No wonder. Notions of private modern corporations as autonomous institutions are hardly more than a century old. To mold the two-century old First Amendment to changing notions of corporations barely a century old would appear to be a matter of legislative rather than judicial prerogative under the argument usually made by Justice Scalia. But here, it is Justice Stevens rather than Justice Scalia who advances this conservative argument, and who thus, exposes the radical nature of the interpretation of the majority (and with it the importance of the new conception of the corporation for constitutional and statutory law). Justice Scalia

---

[48] Id., at 28.

[49] Id., at 29.

[50] Id., at 33–34.

is put in the uncomfortable position of arguing in the style of those he has spent a lifetime criticizing.[51]

Having thus contextualized the constitutional framework in light of a distinctive rationalization of the nature of the corporation, Justice Stevens then turns to the defense of the statute on anticorruption, anti-distortion, and shareholder protection rationales. Like his prior arguments, these are substantially informed by a conception of the corporation as a nexus of contract, a shareholder flow through and a confluence of statutory privilege that militates against treating the entity as an independent organization with autonomous consciousness and speech.

Thus, in constructing his anti corruption argument, Justice Stevens draws on his understanding of the distinctiveness of the corporate nature. "Business corporations must engage the political process in instrumental terms if they are to maximize shareholder value. The unparalleled resources, professional lobbyists, and single-minded focus they bring to this effort, I believed, make quid pro quo corruption and its appearance inherently more likely when they (or their conduits or trade groups) spend unrestricted sums on elections".[52]

One is left here with a different framing structure that marks the relationships between state-corporation-shareholder-citizen-gatekeeper-consumer-society. If there is no corporate democracy because there is no corporation because there are no autonomous sources for institutional activity, then there can be no question about the exercise of speech by an enterprise that is itself merely property. Even less is the need for the protection of speech for an enterprise that is itself little more than the receptacle of a devolution of authority from the state. Indeed in this later case, the argument would suggest that the state is itself controlling speech through the corporate vehicles it ultimately controls. This would produce the ultimate subversion of the state.

Taken together, then, Justice Stevens constructs a solid framework supporting diminished constitutional protection for corporations and enhanced regulatory power by states. But this framework is grounded on notions on corporate nature that privilege the property aspects of corporate nature. It embraces shareholder prominence and the idea that corporations do not speak—they rather magnify the voices of those who control them. As such, they can more readily serve as vehicles to corrupt the political process by disguising the sources of political speech, and amplifying the voices of some individuals over others. It is a framework that suggests that corporations are less 'bearers of rights' than are 'the individuals who hold interests in those entities'. Lastly, it suggests that enhanced regulation is critical to protect shareholders against managers and directors, against whom most shareholders have little real power to control. This is a view of corporations substantially different from that of Justice Kennedy. And it is this difference of view, rather than jurisprudential differences about the nature of the First Amendment, that informs the differences in approach.

---

[51] See, Citizens United, supra, Scalia, J., concurring, at 1–9.

[52] Id., at 64.

Semiotic Elements

Roberta Kevelson reminds us of the rhetorical character of property, including corporations. The relationship individuals have toward property, tangible and intangible, is the consequence of what we say about those objects.[53] Semiotics, then, provides a basis for grasping the way in which things can be reconstructed as other than what they seem,[54] but in ways that also reinforce the common understanding. As Kevelson explained: "All human societies have developed complex systems of both verbal and non-verbal sign systems which are not static but which evolve continuously to correspond with and to represent changing social norms and the evolving, growing social consciousness of any given community."[55] Signs, then, produce meaning, which in turn is meant to deepen a definition and understanding of the sign that aligns with the meaning assigned to it by the interpreters of meaning. Within law systems, this self-referencing and self-reinforcing enterprise, produces both autonomy and definition that is dependent on itself but with references to others.[56]

But that understanding of meaning is itself not understandable in relation to a fixed point of meaning. As Lazzarato recently suggested the exploration of dual registers of corporate semiotics. "The first is the register of "representation" and "signification" or "production of meaning", both of which are organized by signifying semiotics (language) with the purpose of producing the "subject", the "individual", the "I". The second is the machine register organized by a signifying semiotics (such as money, analog or digital machines that produce images, sounds and information, the equations, functions, diagrams of science, music, etc.), which "can bring into play signs which have an additional symbolic or signifying effect, but whose actual functioning is neither symbolic nor signifying ". This second register is not aimed at subject constitution but at capturing and activating pre-subjective and pre-individual elements (affects, emotions, perceptions) to make them function like components or cogs in the semiotic machine of capital."[57]

In this sense, the semiotics of the corporation implicates an understanding of the cultural processes or communication, each of the distinct processes of which is structured by its underlying system of significations.[58] These more precisely suggest

---

[53] Roberta Kevelson: "Property as Rhetoric in Law", 4 *Cardozo Studies in Law and Literature* 189–206 (1992).

[54] "When—on the basis of an underlying rule—something actually presented to the perception of the addressee *stands for* something else, there is *signification*," Umberto Eco: *A Theory of Semiotics*, Indiana UP, 1976, p. 8.

[55] Roberta Kevelson: *The Law as a System of Signs*. Op. Cit.,1988.

[56] Roberta Kevelson: *Peirce Science, Signs*. Op. Cit.: "Justice in an involving, open-ended concept of a global community must be regarded as a method of art and science capable of describing itself." p. 87).

[57] Maurizio Lazzarato, 'Semiotic Pluralism' and the New Government of Signs. Homage to Félix Guattari", (Mary O'Neill, trans.) *EIPCP (European Institute For Progressive Cultural Policies) Multilingual WebJournal*(June 2006). Available http://eipcp.net/transversal/0107/lazzarato/en.

[58] Umberto Eco: *A Theory of Semiotics*. Op. Cit.1976, p. 8.

the polycentrism of the extractions of meanings of the corporation that are at once the construction of what is said about them and what they say about themselves to others.

Theory, though, is hard to understand without context, one that *Citizens United* again provides. Having understood the process of legal signification of the corporation through the opinions in *Citizens United*, the American political elite suggests the complexities of that signification in the arena of cultural communication.[59] The stage for this illustration is provided by the 2012 American Presidential campaign. In the summer of 2012, the former US governor Mitt Romney was on the campaign trail for nomination by the Republican Party as its Presidential candidate. He caused a bit of a stir while campaigning among the people of Iowa in search of credibility and signs of popular support for his presidential ambitions. The object of interest was Mr. Romney's effort to describe his sense of the character of the corporation and to contextualize that characterization within the framework of his campaign policy positions. Appropriately, it seems, the comments were delivered at the Iowa State Fair,[60] an entertainment extravaganza.

As reported by Philip Rucker,[61] the colloquy in context went something like this:

> Romney's appearance at the fair's soapbox grew unusually testy when a few angry people heckled the Republican presidential candidate over his declaration not to raise taxes. They urged the campaign front-runner to increase taxes on the wealthy to help fund such entitlement programs as Social Security and Medicare.
> Romney explained that one way to fulfill promises on entitlement programs is to "raise taxes on people," but before he could articulate his position on not raising taxes, someone interrupted.
> "Corporations!" a protester shouted, apparently urging Romney to raise taxes on corporations that have benefited from loopholes in the tax code. "Corporations!"
> "Corporations are people, my friend," Romney said.
> Some people in the front of the audience shouted, "No, they're not!"
> "Of course they are," Romney said. "Everything corporations earn ultimately goes to people. Where do you think it goes?"[62]

---

[59] Eco correctly distinguishes between systems of signification, which presuppose a cultural semiotics of the sort Kevelson explored, Kevelson, *Property as Rhetoric,* Op. Cit., with systems of communication, which is built on its own semiotics. Eco, *A Theory of Semiotics*, *supra*, at 9.

[60] Romney Questioned on Social Security and Medicare: GOP Presidential Hopefuls Campaign in Iowa, C-Span, Aug. 11, 2012, available http://www.c-span.org/Events/GOP-Presidential-Hopefuls-Campaign-in-Iowa/10737423434–6/ ("Mitt Romney was first up at the Des Moines Register's soap box booth at the Iowa State Fair. During a question and answer session with the audience after his speech, he was confronted by questioners on how to save social security, Medicare and Medicaid without any loss of benefits. He again stated that he will not raise taxes.").

[61] Philip Rucker: Mitt Romney says 'corporations are people' at Iowa State Fair, Washington Post, Aug. 11, 2011, available http://www.washingtonpost.com/politics/mitt-romney-says-corporations-are-people/2011/08/11/gIQABwZ38I_story.html.

[62] Id. An alternative version of the events is described in Michael P. Falcone and Z. Byron Wolf, Mitt Romney At Iowa State Fair: 'Corporations Are People, My Friend', ABC News, August 12, 2011. The moment was also recorded and, to no one's surprise, posted to YouTube: Available at http://www.youtube.com/watch?v=KlPQkd_AA6c.

Romney's remarks were useful, because he was both precisely correct, and sadly misleading. Yet that combination of precision and sad misdirection also marks the legal framework of legal personality in the United States. Romney reminds us, that the issue of corporate personality remains in a state of confusion in the United States. Or better put, Americans have over the last century or more, failed to arrive at any sort of consensus about corporate personality, the nature of the corporation, and develop a coherent legal architecture on the basis of that consensus. As a consequence, Romney has provided a somewhat pathetic articulation both of the confusion in American policy and its significant consequences for discussion.

But semiotic theory reminds us that Romney merely exposed the complex and incoherent relationship among the corporation and those people and things that both interpret the corporate essence and are interpreted in turn by it. On the one hand, Romney was right when he suggested that corporations are people, at least in the sense that in the U.S. corporations are sometimes understood as autonomous institutions capable of formulating and pursuing their own interests (and defending them) necessarily independent of those of its stakeholders, including its shareholders. But Romney was also right to suggest that everything corporations earn ultimately goes to people, at least in the sense that U.S. corporations are sometimes understood as property in the hands of their stakeholders (and principally their shareholders). The corporation, in this case, represents a useful vessel for the aggregation of the collective rights to income, assets and control, of a number of individuals who have come together for a joint enterprise for which the corporation serves as its vehicle. And yet again, Romney was correct to suggest that corporations derive their signification from the state, that is, that the state ultimately defines the character of the corporation through its own intervention in the construction of the entity and the conferral of rights and obligations on the enterprise.

It is in this semiotic context that Romney's remarks acquire a different completion. Romney is correct to observe that corporations are people—to the extent he is seeking to reference the idea that corporations are institutions that exist autonomously from its stakeholders. But that is precisely *not* what Romney appears to mean. He insists that corporations are people, that is: autonomous, because everything corporations earn goes to people—in other words corporations are autonomous entities because they are property in the hands of their shareholders! This effects a perverse conflation between two wholly inconsistent understandings of corporate character. In effect, Romney's description is ridiculous when taken together, but each of its two parts, when considered separately, in themselves are substantially correct. Each is a reflection of equally legitimate understandings of corporate character well embedded in American law, politics and culture. Romney's confusion, of course, and his heroic efforts to perform an impossible conceptual merger, reflects the confused (or perhaps incoherent) state of American approaches to the issue of corporate character.

Put in a different way: the "moment that the game of intertwined interpretations gets underway, the text compels one to reconsider the usual codes and their possibilities. Every text threatens the codes but at the same time gives them strength."[63]

[63] Eco: *A Theory of Semiotics*, Op. cit., p. 274.

The difficulty, apparent in *Citizens United*, is that when multiple games are at play, and the intertwining touches codes and their inverse, the simple process of semiosis loses direction. Romney appears to understand that corporations can be understood both as autonomous institutional actors distinct from their shareholders and as property in the hands of those shareholders. But he doesn't understand (and here he is probably representative of many public officials) that these views are distinct and represent different sets of assumptions about the relationship between corporations, their stakeholders, society and the state. He also cannot resolve the tension inherent in an object, the interpretive fields of which encompass distinct plans of understanding simultaneously. Because that is the ultimate difficulty here—Romney has exposed the corporation and its own inverted *doppelgänger*[64].

We have discovered that the corporation is no longer a corporation as we knew it, but we do not lose or forget the name—corporation. Indeed, the opposite occurs, the corporation becomes a larger space within which meaning is extracted and imposed. The corporation becomes a site, on object, sign and signifier connecting multiple interpretive dimensions. It signifies itself through itself and its relations with its officers, directors, investors, and the state, where meaning proceeds from the corporation outward. But it is also signified through the same relationships, but meaning now proceeds outward from shareholder to enterprise, officers, directors, and the state. Or it can serve as a reflection of the larger corporate body from which it may proceed, where meaning is derived from outside corporation, shareholder, officers and directors, that is, where it proceeds outward from ordering systems of law. The corporation is both the name individuals ("I") live in and also one that is itself an aggregation of this "I." But it is an unstable and dynamic object and sign; not just a name, but also and simultaneously the name of its opposite.

This is the object of semiotics itself: the corporation is constituted as an object by the operation of law, in part, and the aggregated desires of its stakeholders, systematized within the space denominated "corporation."[65] That creation is, in part a function of the extension of the fiction of the legal subject to the corporation. Legal subjectivity is extended to the enterprise autonomously of its constituent parts and its organizational realities—much like the state is understood as distinct from the mass of its citizens from which it derives sovereignty yet upon whom it may act by depriving any of them of life, liberty or property in accordance with the system, the exercise of the rules of which threatens but gives strength to it.[66]

The result is also challenging because the act of incarnation, *of allowing the corporation to stand for something else* produces a wider change in signification and causes tension within interpretive systems grounded in cultures of the living (with the exception of the state). In effect, the incarnation of the corporation (to an extent far more immediate than the similar incarnation of the state) exchanges the living

[64] See W. Menninghaus: *Unendliche Verdoppelung,* (Op. Cit.), 1987.

[65] See, Larry Catá Backer, "The Drama Of Corporate Law: Corporate Narrative Between Policy And Law", 2009 *Michigan State Law Review* 1111, Reviewing: David A. (Bert) Westbrook: *Between Citizen And State: An Introduction To The Corporation.* Boulder, Co, Paradigm Press 2007.

[66] Paraphrasing Eco, Op. Cit. p.274.

for the widening of the grammatical category of the first person singular (the "I") of the triadic relation at the heart of semiotics. But it also hides the first person singular within the intangible aggregation of the corporate form. This also produces an objectification of the individual and the corporation that is distinct from the interpretation of the natural "I". But it also constitutes a part of the "I" of others. The corporate "I" fuels the suppression of the personal "I" and can be suppressed by this personal "I" as well. This produces a metaphysics that can be understood as a normative framework deeply culturally embedded, a politics of thought that illustrates Kevelson's fundamental understanding of the dependent relationships between object, sign and signification, rooted in the perceptions not of the individual but of the mass. Yet as such, it is a fractured political thought space—the masses do not speak in the singular. Objects, signs, and signification are fractured. The facets of this fractured crustal reflects and is reflected by the "I" of itself and of those with which it relates. It is, the corporation, in other words, that illustrates the metaphysical space of *archè* and *telos* (place and purpose) and its inverse, unstructured space without purpose. The modern, macroeconomic, globalizing subject, the "I" to come in the forthcoming decades of the Occident, has to appropriate all features of the corporation as discussed in the above paragraphs. The "I" has to abolish the limits of its own body and to en-*corpor*-ate itself in the subject figure that once was captured by the Leviathan. This *change of corpus* seems to decide about the effects of the semiotic foundations of politics.

Law, Semiotics, and the Corporation: A Politics Paradigm

The semiotic challenges of *Citizens United* are well expressed through the mechanics of law. Considered itself as an object capable of signification, *Citizens United* is providing a metaphysical space that takes its interpretant from *archè* and *telos* to anarchy and nihilism, and vice versa. *Citizens United* presents corporation as a site of primacy and purpose and also as the place without place or meaning. For that purpose three aspects are considered. (a) The first is the relationship of corporation to monitoring and disclosure—acts that both solidify and dissolve the corporation into permeable space in the frame of *constitutional* consequences. (b) The second is the relationship of corporation to the regulatory system it confronts in the context of *regulatory* consequences. (c) The third is the global citizenship of corporations; corporations now represent a new sort of semiotic being both within and outside the state, a layering of semiotic meaning with extraordinary consequences on the penetration of the processes of the American republic by a new construct—not citizen, not foreign.

(Sub a) Constitutional Consequences. Ironically, within all this division, one strong consensus position emerged—all justices other than Justice Thomas agreed on the strong state interest in monitoring and transparency. While this has immediate and specific relevance to the implementation of election procedures, it also has potentially profound importance for corporate law, both within the domestic legal orders of states

and in the construction of transnational systems of corporate governance. In rejecting the challenge to the disclaimer (transparency) and monitoring rules, Justice Kennedy spoke broadly about the value of disclosure as it relates to corporate operation:

Monitoring and disclosure itself provides a sign with a signification much altered by the development of its techniques.[67] Within this construct, *the corporation is object with signification on speech.* In other words: *corporations produce speech.* Thus constructed, as a site for the production of a good that itself is important in the production of an other good—political action—at the heart of the functioning of the Republic (which itself is an interpretive construct)—the corporation becomes central to the production of a political good. "The First Amendment protects political speech; and disclosure permits citizens and shareholders to react to the speech of corporate entities in a proper way. This transparency enables the electorate to make informed decisions and give proper weight to different speakers and messages."

These values appear to represent both a judicial and legislative consensus at the state and federal levels.[68] It suggests that irrespective of the understanding of the nature of the corporation, disclosure, transparency and monitoring are now deemed an essential element in the regulation of the relationships between the corporation, its stakeholders, the state, and other parties. Monitoring and transparency are central to the functioning of entities. It deepens its autonomy from its stakeholders, and furthers the elaboration of the institutional character of the organization. It suggests a direct relationship between theories of accountability for governmental entities and corporate entities. That direct relationship may carry over to other areas of governance–from the imposition of public duties, to the nature of the duties of directors to the enterprise rather than to shareholders as one of many stakeholders in the enterprise.

(Sub b) Regulatory Consequences: Corporations are simultaneously property in the hands of their shareholders and autonomous institutions in their constitution and operation. Still more, corporations exist both as the reification of a nexus or network of contract among the individuals (and other entities) with a stake in its operations, and as a nexus or web of privileges conferred on it (as an entity) by the state through which it is organized and as a result of which it (again as entity) owes certain duties). Yet *poly-contextuality* (even in the organization of corporate governance) *does not necessarily imply anarchy*. Rather, it suggests a complexity in the relationships between the state–as the ultimate national body corporate–and other aggregations of

---

[67] With the advent of the Internet, prompt disclosure of expenditures can provide shareholders and citizens with the information needed to hold corporations and elected officials accountable for their positions and supporters. Shareholders can determine whether their corporation's political speech advances the corporation's interest in making profits, and citizens can see whether elected officials are "'in the pocket' of so-called moneyed interests." 540 U. S., at 259 (opinion of Scalia, J.); see MCFL, supra, at 261.

[68] See Larry Catá Backer: "The Duty to Monitor: Emerging Obligations of Outside Lawyers and Auditors to Detect and Report Corporate Wrongdoing Beyond the Federal Securities Laws" *77 St. John's Law Review* 919 (2003), reprinted 53(4) *Defense L.J.* 671 (2004).

power, which the state may recognize or prosecute.[69] This complexity also suggests that consistency in the construction of relationships between corporations and the state, between legal regimes and corporate organizations may be impossible. Rather it may be more useful to understand corporate character as a function of the relationship within which it is relevant. Thus, for example, as between shareholders and corporations, corporations might be best understood as property with respect to shareholdings, but as entity with respect to the control rights of shareholders. But that flexibility, or multi-contextuality, provides little comfort within the one size fits all framework of conventional lawmaking. Other have suggested that that a hierarchy of character may be necessary, but that the corporate character privileged in any state will be a function of the economic culture of that state.[70]

(*Sub c*) *Global consequences.* Important is here the ability of foreign individuals and states to participate in the American democratic process by acquiring "citizenship" and speech rights through ownership of American corporations. Here *Citizens United* confronts Kevelson's semiotic systemicity in polycentric form. The legal opinion in *Citizens United* permits the construction of an entity that can simultaneously belong in multiple sign-symbol systems. Consider the example of a Chinese national, who is a member of the Chinese Communist Party and duty bound to advance the CCP Party line, purchases a controlling interest in a company chartered in Delaware and operating solely in the United States. Who directs the U.S. corporation? What is the U.S. corporation's citizenship? To what extent can it be separated from its owner, a natural person citizen elsewhere? To what extent does it matter that this owner has a direct and instrumental relationship with a significant stakeholder in the governmental apparatus of another state? The English courts had a solution over a century ago;[71] the company and its shareholder are distinct.[72] Yet the formal interpretation belies a sense that the functional reality will be different—the Chinese owner will treat the U.S. corporation like an instrument of his higher obligations. In the context of Citizens United, would this mean that U.S. law would effectively permit the Chinese government to directly participate in U.S. political campaigns through its direct or indirect ownership of U.S. corporations? Where multiple"I"s are stacked and the stacking applies across borders, the idea of "I" becomes not merely intersubjective but permeable. In that context, lawyers cannot make meaning in one context without affecting others. Decision without semiosis produces confusion.

---

[69] See, Larry Catá Backer: "The Drama Of Corporate Law: Corporate Narrative Between Policy And Law," 2009 *Michigan State Law Review 1111* Op. cit.: suggesting the way that standard ideologies of corporation character provide a basis for legitimating their domestication within legal regimes in ways that exclude the possibility of corporate character not dependent on the state, archetypes for which are the Yakuza and Mafia.

[70] See, Katsushito Iwai: "The Nature of the Business Corporation: Its Legal Structure and Economic Functions". *Japanese Economic Review*, Vol. 53, pp. 243–273, 2002.

[71] Continental Tyre and Rubber Co., Ltd. v. Daimler Co., Ltd. [1915] 1 K.B. 893 (question of the citizenship of a company where it was incorporated in the UK but all directors and all stockholders but one are Germans resident in Germany; the corporation was determined not to be an enemy alien even though most of its shareholders and directors were).

[72] Salomons Case (1895) 2 CD 323.

Citizens United illustrates the inability of law to embrace flexibility in the context of corporate personality. It also shows the continued power of the lack of consensus about a guiding ideology of corporate personality and its regulatory consequences. *Citizens United* is as much about corporate governance as it may be about the constitutional limitations of government efforts to regulate corporate speech. The Supreme Court majority's embrace of an entity ideology ought to provide substantial support for regulatory efforts that seek to deepen the autonomy of the corporate enterprise and weaken governance rules that strengthen shareholder's property rights. The case provides a foundation from which to advance everything from rules that advance shareholder democracy and participatory rights, to the imposition of public obligations on corporate entities. It suggests a policy basis for the separation of corporate governance from the personal and individual interests of shareholders in the protection of their property. As a consequence, it may be possible to conceive of fiduciary duty as extending to other corporate stakeholders. If corporations are not synonymous with their shareholders, then domestic corporations, owned by foreign individuals or governments, may be treated as domestic persons to the same extent of natural persons resident in or citizens of the jurisdiction. Perhaps more interesting, *Citizens United* also suggests a basis, tinged with constitutional implications, for the extension to corporations of direct obligations under international as well as national law. Corporations, understood as entities with a public purpose, may be burdened with public obligations not only under national law, but under international norms as well. Inadvertently perhaps, for it is doubtful that the justices thought in these terms, but no matter, inevitably, the consequence of the embrace of an entity ideology provides a basis for a transnational framework for corporate governance.

Sir Charles Sedley wrote long ago:

> How shall we please this Age? If in Song
> We put above six Lines, they count it long;
> If we contract it to an Epigram,
> As deep the dwarfish Poetry they damn;
> If we write Plays, few see above an Act,
> And those lewd Masks, or noisie Fops distract:
> Let us write Satyr then, and at our ease
> Vex th'ill-natur'd Fools we cannot please. (Sir Charles Sedley, To Nysus, in The Penguin Book of Restoration Verse, 690 ((Harold Love, ed., Baltimore, MD: Penguin Books 1968) (first published cir. 1701))

And, indeed, *Citizens United* presents the reader with a brilliant exercise in "satyr". It certainly can "vex . . . fools we cannot please."[73] A simple question of the availability of legal protection for the production of political speech by an intangible created by the law, the protection of which it seeks, should present a fairly straightforward issue of interpretation, one with well recognized objects and well understood signification of equally well recognized signs. Yet, this suggests the complexity of the simplest

[73] Id.

form.[74] How shall we please this Age? "It is not satisfaction of the will that causes pleasure . . . , but rather the will's forward thrust and again and again becoming master over that which stands in its way. The feeling of pleasure lies precisely in the dissatisfaction of the will, in the fact that the will is never satisfied unless it has opponents and resistance.—"The happy man": a herd ideal."[75] Is law politics, as the CLS discussed and legal semiotics highlights as a central issue; or has the cultural landscape changed—have lawyers remade the world as Kevelson understood possible?

[74] Sam Favale: "Montana Supreme Court Defies Citizens United Decision", *The Wall Street Journal,* Jan. 3, 2012, available http://blogs.wsj.com/law/2012/01/03/montana-supreme-court-defies-citizens-united-decision-upholds-state-ban/ ("On Friday, the Montana Supreme Court restored a 100-year-old state ban on direct spending by corporations on political candidates or committees, saying that the U.S. Supreme Court's 2010 decision in Citizens United v. FEC dealt with federal laws and elections, but the "vast majority" of elections are held at state and local levels," Id.).

[75] F. Nietzsche: *The Will to Power,* Op. Cit., p. 696 (Nov. 1887–March 1888).

Chapter 13
Structuralism and Legal Semiotics

A New World, A New Imagination

Structuralism, although widely neglected in many philosophy encyclopedias, is one of the major foundations for semiotics and has in that context the same importance as phenomenology or analytical philosophy. Structuralism focuses on elements of structures within which the relationships of individuals can function in the boundaries of the structural order created and can be understood only within these structured inter-relationships. Emphasis is on the fact that "everything there is"—also one of Peirce's points of departure—"is *structured* in- and of itself". The repeatedly quoted Paracelsus (1493–1516) already noticed: "nothing is without a sign" and "since nature does not release anything in which it has not marked what is to be found within that thing", concluding that "they all (i.e. "all what is") become known through their *signatum*" (signature). So the *signatura* is an expression for a scientific approach to order what is hidden as the constitutive secret of things, it is also the science of understanding the markers of reality, and it is also the expression for the very act of marking itself. Paracelsus understands that act as the understanding of how things are signed, what *signator* exists, and how many signs are taken into consideration. This is a truly early program for semiotics! And it shows how structuralism and semiotics are tied together.

Like any system, *language* represents an order. That order emerges and is reinforced where the language system differentiates and articulates words and expressions. Speaking is not solely a means of communication, but also creates and maintains a social order through differentiating articulations. The dynamics of that order culminate in one's ability to make and to understand those *differences* as well as their *linking—our language and our world in its entirety are rich because of the human ability to demarcate different signs*. Here is a double operation at work; one pertains to the level of meanings, the other to the semantic elements and their structured patterns. Meaning as a distinct entity beyond a specific context is amorphous, indeterminate and without profile—meaning needs an appropriate context to be effective. A speaker can only demarcate characteristics in so far as he coordinates the basic elements (such as morphemes, words, and parts of sentences) into whole sentences and ultimately to texts. But one is in general

J. M. Broekman, L. Catà Backer, *Lawyers Making Meaning*,
DOI 10.1007/978-94-007-5458-4_13, © Springer Science+Business Media Dordrecht 2013

not aware how a speaker creates through his speech articulation an entire world image.

The activity of structuralism, in particular focusing on processes of analysis and restructuring, goes hand in hand with an emphasis on structures and systems of meanings and expressions [French: *signifié* and *signifiant*, English: *signified* and *signifier*] which are interpreted and maintained as one-to-one relationships. This activity might be a reduction in itself, but it makes the techniques of classical structuralism recognizable. It thus provokes the question whether contemporary thought patterns still operate accordingly, or build upon new forms of thought formation[1].

One of the most intriguing new thought formations is for example in modern genetics. Without computers—symbols of our age, which expresses itself in digital languages—there would not be any genetic knowledge possible. Genetics is based upon a specific view on life through newly acquired knowledge "about a human life-time that reaches from the one-cell egg through adulthood to the grave". This statement was formulated at the occasion of the 50th anniversary of the 'double helix'. This new imaginative force has surprisingly new aspects. There is in the first place a basis in *visualization* through *imaging*, which is solely created through the use of *computers*. This goes hand in hand with new forms of *information* that sustain genetic, medical and other knowledge. "Obtaining the sequence of the human genome is a first step", the *New York Times* wrote at that occasion. "Biologists must now annotate it, or identify the regions of DNA that hold the genes and their control elements. Next come tasks like discovering the variations in DNA sequence that contribute to disease in different populations, defining the proteins produced by each gene, and understanding how the proteins in each cell interact in a circuitry that controls the operation of the genome". It is clear from those statements how genetics operate on the basis of newly adopted principles.

These have a common metaphor in the concept of a Text, or a Book that is written along the lines of the Grammar of Language. Variations in sequences, which define and sustain our understanding of their interaction and their circuitry, are modern expressions for old ideas. That is conceivable in the works of De Saussure and many others who showed interest in the construction of a text or a book. One can often read the same metaphors in the context of genetics. They suggest that the entire evolution of life became written in the four-letter language of the chemical bases. This sounds as if there were no development of knowledge and imagination since the Renaissance! Galilei already suggested how the Book of Nature was written in Circles, Triangles, Pyramids, Cones and Squares. Those who know the rules of their composition and the laws of coupling, he suggested, know all what is knowable. The planets in their cosmological course are just like the individuals in a State or the words in a language. Solely one *mos aedificandi* reigns reality. Is this our contemporary image that rules our epistemology? Does this image *represent* the epistemology of genetics?

The answer is in the negative. The revolutionary viewpoint may still be in the *grammar* as the most elaborate and correct metaphor that represents the dominance of

---

[1] Jan M. Broekman: *Structuralism. Moscow—Prague—Paris*. Op. Cit., 1974.

elementary processes. But that grammar received new and very different connotations and functions. It has been highlighted as an element of the history of semiotics, that the body in its entirety was the subject of healing in traditional medicine. Today, the healing of the body is a matter of equilibrated molecular processes, genetic make-up and the changes and modulations of these sub-processes. That is an indication for the changing grammar in the construction of our knowledge.

As one perceives how diseases can be healed *under the condition that the body is understood in terms of genetics*, one discovers the key for all relevant discourses based upon domain knowledge. All aspects of such a new key have an epistemological requirement to detect the acceptance of (self)-expressiveness in terms of the specific field (domain) of knowledge. That knowledge has global dimensions despite its fascinating and profound specificity. The breathtaking newness is in the *combination of the global and the specific*. A global scale has limited insights and knowledge conditions of specific sciences as its basis rather than as its disadvantage. This epistemological turn changes the use and interpretation of the traditional concept of "structure".

Lévi-Strauss described how people in a Latin-American tribe painted their faces in perfect geometric figures without knowing any geometry. Those figures were not only elements of an encompassing epistemology, but they formed also an epistemological structure. His widely acclaimed discovery was that such facial paintings belonged to what he called 'the logical syntax of social reality'. The images seemed compatible with structures of parenthood and family-relations practiced by other tribes in Africa and other parts of the world. His observations and theory show how a system of relations can be independent from the observer as well as the object. Now, what has this observation in terms of "structure" to do with epistemology as a generic problem of cultural philosophy? Is it also a philosophical problem in a stricter sense of the word? The DNA double helix *structure* determines family relations and parenthood problems, as medicine tells us today. It became expanded through genetic counseling. So, one should consider the question in what regard the concept of a *structure* is compatible with or different from the epistemology in structuralism from Jakobson and other Moscovites to Barthes or Lévi-Strauss in France.

We must conclude, that the dimensions of our knowledge and of the basic observation of this knowledge in a philosophical discipline called "epistemology" have considerably changed since the first formulations of structuralism. The concept of 'grammar' is a rich metaphor, which tries to embrace all those issues and their system. Knowledge is nowadays conceived as dependent upon globally accepted techniques, as are for instance effective in the case of genetics. There is simply no way to imagine a genetic fact or research on virtual dimensions that is limited to *national* boundaries of knowledge and applicable only to a *limited* numbers of citizens. There is also no way to understand electronic communication, virtual procedures or communication types without *global* electronic access on the basis of steadily growing computer applications. However, this universal feature of modern knowledge is not suggesting a complete anarchy, nor abolishing local (domain) knowledge(s). It is true that specific conditions create specific types and fields of knowledge, which all have to become internalized by the users. Does this also influence the notion of "structure" itself? Perhaps we now need to speak of structure in the plural, existing simultaneously and in constant communication, stacked one atop the other, across each other and in constant movement. The result is communication, porosity and collision. Kevelson's semiotic systemicity is now at the center of meaning making but in polycentric form.

To live in a global society requires new learning processes. Our concept of universality is renewed in epistemological contexts, but that renewal leads to important challenges for citizens who unfold their public life in a modern society. It shows how "structuralism" implies learning a new key. That new key is clearly perceivable in what was called *neo-structuralism* in the 1980s of the past century, closely connected with ideas on *deconstruction* as well as recent articulations of *hermeneutics, semiotics* and *phenomenology*. Do not forget how all those brand names of philosophical views belong to a clearly detectable discourse in occidental culture: the discourse of reason, in which Kant already underlined the split function of its central subject, the "ego". A perhaps most central question semiotics poses here, is semiotics, with signs and meaning in the forefront, is condemned to that very same discourse. This leads to the problem how human sciences are thought, in what form and under what conditions.

Post-modernity and Semiotics

Three important methodological issues thus dominate our recent understanding of structuralism. One is on its cultural and *epistemological* background, a second is on the emphasis on *surface structures* and their importance for understanding reality and a third focuses the tendency to perceive human sciences as a unity in itself in close *intertwining* with possibly all other sciences.

(1) Both traditions, the Anglo-American tradition on the one hand, and the French and German tradition on the other, concur parallel to (legal) semiotics in the insight that meaning and sense belong to a language, which mirrors, represents and maintains a particular social and cultural order. But they do not do away with political traditions that want to fulfill the task to safeguard modern concepts of humanism on the basis of social, cultural and individual freedom. As a consequence, one should conclude that structuralism unites two European traditions in understanding human subjectivity. *It seems however, that it did not.* Why this is so, may be a matter of political and of philosophical inspiration. It is fascinating to experience, that languages—the embedding of meaning and sense—in their turn depend upon the superstructures of politics and history, not to mention a globalizing economy. This is a great challenge for semiotics. Legal semiotics is unthinkable without such superstructures, although it is at the end not a political discourse in its own right! The divide between the French and German philosophical perspectives relates beyond doubt to the history of World War II and the typically German experience of the Cold War period after 1945. Those historical effects pertain to the understanding of the subject position in philosophical perspective and in life,

whereas both discourses were confronted with varying regime systems and economic powers.

(2) The second feature is in the specifics of epistemology and their particular focus on surface structures as an indicator for more encompassing knowledge. An example is in mapping procedures. These mapping manners are designed to visualize and create images, which can reach from deep levels to the surface of reality and focus structures. Greimas' squares are an example, however, compared to computer-generated images a quite primitive attempt, which indeed shows the operational impact of surface structures. Structural elements that change place or position leave traces in the surface-structure to mark their original position in depth-structures. Those traces show how surface-structures are not just incidental forms and do not carry a meaning just for the surface appearances. Below each level of perceived reality exists a wealth of meaning. Because of this, we experience how much reality often remains unaccounted for in our everyday treatment of common appearances. Spoken in general, surface-structures challenge semantic interpretations. Linguistic surfaces only indicate the importance of underlying structures in analytical as well as in synthetic respect. However, the concept of a structure is here still in perfect harmony with the classical definition in Schleiermacher's hermeneutics, who suggested already in the nineteenth century that a structure is a system of relations between elements, which all have a meaning *because of their difference* to others. *Structuralism attempts to reach beyond this classical view without, however, abolishing the importance of "structure" as a basic concept.*

(3) A third dimension of structuralism is how it underlines the need to unfold its methodology in *human* (including law and legal discourse) discourse as an encompassing and whole discourse. That approach strives in the first place for the highest possible integration in the so-called human sciences. Historical observations, cultural data and social perspectives need such an integrated view in order to meet the complex realities of life. However, this includes also a renewed interpretation of the classical divide between the human- and the physical sciences. It is important how that divide appears irrelevant and old-fashioned in contrast with the global importance of computer sciences and digital reality.

We should also mention the unfolding of what is fashionably called "post-modernity". Any general observation pertaining to the culture of the Occident would emphasize the importance of its self-interpretation. Western culture mirrors, in other words, its main features in its own and very special conceptualization of a "Self" since approximately the fifteenth century. The Occident understood that "self" since those years as a unity, in particular as a religious, philosophical and cosmological principle and most recently also as represented by a unified science, a technology, its applications and social consequences included. A first breach with that idea of unification was perceivable in Western metaphysics, in particular the thought patterns of Hegel, Marx, Nietzsche, or Freud. This inspired many thinkers of classical structuralism and deepened later in "post-modernity".

Structuralism was not only a new methodological approach to classical questions and problems, but also a forceful challenge to social order. The aim of neo-structuralism is not to further, deepen or enhance the specific principles of structuralism, but to change the occidental self-understanding by means of *a new positioning in modern history* with, as a consequence, a renewed reflection upon the use of the term 'modern' itself. Post-modernity should be its literary expression. No movement that bears the name structuralism, neither in Moscow, in Prague or in Paris, would place its theoretical approach to literature, logic or language in the broad perspective of a crisis in Occidental culture. Neo-structuralism developed this new feature. It described what many migrants in the European Union and ultimately all inhabitants of the Union who acquired Union citizenship experienced in their public life spheres. The deep sense of such post-modern reality is throughout that *belonging* is a matter of *being in exile*. That is in the deepest sense of the word their proper experience, which includes the reality of a continuous threat of crisis in cultural patterns.

"Post-modernity" should therefore not only be understood as a matter of positioning in history, or as a concept of a specific philosophy of history, but first and foremost of *a crisis management with respect to its proper history*. In that continuous presence of crisis interfere the new legal dimensions of Union life, supported by the constitutional dimensions of the Treaties as well as the Charter on Fundamental Rights, 2000. To mention the latter is to remember the ideological and historical position of neo-structuralism, its need to develop a view on the subject's freedom in global frameworks of power. But even here, neo-structuralism's dependence on the ideology of the state tends to limit its vision in a world in which the state itself has been de-centered and other sources of relations now intrude. Thus, for example, corporate social responsibility charters guaranteeing workers down a corporate supply chain certain rights derived from international norms and corporate business custom may also apply to define the subject's freedom in global frameworks of power.

In structuralism is an awakened and alerted awareness about the historical determination of self-interpretation and scientific knowledge. Post-modernism is the catchword for this sensibility. Moreover, it is the condition under which the concept of a structure can become re-interpreted. A major element of that condition is the above-mentioned change in Western metaphysical orientation. The scope of that change reaches from (1) philosophers and ordinary citizens losing a basic trust in the pre-established social order and the concept of order itself, to (2) a challenge resulting from newly designed scientific knowledge and its inherent ontological presuppositions. It shows that the post-modern situation has emerged from *within* modernity, and consequently remains a historical fact in its own right. The concept of history has decidedly changed in this context. The positioning of neo-structuralism in post-modernity is not a vague literary articulation or a fashionable expressiveness. On the contrary, the epistemological consequences of determining a time period in modernity gave rise to the question how to perceive neo-structuralism structurally. How can one, with the concept of 'structure' as a major instrument, discover and define structuralism as a phenomenon of post-modernity?

A most outstanding issue is the possibility to draw time fragments apart, since any process of divergence creates self-awareness. In other words: insights, which occur *today*, are different from those that may occur *tomorrow*. But the difference between the two provokes important semiotic and semantic consequences. If there is a predominant consciousness that *today* is decidedly *not* tomorrow, then the diversification (or even opposition) of the two is a key to understand the position of structuralism in good Greimasian thinking. The insight is that *today without tomorrow or yesterday,* has no meaning or sense. The same is true for *signs*. Merleau-Ponty once stated how he learned from De Saussure, that "signs taken individually one after one did not have any meaning". Peirce would have agreed wholeheartedly! What seems true for signs is also true for days, historical periods and places in the stream of consciousness and self-understanding. A "structure" has no distinctive content in itself. It *is* content in so far as its pattern of organization is perceived as a property of our reality. Applied to our distinction between modernity and post-modernity, one could not only highlight the importance of the differentiation as such, but also venture the idea that the full meaning of all our thought-activities relates to the self-determination of those thoughts in a precise historical context. *Structuralism is thus not defined by contents of "structure" in the first place, but by its place and occurrence in post-modernity.* A structure is never a universal point of view, which functions as an archimedic place from where interpretations of consciousness and the reality of the world occur. An "infinite consciousness" does not exist.

The Structure of Communication

Derrida's book on *Grammatology* suggested how the European tradition connects the human *voice* with the *breath* rather than the *writing*, with the *spiritual* rather than the *material*. This is a precious insight that also should inspire lawyers, because who is hearing sounds, listens to a voice. Listening is different from hearing as *'Verstehen'* differs from *'Erkennen'*. To listen is a spiritual occurrence and includes understanding and interpretation, whereas the hearing is mainly a physiological fact. That issue is not purely a matter of semiotics or of the cyberspace features of electronic communication, but refers to the vital question "*what is communication*", a question of pivotal importance for law and legal practice.

Is "the structure of communication" not a contradiction in itself, or at least a combination of incompatible elements? A structure is not closed. How is a structure that features communication to be understood if it is almost naturally viewed as closed? Its implicit model is at stake and criticized especially where the Sender-Receiver or Speaker-Hearer Model is dominant, in particular in Anglo-Saxon theories and philosophy. All communication implies a paved path from (a) to a (b), be it a *subject* to an *object*, a *self* to an *other*, or a *sign* to a *sign*. Derrida underlined the latter and states that there exist no communication models without signs. Each communication transmits the identity of a signified object from one subject to another. That transmission (the *passage*) is not identical with a simple signifying operation. It seems that there is no signifier for a passage. Subject and object are presupposed to be independent entities in these models.

However, those models can by no means guarantee a semiotic parallel or any other compatibility between the two. Differences that cause the formation of signs do not create the structure of communication, as one could readily deduct from De Saussure's linguistics. *Signs are like human individuals; they need others to be or become selves.* There is no decoding of signs without a text, signs receive their meaning because of their place and function in the universe of signs—the same is the case with texts. *The identity of texts, or signs, results from the infinite differences among them.*

Views Behind Appearances

"A view behind the appearances"—it is a privileged instrument in a semiotic mode. But it has only a sound philosophical sense if structures are recognizable in non-apparent and deep layers of reality. Those are perhaps solely accessible by means of linguistic articulation and (re)-construction activities. Language is a most important mental construct, as Husserl explains and Derrida, Lacan, Foucault or Piaget reformulated. It sets man apart from other organisms and functions as the basic tool of thought and reason, as Aristotle already suggested. Let us consider the fact that the *view* behind appearances is not an *optical* but a *linguistic* option, an articulation of perception in words! But that articulation is not an innocent mark of the human mind.

Hermes' name symbolizes an art of understanding and interpretation, which is highly appreciated in the human sciences today. However, it is also a turning point in their practices. One should not neglect that structuralism contains elements of what was in Occidental philosophy named *hermeneutics*. Is there any knowledge feasible or any certainty reliable, which is not produced by Hermes' function as a messenger between spirit and matter? Members of the *Tel Quel* group in Paris debated vehemently around 1970 whether the meaning of a literary fragment depends on its contextual function. Structuralism researches that words, metaphors or dialogues acquire a specific meaning through their relations with other literary constituents. Language is the *material*, literature the *opus* and interpretation the *modus operandi*—that is the platform, which did not change.

Today we would underline how Hermes belonged to Indo-Germanic language patterns, which treat *time* as a *space* and a *thing* and consequently treat *periods* in time and history as *quantities* or *domains*. The exchange-mechanisms that played such a dominant role in analytic structuralism had their origin in this language pattern. The Occident treats human activities as a matter of subjects facing a world of objects as if this activity has the highest position in the ranks of human values. A view beyond the appearances of reality focuses common foundational values in society. *Meaning*, *interest* and *ontological ground* are elements of that value system, but they are certainly not fixated elements of a cosmic order. Categories such as *agens* and *movens*, *causa* or *Creator Spiritus* articulate themselves in the profile of the technical Occidental culture. Such foundational values govern the nature and limits of language, expression and communication, but are they also the limits of hermeneutics? A general awareness of limits dominates modernity. Modernism focuses differences between limited discourses, structures of limited domains of knowledge and ultimately of difference as such.

Structuralism purifies its metaphysical implications when it enters post-modernism. Language cannot be treated as a value-free and uncommitted image, an expression of life as it really is—it has to ceaselessly invent a new semiotic relevance of *image*, *expression* and *representation*. Such semantics are a true expression of post-modernity in Occidental cultural life, a fact that unfolds in North American discussions on *diversity* (in legal arrangements) as well as in the European Union's strivings (in political arrangements) towards a balanced *multiculturalism*. Once the doubts pertaining to language become a social practice, the foundations of how to represent reality tremble. Doubts and discussions on accurate representation make clear how ethnocentric individuals are in their acquiring and management of knowledge. That goes with an important incoherence in their epistemological views, which tend to balance their daily lives by means of oversimplification. Is this just a criticism of cultural attitudes? Ask Hermes.

What is the meaning of his words? Does he carry specific meanings in specific words so that he engenders an insight in complex language patterns? Can a single utterance have such a definitive meaning for an individual—for Hermes himself as well as for his listeners? Hermes experiences how words always mean more and less then the context suggests in which they are spoken or written. This consideration is a post-modern sensibility. Human consciousness and its history expressed in words of a language transcend an individual's experience. The plural seems founded in unfamiliar meanings and a bewildering mixture of consciousness and unconsciousness. Nietzsche, Freud, Lacan and others expressed the often quoted experience of Hugo von Hofmannsthal about how "we are not at home in our selves"—and will never be, as post-modernity states, overlooking human history. Truth is plural, and that experience shows how the human condition is not entirely located in only one specific language, cultural system or value. That is the post-structuralist contribution, "I think that the essentially local character of the critique in fact indicates something resembling a sort of autonomous and non-centralized theoretical production, or in other words a theoretical production that does not need a visa from some common regime to establish its validity".[2] When determining the essence of a human being, it is as if location is not a criterion at all. In any case, they are not imprisoned in words with limited meanings.

Semiotic Epistemology

> *Writing, even great writing, is inevitably*
> *to some degree a local concern, in a way that music*
> *simply isn't. Our novels may not be read in Alpha Centauri,*
> *but it seems possible that some of our music will be played.*
> *(Michael Cunningham)*

[2] Michel Foucault: "Society Must be Defended" *Lectures at the Collège de France 1975–76* (David Macey, trans., Bertani & Fontana, (Eds.) NY 2003. p. 6.

The emphasis in "structuralism now" is on epistemology, on our theories of knowledge, which have always fascinated occidental philosophy. Is there any sensibility for truth in our days, when we have to leave the local domain in order to find a humane essence in the plurality of life? Not *the* truth, but truth as a phenomenon that manifests itself, overwhelms the perceiver, the listener, the thinker. It emphasizes the necessary preparedness for a change in attitude, a change towards a world without fixated dimensions, which is a major problem in all perceived contexts of multiculturalism. So, what is a transcendental structure? It seems a surpassing of domain structures located in discourses, scientific frameworks and standardized observations. All in all, one must conclude, it is not an "is", although it is unthinkable without the anthropomorphic language of the "is". Was "being" not always a hinge of Western philosophy?

The question "How to know knowledge?" has become an operational topic in the arts, in philosophy or the sciences. Structuralism is nowadays only one of the catchwords for those types of operations and an endeavor rather than a point of view based on a stable theory of knowledge, an intellectual orientation rather than a result from linear logical deduction. It is a virtue of the novel to suggest this to the reader. More than five decades later, we have every reason to go along with Roland Barthes and speak about structuralism as a specific intellectual *activity*. Do not forget how that activity already focused the reconstruction of an object in such a way that the rules according to which it functioned became apparent. The structural man (Barthes' still relevant expression) is like a player: he takes apart and puts together so that he creates a world, which resembles the first, the so-called original. Some may develop a bird's-eye view on structures or structuring processes in reality, and speak of transcendental structures as a *super*structure. Others embrace a different metaphysical notion and prefer the use of an *infra*structure. No matter, whether an embracing or a foundational function is viewed. Both use that word as distinct from a theory or a concept, and in doing so abolish the direct applicability and representational character of words and language. The dissipation of such proper names as a direct reference is a major feature of structuralism now. That activity has a different character and seems embedded in scientific rather than purely philosophical discourse.

Epistemological strategies are embedded in the mainstream of Occidental culture. The *silencing of philosophy* in that culture is an *intensification of philosophy* in the form of scientific articulations. Is that the closure of a culture? One is attempted, especially under the pressure of publications announcing the end of Western culture, to bring these issues together. However, it is said that thinking in terms of an *ending* (coming to-, or striving for an end) is typical for Occidental life. The Occident, the West is an image of the point of compass where the sun sets. Decline is an element of psychological and geographical localization, as Valéry stated. Is Spengler's famous *Decline of the Occident* a contradiction in itself? What belongs to the Occident, or the West, declines anyway!

Those concepts do no longer contribute to an adequate description of Western culture. A global culture is signalized, multiculturalism is in effect, a transatlantic marketplace emerged—all these marks display their Anglo-American watermark as soon as their names are written. However, there is more. It may no longer be possible to think in terms of single cultures—that is post-structuralism's great insight. Even the multi-culturalism of conventional Occidental socio-political structures is grounded on a singularity (the idea that multi-subcultures exist within an overarching master narrative that is itself an expression of porosity within limits; an idea also echoed in early Habermas). Semiotics reminds us that there may be a symbolic and interpretive category—neither culture nor multi-culture. The geography diminishes whereas the names and spirit of place do no longer indicate a philosophical viewpoint or frame of thoughts. There are fundamental changes in the Occident, as far as such traditional values and practices like *labor*, *property* and *identity* are concerned.

Dostoevsky mentioned once that he liked to read newspapers. In contrast to his personal literary work, daily papers present stories without connection. The pages on a paper are not conceived in a logical or causal frame but serve the charm of their layout and the thrill of the moment. This is indeed very different from traditional values such as sense and essence, respect for history and relations not momentarily produced but grown and developed. But that spiritual dimension is lost where labor changes into services, history into a composite of stories, time into a collection of moments and substance into assemblage. Beyond substance, cars, buildings, houses, town, computers, scientific theories, philosophical ideas are assembled. Each individual possesses his or her car, building, computer, which is instantly composed in accordance with one's rights, wishes and desires. Take the Lexus car: assembled by robots from parts that were assembled at unknown locations from unknown parts. Books like a Dell computer: composed after wishes on a web site, brought into existence only as a composite. Structuralism persevered; its silence about guiding ideas and principles suggests the perfection of the idea.

Criticism suggested already in the fifties of the past century that structuralism annihilates the fundamental questions of meaning and sense in life, society and science. Contemporary structuralism does not do away with that critique, although the cultural embedding for that critique seems to dissipate, in particular through semiotics and deepens the self-understanding of Occidental culture. But CLS and the post-structuralist criticism of structuralist foundations tended to forget Nietzsche's important insight: the fact that all structures are indefensible does not produce nihilism—the absence of structure; it may instead produce (and necessarily so according to Nietzsche himself) choices among structure. Here the focus of the semiotic square turns, and for legal semiotics the conclusion is unavoidable—lawyers will make the world; that world will inevitably fail to attain "truth" and will be remade again. The battle lines are choices of meaning and structures of frameworks. Semiotics provides the lawyer with the necessary tools for framing issues inside (meaning within structure) and for bridging structures (meaning across structure). The first would go to the question of ambiguity (in statute or contract) within the logic of law structures; the second would go to the question of communication and harmonization (international corporate social responsibility; obligations of corporations operating within a state) between autonomous system frameworks.

Part IV
Doing and Saying Legal Semiotics

Chapter 14
The Legal Semiotic Modus Operandi

Doing and Saying

Three critical positions of legal semiotics in the waning of the CLS were highlighted as discussions within US Common Law legal scholarship. They all focus on *a lawyer's attitude*: (1) one in so far as legal meanings are installed in the lives of ordinary citizens, (2) a second on a lawyer's possible connection between a progressive standpoint in politics and semiotic knowledge or experience, whereas (3) a third made clear that legal education is inherently a process of attitude formation in view of future legal practices, so that the process itself remains in the realm of theory-formation. That particular focus shows clearly the relevance of Mr. Jourdain's parallel situation. He did not know that he wrote prose—do lawyers know that they write and operate semiotics? All three aspects, which fascinated CLS scholars, one must conclude, are at distance from this parallel as well as the practice of law.

They hardly touch the question *how to proceed practicing the law when a lawyer has acquired semiotic knowledge and skills*. That is the direct effect of considering the legal semiotic modus operandi. Does the latter have any chance to intrude on the close relationships between legal theory/jurisprudence on the one hand, and the practice of the law on the other? Or do these remain two different languages, two different types of activities, two variant attitudes so that even a legal semiotic approach remains confined to the field of legal theory caused by a predominance of the non-law referent?

The question includes a general (in particular philosophical) issue that has problematic character: can *what we do* ever be understood and expressed in terms of *that doing itself* and not exclusively in terms of theories about what we do? Is the lack of completely mastering the relevant expressiveness impeding a lawyer's self-awareness, as in the case of Mr Jourdain ? Should Mr. Jourdain be content to understand little more than technique (the rules of prose and poetry) ceding guidance on the forms themselves to the Master Philosopher? The doing might be embedded in a language—a talking to yourself, for instance, an inner dialogue—which is only partially a means of communication, so that what we do is only partially expressible in terms of our narration of what we do or did. Semiotics unveils this fascinating problem: the absence of the possibility to determine a referent dominates the

J. M. Broekman, L. Catà Backer, *Lawyers Making Meaning*,
DOI 10.1007/978-94-007-5458-4_14,

linguistic situation. That is a fundamental problem when considering the semiotic modus operandi, which at the same time challenges us to perform semiotic knowledge and skills with precision and accuracy. Especially a lawyer, whose work unfolds in words and meanings, is vulnerable in that regard.

Texts-A Legal Semiotic Modus Operandi

Semiotic steps in legal work are *steps to take in texts*. Before lawyers write, bring a pen to paper or move a finger towards a keyboard, they *read*. What they read, even if it is a string of incoherent words, can be named a *text*. Everything Peirce brought to the fore about the sign and its triadic embedding or Greimas suggested about the multifaceted character of texts, belongs to a lawyer's semiotic approach. These suggestions should be adapted, sharpened *and become an element of lawyers' self-awareness and professional attitude*. That is the key to the legal semiotics modus operandi: there is no complicated application of sophisticated methods required but rather the sharpening of awareness about reading and, in the first place, about texts. To be a lawyer begins with listening to- and reading spoken and written texts. The ways semiotics can be fruitful in a legal context is with focus on the specific character of texts. Related issues such as the construction of Greimasian squares, the semiotic analysis of meaning and discourse, the underlying values of an operating legal discourse or the unison structures of legal cases can further complete semiotic light on the performance of legal handwork. The multilayered character of texts being necessary components of discourse seems evident: And the object can be quite pragmatic—for Mr. Jourdain the better wooing of a mistress; for the lawyer the better management of words in the service of clients and in fidelity (or opposition) to the structures and logics of the system in which she operates.

But what are the semiotic consequences for legal discourse? One should consider how a legal-semiotic modus operandi has the following components/procedures vis à vis a legal text. These should be recognized in the first place, whereas it is clear to a lawyer that they are taught to him as one of the principal backbones of his legal work. In making those steps relevant for legal semiotics, they unveil how he—like Mr Jourdain unknowingly spoke prose—already acts in many semiotic ways, unknowingly and classifying his steps as fundamental for legal handwork. Once transposed into semiotic dimensions, they show another relevance for the same practical questions. General and preparatory steps, which are all in one way or another textual, are:

1. Identify the *message*. Find and describe that central message in the text by means of concise language and highlight the main issue at hand. Try to already construct a parallel series of remarks pertaining to that message in terms of everyday language and of terms you would use as corresponding legal expressions.
2. Identify the *signifiers*. Formulate what they do in this text context and determine their meaning(s). Be aware that a network of signifiers can be detected in natural

language and another, most probably more restricted, network of signifiers in legal language.
3. Identify the *signifieds*. How do they function as a receptor of meaning that is conveyed to the reader/receiver? Together with that, try to understand precisely what the latter understands as the meaning at hand, and whether that is identical, equivalent or different from the meaning(s) in the legal expressiveness you read.
4. Identify the *paradigms* at hand, such as pairs, oppositions, or categories, including their psychological or sociological signification. Have a constant eye for the language used, whether it is a natural language, a legal language or any mixture and perhaps a suggested translation of the one into the other.
5. Identify the *syntagmata*. A syntagm is a string of words or phrases, a collection of statements or propositions that form a specific unity. Find the direct and the indirectly implied messages, which you can identify. Be aware how syntagma form clusters in legal discourse, which often times want to be understood as a *sign*. Linguistic components, such as words, de- and connotations, literal and symbolic messages play altogether a constitutive role.
6. Identify the *principle* (often represented by a syntagma) that functions in the text or message such as: "justice" or "peace keeping", "equilibrium" etc. Those expressions fulfill not only a sign-function, but they represent many times an entire ideological proposition, meant to have a strong rhetorical power. It is of rhetorical importance to find how these elements in the text are tied together and form a distinctive pattern. This importance could be characterized as part of the management of the text construction. That leads to more encompassing strategies in legal discourse, often suppressing discourse elements of natural language.
7. Identify the specific *legal features* at work, reaching from message description to legal management analysis of the text.

Syntagma and Sign

Texts are not harmless communication instruments—they *represent* all sorts of viewpoints, values, convictions, worldviews in the form of words conveyed at first sight, and even those words represent in their turn what is beyond their annotations in a dictionary. Vices and virtues of texts are in their representation—do texts really represent what is exterior to them, or is there more to discover? One of the most obvious issues is that texts are never natural facts but rather *organized significations*; in other words: not *natural*- but *institutional* facts. Is their birthplace in institutions, their manifestation is also unfolding within the realm of an institution. The latter observation is at issue in the ordinary wisdom embedded in linguistic expressions such as "at first sight", which implies that there are always other sights involved. Or take a related wisdom in the sentence about a certain phrase: "read it, it does not say what it says".

The difference between syntagma and sign—a linguistic unit and an individual sign—is of interest here. A syntagma is a string of words that forms a part of some larger linguistic unit. A sign is in our daily understanding represented by one word: stop, go, turn, come, stay, here, etc. But there is the remark of Peirce, (who complicates and at the same time clarifies the issue) suggesting: "a sign on its own is not a sign". That remark pertains to the difference between a syntagma and a sign and challenges our understanding of signs via triadic rather than via dualistic relations. If a sign on its own is not a sign, then a sign is a sign due to its relations with other elements of a string, to which a sign belongs—a string either of spoken/written or of unspoken words. So if a sign is indeed not a sign when it is on its own, a sign is a sign thanks to its visible or invisible syntagmatic character, ultimately meaning that signs are texts, mostly embedded in texts. The sign-issue shows that texts are indeed multi-layered semiotic jewels, and excel in *not* only being what they seem to be, and *not* only saying what they seem to say. Hence the differentiation between *surface- and deep structure* of texts in general, and of texts in legal discourses in particular.

'Deep' as metaphor

> The problems arising through a misinterpretation of our forms of language have the character of depth. They are deep disquietudes; their roots are as deep in us as the forms of our language and their significance is as great as the importance of our language.—Let us ask ourselves: why do we feel a grammatical joke to be deep. (And that is what the depth of philosophy is.)
> (Ludwig Wittgenstein, *Philosophical Investigations*, 1953, § 111)

One should not forget that our language about *surface- and deep structure* of texts is *metaphorical*. Many philosophers have understood that the metaphor was in use because of the complexity and the difficulties to access linguistic articulation pertaining to the concept of a text. The depth of the deep structures seems unfathomable, and dimensions, which remain unnoticed or are only accessible in an indirect manner in a text, seem numerous. That is the more, since 'deep' suggests often 'hidden' or even 'private', for instance where deep reasons in the context of textual articulations are often principled and connected to moral consequences when openly interfered. Texts can furthermore show divergences in world-view, which remain better hidden under the surface of the words, or real conflicts in social life break out. One of many examples is in practically identical texts on the status of Jerusalem forwarded with complete opposite connotations and political results by Jewish and Muslim authors. One has to conclude, that the suggestion of textual deep structures forces us to acknowledge at least two complicated issues, which are both important for semiotic analyses and in particular the semiotic modus operandi in legal discourse: (a) although surface- and deep structures suggest a certain two-dimensionality, texts are in essence three-dimensional linguistic entities; (b) and show a complicated process character, within which time plays a dominant and often misunderstood role. Hence Wittgenstein's remark:

> But you talk as if I weren't really expecting, hoping, *now*—as I thought I was. As if what were happening *now* had no deep significance.–What does it mean to say "What is happening now has significance" or "has deep significance"? What is a *deep* feeling? Could someone have a feeling of ardent love or hope for the space of one second—*no matter what* preceded or followed this second?—What is happening now has significance—in these surroundings.

> The surroundings give it its importance. And the word "hope" refers to a phenomenon of human life. (A smiling mouth *smiles* only in a human face.) (L. Wittgenstein: *Philosophical Investigations,* Oxford UP 1953, § 583.)

Kristeva[1] once made a very radical remark, which embraces the issues under (a) as well as under (b). She suggests, that *a text is in fact not a linguistic phenomenon* (although we normally understand it that way), a structured signification presenting itself in a linguistic corpus perceived as a *flat* structure—instead *a text is the engenderment of a linguistic phenomenon.* We have to consider the issue at an abstract level and withdrawing from particular texts in specific discourses such as the legal to fully understand the issue, and from speculations about holographic representations of texts. The difficulty of understanding the limitations inherent to a surface structure of a text is (among others) in the fact that we do not yet dispose of holographic text images although we already speak as if they exist in our mind. Read our great poetry—or: are Shakespearean plays not staging thoughts in holographs?

Kristeva concludes that any engenderment of texts inscribes itself in a linguistic phenomenality and shows therefore always a surface-text (which she calls phenotext). The latter encounters us for instance as printed, but the print is not a guarantee that we can read that text. A text is only readable if we descend vertically through its genesis via its linguistic categories as well as the topology of its signifying acts, which is what is commonly perceived as 'deep'. This must fascinate each lawyer, because his or her descend through legal-linguistic categories and signifying acts is a voyage via two of the main axes of jurisprudence, being topology and category. This particular view on the engenderment of a legal text includes an awareness of the specificity of the tissue of legal language and of the textual genesis of the "I" that promotes itself as the privileged reader of the text. That voyage in- and of itself is a process that creates the deep structure (called geno-text)[2]. Be aware, that there are obviously two different components here: the text as surface differs from the text as deep structure in that the first is promoted in the public space (ultimately as printed) and that the second is resulting from a vertical process, which produces the voyaging "I" during the engendering process as the text's constitutive power. We conclude, that any text thus embraces two processes: the public and the private, the "they" and the "I". The coherence of the two decides about the ultimate signification

---

[1] Julia Kristeva: "L'engendrement de la formule" in: *Semeiotikè. Recherches pour une Sémanalyse.* Paris 1969, 278, 286.

[2] A good example might be the "oral argument" in a US Supreme Court, which precedes the ultimate, written judgment, printed and definitive, a surface structure in itself, comprising both the majority and dissenting opinions, applied more fully in the discussion of *Citizens United, supra,* Chap. 12. The oral argument could be seen as a specific, "highly stylized" discourse within legal discourse in its entirety, a specific area in which, as Chief Justice John Roberts Jr. claims: 'justices are debating among themselves and just using the lawyers as a backboard'. It is often highlighted that oral arguments are less important than the written briefs, the spoken words carrying less weight than the written. This shows how legal texts emerge from a complex context of meanings—an emergence, which in itself seems "good for law". See A. Liptak: "Are oral Arguments Worth Arguing About?" in *The New York Times,* May 6, 2012.

of the text, through which becomes clear how generating a signifying system leads to a pheno-textual manifestation.

Symbolic and Ideological Components

Based on the various linguistic categories—those of the artificial legal discourse not in the least—one must conclude that geno-text in law and legal discourse seems in particular determined by symbolic and ideological components; both play therefore an important role in the engendering of a pheno-text of jurisprudence. Predominant ideologies in a period of a culture can determine all processes that normally reflect in the tissue of the language of he time. The realist ideology, that literature must represent a reality of non-literary character is then concordant and at the same time in opposition with legal discourse. Law suggests to the world of everyday life that its literary dimensions represent the reality of that world, but at the same time needs to oppose this naïve realism. It does so by means of generating a rhetoric in which a world is formulated in legal terms and concepts, which are not belonging to a natural but to an artificial, professional and therefore institutional character. This double standard of meaning shows that legal texts are major elements in socially important and distinct transformations of meaning, which are on the one hand influenced by and on the other create what Lacan called 'master discourses'. Legal discourse thus belongs to our modern accelerating production of symbolic discourses. That is a common feature of the textual processing of signification complexes in which names, formulas and other signifying indications live a relatively independent life, and thus serve successive ideologies. These live their lives in all seven steps jurists take when confronted with semiotic analyses: analyses of what they perform in legal and non-semiotic frameworks, and now should heighten their awareness of.

That could be the reason why Greimas distinguishes, like Kristeva, between superficial- and deep textual structures to show how there are *essential steps in the voyage from immanence to manifestation*, which undoubtedly will provoke a semiotic awareness in the legal mind. The latter wants to focus on the text as manifestation solely, and therefore on a semiotic grammar system that arranges the contents susceptible of manifestation into discursive forms. Do not forget that lawyers produce and organize significances. Although these include perhaps quasi-universals (what they often do in the language of jurisprudence), they remain particular to any type of language, included artificial languages such as law's language.

Order

The relations between surface and depth suggest furthermore an *order*. Reading requires for instance the voyage from surface or manifestation to depth, whereas writing is often seen as an activity to reach from depth to surface. The same comes up in cases of causation, of analysis and the like. Is that correct in semiotic perspective?

Is it correct to suggest that an analysis should begin at the manifestation level and then go 'deeper', or that an author in legal discourse—for instance a judge forming his Court's final opinion—has to move inversely from a depth- to a manifestation text production? It is interesting to notice that these moves appear in the mind of the average spectator. They are fascinating because on the one hand they seem a method of immersion in hardly accessible regions from which the author emerges as a hero, thus demonstrating how hardships lead to artistic or even legal-institutional freedom.

In reviewing a film of Frederick Wiseman, the inverse comes to the fore.[3] O'Brien describes in his review how Wiseman works—inversely—from deep structure to manifestation. He films over a period of weeks whatever captures his interest, and then out of that footage he constructs, over a period of many months, a film. "This process can be seen as a trebly affirmed exercise in artistic freedom", O'Brien concludes. "The subject can be practically anything; any aspect of that subject may be filmed; and the results are selected and combined at will, without hewing to any preconceived plot or message: 'I try to approach the shooting with a clear but empty head . . . It is only during the editing that I discover the themes and structure of the film' Wiseman adds. "O'Brien tells us: "Others make outlines and then film them. Wiseman describes a paradoxical reversal: first he films, then he decides what film there is to be made. Fundamental questions of significance and intent are uncovered last of all". This reverse is a challenge for semiotic approaches of legal texts. Lawyers should perhaps practice their reading of legal texts not as firmly fixated predetermined regular textual pattern with institutional qualities, but as a subject that can be practically anything—which is a behavior far beyond the rules of how lawyers should read and behave otherwise within the boundaries of legal discourse.This was focused where legal texts were characterized as 'articulating surfaces' within the complexity and firmness of law and legal discourse. Important is to underline that both the signifier and the signified produce themselves within the framework of a text, so that the heart of each text should be perceived in terms of being a semiotic production unit. Any theory of signifying is thus (a) a process and (b) a practice. The two focus on meaning—no matter whether meaning results from direct representations or from an elaborate engenderment. One should thus conclude, that texts *become* a linguistic phenomenon, and they do so by means of a passage through any type of engenderment.

A good non-legal example is, how we consider in everyday language our genetic predisposition as an issue that belongs to the deep structures of our life story, and the behaviors that are probably resulting from those patterns as belonging to the surface. The coherence of those two seem in philosophical terms a matter of substance and theory, or naturalness and the artificial. However, that order is not a dogma, and one does not absolutely need to transit from the natural to the artificial or vice versa. Greimas' work with polarities, opposites and their relations, made visible by means of squares, leads to fortify that questioning of a long and generally cherished dogma.

[3] Geoffry O'Brien: "Crazy Horse" in: *The New York Review of Books,* LIX, No. 5, p. 20.

Chapter 15
The Legal Semiotic Modus Operandi: Squares

As a most stimulating example, we quote here from the prize-winning article of Michelle Wirth JD[1] some considerations related to the above steps. The article applies semiotics to the Pennsylvania Supreme Court case *Ferguson v. McKiernan*[2] to reveal the shift in social context that made the lines of legal reasoning behind the outcome appear "self-evident" for lawyers and the public.

The Signifiers

1. First there is the preparatory step as the *broader context of the issue* at stake is formulated:

   > The Pennsylvania Supreme Court's opinion in the above-mentioned case *Ferguson* highlights a gap between the legal master discourse and the social master discourse regarding reproduction via use of technology and private contracts establishing obligations and privileges toward the resulting offspring.

2. Then follows precision in terms of legal language:

   > In *Ferguson*, the Pennsylvania Supreme Court points to the use of technology in the sperm donation process as the sign, or what the American judicial system calls a "factor," that determines what theory of analysis it will use to decide whether a sperm donor is obligated to provide financial support for a child conceived using sperm from the donor.[3] If the court determines that the child's conception most resembles conception achieved through use of an "institutional sperm bank," then the court applies "contract" theory analysis.[4] Under this analysis, in this case the sperm donor would have no obligation to support the child and the child would have no right to receive support from the sperm donor. If, however, the Court determines that the method of the child's conception most resembles "traditional sexual reproduction," then the Court applies a "best interests of

[1] Michelle Wirth: "Who's Your Daddy? Or: Using Semiotic Tools to Deconstruct Legal Determinations of Who Holds Parenthood Obligations and Privileges". In: *International Journal for the Semiotics of Law,* Vol. 22. No.1, 2009, p. 83 ff. and: Jan M. Broekman & Francis J. Mootz: *The Semiotics of Law in Legal Education*, Springer 2011, Ch. 9.

[2] *Ferguson v. McKiernan*, 940A.2d 1236 (Pa. 2008).

[3] *Ferguson*, 940A.2d at 1245–46.

[4] See generally, *Id.* at 1242–43, "Sperm Donor's" argument.

J. M. Broekman, L. Catà Backer, *Lawyers Making Meaning*,

DOI 10.1007/978-94-007-5458-4_15,

the child" theory of analysis.[5] Under this analysis, in this case the court would find that the sperm donor has an obligation to provide support to the child, and the child has a right to receive support from the sperm donor.[6] The court stated it believes these "two distinct views . . . to be self-evident."[7]

3. Then there is special attention for the proper identification of the signifiers in case:

Signifiers are those terms used in the message, which give the message meaning in the sense that if you used the opposite of the term, you would change the meaning of the message. Given that signs are created by contrasting something to "all that it is not", the opposites of the signs are also useful signifiers to examine. The court's opinion may contain synonyms of, or adjectives that modify, these signifiers that can illuminate their meaning. Combined, we will call these surface-level signifiers.

4. And finally, there is a preparatory list of surface-level signifiers, conceived as a preparation for the Greimasian square

Dichotomies	
Sign	Jural-Opposite
Legal Master Discourse—Present Case	
Private sperm donation	*Public sperm donation*
"Conception outside the context of institutional sperm bank" = *Known Donor* + fertility clinic	"Conception inside the context of institutional sperm bank" = *Anonymous Donor* + fertility clinic
Direct contract between Donor and Donee	No Direct contract between Donor and Donee
One contract, between Donor & Donee: Donor not obligated to support child; in exchange, Donor gives up claim right of privileges toward child; Donee does not have to share claim right of privileges toward child; in exchange, Donee gives up right to seek financial support for child	Two Separate Contracts: between Donor and Sperm Bank; and Sperm Bank and Donee; Donor not obligated to support child; in exchange, Donor gives up claim right of privileges toward child; Donee does not have to share claim right of privileges toward child; in exchange, Donee gives up right to seek financial support for child
Social Master Discourse—Present Case	
Sign	*Social-Context Opposite*
Contemporary society	Old-fashioned society
Inescapable reality	Escapable reality

[5] *Id.* at 1246 (stating, "In the case of traditional sexual reproduction, there simply is no question that the parties to any resultant conception and birth may not contract between themselves to deny the child the support he or she requires. *See, e.g., Knorr, 588A.2d at 505* ("[Parent's] right to bargain for themselves is their own business. They cannot in that process set a standard that will leave their children short."); *Kesler, 744A.2d at 796.*")

[6] See *Id.* at 1249, dissenting opinion, stating "*Section 5102* of the Domestic Relations Code prescribes that "[a]ll children shall be legitimate irrespective of the marital status of their parents," and, subject to limited exceptions not applicable here, "in every case where children are born out of wedlock, they shall enjoy all the rights and privileges as if they had been born during the wedlock of their parents [.]" *23 Pa.C.S. § 5102(a).*"

[7] *Ferguson*, 940A.2d at 1246.

Social Master Discourse—Present Case	
Sign	*Social-Context Opposite*
"Would-be" mothers (market for sperm-without-claim-rights)	No "would-be" mothers (no market for sperm-without-claim-rights)
Privileged (right) to Raise a Child	Not Privileged (no right) to Raise a Child
"All-manner of arrangements" (re: contracts delineating obligations to support and claim rights to parental privileges)	Proscribed limits on available arrangements (re: contracts delineating obligations to support and claim rights to parental privileges)

The jural-opposites are context-specific; they are not naturally occurring or even necessarily commonly recognized opposites. The second half/ dichotomy in the pair can change depending on the context.
"Fertility clinic" = Conception via clinical means, i.e. use of either "artificial insemination" or in vitro technology.

Pairing, Squaring

5. With this list in mind, the pairing of the terms in case is researched and the square can thus been designed as a string of pairings. Wirth suggests:

> *Pair the surface-level and sub-level signifiers into dichotomous relationships*, such as pairs, oppositions, and inverses, jural-correlatives and jural-opposites. Evoke the signifier that completes the pair even if it is not explicitly mentioned in the message:

Donor	Not-Donor
Man	Not-Man
Father	Not-Father
Woman	Not-Woman
Mother	Not-Mother
Parent-Child Relationship	No Parent-Child Relationship
Sexual reproduction ("traditional sexual reproduction"	Clinical reproduction ("institutional sperm bank")
Institutional sperm bank	Private sperm donation
Anonymous Donation	Not-Anonymous Donation
Dependent Child	Not-Dependent Child
Conception with agreement	Conception without agreement
Contract regarding support	No contract regarding support
Enforceable as a matter of law	Unenforceable as a matter of law
Fertility Technology Legal	Fertility Technology Illegal
Creation of Paternal Anonymity Legal	Creation of Paternal Anonymity Not-Legal
Paternal Identity Attainable	Paternal Identity Not-Attainable

This list can be used to create a square of two conceptually related pairs. Squares can be connected as rectangles or otherwise serve as the foundation of a map of relationships[8]. The effects are in the reading and in particular in the resulting comprehension of the reader. More importantly, it facilitates an analysis of choices and

[8] A final square that closes these instructive remarks can be consulted In: M. Wirth: "Semiotics of Parenthood in Semiotic Perspective", In: Broekman/Mootz, Op.cCt., p. 168.

structures within which a decision will be made—the point within these rectangles of possibilities that the authoritative interpretant (the court) will settle. From there the relational rectangles can be situated and the lawyer will have a basis for starting an analysis of the succeeding relational rectangles possible (that is, she will be ready to use precedent to advance, defend, constrain or reject the prior holding).

Wirth' remarks support a more precise understanding pertaining to the construction of squares in the sense of Greimas. General meanings, Surface- and Deep-structured meanings and many other issues as well as underlying values and parallel cases are open for research and discussion with the squares as notes.

Chapter 16
The Legal Semiotic Modus Operandi: Names

Names

The semiotic modus operandi in legal discourse relates more often than observed to *names* and *naming/name giving*. Names are crucial in specific domains of law, in particular in case law of Courts—both in Civil Law as in Common Law. Recent political and legal developments have considerably emphasized the importance of this name giving: *new Courts* have been installed all over the Western hemisphere, and *new political unifications* created Courts focusing on case law, as the European Court of Justice and the EU Court of Human Rights showed. With them, the legal cases name giving has been unaltered; the process remains beyond reflection and is not subject of any analysis.

Three general aspects are directly important for the semiotic modus operandi in this context: (a) legal cases bear mostly proper names, (b) the political dynamics of names given to cases relates to questions of linguistic expressivity, and (c) all names, legal names included, serve the formation of stably fixated reference systems to avoid impressions of arbitrariness.

Let us not forget—it was emphasized in the sixth chapter—that *names* belong without exception to a *social structure,* and such a structure is definitively more than a single conversion of speech acts. Speakers and hearers, senders and receivers depend on contents and structures of that *milieu*, and all of them characterize the presence of an individual. Not we ourselves, but *others* gave us a name and taught us its language, and they did so within the scope of law and legal discourse. Names profiled us and set us free from an unidentified life under the condition that we embrace a legally valid identity. We are indeed seldom aware of law's creation of identity-appearances when we see a face, look at a passport picture or hear a name. And even less often, we are aware that we organize important parts of our life the way law organizes its institutions and discourses: by means of identity creation—a process in which name giving is essential. Names bridge the gap between nature and culture, but also, very powerfully, between the observable and the understandable. Names make the observable also understandable and, in doing so, represent an order of the world.

J. M. Broekman, L. Catà Backer, *Lawyers Making Meaning*,

DOI 10.1007/978-94-007-5458-4_16,

Legal cases bear a name created by codes of court activities and law books and their names identify their place in the discursive order of jurisprudence—an order that sustains the meaning-making task of lawyers. But it also serves as a marker for constraints on meaning majking—the case name is a reminder of the contingency of the meaning' application. It is focused on the principles before the judge; it need not extend farther. Its application must be sustained through another performance of meaning among another group identified by name. Statutes speak to all subjects; cases to the litigants. Meaning making now is seen to take on a territorial aspect that mimics the territorial orientation of the state within which meaning can be given.

Thus, names can be understood as a general medium from which to make meaning in social life and as the essence of human relations. That is an important but mostly neglected issue in legal semiotics, because names show us where and why we live with our images—images of our selves as well as images of our socially important means, among which legal cases play a role far beyond legal discourse. Names are embedded in language whilst the brain relates to linguistic components with their consciousness base. So the question arises what it means when we suggest that we 'linguistically connect to others'. Names play an important role in that context. Signs, as Peirce clearly underlined, are never alone, and so are names: they are always entangled in patterns and networks of human relations. They are meaningful because they are *given* a meaning. That is important where the process of language acquisition is at stake. The understandable becomes understood and interpreted when the constitutive forces of signs are set free in an acquired linguistic competence.

The Latin understanding of the term *casus* concerns the inflection of a verb. In this light a case is a particular situation, an example or a comparison, but also an element of relationships, in particular of a word with other words in a syntagma. What is valid for linguistics, seems also to be valid for legal language, it holds equally well for the linguistics of a trial, a legal inquiry, a lawsuit or the legal determination of guilt. Cases in law relate to the standing jurisprudence, the doctrines, statutes and other fixated texts. This shows their belonging to an artificial discourse; cases are at distance from everyday reality, they play a particular role *in* that reality without being *of* that reality. They are the construction of specialists and of institutionally entitled actors[1]. Names are of central interest: the Stoic interpretation and the Latin expression even identify *name* and *case*. This is clear in law as well as medicine; the latter discourse has cases named after the clinical picture, which is referred to. Patients and legal subjects guarantee the true existence of the case and the appropriateness of the knowledge involved as expressed in the name giving. As a consequence, the legal subject—itself a bearer of rights and duties—makes the case bear his name, which is also its name. Yet it the name nearer does not completely control her name; the state provides a framework for managing names; first by demanding that a name be given, then by managing the use of the name and then by controlling changes in the name (through marriage, divorce or willful act). There is power in a name, and the state has to come extent also coopted that power for its own purpose, a state of things

[1] Parallels between legal cases and medical cases are surprising. See Jan M. Broekman: *Intertwinements of Law and Medicine,* Op. Cit. 1996, Ch. III.

discussed more precisely below. It is in this context that one can understand more deeply the insight that names may be identical and yet totally different, as they belong to two languages; tow owners, two "I"s. The naming is hence at the heart of law's meaning and not just a resource to a multilayered communication. This semiotic power honors the narrative structures of law and legal discourse, and emphasizes their importance.

Cratylus

It fascinates that a text written around 360 BC introducing Socrates, Hermogenes and Cratylus as dialogue partners, seems to focus on the same questions we cherish today when talking about words, names and language. Plato's Cratylus leads us upfront to positions, which we ardently debate in sciences, philosophy or politics approximately 2,5 millennia later: have names, or for that reason linguistic expressions in general, their birthplace in nature or in habits? So the dialogue begins with Hermogenes outlining a sharp contrast between the conventionalist and the naturalist thesis:

> Her. I should explain to you, Socrates, that our friend Cratylus has been arguing about names; he says that they are natural and not conventional; not a portion of the human voice which men agree to use; but that there is a truth or correctness in them, which is the same for Hellenes as for barbarians. Whereupon I ask him, whether his own name of Cratylus is a true name or not, and he answers "Yes." And Socrates? "Yes." Then every man's name, as I tell him, is that which he is called. To this he replies—"If all the world were to call you Hermogenes, that would not be your name." And when I am anxious to have a further explanation he is ironical and mysterious, and seems to imply that he has a notion of his own about the matter, if he would only tell, and could entirely convince me, if he chose to be intelligible. Tell me, Socrates, what this oracle means; or rather tell me, if you will be so good, what is your own view of the truth or correctness of names, which I would far sooner hear. (Plato: *Cratylus* Transl. Benjamin Jowett. www.classics.mit.edu/Plato/cratylus. html.)

Socrates tries to do what we all do in such questionable situations: he attempts to look at the reality of language in everyday life to solve the tensions between the conventionalist and the naturalist position. The argument approaches clearly the defense of the naturalist viewpoint, because reading reality is also in this particular dialogue position a reference to naturalness.

> Soc. Son of Hipponicus, there is an ancient saying that "hard is the knowledge of the good." And the knowledge of names is a great part of knowledge (...) I do not know the truth about such matters; I will, however, gladly assist you and Cratylus in the investigation of them. When he declares that your name is not really Hermogenes, I suspect that he is only making fun of you;—he means to say that you are no true son of Hermes, because you are always looking after a fortune and never in luck. But, as I was saying, there is a good deal of difficulty in this sort of knowledge, and therefore we had better leave the question open until we have heard both sides.

The naturalist says: your name cannot be true because the natural habits of its bearer do not confirm what the name should express. You, Hermogenes, cherish an attitude of always looking to enrich yourself without giving Tyche (the Goddess of fortune) a glance! "In the depth of your character, your nature, is no reliable reference to your name"—Socrates suggests, and therefore your name is a joke. Harsh words are not exceptional once the abyss between the two notions becomes subject of discussion—that is the case in law, as it is in physics, medicine, bioethics or philosophy. So Hermogenes tell his dialogue partners,

> Soc. I cannot convince myself that there is any principle of correctness in names other than convention and agreement; any name which you give, in my opinion, is the right one, and if you change that and give another, the new name is as correct (. . .)

Whereupon Socrates—who clearly leads the dialogue through the entire history of Greek philosophy and from viewpoint to viewpoint, never being fixated on one or another—leads to the intertwining of name giving and speech activity: to social positioning and the maintenance of social skills in the hands of the name-*givers* themselves. The discussion between two fixated positions, a naturalist and a conventionalist, may be politically or even rhetorically stimulating but is philosophically untenable. Socrates will in the course of his dialogue not embrace one of them, because to frame the issue at stake in such an opposition of viewpoints is definitively incorrect. We, in our days and our philosophical experiences can only agree:

> Soc. And is not naming a part of speaking? For in giving names men speak.
> Her. That is true.
> Soc. And if speaking is a sort of action and has a relation to acts, is not naming also a sort of action?
> Her. True.
> Soc. And we saw that actions were not relative to ourselves, but had a special nature of their own?
> Her. Precisely.

Speaking names is a matter of speech, of language, of culture, and names as well as name giving have sense only as a part of such broader frames:

> Soc. And now suppose that I ask a similar question about names: will you answer me? Regarding the name as an instrument, what do we do when we name?
> Her. I cannot say.
> Soc. Do we not give information to one another, and distinguish things according to their natures?
> Her. Certainly we do.
> Soc. Then a name is an instrument of teaching and of distinguishing natures, as the shuttle is of distinguishing the threads of the web.
> Her. Yes.
> Soc. And the shuttle is the instrument of the weaver?
> Her. Assuredly.
> Soc. Then the weaver will use the shuttle well- and well means like a weaver? And the teacher will use the name well- and well means like a teacher?

Whilst thinking with Socrates, we are already at distance from fixated and isolated principles or any ideological viewpoint a partner in the dialogue *must* appropriate. Focus is on the skills of the name giver as well as on the receiver of the names concerned. That is an extended view on the conventionalist thesis, with focus on the context rather than on singular structures of individual speech acts. Be surprised: here Socrates makes again an important move:

Soc. Cannot you at least say who gives us the names which we use?
Her. Indeed I cannot.
Soc. Does not the law seem to you to give us them?
Her. Yes, I suppose so.
Soc. Then the teacher, when he gives us a name, uses the work of the legislator?
Her. I agree.
Soc. And is every man a legislator, or the skilled only?
Her. The skilled only.
Soc. Then, Hermogenes, not every man is able to give a name, but only a maker of names; and this is the legislator, who of all skilled artisans in the world is the rarest.

Now follows the heart of what we call today legal semiotics:

Soc. And how does the legislator make names? And to what does he look? Consider this in the light of the previous instances: to what does the carpenter look in making the shuttle? Does he not look to that which is naturally fitted to act as a shuttle?
Her. Certainly.(...)
Soc. Then, as to names: ought not our legislator also to know how to put the true natural names of each thing into sounds and syllables and to make and give all names with a view to the ideal name, if he is to be a namer in any true sense? And we must remember that different legislators will not use the same syllables. For neither does every smith, although he may be making the same instrument for the same purpose, make them all of the same iron. The form must be the same, but the material may vary, and still the instrument may be equally good of whatever iron made, whether in Hellas or in a foreign country;—there is no difference.
Her. Very true.(...)
Soc. And the legislator, whether he be Hellene or barbarian, is not therefore to be deemed by you a worse legislator, provided he gives the true and proper form of the name in whatever syllables; this or that country makes no matter.

Two changes are taking place under the surface of this text. The first is about the concept of "nature", the second on "speech" or "language".

(a) A short consideration about the first is, that "nature" no longer functions as what is meant in the Latin expression 'natura naturans' (nature in and of itself) but as indication for the 'skilled name giver'. Not the structure but the context of his skills is highlighted in the dialogue of Socrates. One could say that the skill-context of the name giver focuses on the Ancient Greek idea of the Good: the word 'nature' approximates the concept of the 'Good', which is also understood as the 'One'[2]. This does not automatically annihilate the naturalist position and further a conventionalist thesis. Gadamer remarked how the Greek accepted our speech practices to remain *by analogy* when reference to the Good was made. The Good (here in the form of the Skilled name giver) can never be expressed directly and definitively and should remain a language *modo obliquo*. The Good is the One and the One is the Good. Remember, that our number 'one' was for the Greek not an 'arithmos', a unity of multitude, but only a constituent element for numbers.

[2] See H.-G.Gadamer: *Die Idee des Guten zwischen Plato und Aristoteles*, Heidelberg 1978, p. 22. (*The idea of the Good in Platonic-Aristotelian Philosophy*, Yale UP, 1988).

Their smallest number was 'two': all numbers must be Unity and Multitude at the same time. The transition from 'nature' to 'Good' is clear: *first*, the inexpressibility of 'nature' meets that of 'Good' by analogy and absence of immediacy of expressiveness; *second*, the gift/skill of name giving seems a form of participation in experiencing the 'Good' and takes place before any pragmatism can unfold[3].

(b) The second change in the course of the argument pertains to the level of language. As soon as the expressions 'nature' and 'language' are brought together, reference to what is called a 'natural language' takes place. But the 'natural' character of a 'natural language' is rather a matter of convention than of 'nature' in the sense of the *natura naturans*.

Do not forget what was explicitly outlined in chapter five of this book: a natural language is a language learned by birth, and is thus a matter of education, guidance, convention, the Law. Important in this regard is, that the concept of 'natural language' brings a widened understanding of language with it: human communication as linguistic communication can take place in a variety of languages—not only a variety of mother tongues but also of natural- and artificial languages, as well as their mixtures. Socrates' reference to the lawmaker as a name giver does not take the latter remark into consideration, although this is essential in his dialogue context. We show this relevance in the heart of the question why legal cases bear names.

Cases, Names

Why and how do legal cases bear names? The question is not on any program of a Law School, nor subject of any Legal Semiotics program. Legal cases seem to bear names naturally. And they are most of the times *proper names*. Yet, one could already ask whether the process of name-*giving* is not an outstanding argument in favor of the conventionalist thesis as mentioned in the Socratic discussion. A name cannot be given, and thus not function, beyond a (cultural, linguistic) context, one must say: and that is the conventionalist perspective with emphasis on *habit* in a Peircean sense of the word. Moreover, habits play in legal discourse an outstanding role—they form the backbone of a lawyer's production of firmly fixated predetermined regular textual patterns in accordance to institutional rules.

It is exactly in this framework that Civil Law—as well as Common Law countries, India, the Philippines, African countries, Japan and elsewhere *the name giving to cases* is regarded as *a matter of (legal) style* for Court documents and case opinions. Citation rules, which include the names given, find their origin in this creation and determination of style, although the name giving should not be understood as identical with the citing. Basic for this style is almost universally the use of proper names, those of the parties concerned or those of any other institutional use of a

[3] Consider the argumentation on 'nature' in a conceptualization of names as sound-mimesis in: G. Genette: *Mimologiques, Voyage en Cratylie*, Paris 1976 Ch. 1.; Engl. Tr. By Thaïs E. Morgan: *Mimologics,*UP Nebraska 1995.

proper name. These names are indexed on the >World LII< website, the site of the "Legal Information Institute", they are in the US LII with the US Supreme Court decisions indexed by means of the party names, in the "Oxford Standard for Citation of Legal Authorities" and in the US "Historic Supreme Court Decisions" which also orders cases by party names[4]. These references show indeed a mixture of citing and name giving, which is understandable in the context of the rigidly maintained rules of constructing legal discourse.

But: *what is the inherent semiotic power in the name giving to cases*, seemingly an act without apparent interest? That question leads us to the cases, which bear given names.

First of all, legal cases are not mini-novels. They form another type of literature—do they also form another type of language? They certainly do. Here is the key to understanding the shortcomings of the Socratic dialogue: there is in that conversation no differentiation of language and the conversation goes on as if such a differentiation is not necessary because everything goes—but: everything goes only in a natural language. Does everything go on that specific linguistic level? That is the concealed issue in the Socratic mention of the law, legal discourse and the lawmakers' authority.

> Soc. Then, Hermogenes, not every man is able to give a name, but only a maker of names; and this is the legislator, who of all skilled artisans in the world is the rarest.
> Her. True.
> Soc. And how does the legislator make names? And to what does he look?

The first thing to answer is: he does look at the properties of legal language. But then we should ask whether there is a decisive difference between the natural- and the legal language in which and about which the dialogue speaks. The answer is in the affirmative: the latter is an artifice within- and with use of components of the first!

> Soc. Then, as to names: ought not our legislator also to know how to put the true natural names of each thing into sounds and syllables and to make and give all names with a view to the ideal name, if he is to be a namer in any true sense?

He surely should, because mastering a natural language is always a precondition for managing an artificial language. This diversification is the key to a legislator's activity in the natural as well as the legal language.

We thus have to consider that the proper names, which function as names for legal cases, are no longer proper names in the sense of a natural language.

In other words, proper names as names of legal cases are not proper names of everyday life but became components of legal language! Their meaning is *legal*, and thus at distance from everyday language. This implies a first semiotic insight: names of cases do much more than belong to the solution of a conflict legally; they do strongly *indicate* that the conflict solution is legal by its very nature. To read the proper names of a legal case is not to read the names of he named individuals but to read legal discourse.

---

[4] Law.cornell.edu/supct/cases .

At a still larger distance to the Socratic discussion is a more definitive semiotic conclusion about cases bearing (proper) names. Their names give them the ultimate textual character of legal discourse:

The surface structure of law and jurisprudence seems uniquely fixated by means of case names.

Three semiotic functions come together: the names are (a) an *index* of law in legal discourse; (b) they are a *sign* of law in society and (c) a *symbol* of law's presence in occidental culture. This togetherness of index, sign and symbol is the semiotic specificity of legal discourse related to the names of cases in law. The legal semiotic modus operandi excels in the analytical understanding of the cohesion of those three. All three terms are prominent contributions to semiotics in the philosophy of Peirce.

An *index* is one of the ways in which a sign may be related to its object, he explains. Indexes are also called indexical signs—they are those signs through which actual signs are connected with its object. This basis for legal reasoning itself remains in the dark, and does not belong to theoretical or jurisprudential reflections. Only legal semiotics clarifies those relations within sign functions in law. Signs in law relate on the basis of resemblance (icons), of habit (symbol) and of indexical character in which a sign vehicle represents it object by means of an actual connection, in this case the *name*.

A *sign* is that what stands for something else—an umbrella term under which many subtypes are hidden, mostly through creating a reference to signification(s). Everything can be a sign so that significance is about the relationship between a sign and what it signifies, intends, expresses or means. That is the case with the naming of cases without which those cases could never function as an index—as the LII, the Citation- and the Historic Listing of cases in jurisprudence show. Legal discourse functions here as the decisive institution, its case names *may* act as signs *without* any respect to the human agent as its originator. The proper names of living (or past) individuals are clearly not relevant; their meaning fulfills (since the moment of the original complaint) another role. The names are signs, which are *always* signs once they acquired their signification in the name giving process; signs of jurisdictional limits (cases, not statutes or orders, of the character of the dispute, of the limits of the powers of the interpretant, and of the system within which signs themselves are interpreted. The human mind is understood as the sole agency through which signs signify.

A *symbol* is a distinctive semiotic component here, because names are connected with law and legal discourse by virtue of habit formation or convention. The latter is strongly present in legal discourse because of its artificial character: historical and actual decisions about meanings and habits create the web of meanings and significations that form the deep structure of law. The symbolic feature present in the name giving to legal cases interests furthermore in a complementary semiotic meaning of the term 'symbol' in so far as it designates a social order as an arena into which humans are initiated and in which they must act. This dimension throws an additional light upon Peirce's remark, that a sign alone is not a sign. The symbolic dimension is necessary to keep law and order related to human activity and to the system from which legal meaning is derived and constrained (knowledge of both of which is essential for lawyers seeking to consciously make meaning, and intuitively understood by lawyers reprising the role fo Mr. Jourdain in the legal field). The structure of symbol meaning has a double sense: one is the primary, direct, literal, and the other the secondary, indirect and figurative. The latter can only be understood through the former. A general observation shows the symbol as keystone of all hermeneutics, because the latter unveils the concealed sense inherent in direct meanings. It implies that relations between symbol and sign are, particularly in semiotic, very strong and equally complex. A traffic sign, for instance, can be the symbol of a (local) culture and of nationally established behavior habits; the arbitrariness of the sign-matter (De Saussure) is in legal practices transferred to the symbol—a transference that needs semiotic attention.

By means of summary, we come to the following points of semiotic attention in the case-name relation

1. The fact that legal cases (not unlike medical cases) bear names is not indifferent in semiotic hindsight.
2. Semiotic attention and skills do always uncover the meaning of a legal-practical activity, which is normally taken for granted. This includes the naming, citing and ordering of legal cases.
3. Names of cases are a *sign* in semiotic perspective via their particular relation to *index* and *symbol*. This is not due to any theoretical consideration but because the sign character of names bridges the socially important abyss between everyday language and law's artificial discourse. Symbol implicates meaning and place because semiosis speaks to system as well as local meaning.

Chapter 17
Artificiality and Naturalness—The Tyche Deity

> Let us not pretend to doubt in philosophy
> what we do not doubt in our hearts.
> (Ch. S. Peirce 1903)

Two intertwining characteristics form the basis of today's semiotics of law, especially in US legal semiotics[1]. The first can be found in the work of Peirce who developed in the late 1860s a general theory in which he forwarded the view that 'man is a sign'—an observation immediately relevant in law and legal discourse. The second is in the use of linguistic expressions such as 'word', 'community' or 'discourse'. The daring aphorism 'man is a sign' was for Peirce an element of a more encompassing theory, which he called 'evolutionary cosmology', and in which law seems to be almost naturally incorporated. It supports Peirce's idea that all knowledge results from a process of inference—from presumptions, deductions and conclusions, so that signs are always involved in epistemological questions, as they are in issues of legal theory.

Evolutionary Cosmology

A basic concern in Peirce's philosophy is in plying chance together with continuity. The togetherness of these two is omnipresent in his thoughts. We cannot live, think and know without continuity, he says, which means that past ideas must be present in every movement of our mind, although in often totally different forms. However, novelty exists by the grace of chance rather than of continuity. The tension between chance and continuity is therefore almost immeasurable, and took almost the philosopher's entire lifetime. He described as early as in 1891 how the next step in the study of cosmology must be to examine the general law of mental action—In doing this, I shall for the time drop my *tychism* out of view, in order to allow a free and independent expansion to another conception ... I mean the idea of continuity,

[1] Earlier fragments of this Chapter are published: "Tyche in Law" in *Liber Amicorum René Foque,* Ed. Larcier, Brussels 2011, and: "A Goddess for semiotics of law and legal discourse" in *DADA-Rivista di Antropologia post-globale*. A. Palmisano (Ed.) Trieste 2011.

J. M. Broekman, L. Catà Backer, *Lawyers Making Meaning,*

DOI 10.1007/978-94-007-5458-4_17,

he writes literally. Tyche guided Peirce's fascination with chance and continuity. He looks her in the face when he concludes "... that there is but one law of mind, namely, that ideas tend to spread continuously and to affect certain others which stand to them in a peculiar relation of affectibility. In this spreading they lose intensity, and especially the power of affecting others, but gain generality and become welded with other ideas."[2]

A majority of philosophers, linguists, social scientists, and anthropologists on both sides of the Atlantic use and explore the expressions 'word', 'community' and 'discourse' and weigh their consequences. This unites Peirce with those who contributed to 'symbolic interactionism' and others such as Lévi Strauss, Greimas, Kristeva, Lacan, Barthes or Eco—to mention only a few names. Peirce wrote already around 1903: "... it is sufficient to say that there is no element whatever of man's consciousness which has not something corresponding to it in the word ... the word or sign, which man uses, is the man himself. For, as the fact that every thought is a sign, taken in conjunction with the fact that life is a train of thought, proves that man is a sign ...". He had earlier noted circa 1892, "All communication from mind to mind is through continuity of being. A man is capable of having assigned to him a role in the drama of creation, and so far as he loses himself in that role ...".[3] This role only unfolds in a community: "A man has consciousness; a word has not, ... our thought is an index for itself of itself on the ground of a complete identity with itself. But so is any word or indeed any thing, so that this constitutes no difference between the word and the man." Word and man depend on their community in which they find support for their articulation: "... reality depends on the ultimate decision of the community; so thought is what it is, only by virtue of its addressing a future thought which is in its value as thought identical with it ... so that it has only a potential existence, dependent on the future thought of the community."[4]

Word and community, together understood as signs of man's essence, suggest contemporary uses of the concept "discourse." A discourse is, as Morris explained in the 1930s of the twentieth century, on the one hand a coherent series of articulations through the use of a natural-, and on the other through the use of an artificial language[5]. Legal articulations are a unique case. Legal discourse is an artificial language discourse created through the management of natural language components. This *unique combination of artificiality and naturalness* forms a philosophical challenge that semioticians as well as philosophers of law have to face. It is no surprise that the Ancient Greek Goddess *Tyche* is mentioned when this powerful combination, and in particular these two intertwined with continuity, plays a role in semiotics—as Peirce has shown in almost his entire lifetime.

---

[2] Peirce: CP 6, 103.

[3] Peirce: CP 5, 314 and CP 7, 572.

[4] Peirce: CP 7, 585, and CP 5, 3.; Ch. Morris: *Signs, Language and Behavior*, New York 1955[2], p. 130, and: *Signification and Significance,* Cambridge MIT, 1964, p. 60 f.

[5] Morris: Op. Lit., p. 131.

Tyche

Tyche knows how fate and fortune are both powerful discourses loaded with frantic explanatory energy to envision the many courses of events in human life. *Ob*sessed with fortune is *pos*sessed by fate; and *ob*sessed with fate is *pos*sessed by fortune, she tells us. Our classification of fate or fortune depends upon the cultural asymptotes we use for their articulation.

Chance plays a dominant role in our articulations and consequently in all our linguistic achievements—in particular when we evoke reality as a most natural component of our discourses. Without chance is no change, no growth, no newness or understanding by means of an open discourse. *Is fate growth?* We hesitate to admit and do not always understand or articulate properly. But the same is true for Fortune, although perhaps different. Difference is in the soul of the Goddess; a schism is the source of her energy because none of her positive actions are without destructiveness. That is also the reason for her divination: her schism is too far from articulate discourse to have it function in a direct manner. The outcry for a sign shouts down her incomprehensible schism. "Give us a sign ..." is a well-known formula that halts our articulation of the flux of events—be they fateful or fortunate.

Do we therefore also share an obsession with Fortune along with the ancient Greek during the IV century B.C. and in fact during the entire Hellenistic period? The question joins a riddle: since the statue of Tyche in Antioch around 300 B.C. was erected, approximately 500 years later another statue was set up in the distant village of Dura-Europos. Such considerations lead to the 1994 exhibition in the Yale University Art Gallery, organized by Suzan Matheson and her staff, supported by J.J. Pollitt's 1986 publication *Art in the Hellenistic Age* in which Tyche was mentioned as one of the driving forces in Hellenistic public life and thoughts.[6] The exhibition, entitled *An Obsession with Fortune*, shows us how the Greek Goddess and her Roman appearance Fortuna linked occurrences of equivocal fortune to Deity. The same instability of human affairs and courses of history are essentially ours. But we have no Goddess anymore to blame for inconsistent governance or unfortunate decisions, so that only presidents and politicians (which we mostly consider as a token of inconsistency or a coin in social merchandise) are left.

In other words, the Greek in the fourth century B.C. did deify chance, fate and fortune, instead of entrusting them in the hands of politicians; perhaps one can think of this, by analogy to modern conventional approaches, as a constitutionalization of an aspect of the social condition. No wonder that the relations between Tyche and Law seem close. We gain knowledge from the exhibition and its catalogue with regard to many aspects of this relationship, especially how long it took before the deification of

[6] Susan B. Matheson [c.s.]: *An Obsession with Fortune: Tyche in Greek and Roman Art.* Yale University Art Gallery, 1994. J.J. Pollitt: *Art in the Hellenistic Age,* Cambridge UP, 1986, -idem-: "An Obsession with Fortune", in: *Yale University Art Gallery*, 1994, p. 13 ff. See also: Lisa R. Brody & Gail L. Hoffman: *Dura Europos. Crossroads of Antiquity*. Exhibition at the McMullen Museum of Art; Boston College, 2011. See also: Lucinda Dirven: *The Palmyrenes of Dura-Europos*, Brill, Leiden 1999, p. 103.

Tyche occurred. The implication of city and political life in an individual's fortune is another aspect in that context, as is the character of public life around Tyche. All these themes play, remarkably enough, also a role in the philosophy of Charles Sanders Peirce—not in his *pragmatism*, but mainly in his *semiotics*, which he determined as being the science of signs and meanings. Meanings focus in particular on the core issues of law and legal thought patterns and form a coherent process of meaning *making* (*Tuchios* [Gr]= maker) as studied in the *legal* semiotics of Roberta Kevelson.

Polybios (200–118), the Greek historian and politician gave in his *Histories* a famous account of the period between 220 and 146 B.C. and in doing so wrote a text that inspired Montesquieu's *Spirit of the Laws* which in its turn stirred the *American Constitution*. He described Tyche as "who makes no treaties with this human life of ours, who devises all sorts of new twists to confound our calculations, and who shows her power in completely unexpected ways ...". He based his writing on his experiences with history and the nature of man rather then on the factual features of the Goddess. How much experience, how many unexplainable life occurrences, how much of a lifetime do these words require before they can be written and understood? His lines are on personal experience and the grasping of a situation plus awareness of an individual's socio-historical dimension and its transfer from one generation to another: for short, the stuff from which history is made. In other words, he shows a new self-understanding in the meaning making of social change in one's life. The character that disturbs it should by definition not be a Deity! And yet?

"Fortune is quite capable of wiping out reasonable expectations with unforeseeable turns of events and if she gives aid to anyone and tips her balance in his favor, she will eventually, as if she regretted the help, tip the scale against him and instantly ruin his successes." Why does Polybios coin these words about her?[7] *Anxiety must have been the hallmark of the Hellenic society who created such a Goddess*! Histories of the Macedonian King Perseus provided an example of how a superbly high-rising position ends up in humiliation. Not only individuals, but also entire countries show that pattern: they flourish in one century and are annihilated in the next—Romans provide an example when their empire became destroyed in the end. No wonder that Matheson describes Tyche long before she became divine (after many centuries in which poets and philosophers contemplated her in verses and tractates) as a determinate feature of life encapsulated in a word that stood for chance or fortune. She dates Tyches' divinity to the fourth century B.C. but traces her existence back into earlier centuries where she can be found as a linguistic expression, a water nymph, a cult object—until she calls herself in the fourth century "a divinity (theos) and the director and manager of all things"[8].

The case of Tyche is not a simple process of name giving, it is a process of *meaning making* that finds it peak in deification: where man understands that he is no longer able to keep fate or fortune in his hand, these two are relocated in other semantic dimensions. Archilocus (680–645) is said to be the first Greek poet who wrote his lyrics using the first person singular. That implied an important step in his

---

[7] Pollitt: *An Obsession.*, Op. Cit., p. 13.

[8] Susan B. Matheson: "The Goddess Tyche" in: *An Obsession ...*, Op. Cit., p. 19 f.

profiling of Greek character; in particular in as far as identity formation is concerned. It interests that Werner Jaeger refers to his poetry because the poet "encourages his friends to endure misfortune patiently or tells them to leave everything to the gods. *Tyché, Fortune, and Moira, Fate, give man all he has.* The gods often lift up men who lie on the ground in disaster, and often cast down to the earth men who stand firm". All these phrases occur in later Greek thought about the power of Tyche. "Archilocus' religious thought is rooted in the problem of Tyche, and his knowledge of God is knowledge of Tyche", Jaeger underlines. [. . .] The Greeks, as they learnt to understand the problem of human freedom, penetrated deeper into the mystery of Tyche."[9] That is an important aspect of understanding Tyche with regard to fate and freedom: the aspect of *endurance*. It says: freedom is not solely the result of individual decisions in life or of social commitments; the share of passivity in acquiring freedom is important. But (1) *endurance* and (2) *profiling actively a "first person-identity"* are in contrast, although both are of essence for social behavior.

So there is another aspect to mention. How can endurance be possible when the complexities of daily life (communication and understanding included) do not allow us to withdraw from a powerful personal identity? Tyche bridges the distance between *endurance* and *a self* by means of *signs,* which carry her image and are meant to be *in the hand of everyone*. This is why she played a role in even the most remote Hellenistic cities. Pollitt provides the archeological and historical data about the important public sculptures of Tyche (especially the Tyche of Antioch by Eutychides) and the many subsequent images of the Goddess that fit in with its semiotic explanation: was her character devastating, her image was omnipresent. "The personification of cities and countries as females wearing 'city wall' crowns was a type already established for use on coinage in the fourth century B.C.". In the days of her divination, Tyche spreads her image. "It is important to emphasize that while these Tyche figures had an allegorical content that was typical of their age, and that while they probably served the same function that flags and state seals do in our own time, *they were not simply symbols*. (. . .) the fortune of a city was understood as something very real, even if unknown. (. . .) figures of Tyche may have taken on a kind of magical quality, like good luck charms". Miniature figures of Tyche were "probably both amuletic and apotropaic, images both of hope and anxiety", Pollitt adds.[10]

The long period before the ultimate deification of Tyche in the fourth century B.C. leads us to recognize that (1) a man's individual fate and fortune is embedded in town and country, and therefore socially engendered beyond his personal power, and (2) that signs of a man's fate and fortune remain metaphorically and materially in his hands—which implies an ultimate personal appropriation despite the quirks of the Goddess.

---

[9] Werner Jaeger: *Paideia: the Ideals of Greek Culture*. Vol. I, Oxford UP New York 1945, p. 124.

[10] Pollitt: *An Obsession . . .*, Op. Cit., p. 14, 15.

City Fortune

Tyche is not the Goddess of exclusively individual disaster and personal fate. She wears a *mural* crown to show her protection to the cities in the Greek and Roman world, to rein the fortune of those cities that were for her almost personified organisms. These ties between individual and social structure confirm an individual's engenderment in social life—a theme at the basis of even our contemporary understanding of signs and meanings in life. Without bounds with a city life, one concludes, a Greek personality could not unfold. Hence the intensity of Tyche's presence in times of balanced prosperity as well as in times of discontinuity or fatal blows in political lives of persons and cities. Tyche was the axe of meaning making in all circumstances—had she not proclaimed to be "the director and manager of all things"?

Pieter Broucke describes in the Yale exhibition catalogue how statues representing Tyche were erected all over the Hellenistic regions, at its peak when Praxiteles sculptured in the fourth century B.C. the Tyche of Megara and set it up near the temple of Aphrodite[11]. But statues are, of course, a dissipating minority of signs in comparison with the coins that helped circulate the image of Tyche in the hands of numerous citizens during several Hellenistic centuries, even surviving conversion to Christianity in later ages. Greek coinage thus created a fixed and supportive scheme of reference for the behavior of citizens.

Clearer feelings of chaos came to the fore when the political landscape changes and cultural diversity, anonymity and cosmopolitism appears. Broucke: "Stability and order [. . .] were replaced by feelings of chaos and insignificance, as well as by the acknowledgement of the constant possibility of a reversal of both personal and communal forces. Within this new Hellenistic world order Fate came to occupy a crucial position. The personification of the source of that uncertainty, Tyche—fate, destiny, or fortune—became an essential and ubiquitous element in Greek culture." We feel the constancy of possible reversals also in our days and agree with what no longer appears as solely an observation of Ancient Art or Classical Archeology: "The surge in attention given to a city's Tyche was, thus, characteristic of the uncertain times."[12] This determines modern legal and political thought and the role of change therein, as we learn from contemporary philosophy. Coins and their Tyche figure are still a token of possessing fate and/or fortune in the hands of citizens who struggle to hold on to their identity.

Tyche Personal and Public

All Tyche fused personal and public fates and fortunes and determined the flux of life. The many coins in the hands of individuals populating the Ancient and the Hellenistic world showed two motives: the *face* as an indication for the private, and

[11] Pieter B.F.J. Broucke: "Tyche and the Fortune of Cities in the Greek and Roman World", in: *An Obsession . . .*, Op. Cit., p. 35–49.

[12] Op. Cit.: p. 37.

the *murals* for the public dimensions of life. That eloquent image had central meaning with regard to the general image of man and of Tyche. So one will never encounter one Tyche solely for individual- and another for exclusively public issues. Lives of individuals and lives of the cities are one life structure, which at a certain moment of history also grounds ideas about democracy. Inscriptions are found on which Tyche is linked with Eirene and with Demokratia, and the three were together (not one of them alone; never one after the other) deified in the fourth century B.C.[13]. To enjoy good fortune, one has to be someone *of* a public—without public/city ties one is not a 'someone' who can enjoy. It's all a matter of engendering an identity: enjoyment of fortune or fate needs a social structure; individual fate and fortune are in essence public and only as public features can they be individual. Took the *public Tyche* a personal aspect on, then the *personal Tyche* was always public—each city had its own Tyche, and cities were bearing their proper name together with their Tyche, in order to show the world their specific features. The Tyche of a city could very well conflate with the Tyche of the Demos, so that all features of Tyche, good and bad, can unify individuals in their immediate social structure. Tyche's blending with other deities contributed to reconciliation and even integration of diverse societies within a state, as some inscriptions suggest. A Tyche as *Oikoumene* is therefore throughout possible: a ruler's city Tyche can imagine to become ruler of the entire inhabited world, as the Ptolemies once dreamed.[14]

An individual fortune is thus solely anchored in the prosperity of the common. That thought fits more than one consideration of Jaeger, who in the context of Archilochus' philosophy and lyrics suggests: "It is a universal conception that there is a 'rhythm' in all human life" and Tyche's deity is grounded in that fact. He thus recommends to exercise self-control and "to avoid excessive joy or grief, to feel excessive emotions for the happiness or unhappiness that comes from destiny". Addressing Tyche must awaken that spirit: the rise and fall of human fortune belongs to the 'rhythm' of human life itself. 'Rhythm' should not be interpreted in terms of 'flux' or movements of music and dance, but as a succession of 'tableaux', of 'forms'. Jaeger underlines: "rhythm then is that which imposes bonds on movement and confines the flux of things"—a thought, which Aristotle indicated as *schema*.

Consider how prosperity and fate, fortune and uncertainty are deified because they do not have the measures of a human hand. The coins that represent them can only be a modest token of us possessing fate and fortune, and the concept of possession itself may not be fit to embrace all dimensions at hand. The same is true for our speech that by means of words tries to fathom fortune or measure fate. Speech is a form of *sympatheia*, which is precious, albeit often completely inappropriate to all of us. Speech is passion and emotion when the doom sent by the gods is envisaged. We speak here about a first form of tragedy. Jaeger remarks: "Without the problem of Tyche or Moira (which had been brought home to the Greeks by the Ionian lyric poets) true tragedy would never have developed [. . .] the plot remained first and foremost a description of human suffering, a fuller and nobler expression of the

[13] Matheson, Op. Cit., p. 19.

[14] Amy C. Smith: "Queens and Empresses as Goddesses", in Brody & Hofman, Op. Cit., p. 91.

high idea of God's power over man's life".[15] Tyche reigns in function of the high power in life, a function she shares with Law. Everyone who has been thinking about the relations between Tyche and Law has noticed that double face. Tyche and Law have their own idea about ground lines of order in human life, which often differ from daily hopes and experiences. The latter had nothing but coins as a sign of its inarticulate consciousness about those dimensions. On the other hand, Tyche knew what Law (here we do not refer to Diké who was often thought to be related to Tyche) could not know: that *a moment of chance determines the course of life beyond the grip of law and legal discourse* on that life. Law does not consider *determination through chance* because it does not recognize any such power. An essential difference between Tyche's and Law's discourse is in the *openness* of the first and the *closeness* of the second. Awareness of Tyche in modernity focuses on such tensions.

Peirce's Goddess

> Try to verify any law of nature and you will find that
> the more precise your observations,
> the more certain they will be to
> show irregular departures from the law.
> (Ch. S. Peirce 1893)

If Tyche is still a Goddess in our contemporary philosophy, then she is Deity of THE OTHERNESS OF ALL THINGS. That otherness takes all forms of discourse, and concern an opposite, a negation, a ground, a contrast, a shadow, an unexpected, a clown, a trickster, an absence, the true and the false and many more. Peirce, who is called the most original of American philosophers and their greatest logician, incorporated Tyche for laying the groundwork of his principle of *continuity* (logical as well as ontological), which includes Tyche's (re)-presentation of Otherness. In doing so, Peirce unfolded many features that are relevant for the foundations of a philosophy of law and legal discourse in her shadow[16].

First, there is an essay as early as from 1867, which Peirce considers as being a part of "the substance of my central achievement", Peirce's biographer Joseph Brent highlights. That substance is *not* his *pragmatism*[17] but rather his *tychism* and its other pole, *agapism* or 'evolutionary love'. He called the principle of continuity: *synechism. Tychism* and *agapism* were therefore complementary phases of the *synechistic* law of mind, which for him was at the same time the law of nature. Their relation to pragmatism is a key for the understanding of Peirce's philosophy, the

---

[15] Jaeger, op. cit., p. 250, 251. See also: Olga Taxidou: *Tragedy, Modernity and Mourning*, Edinburg UP 2004.

[16] Charles Sanders Peirce: "A New List of Categories" in: *Proceedings of the American Academy of Arts and Sciences*, CP 7, 287–298; also: Joseph Brent: *Charles Sanders Peirce. A Life*. Indiana UP, 1993, p. 69; and also: John K. Sheriff: *Charles Peirce's Guess at the Riddle*, Indiana UP 1994.

[17] For which Peirce is still known as a companion of William James, and which constitutes an elaborately discussed theme in legal philosophy.

more since *pragmatism* was designed long after his conceptions of *tychism, agapism* and *synechism.*

Second, the temporary and sudden publicity given to *pragmatism* covered Peirce's deep and lasting concern about the unity of ideas—a problem that Tyche exhibits in each of her disturbingly many and various contradictions. To unravel *the connectedness of things* appeared for Peirce the truly philosophical task to complete. He thus considered more than any other Occidental philosopher in the nineteenth and twentieth century how in the Ancient Greek world Tyche became worshipped: if one cannot take fate and fortune in hand, one should exchange coins bearing her image from hand to hand. Those coins are *signs* involved in the creating of *meaning*—an essential element of Peirce's project, which recalls us our outcry: "Give us a sign. . . !".

Thirdly, 'synechism' is on the interconnectedness of things. Our language/discourse articulates interconnections via activities of the mind, accompanied with and most often created by *signs*. Peirce claims that signs are neither a reproduction of reality nor a copy of what they signify—they are *constructions,* like maps, icons or plans of action and do therefore not limit their function to linguistic articulation. His philosophy insists on the emergence of novelty/newness as a principle upon which our conceptualizations (which erroneously tend to bring reality to the fore as if there exist 'words for things') are based. These require that we bring novelty in harmony with already existing identities, a problem that Pierce treats under the heading of the concept 'continuum'[18]. He unfolds his doctrine of Pure Chance as a factor in the context of *Becoming*, and thus—as Kevelson notices—establishes semiotics as a process of growth of thought. A sign is the fulfillment of Tyche's capacity to master inconsistence in connection with consistency: as an opposite, a breach, a trickster, a falsification, a fool, an incomprehensible, an unforeseen, or an injunction in the surface of our text, speech or action. That conceptual appearance of a sign including its very opposite is a phenomenon under the phenomena with which we are confronted. But a sign makes us only understand its conceptual representation, and *not* the thing it represents—of which we can perhaps only approximate some knowledge. Do not forget how Tyche means that the real is precisely *not* what is immediately before us, nor what seems predestined and ordered through laws. "Read me: there is not what is written there!" The real is what emerges in new relational patterns—one of Tyche's vibrantly modern features is a *pattern philosophy*![19]

Fourthly, what we think to know as real is the reality we represent by means of linguistic articulation. Reality is thus at any given time incomplete and inaccurate, even with a logic capable of prediction: "only an inductive mode of inference can advance our knowledge of the world as it is becoming", Kevelson comments.[20] With conceptualizing a sign we enter an *unlimited* process of semiosis, as not only Peirce

[18] Kelly A. Parker: *The Continuity of Peirce's Thought,* Vanderbilt UP 1998. Ch. 4 & 8.

[19] William Gibson: *Pattern Recognition.* Berkley/Penguin 2005*;* Daniel C. Dennett: "Real Patterns", in: *The Journal of Philosophy*, Vol. 88, No. 1. P. 21 f.

[20] Roberta Kevelson: *Peirce, Paradox, Praxis.* Mouton de Gruyter 1990, p. 310.

but later also Eco and Colapietro conclude[21]. That has a far-reaching conclusion for the presence of reality as a concept in our discourses and the role of chance therein: since there *are* no signs, and nothing *is* a sign, everything *can become* a sign so that there are ultimately only sign functions, and these are only temporarily exercising such a function, Peirce suggests. *Does only Tyche's seduction show us reality; so that reality and chance seem to be double-faced articulations?* "The real, then, is that which, sooner or later, information and reasoning would finally result in, and which is therefore independent of the vagaries of me and you", he writes. The very origin of reality shows that this conception essentially involves the notion of a community, without limits and capable of a never-ending increase of knowledge. Hence Peirce's conclusion: "There is nothing, then, to prevent our knowing outward things as they really are, and it is most likely that we do thus know them in numberless cases, although we can never be absolutely certain of doing so in any special case"[22].

We cannot remain steadfast with any doctrine of necessity or of determinacy because of the complex games Tyche plays with us. The combination of steadiness and chance is her major theme. Any moment she interferes, there is change, growth, turn and twist or unforeseen development. Peirce underlines: "Everywhere the main fact is growth and increasing complexity. [...] By thus admitting pure spontaneity of life as a character of the universe [...] I account for all the variety and diversity of the universe, in the only sense in which the really sui generis and new can be said to be accounted for. The ordinary view has to admit [...] that variety can spring only from spontaneity, or else shoves it back to the beginning of time and supposes it dead ever since."[23] And he completes on the very same page "Yet chance is explanatory of change, which is a fact".

Fifthly, this insight leads Peirce to his *evolutionary semiosis*; only that view seems apt to appropriately consider its character of infiniteness. It appears in the understanding of the sign under the guidance of Tyche and in the insight how signs are only possible in an open-ended, nonfinite, complex and evolving process with chance as one of its this as clearly as he can: "I start by defining what I mean with a sign. It is something determined by something else its object and itself influencing some person in such a way that that person becomes thereby mediately influenced or determined in some respect by that Object." He could do so only after having described in 1901 how anything which determines something else to refer to an object to which itself refers in the same way, that something else must becoming in turn a sign, and so on. Emphasis is on the last three words: the 'and so on'. The latter suggests that it is questionable whether consciousness can ever be seen as essential to the understanding of a sign, since there is always a determination of a sign of the same object at work of which it is itself a sign! There is virtually an endless series of signs when a sign is understood, and a sign never understood cannot be

[21] Umberto Eco: *A Theory of Semiotics*. Bloomington. Indiana UP. 1979, p. 69, 120 ff. See also: Vincent M. Colapietro, *Peirce's Approach to the Self. A Semiotic Perspective on Human Subjectivity*. New York, 1989, p. 35 f.

[22] Peirce, CP 5, 315 f.

[23] Peirce, CP 6, 58 f.

said to be a sign. Signs are the outcome of evolutionary processes and understood only in terms of chance. If we do not accept chance, we cannot understand signs! There exists a remarkable tension between chance and design, between novelty and habitual patterning for Peirce. And what is discovered as essential in the concept of a sign is also of essence for the entire project of *semiosis*. What about law and legal discourse?

Tyche in Legal Discourse

Does Tyche fit in *legal* discourse? She might be shy to forward an opinion, because her role in legal discourse would perhaps be different from the role she plays in general culture or history, although *Diké* was her companion deity and both guarded a city's good fortune. Her other equivalent was Demeter, the Goddess of grief and good harvest, nurturer of mankind who could empathize with grief, having experienced it herself. Those two also relate her to law, so that we could see that Tyche fits in legal discourse under the condition, that we understand law as *a system of signs* and that we do not perceive law as a *closed discourse* imprisoned in a self-referential character.

Neither the Goddess nor Peirce focused on law and its practices. Their fascination was with nature, history and mankind in general to which law belongs. But Peirce shows clearly that our understanding of the law depends on the relation between propositions of universal and/or of particular character, and that is a *semiotic* issue. *Legal* laws are *particular* (even when they seem to be general within their own discourse) and here are Tyche's character as well as Peirce's plea for 'coherence *together with* chance' important. Kevelson calls his plea a "'hotbed' of possibility" of greatest importance for modern law[24]. She thus characterizes "the attempt to transform the idea of law from a universal proposition which is indefinite and vague to a particular proposition which is definite and resolved of vagueness" as a stumbling block[25] that Austin and others met when discussing legal positivism and determinism. The voice of Tyche changes our view on the relationship between universality and particularity from *deterministic* to *chance-related*, as Peirce has shown in most of his works[26].

Peirce's thoughts concern a hitherto unwritten study on legal philosophy. Fisch underlined their relevance for the foundations of law and legal discourse: "I argue that Peirce had a much greater and lifelong interest in law and in social philosophy than has hitherto been recognized". He placed Peirce's concern with law and legal thinking in a biographical perspective. "Philosophers of law" Fisch writes, "have often remarked

---

[24] Roberta Kevelson: *The Law as a System of Signs*, N.York 1988; —id.: *Peirce and the Mark of the Gryphon,* N.York 1999; —id.: *Peirce, Paradox, Praxis,* N.York/Berlin 1990. —id.: *Inlaws/Outlaws,* Peter Lang, Lisse 1977; —id.: *Peirce, Science, Signs,* N.York/Bern 1996.

[25] Kevelson, *Peirce, Paradox, Praxis,* Op. Cit., p. 173.

[26] Peirce, CP 5, Ch 5, and CP 6, §§ 32, 51 f, 63 f, 200 f, 204, 270, 336.

that there were several distinguished lawyers in the Metaphysical Club in which pragmatism was born, and have traced connections between pragmatism and 'legal realism'; but more recently Roberta Kevelson and others have found relevance to legal reasoning in a much wider range of Peirce's work on logic."[27] *Legal semiotics* as prepared in Peircean logics, metaphysics and pragmatism, are the spirit and the form of such a philosophical endeavor. Peircean thoughts and Tyche's inspiration profile a legal philosophy in at least the fields of meaning and argument, chance, and the open character of discourse.

We are not used to be living with the idea that every discourse must be perceived as a place where meanings are made, ideas grow and novelty occurs. Tyche reins every possible discourse—*legal* discourse not in the least. Are the three C's that excel in Civil Law: completeness, coherence and consistency[28] of the legal system requirements that do not leave room for the Goddess? Certainly not. Those criteria are in essence *rhetorical*. They fortify the narrative that keeps *law as an institution* alive. Tyche taught us to appreciate habit formation. Here she does, and she does very effectively with regard to legal argumentation.[29] The semiotics of argument in law and legal practice demonstrate how arguments are offered as if they were facts, but once we are clear about how inconsistency creates consistency, incoherence causes coherence or incompleteness functions as an element of completeness, as Greimas would suggest[30], we understand how arguments are *made* (and not simply re-presented) within the boundaries of the discourse. When Peirce participated in Harvard's Metaphysical Club in 1872, Sir Frederick Pollock had just written some untimely lines, stating: "Law in the widest sense is a condition or assemblage of conditions under which the evolution of things proceeds..."[31]. James Boyd White offers a recent example when he reflects upon how constituting *a culture of argument* inspired modern US society by means of a text named "The Constitution". He concludes how "this is thus in a literal sense a rhetorical constitution: it constitutes a rhetorical community, working by rhetorical processes that it has established but can no longer control. *It establishes a new conversation on a permanent basis*."[32]

---

[27] M.H. Fisch, *Peirce, Semeiotic and Pragmatism,* Indiana UP 1986, p. 13, 438. The "Metaphysical Club" is a philosophical club with the future Justice O.W. Holmes Jr, the psychologist William James and with Charles Sanders Peirce, established in January 1872 in Cambridge, Mss and dissolved in December 1872. When Peirce arrived at Johns Hopkins University in 1879, he founded a new Club there, which existed six more years.

[28] John H. Merryman: *The Civil Law Tradition,* Stanford UP 1985 (2nd Ed.) Ch 2; Ch 5.

[29] I. A Richards: *The Philosophy of Rhetoric,* Oxford UP 1936, Ch. 2.

[30] Algirdas J. Greimas & François Rastier: "The Interaction of Semiotic Constraints" in: *Yale French Studies,* Vol. 41, 1968. (See this book Part II, Chapter 5)

[31] F. Pollock: "Law and Command", in: *Law Magazine and Review*, 1872,1. p. 189 f.

[32] James Boyd White: *When Words Lose Their Meaning,* Chicago UP 1984, p. 246 f. See also Chaim Perelman: *The idea of Justice and the Problem of Argument*, London/New York 1963, and Perelman/Olbrechts-Tyteca, *The New Rhetoric: A Treatise on Argumentation*, Notre Dame UP 1969. Notice the proximity to I. Prigogine & I. Stenger: *Order Out Of Chaos,* Glasgow 1984.

Arguments establish law and legal discourse during the process of meaning making which unfolds whilst solving an incidental case[33]. But Tyche desires, that this meaning making is a process beyond discursive coercion. That becomes clear *when she shows her whimsy character*, for which we give a Greek and a modern example. Werner Jaeger tells us an example that circulated in the Ancient Greek world: "In Xenophon's portrait of Cyrus, [...] Cyrus is a Persian Alexander. Only his fortune, his tyché, was different from his Macedonian parallel. The spear, which pierced him, might have killed Alexander. If it had not taken Cyrus' life, the Hellenistic age would have begun with him, and would have followed a different course. [...] Greek culture, through its intellectual content and its form, always imparts to every other élite something, which that élite does not possess, but thereby helps it to develop itself too"[34]. Greimas would have constructed one of his squares to show the play of opposites of meaning and their creative integration. More than two millennia later, Paul Auster[35] introduces Miles, the central figure of his 2010 novel, who is a victim of chance and waits for his Tyche without knowing that he already met her: "Whenever he thinks about that day now, he imagines how differently things would have turned out if he had been walking on Bobby's right instead of his left. The shove would have pushed him off the road rather than into the middle of it, an that would have been the end of the story, since there wouldn't have been a story... ". However, we say from the lesson Tyche taught us: there is *always* a story.

"One should beware of believing that the inventive mind operates according to chance"—this sentence of the French Enlightenment philosopher Destutt de Tracy serves Greimas as motto for his 1968 essay. Do not forget that Tyche was named 'the constellation virgo': she determines how an *order of things* emerges, and encounters us with vision, feeling and spontaneity where human creativity unfolds. She was for that reason a guide for Peirce in the context of understanding his own personal fate as well as the development of his ideas about an evolutionary cosmology, which colored his lifelong interest in philosophy and logic. In *Evolutionary Love* 1893[36] he suggests how all forms of evolution are tied to Tyche's force that reins over a person in his or her social context, thus influencing and often even determining the development of a human character: *any self is for itself a sign*. "Every thought, or cognitive representation, is of the nature of a sign. 'Representation' and 'sign' are synonyms. The whole purpose of a sign is that it shall be interpreted in another sign; and its whole purport lies in the special character, which it imparts to that interpretation. When a sign determines an interpretation of itself in another sign, it produces an effect external to itself [...] not in this or that metaphysical sense, but in an indisputable *(read: argumentative, rhetorical)* sense. [...] Thinking is a kind of action, and reasoning is a kind of deliberate action; and to call an argument

[33] Jan M. Broekman & William A. Pencak: *Lawyers Making Meaning. The Roberta Kevelson Seminar on Law and Semiotics at Penn State University's Dickinson School of Law,* IJSL Vol. 22, Nr. 1, 2009. See in that issue D.J. Brion: "Trial Argumentation: The Creation of Meaning", p. 23 ff.

[34] Werner Jaeger, Op. Cit., Vol. III, p. 161.

[35] Paul Auster: *Sunset Park*, Henry Holt & Co. 2010.

[36] N. Houser & Chr. Kloesel (Eds), *The Essential Peirce*, Vol.1. Indiana UP 1992, p. 362.

illogical, or a proposition false, is a special kind of moral judgment, and as such is inapplicable to what we cannot help. This does not deny that what cannot be conceived today may be conceivable tomorrow. But just as long as we cannot help adopting a mode of thought, so long it must be thoroughly accepted as true. Any doubt of it is idle make-believe and irredeemable paper"[37]. This self-understanding is based on insight in *order* tout court, an order that expands itself in the forms of argument and accelerating reasonableness.

The *openness* of a discourse, Tyche teaches legal philosophers, *is not a condition for, but itself the result of chance*. Kevelson has in her semiotic interpretation of law spent much energy in discussing the *open* character of law's discourse. She clarifies that any legal argument is in need of a narrative space located between chance and necessity and within which Tyche is the most important performer. Peirce would have agreed and repeated how every thought-life of a person is a sign. We know from Fisch that Peirce found in a book on Plato how Socrates defined thought as 'a conversation of the soul with itself' and so he wrote in the margin: "This is, I think, Plato's greatest contribution to thought".[38] All thought is dialogic by nature, he would underline, and characterizes all signs, signification- andS meaning- making. A thought is like a word is like a sign: they cannot exist in the isolation of their own self. Tyche guarantees the Otherness they need to become; only chance causes novelty and continuity. It interests how thoughts of Peirce fit almost seamless to the subject "*Tyche in Law*". Inspired by his philosophy, we conclude with a few keywords to describe her position in legal discourse more precisely.

First, there is the *openness of discourse*. Kevelson characterizes the field within which the issue is most thoroughly debated, the field of '*autopoietics*,' as "a rather old hybrid of semiotics, bent in an unusual way".[39] Its self-reflectiveness parallels Peirce's dynamics of inquiry—a process that plays for him a dominant role in science and thought. Tyche would not accept this single focus on discourse as 'a self that plays the game of reflection on itself'. If such reflectiveness in law occurs, it does not create closeness by means of doubling itself, but on the contrary new habits of thought so that reflectiveness includes novelty and obeys the prescriptions of Tyche. She cares that openness shows itself even in reflection, so that chance, spontaneity, irregularity and lawlessness remain constituent particles of law's discourse. A legal philosophy should not consider lawlessness as a deviation or exception but as a regularly force of law.

Second, the philosophical discussions about (in)-determinism are still relevant. Peirce's happy relationship with Tyche shows the intensity with which to contemplate the issue in legal context. What happened in the aftermath of the US Civil War brings an implicit theory of law to the fore that has evolved from *argument*, in particular from arguments that produce dissent, discontent and conflict. A parallel could be in recent dimensions of European Union Law, where dissent and discontent also bring novelty and hitherto unknown legal insights and procedures. Tyche asked Europeans

[37] Peirce, CP. 8, 191.

[38] Max H. Fisch: *Peirce, Semeiotic, and Pragmatism*, Op. Cit., p. 442.

[39] Roberta Kevelson: *Peirce and the Mark of the Gryphon*, Op. Cit. p. 160.

to digest her whimsy character features in law for instance, when they become confronted with ADR or ODR.[40] Kevelson's semiotic insight can become real on both continents: *a People divided can nevertheless be One!* And, not unlike a sign, the One can bring division again, which results in a new One, etc. ad infinitum. That is, again, at home in Peirce's thoughts when he advances how *Secondness* (the medium between *Firstness* and *Thirdness*) is characterized by creative conflict, so that law produces sequences of impressively different layers of reality, and does not solely reflect upon them.

Finally, one concludes perhaps surprised, that *Tyche highlights the dialogic dimensions* of legal relations in society. She was after all a Greek Goddess, and knew by experience how Socrates (in the *Theaetetus* and the *Sophist*) mentioned that *all thought is dialogic by nature*. She adds to this context (Peirce noted this as if he was her secretary) the pivotal importance of the Sign, and concludes that the Self is always a sign for the Self. The first sign in practice for law is a Self! That semiotic understanding of the Self is the riddle Tyche has left for twenty-first century lawyers. That seems a task of exceptional gravity when chance, dissent and conflict become novel components of law in times of revolutions and decline of the Nation State.

Tyche brings us to Peirce in a much deeper and more bewildering sense than we ever thought of. Chance and change are notions awakened by Tyche's whimsical character. Therefore, these can never become stable and fixated elements of a theory, one is attempted to say. In Peirce's references to Tyche, in particular in the development of his own tychism, he acquired by no means a final form of his 'evolutionary cosmology'. Again: to have Tyche function in the context of a stable philosophical project seems incompatible with her eccentric nature. Peirce experienced that from the very beginning, and in particular in the long period of his life in Arisbe, where he studied Greek philosophy with great intensity.

Can Peirce's reflections on Kant, on Kantian categories, on Categories as such and on the Triadic nature of ontology or on concepts such as chance and continuity, be considered as building blocks of a system that includes Tyche? The question is the more pressing where she is mirrored in the socio-legal situation of today's society and its political culture. Hence the pressing interest in the semiotic foundations of politics, both philosophical and legal-theoretical. In times of a decline of the nation state, of governance not by governments but by global corporations defending their interests even under the heading of 'human rights' concepts, Tyche's eccentricity, as Chap. 9 suggests, catches the eye.

We should not qualify Tyche's spirit negatively. She inspires us to understand the restlessness of life, but gives us not the power to understand life in these terms of restlessness. Hence Peirce's focus on chance, without which no change or surprise can enter the stage of our knowledge and understanding of world history. Is Tyche's deification a way of overcoming the dyadic character that reins all our knowledge, in particular our philosophical understanding of reality? Does her deification contribute

---

[40] Which could very well be examples of Law's Chaotic Order, suggests Denis J. Brion: "Chaos-What Judges and Juries Do", in W. Pencak & J.R. Lindgren: *New Approaches to Semiotics and the Human Sciences,* Peter Lang 1998, p. 33.

to this fundamental change in our approach, described by Peirce in his letters to W. James in which he suggests that he may have found the key to the secret of the universe? "The guess of the secret of the Sphynx", he calls it. *Synechism* originates here, eventually called *tritism*: each opposition needs mediation, a "tripling". The process of deification could therefore be characterized as a forwarding of that tritism, a truly transcultural, and cosmic principle. Hence Peirce: "... skepticism about the reality of things—provided it be genuine and sincere, and not a sham—is a healthful and growing stage of mental development". Note, that evolutionary cosmology is made possible by discovering the structure of the triadic, not inverse: the triadic notion is not coming before and not preceding, cosmology. This Peircean type of cosmology is a fruit of his insight into the triadic structure of understanding everything. In law, we mention the modern striving for an interpretation of doctrines and principles in terms of human interpellation and affection. Indeed: the False, the True: Peirce is not interested in features of the concept of chance, or in prophecies about its eventual effects, but in the functions of chance in a philosophy focusing on interrelations of things, events, meanings and discourses. It implies Peirce's interest in change as a product of chance, in the foundations and the logics of chance, in growth, and evolution.

The influence of Tyche is important because it makes his philosophy fruitful for exploring its affinity with legal thinking—in competition with logic, whilst he fully understands that legal logic is not formal logic. This conclusion does not only fit to the strictly philosophical works of Peirce (in particular his pragmatism) but in a broader sense the area of legal semiotics as such. Semiotics reads the artificiality of law's discourse within the framework of linguistics. The difference between a lawyer's word and words spoken in everyday life focuses on the character of those languages we call 'natural'. The central question in this book is therefore about the relation among artificiality and naturalness. Is our speech 'natural'? Ask Mr Jourdain, ask Peirce in his backyard hearing the train whistle, ask a lawyer. Is he the *SEMEIOTIKOS* of our days? Tyche would have answered that question.

Chapter 18
A Legal Semiotics Vocabulary

The following are some of the most predominant concepts that can be found in a vocabulary of legal semiotics in practice. Semioticians debate the meaning and definition of these concepts inspired by linguistics, medicine, social sciences, politics and law. Notice, that those of them who focus on law and legal discourse do in the overwhelming majority of cases *not* practice law. Practitioners of law do in general not participate in this type of reflection.

John Locke's idea, that distinctions not only create differences, but through the creation of differences also unite and connect in a *sign*, is practiced here. He suggested that signs are cognitive instruments "whereby Notions and Knowledge and the Thoughts of Men's Mind are conveyed from one to another". That conveyance bridges and ultimately unites the attitude of legal practitioners and those who practice semiotics. This *Vocabulary of Legal Semiotics* does not mention legal terms but only semiotic expressions that are involved in most legal uses. It is rather a specification for lawyers' uses of the more general and foundational "Glossary of Semiotics" of Vincent M. Colapietro, Paragon House, New York 1993. And even those topics can be deepened through further exploration of (among others) W. Nöth: *Handbook of Semiotics* (1990, 1994), Ducrot & Todorov: *Dictionnaire encyclopédique des sciences du langage.* (1972), T. Honderich (Ed.): *The Oxford Companion to Philosophy,* (1995) or Th. Sebeok (Ed.) *Encyclopedic Dictionary of Semiotics, Approaches to Semiotics.* (1986, 1994).

The list originates mainly from linguistics, philosophy, sociology and communication sciences. That is no surprise, since law has closest ties with language and serves communicative/informative purposes. It shows again how issues beyond legal practice are nevertheless important for legal discourse in its entirety. To enhance the experimental applicability of these major concepts, *provisional descriptions* are provided in order to make this vocabulary of semiotics and legal semiotics useful for legal practitioners.

Code — Codes are rules for converting and thus for changes of informational elements, such as a letter, word, or even text fragment, so that it will be used in another informative context, which can also exist in letters, words or texts. That change of context is an important issue in semiotics and law. The relevance of a code in legal semiotics

J. M. Broekman, L. Catà Backer, *Lawyers Making Meaning,*
DOI 10.1007/978-94-007-5458-4_18, © Springer Science+Business Media Dordrecht 2013

is important; codes are the heart of meaning making and meaning management in Civil as well as in Common Law. In particular the Civil Law depends on codes that regulate—often in rigid prescriptive manners—the communication between subjects of law. The words of Article 4 in the Napoleonic Code, which proclaim the judge who refuses to judge/speak to be guilty of denial of justice, are a famous example. The Common Law focuses on a code as a compilation of laws, so that most jurisdictions have codified their laws as a means to understand them as a textual unity, as a guide to the professionals and a basis for action. It is of semiotic importance how in the Common Law the Code has changed into the "Model Rules of Professional Conduct".

Connotation — Indicates a mixture of different meanings, for instance the contrast of a word or phrase with its literal meaning. Connotation is often contrasted with denotation, the things a word refers to. A connotation essentially determines how something can or should be associated with a word or phrase, an implied value judgment or a feeling.

Discourse — (Lat. *Discurrere*) A discourse comprises linguistic units, especially written or otherwise documented speech acts. These units can compose a variety of sentences, conversations, arguments or speeches. Their analysis is differentiated into *Discourse Analysis* (comprising language [*langue*] and speech [*parole*]), *Narrative Analysis* (pertaining to narrations as elements of discourse) and *Conversation Analysis* (sociological research on material elements of conversations, such as videos and tapes). Kristeva, when offering a typology of discourses, highlights *monological* discourse. She so differentiates between an epic, historic and scientific discourse. (Kristeva, 1980) The concept of "*legal* discourse" (Charles Morris, 1955) is extremely important in semiotics. In the light of legal semiotics, a legal discourse can be defined as "a well-structured totality of specifically legal speech acts".

Icon — *icon*, *index* and *symbol* [see below] are three terms in the philosophy of Peirce to indicate how a sign vehicle represents its object; in the case of an icon by means of resemblance or similarity. Lawyers often take this type of representation as given by nature and do not reflect upon the precise and limited meaning of this representation. An icon is thus one of the most fundamental divisions of signs in general. In law (for instance in criminal investigations), similarity is regarded as a strong motive in its own right, without reference to considerations why and in particular how it belongs to the more general issue of the many relationships between sign and object—one of the basic themes of the philosophy and semiotics of Peirce.

Index — an actual and/or physical connection is also in legal reasoning an important issue to consider. For Peirce, the index is one of the ways in which a sign may be related to its object. Indexes are also called indexical signs—they are those signs through which actual signs are connected with its object. This basis for legal reasoning itself remains in the dark, and does not belong to theoretical or jurisprudential reflections. Only a legal semiotics clarifies those relations within sign functions in law.

Linguistics — A discourse on language, theoretical or applied. A person engaged in this particular discourse is a linguist. Language structure (grammar) and linguistic meaning (semantics) are major components. Grammar encompasses morphology (formation and alteration of words) and syntax (the rules that determine the way words combine into phrases and sentences). Applied linguistics puts linguistic theories into practice in areas such as foreign language teaching, speech therapy, translation and speech pathology, or analysis of law and legal discourse.

Meaning — A relationship between *signs* and the kinds of things they refer to, intend, express or signify. One term necessarily causes something else to come to the mind in consequence; a sign is hence understood as an entity that indicates another entity to some agent for some purpose. Signs exist only in opposition to other signs. One issue has meaning only because it is *not* another. F. de Saussure defers meaning to the sign itself: meaning is ultimately the same thing as the sign, and *meaning* means that relationship between signified and signifier. This, in turn, means that all meaning is both within us individual and communal.

Message — An object of communication, providing information or being information itself. So its meaning depends upon its context; the term may apply to both the information and its form. The core subject matter of semiotics is the communication of messages. In communications sciences, a message is information sent from a source to a receiver. Semiotics does not accept this philosophical scheme as its point of departure and regards the sender/receiver model as inadequate. The position of the sender (the "I") is more complex and so is the position of the receiver: Lacan and many others have demonstrated the inherent complexities. An important semiotic question in this context is, that messages in legal discourse are constantly in a flow of transformation (for instance messages becoming a command) and thus change the discourse character of law.

Metaphor

> Metaphor is the juxtaposition of disparate elements of the world in which an unsuspected commonality, an illuminating partial likeness, has been discovered, and the more unlikely the juxtaposition, the greater the consequent sensation of the unifying of the world. . . .
>
> Leon Wieseltier on Saul Bellow, Nov. 2010

A metaphor relates two or more seemingly unrelated subjects, and describes a first as *being* or *approximately being equal to* a second. Properties of the second are used to enable the description of the first. Metaphor is more forceful and assertive than analogy, although the two are highly similar and often confused. Metaphors can be distinguished from other rhetorical concepts such as metonymy, synecdoche, simile, allegory or parable. Legal semiotics judges the uses of metaphor in the rhetoric of law quite differently. The displacement of words, which is the issue here, is in classical theories considered as a purely verbal matter. Legal semiotics, however, focuses on *meaning* as the major subject of that displacement, thus pointing at the transaction between contexts, which takes place in the emergence of metaphor. The metaphors of law and language derive from comparison, and that is in fact a matter of thought formation. Lawyers should thus raise their implicit recognitions into explicit distinctions and, in doing so, create a platform for legal thinking that represents much more than a sampling of shortcuts for the pragmatic mind. Pragmatism should never become identical with the worship of shortcuts.

Metonymy The substitution of one word for another with which it is associated. Metonymy uses a single characteristic to identify a more complex entity; it is basic to cognition. It is common to take one easy-to-perceive aspect of something and use that aspect to stand either for the thing as a whole or for some other aspect or part of it. Semiotics of law researches whether the use of metonymy structures doctrinal discourse.

Paradigm Practices of knowledge-formation, which define a scientific discipline during a particular period of time. Thomas Kuhn defines a scientific paradigm as: *what* is to be observed and scrutinized, the kind of *questions* that are supposed to be asked, *how* these questions are probed for answers and are structured, *how* the results of scientific investigations should be interpreted, *how* an experiment is to be conducted, and *what* equipment is available for it. A prevailing paradigm often represents a more specific way of viewing reality in general and in everyday language than a general scientific method. A matter of legal semiotic analysis is, whether legal discourse can be understood or functions as a specific

Reference Reference pertains to the range of objects to which a sign points, in contrast to the meaning or signification of a sign. What refers to or designates something, acts as a connection or a link between two things. The objects it links may be concrete or abstract (such as data, thought, or memories). The object which is named by a reference, or to which the reference points, is called the referent. In semantics, reference is generally construed as the relation between nouns or pronouns and objects that are named by them. Frege distinguished between sense and reference because of the problematic character of that relation. A semantic sign can be considered a subset of the linguistic sign, which was first analyzed by de Saussure. A sign contains the *signified* (a thought which represents an object), and the *signifier* (the sound or written word). Both share the actual physical object as referent. It seems evident, that referential activity and the construction as well as the management of signs are in the lights of semiotics the pillars of legal discourse, both as an object of theoretical analysis and as a specific discursive strategy in law and legal practice.

Rhetoric — From Homer, Ancient- and Classical Greek culture, the Sophists and European Middle Ages, rhetoric was about public speaking that influences the coherence of society, approximating public virtue, logos and discourse, not in the least in view of law. Modern rhetoric underlines the importance of language and persuasion in increasingly mediated environments. And rhetoric enriches our understanding of linguistic communication: "A rhetorical figure is a situation in which language means something other than what it says" (Culler1981). Rhetorical analysis considers how communication media have a persuasive impact on us. Behavioral sciences, literary criticism and ancient rhetoric sustain today's interested in human symbolic behavior. Legal semiotic not only studies these developments in law and legal judgment, but also highlights the institutional aspects of law in which rhetorical figures unfold in legal practice.

Semantics — The study of meaning expressed in a language, code, or other form of representation of information. Semantics is contrasted with two other aspects of meaningful expressivity, namely, *syntax*, the construction of complex signs from simpler signs, and *pragmatics*, the practical use of signs by agents or communities of interpretation in particular circumstances and contexts. Semantics may also denote the study of meaning within systems of signs. Of central interest for law and semiotics is the relation between a sign and its object, always including objective reference, called its *denotation*. Sometimes one refers to the relation between a sign and the signs that serve in its practical interpretation as its *connotation*. But the application of *semantics* seems restricted to the denotative aspect especially in the formal semantic, pragmatic, and semiotic traditions.

Semiotics — The study of signs and symbols, both individually and as groups,

(Semiology) functioning in sign systems. This includes the construction, engineering and understanding of meaning, mainly as an epistemological processes. Semiology is important in law and legal anthropology as well as logics. The latter pertain to areas belonging also to the natural sciences – such as how organisms make predictions about, and adapt to their semiotic niche in the world. In general, semiotic theories take *signs* or sign systems as their object of operation. There is no appropriate theory of law without reference to its legal semiotic dimensions.

Semiosis Charles S. Peirce's term for any process that involves *signs*, sign actions and sign processes, in geneeral including the production of meaning. Semiosis is the expression that indicates a *performance* of involving signs. Although one can communicate unintentionally, individuals usually speak or write to elicit some kind of response. But semiosis does not provide an explanation of how it *produces* its effects.

Semiosphere The sphere of semiosis in which the sign processes operate in reality, understood as sets of interconnected *Umwelt*s, an Umwelt being reality, made available for an organism via perception and operation (J. v. Uexküll). That concept relates to the idea of *Lebenswelt*, which is the source for action and reflection, life as the most encompassing context. Umwelt and Lebenswelt are actually considered as part of biosemiotics (Sebeok). A semiosphere comes into being when Umwelts are communicating. A community of organisms occupying the semiosphere will be relevant for semiotics. But organisms create the signs, which will then become the constituent parts of the semiosphere. This is basic for the continuous creation of new environments. It would be highly interesting to note, that society contains various social Umwelts, who may form a social semiosphere and from which law may be regarded as important. Sociosemiosphere and biosemiosphere thus form a unity, which trough semiosis has today great explanatory power.

Semiotic Square A visual representation that classifies concepts relevant to a given opposition of concepts, such as feminine-masculine, beautiful-ugly, etc. and extends the relevant ontology (Greimas), so that one pair of concepts ultimately reveals minimally six implied concepts. The square inspires important work of legal semioticians, like Bernard Jackson.

Semiotic Triangle The figure that explains the relationship between Concepts, Symbols (or signifier) and Objects (or signified). The relations between real objects, symbols and thoughts are in our times discussed in semiotic perspective by Charles W. Morris and Charles Sanders Peirce. Differences between objects, concepts and symbols are symbolized in the triangle. Of central interest is the observation that no symbolic representation of an object can ever be directly referring to the object, but only through concepts. The relation between Symbol and Referent is thus an implied relationship. Peirce is closely associated with the triangle because of his focus on signs, so that his works form an important source of inspiration for legal semiotics.

Sign (Sign System) Components of semiotics, epistemology, logic, and philosophy of language. They all deal with signs, what they are and how they signify. There are extremely close ties between *signs* and *signification.* Everything can be a sign (Peirce), and significance is about the relationship between a sign and what it signifies, intends, expresses or means. Things *may* act as signs *without* any respect to the human agent as its originator. There are furthermore signs, which are *always* signs, and there are signs that *have* to acquire their signification. The human mind is understood as the sole agency through which signs signify. Human language and discourse, communication, philosophy, science, logic, mathematics, poetry, theology, and religion are fields of human study and activity where grasping the nature of signs and symbols and patterns of signification may occur. One of the major insights is (as Kevelson showed) that law could be interpreted as a discourse-depended system of signs.

Signification (Signifier, Signified) Signification is the essential process in understanding and managing signs in so far as there is no sign without the signification of another sign. The "being a sign" is a matter of signification (the achievement) and signifying (the process); what the sign is therefore is the signified (a natural or cultural object). Maintaining conventional signs could be the ultimate goal of legal engineering in and through legal language (which is not in natural language, although the vocabulary seems natural, the meanings are cultural and often institutionally anchored. Philosophy of language and psychology are neighbors in explaining signification. The first excels in understanding meaning, the other in exploring issues such as expression, intentions or communication. Whatever belongs to signification is ultimately the engendering of relationships between signifier and signified. Semiotic analyses of legal discourses reengineer those relationships, their implications and social effects.

Structuralism A mainly philosophical approach to explore the predominantly *structural relationships* between elements in language, literature and other fields upon which networks are built. Meaning is produced pertaining to an individual, a system, or a culture through these networks. This meaning (not subjectivity) frames and motivates the actions of individuals and groups. Structuralism as an academic interest peaked in the late 1960s and early 1970s. Structuralism in linguistics influenced semiotics until our days, both regarding real- and virtual realities. Russian formalism, Prague structuralism and Parisian literary criticism and anthropology are major stations in its development. Structuralist influences on legal theory inspire legal semiotics. Important in that context are: (1) the perspective on "Law" as a specific *discourse*, (2) a renewed interest in legal hermeneutics, in particular for the properties of legal *texts*, who forward "inter-textuality" rather than strictly "one-text" interpretations,

(3) the idea that legal activities are in essence *linguistic* activities or language operations, (4) a revitalized attention to the structural *engineering* of the legal discourse in contrast to reshuffling fixated contents such as precedents, rules etc.

Structure How an issue, such as a story, a narrative or other texts, is related to all types of reality based on information and knowledge. A structure is thus a result of the composition of knowledge by means of perceiving elements and their combinations. Structures become visible in the recognition, observation, nature, and stability of patterns and relationships of entities. The *structural content* functions as the information, which the structure represents or is. This insight is a building block for a theory of general semantics. A structure defines furthermore what a system is made of: a configuration of items. Structures are generally spoken a collection of inter-related components, and form for instance a hierarchy or a network of relationships.

An actual debate is occurring on the understanding of a structure, the share of intelligent (re)construction and that of reality beyond human intelligence. The problem of representation forms the background of those epistemological issues. One could say that a structure, being itself an order, shows "order in reality" without deciding whether this is the result of pure reality or of human consciousness. Legal semioticians tend to see legal structuring as a narrative activity, even the formation of narratives, which takes a reference to reality for granted, if not an absolute condition.

Symbol The structure of a meaning with a double sense: one is the primary, direct, literal, and the other the secondary, indirect and figurative sense. The latter can only be understood through the former. A more general observation shows the symbol as keystone of all hermeneutics, because hermeneutics unveils the concealed sense inherent in direct meanings. The relations between a symbol and a sign are, particularly in semiotic, very strong. A traffic sign, for instance, can be the symbol of a (local) culture and of nationally established behavior habits; the arbitrariness of the sign-matter is often transferred to the symbol.

Symptom Since Galen and his medical semiotics, a symptom was a feature as noticed by doctor and patient. But that feature is the product of human intelligence, in particular a semiotic approach to reality, and not a natural datum. Medical doctors and patients notice differently and often also give different names. The semiotic tradition tells that the patient gives a sign or signal, which is understood by the doctor as a symptom if he disposes of a well-ordered structure of medical phenomena. In that case, the sign can be placed and thus named 'symptom'. The therapy unfolds from signs on and proceeds via the knowledge of symptoms. Not the *nature* of the sign or symptom, but the observer decides about sign or symptom. In engineering, like in medical semiology, a symptom may be used to refer to an undesired effect occurring in a system.

Syntax — One of the fields of linguistics that is very close to semiotics, it deals with the types and kinds of expressions in a language. It is founded on the Greek notion of 'syn' and 'taxis'—together and arrangement. Expressions are used according to rules, which govern them, especially their combinations together in sentences and texts. Sentences (phrases) and terms are considered the basic elements of speech and discourse. The contrast between *syntax*, the mechanics of a language used to convey information, and *semantics*, the actual meaning of that language, is inherent to semiotic analyses. It is in any document on the web that does not contain special tagging to convey meaning, so that virtual meaning is, in contrast to meanings conveyed by a human individual, difficult to analyze by means of a computer program.

Text — A structured unity of words, signs and symbols written in any language or other form of communication, in particular electronic forms. In semiotics, texts are taken for signs that are transmitted, and texts are used and interpreted as such signs—often beyond purely linguistic units. This leads to communication theory as well as text hermeneutics, which often reach beyond the boundaries of language, for instance when they also pertain to buildings, landscapes and the like. All accede layered meanings to texts: read the text, and understand that there exists not only what is written! Greimas and Kristeva suggest that texts witness a specific type of social and intellectual productivity, which is called 'writing' or even 'literature'. Sentences or phrases are therefore more than signs; they have a semantic relevance in themselves. Texts should be understood as formulae of significance in a natural language or, broader, in landscapes created by human ingenuity.

References

On The Roberta Kevelson Seminar

Broekman, Jan M., and William A. Pencak, eds. 2009. Lawyers making meaning. The Roberta Kevelson seminar on law and semiotics at Penn State University's Dickinson School of Law. *International Journal for the Semiotics of Law* 22 (1): 1–123.

Broekman, Jan M., and William A. Pencak, eds. 2010. Signs of law. The Roberta Kevelson seminar on law and semiotics at Penn State University's Dickinson School of Law. *International Journal for the Semiotics of Law* 23 (1): 1–142.

Broekman, Jan M., and Francis J. Mootz III, eds. 2011. *The semiotics of law in legal education*. Dordrecht: Springer.

Wagner, Anne, and Jan M. Broekman, eds. 2010. *Prospects of legal semiotics*. Dordrecht: Springer.

On Roberta Kevelson

Kevelson, Roberta.1988. *Law as a system of signs*. New York: Plenum Press.

Kevelson, Roberta. 1998. In *Hi-Fives. A Trip to Semiotics*, ed. R. Kevelson. New York: Lang.

Kevelson, Roberta. 1999. *Peirce and the mark of the Gryphon*. New York: St Martin's Press.

On Charles Sanders Peirce

Houser, Nathan, and Christian Kloesel, eds. 1992. *The essential Peirce. Selected philosophical writings* vol. 1 (1867–1893). Bloomington: Indiana University Press.

Houser, Nathan, and Christian Kloesel. eds. 1998. *The essential Peirce. Selected philosophical writings* vol. 2 (1893–1913). Bloomington: Indiana University Press.

Brent, Joseph. 1993. *Charles Sanders Peirce. A life*. Indianapolis: Indianapolis University Press.

Of US Legal Scholars (Key Articles)

Balkin, J.M. 1990. The Hohfeldian approach to law and semiotics. *Miami Law Review* 44 (5): 1119 ff.

J. M. Broekman, L. Catà Backer, *Lawyers Making Meaning*,
DOI 10.1007/978-94-007-5458-4,

Balkin, J.M. 1990/1991. The promise of legal semiotics. *Texas Law Review* 69:1831 ff.
Balkin, Jack M. 2008. Critical legal theory today. In *Philosophy in American law,* ed. Francis J. Mootz III Oxford: Oxford University Press.
Kennedy, Duncan. 2000–2002. Semiotics of critique. *Cardozo Law Review*. 22:1151 ff.
Paul, Jeremy. 1990–1991. The politics of legal semiotics. *Texas Law Review* 69:1779 ff.

On the Theme in General

Eco, Umberto. 1979. *A theory of semiotics*. Bloomington: Indiana University Press.
Francis J. Mootz III: *Rhetorical knowledge in legal practice and critical legal theory*. Alabama: Alabama University Press.
Jackson, Bernard S. 1997. *Semiotics and legal theory*. London: Kegan Paul. Reprint Deborah Charles Publ.
Milovanovic, Dragan. 2003. *An introduction to the sociology of law.* New York: Criminal Justice Press.
Pencak, William A., and Ralph Lindgren. eds. 1998. *New approaches to Semiotics and the human sciences.* New York: Lang.
Pencak, William A., and Cindy Palecek. eds. 2002. *From absurdity to Zen. The wit and wisdom of Roberta Kevelson* New York: Lang.
Sebeok, Thomas A. 2001. *Global Semiotics*. Bloomington: Indiana University Press.
Unger, Roberto Mangabeira. 1986. *The critical legal studies movement.* Harvard: Harvard University Press 1983.
White, James Boyd. 1973. *The legal imagination*. Boston: Little Brown & Co.
White, James Boyd. 1984. *When words lose their meaning*. Chicago: Chicago University Press.
White, James Boyd. 1990. *Justice as translation: An essay in cultural and legal criticism*. Chicago: Chicago University Press.

On This Book

Akrich, M., and B. Latour. 1992. A summary of convenient vocabulary for the semiotics of human and nonhuman assemblies. In *Shaping technology/building society: Studies in sociotechnical change*, eds W. Bijker, and J. Law Cambridge: MIT Press.
Ali, Benmakhlouf. 2011. *L'identité. Une fable philosophique.* Paris: Partner University Fund.
Apel, K.-O. 1973. *Transformation der Philosophie, Band II: Das Apriori der Kommunikationsgemeinschaft*. Frankfurt a. M.: Suhrkamp.
Aristotle. 1912. *A treatise on government.* William Ellis, trans., London: JM Dent.
Bergh, G.C.J.J. van den. 1994. De taal zegt meer dan zij verantwoorden kan. In *Ars Aequi Libri.* Netherland: Nijmegen University.
Bergh, G.C.J.J. van den. 1996. Jacob Israel de Haan's Legal Significs. *International Journal for the Semiotics of Law* IX(25).
Bergh, G.C.J.J. van den, en Jan M Broekman. 1979. *Recht en Taal.* Kluwer.
Bernsau, Klaus M. 2009. *Corporate semiosis instead of corporate communication: How to apply semiotics pragmatically in the field of entrepreneurship and management*. Spain: Coruña Sept.
Balkin, J. M. 2008. Critical legal theory today. In *Philosophy in American law*, ed. Francis J. Mootz III. Oxford: Oxford University Press.
Balkin, J. M. 1990. The Hohfeldian approach to law and semiotics. *Miami Law Review* 44(5).
Balkin, J.M. 1990/1991. The promise of legal semiotics. *Texas Law Review* 69.
Balkin, J.M., and B.S. Noveck, eds. 2006. *The state of play. Law, games, and virtual worlds.* New York: New York University Press.

Brion, D.J. 1998. Chaos-what judges and juries do. In *New approaches to semiotics and the human sciences,* eds. W. Pencak, and J.R. Lindgren. New York: Lang.

Brion, D.J. 2009. Trial argumentation: The creation of meaning in: *Lawyers making meaning*. The Roberta Kevelson Seminar on Law and Semiotics at Penn State University's Dickinson School of Law, IJSL, vol. 22, no. 1.

Brody, Lisa R., and Gail L. Hoffman 2011. *Dura Europos. Crossroads of antiquity*. Boston: Boston College.

Broekman, Jan M. 1963. *Phänomenologie und Egologie*. Den Haag: M. Nijhoff.

Broekman, Jan M. 1979/1980. Betere taal is beter recht. *Wijsgerig Perspectief op maatschappij en wetenschap* 20 (2).

Broekman, Jan M. 1984. Justice as equilibrium. *Law and Philosophy* 5.

Broekman, Jan M. 1988. Semiology and medical discourse. *Methodology and Science, International Journal for the Empirical Study of the Foundations of Science and their Methodology.*

Broekman, Jan M. 1985. The minimum content of positivism *Rechtstheorie* XVI (4).

Broekman, Jan M. 1990. Holism, law, and the principle of expressibility. *Rechtstheorie* 28.

Broekman, Jan M. 1994. Legal discourse and legal facts. In *EYSL, European yearbook in the sociology of law*, eds. A. Febbrajo, and D Nelken. Milano: Giuffré.

Broekman, Jan M. 1996. *Intertwinements of Law and Medicine*. Leuven: Leuven University Press.

Broekman, Jan M. 2003. *Structuralism. Moscow, Prague, Paris.* Freiburg 1971; Amsterdam 1973; Barcelona 1974; Dordrecht 1974; Renmin UP 1st ed. 1983; 2nd ed.

Broekman, Jan M. 2008. *Binding words, unfolding selves*. New York: iUniverse.

Broekman, Jan M. 2010. Firstness and phenomenology. In *Prospects of legal semiotics,* eds. A. Wagner, and J.M. Broekman. Dordrecht: Springer.

Broekman, Jan M. 2011. Individual, state and the semiotics of anarchy. In *Law at the end of the day*. Larry Backer's blog.

Broekman, Jan M. 2011. Signs, diversity and tolerance. *The Journal of Comparative Law.*

Broekman, Jan M., and Anne Wagner, eds. 2010. *Prospects of legal semiotics*. Dordrecht: Springer.

Broekman, Jan M., and William A. Pencak. 2009. *Lawyers making meaning*. The Roberta Kevelson seminar on law and semiotics at Penn State University's Dickinson School of Law. *International Journal for the Semiotics of Law* 22(1).

Broekman, Jan M., and William A. Pencak. 2010. *Signs of law*. The Roberta Kevelson seminar on law and semiotics at Penn State University's Dickinson School of Law. *International Journal for the Semiotics of Law* 23(1)

Broekman, Jan M., and Francis J. Mootz III, eds. 2011. *The semiotics of law in legal education.* Dordrecht: Springer.

Catá Backer, Larry. 2000. Chroniclers in the field of cultural production: Interpretive conversations between courts and culture, *Boston College Third World Law Journal* 20:291.

Catá Backer, Larry. 2003. The duty to monitor: Emerging obligations of outside lawyers and auditors to detect and report corporate wrongdoing beyond the federal securities laws. *St. John's Law Review* 77.

Catá Backer, Larry. 2003. "Retaining judicial authority: A preliminary inquiry on the dominion of judges." *William & Mary Bill of Rights Journal* 12:117.

Catá Backer, Larry. 2006. Corporate institutionalism and fiduciary duty: On professor Katsuhito Iwai's nominalistic and realistic corporations model. Blog: *Law at the End of the Day* July 10.

Catá Backer, Larry. 2008. Symposium: Law and the state in the transnational legal order: "Reifying Law: Understanding Law Beyond the State." *Penn State International Law Review* 26 (3): 521.

Catá Backer, Larry. 2009. The drama of corporate law: Corporate narrative between policy and law. *Michigan State Law Review* 1111.

Catá Backer, Larry, 2012. Governance without government: An overview. In *Beyond territoriality: Transnational legal authority in an age of globalization*, eds. Günther Handl, Joachim Zekoll, and Peer Zumbansen. Leiden: Brill Academic Publishers.

Chandler, Daniel. 2002. *Semiotics: The basics*. Abingdon: Routledge.

Chomsky, Noam. 1969. *Topics in the theory of generative grammar.* Lectures Indiana 1964 re-published in the *Janua Linguarum,* Series Minor No. 56, Mouton, Paris: The Hague.

Clarke, D.S. 1987. *Principles of semiotic*. London: Routledge.
Cobley, P., ed. 2001. The Routledge Companion to Semiotics and Linguistics London: Routledge.
Colapietro, Vincent M. 1989. *Peirce's approach to the self. A semiotic perspective on human subjectivity*. New York: State University of New York Press.
Colapietro, Vincent. 2008. Peircean semeiotics and legal practices. *International Journal for the Semiotics of Law* 21 (3).
Danesi, Marcel. 2004. *Messages, signs, and meanings*. Toronto: Toronto University Press.
Deely, John. 1994. Membra Ficte Disjecta (A disordered array of severed limbs). Editorial introduction to the electronic edition of the collected papers of Charles Sanders Peirce.
Deledalle, G. 1990. Victoria lady Welby and Charles Sanders Peirce: Meaning and signification. In *Essays on Significs*, ed. H. Walter Schmitz. Amsterdam: John Benjamins.
Dennett, Daniel C. 1991. Real patterns. *The Journal of Philosophy* 88 (1): 27–51.
Deresiewicz, W. 2011. The graduates. *The New York Times Book Review.*
Dworkin, Ronald. 1985. *A matter of principle*. Harvard: Harvard University Press.
Edelman, Gerald M., and G. Tononi. 2000. *A universe of consciousness. How matter becomes imagination*. Basic Books.
Favale, Sam. 2012. Montana supreme court defies citizens united decision. *The Wall Street Journal*, Jan. 3.
Fisch, Max H. 1986. In *Peirce, semeiotic, and pragmatism,* eds. Ketner and Kloesel. Bloomington: Indiana University Press.
Fleet, Paul Van. 2011. Tarski, Peirce and Truth—Correspondences in law. In *The semiotics of law in legal education*, eds. Jan M. Broekman, and Francis J. Mootz III. Dordrecht: Springer.
Freud, Sigmund. 1960. Zur Einführung des Narzissmus. *Gesammelte Werke, Werke aus den Jahren 1913–1917*, London: Imago.
Fyodor, Dostoyevsky. 1846. *The double: A Petersburg poem*. (Constance Garnett, Tr.).
Gadamer, H.-G. 1988. Die Idee des Guten zwischen Plato und Aristoteles (trans: The idea of the good in Platonic-Aristotelian philosophy), p. 22. Heidelberg 1978. London: Yale University Press.
Georgio, Agamben. 2009. *The signature of all things. On method.* New York: Engl. Ed.
Genette, G. 1995. *Mimologiques, Voyage en Cratylie*, Paris 1976 Ch. 1. (Engl. Trans: Thaïs E. Morgan: *Mimologics*). Nebraska: UP.
Gifis, Steven H. 1991. *Law dictionary*. Barron's Educational Series.
Gillespie, Alex. 2009. The intersubjective nature of symbols. In *Symbolic transformation: The mind in movement through culture and society*, ed. Brady Wagoner. London: Routledge.
Greenberg, Paul. 1968. The semio-grads. *The Boston Globe*, 16/5/2004.
Greimas, Algirdas J., and François Rastier. 1968. The interaction of semiotic constraints. *Yale French Studies* 41.
Grupo de Estudios Percianos at the Universidad de Navarra (Spain). Available (in English and Spanish) at http://www.unav.es/gep/index-en.html.
Groudine, Candace J. 1980. Authority: H.L.A. Hart and the problem of legal positivism. *The Journal of Libertarian Studies* IV:273.
Guberman, Ross M., ed. 1996. *Julia Kristeva Interviews*. Columbia: Columbia University Press.
Gudel, Paul J. 2010. The skepticism of critical legal studies and the function of moral discourse. Oct. 2010, p. 75. http://works.bepress.com/paul_gudel/6.
Haan, J.I. de. 1916. *Wezen en taak van de rechtskundige significa*. Amsterdam: Van Kampen.
Haan, J.I. de. 1916. *Rechtskundige significa en hare toepassing op de begrippen"aansprakelijk, verantwoordelijk, toerekeningsvatbaar"*. Amsterdam: Versluys.
Hardwick, Ch.S., and J. Cook, eds. 1977. *Semiotic and significs. The correspondence between Charles S. Peirce and Victoria Lady Welby.* Bloomington: Indiana University Press.
Hart, H.L.A. 1994. *The concept of law.* 2nd ed. Clarendon: Oxford University Press.
Hart, Betty, and Todd R. Risley. 1995. *Meaningful differences in the everyday experience of young American children.* California: Brooks Publishing Company.

Hart, Betty, and Todd R. Risley. 1999. *The social world of children learning to talk.* California: Brooks Publishing Company.

Hausman, Carl R. 1997. *Peirce's evolutionary philosophy*. Cambridge: Cambridge University Press.

Hawkes, T. 1977. *Structuralism and semiotics*. California: California University Press.

Hirschl, Ran. 2004. *Toward juristocracy. The origins and consequences of the new constitutionalism.* Cambridge: Harvard University Press.

Hofmannsthal, H. von. 1979. *Erfundene Gespräche und Briefe.* In *Gesammelte Werke,* eds. B. Schoeller, and R. Hirsch. Bd VII. Frankfurt a. M.: Fischer.

Iwai, Katsuhito. 2002. The nature of the business corporation: Its legal structure and economic functions. *The Japanese Economic Review* 53 (3).

Jackson, Bernard. 1997. *Semiotics and legal theory*, London 1985. Reprint Liverpool, UK: Deborah Charles.

Jackson, Bernard S. 2010. Legal semiotics and semiotic aspects of jurisprudence. In *Prospects of Legal Semiotics,* eds. Wagner, and Broekman. Dordrecht: Springer.

Jaeger, Werner. 1945. *Paideia: The ideals of Greek culture.* (3 vols) vol. I. New York: Oxford University Press.

Jeffrey, Eugenides. 2011. *The Marriage Plot.* New York.

Janik, A., and St. E. Toulmin. 1996. *Wittgenstein's Vienna.* Chicago: Ivan R. Dee.

Johnson, St. 2011. I was an under-age semiotician. *The NY Times Book Review.*

Jones, Nigel. 1987. *Hitler's Heralds: The story of the Freikorps 1918–1923.* New York: Dorset Press.

Jones, Susan 2004. Michael Moore film violates campaign finance law, group alleges (formerly *Conservative News Service; now Cybercast News Service*).

Joseph, Brent. 1993. *Charles Sanders Peirce. A life.* Bloomington: Indiana University Press.

Joseph, John E. 2012. Meaning in the margins. Victoria Lady Welby and Significs. *Times literary supplement*, p 14/15.

Joseph, Brent. 1997. Pursuing Peirce. at *http://members.door.net/arisbe/menu/library/aboutcsp/brent/pursuing.htm.*

Kant, I. 1870. *Zum Ewigen Frieden. Ein Philosophischer Entwurf.* 1795, ed. J.H. von Kirchmann, 6 vols. Berlin: Forum-verlag.

Kant, Immanuel. 1990. Kritik der reinen Vernunft (1781) (Critique of pure reason, Meiklejohn, Ed., Amherst).

Kantorowicz, Ernst H. 1997. *The king's two bodies: A study in medieval political theology.* New Jersey: Princeton University Press.

Kennedy, Duncan. 1991. A semiotics of legal argument. *Syracuse Law Review* 42 (75).

Kennedy, Duncan. 2000–2002. Semiotics of critique. *Cardozo Law Review* 22.

Kevelson, Roberta. 1977. *Inlaws/Outlaws.* Lisse: Lang.

Kevelson, Roberta. 1988. *The law as a system of signs.* New York: Plenum Press.

Kevelson, Roberta. 1990. *Peirce, paradox, praxis.* New York: Plenum.

Kevelson, Roberta. 1992. Property as rhetoric in law. *Cardozo Studies in Law and Literature* 4.

Kevelson, Roberta. 1996. *Peirce, science, signs.* New York: Lang.

Kevelson, Roberta. 1999. *Peirce and the mark of the gryphon.* New York: St. Martin's Press.

Kramer, Stephen D. 2006. *Sovereignty: Organized hypocrisy* 1999. New Jersey: Princeton UP.

Kristeva, Julia. 1969. L'engendrement de la formule. In *Semeiotiké Recherches pour une Sémanalyse*. Paris: Seuil.

Kristeva, Julia. 1980. Desire in language. *A semiotic approach to literature and art.* New York: Columbia UP.

Lucinda, Dirven. 1999. *The Palmyrenes of Dura-Europos.* Leiden: Brill.

Lacan, Jacques. 1953. *Some reflections on the ego.*

Lacan, Jacques. 1977. *Écrits. A selection.* London: Tavistock.

Lazzarato, Maurizio. 2006. Semiotic pluralism and the new government of signs. Homage to Félix Guattari, (Mary O'Neill, trans.) *EIPCP (European Institute For Progressive Cultural Policies) Multilingual WebJournal.*

Levinas, E. 1961. *Totalite et Infini. Essai sur L'extériorité. Phaenomenologica*. Bd 8. Den Haag: Nÿhoff.

Levinas, E. 1963. *Difficile Liberté*, ed. Michel. Paris: Albin Michel.

Levinas, E. 1972. *Humanisme de l'Autre Homme*. Paris: Livre de Poche.

Llewellyn, K. 1960. *The common law tradition*. Boston: Little Brown.

Lieb, E., ed. 1953. *Charles S. Peirce's letters to Lady Welby*. New Haven: Conn.

Martin, L.H., H. Gutman, and P. Hutton, eds. 1988. *Technologies of the Self: A seminar with M. Foucault*. Amherst, MA: Massachusetts UP.

Matheson, Susan B. 1994. *An obsession with fortune: Tyche in Greek and Roman art*. New Haven, CT: Yale University Art Gallery.

Menninghaus, W. 1987. *Unendliche Verdoppelung. Die frühromantische Grundlegung der Kunsttheorie im Begriff absoluter Selbstreflexion*. Frankfurt a. M.: Suhrkamp.

Merrell, Floyd. 1983. *Pararealities. The nature of our Fictions and how we know them*. Philadelphia: John Benjamins Pub Co.

Merrell, Floyd. 2001. Charles sanders peirce's concept of the sign. In *The routledge companion to semiotics and linguistics*, ed. P. Colbry. London: Routledge.

Merryman, John H. 1985. *The civil law tradition*. 2nd edn. Palo Alto, CA: Stanford UP.

Michel, Foucault. 1963. *Naissance de la Clinique – Une Archéologie du regard medical*. Paris: PUF.

Michel, Foucault. 1984. Qu'est-ce que les lumières? 1978, What is Enlightenment? In *The foucault reader*, ed. P. Rabinow

Michel, Foucault. 2011. *The government of self and others*. Picador: *Lectures at the College de France*, 1982–1983.

Milovanovic, D. 2003. *An introduction to the sociology of law*. New York: Criminal Justice Press.

Mootz, III Francis. J. 2006. *Rhetorical knowledge in legal practice and critical legal theory*. Alabama: Alabama UP.

Morris, Ch. 1955. *Signs, language and behavior*. New York Prentice-Hall Inc.

Morris, Ch. 1964. *Signification and significance*. Cambridge, MA: Cambridge MIT.

Nietzsche, F. 1968. *The will to power* (trans: Walter Kaufmann, and R.J. Hollingdale), ed. W. Kaufmann New York: Vintage.

O'Brien, Geoffry. 2012. Crazy horse. *The New York Review of Books*, LIX:5.

Parker, Kelly A. 1998. *The continuity of Peirce's thought*. Tennessee: Vanderbilt UP.

Paul, Bains. 2006. *The primacy of semiosis: An ontology of relations*. Toronto: Toronto University Press.

Paul, Auster. 2010. *Sunset park*. New York: Henry Holt & Co.

Paul, Jeremy. 1990–1991. The politics of legal semiotics. *Texas Law Review* 69.

Peirce, Ch. S. *A new list of categories. Proceedings American Academy of Arts and Sciences* VII.

Peirce, Charles Sanders. 1931–1935. *The collected papers of Charles Sanders Pierce*, eds. Charles Hartshorne, and Paul Weiss, I–VI. Cambridge Ma: Harvard University Press.

Peirce, Charles Sanders. 1958. *The collected papers of Charles Sanders Pierce*, eds. Arthur W. Burks, VII–VIII. Cambridge Ma: Harvard University Press.

Peirce, Charles S. 1998. *The essential Peirce, selected philosophical writings. The Peirce edition project* (ed). Bloomington: Indiana UP.

Pencak, W.A. 1993. Peirce and Arisbe. In *History, signing in*. New York: Lang.

Pencak, William A. 1998. A conversation with Roberta Kevelson. In *New approaches to semiotics and the human sciences*, eds. Pencak and Lindgren.

Petrilli, S. 2009. *Signifying and Understanding. Reading the works of Victoria Welby and the signific movement*. Berlin: Mouton de Gruyter.

Perelman, C., and L. Olbrechts-Tyteca 1969. *The new rhetoric: A treatise on argumentation*. Notre Dame, IN: Notre Dame UP.

Perelman, C. 1945. *De la Justice*. Brussels (Eng. Transl. 1963).

Perelman, C. 1963. *The idea of justice and the problem of argument*. London: Routledge.

Perelman, C. 1990. *Ethique et Droit*. Brussels.

Perelman, C., and L. Olbrechts-Tyteca. 1969. *The new rhetoric: A treatise on argumentation.* Notre Dame, IN: Notre Dame UP.
Plato: 360 BC *Cratylus* Transl. Benjamin Jowett. >www.classics.mit.edu/Plato/cratylus.html<
Pollitt, J.J. 1986. *Art in the hellenistic age*. Cambridge: Cambridge UP.
Pollitt, J.J. 1994. *An obsession with fortune*. New Haven: Yale University Art Gallery.
Pollock, F. 1872. Law and command. *Law Magazine and Review* 1.
Prigogine, I and I. Stengers. 1984. *Order out of chaos.* Scotland: Glasgow.
Richards, I.A. 1936. *The philosophy of rhetoric.* Oxford: Oxford UP.
Robbins, Ira P. 1999. Semiotics, analogical legal reasoning and the Cf. citation. *Duke Law Journal* 48.
Roland, Barthes. 1977. *Fragments d'un discours amoureux.* Paris: Paris Du Seuil.
Roland, Barthes. 1985. Sémiologie et Médicine. In *L'aventure sémiologique*. Paris: Paris Du Seuil.
Sacks, Sam. 2011. Sense and semiotics. *The Wall Street Journal*, Oct. 8/9.
Saussure, F. de. 1972. *Cours de Linguistique Générale.* New edn, 27–35. Paris. English transl: *Course in general linguistics*, ed. Roy Harris. Chicago: Open Court, 1983.
Schmitz, H. Walter. 1892–1926. *De Hollandse Significa. Een reconstructie van de geschiedenis van 1892 tot 1926.* Assen 1960. German edn 1985: *Verständigungshandlungen—eine wissenschaftshistorische Rekonstruktion der Anfänge der signifischen Bewegung in den Niederlanden.*
Schmitz, H. Walter, and E Heijerman, eds. 1986. *Significs, mathematics and semiotics. The signific movement in The Netherlands.* Münster: Nodus.
Sedley, Sir Charles. 1968. *To nysus.* In *The penguin book of restoration verse*, ed. Harold Love, 690. Baltimore, MD: Penguin Books (first published cir. 1701).
Searle, John R. 1969. *Speech acts. An essay in the philosophy of language.* Cambridge: Cambridge UP.
Searle, John R. 1979. *Expression and meaning*. Cambridge: Cambridge UP.
Segal, David. 2011. What they don't teach law students: Lawyering. *The New York Times*.
Sheriff, John K. 1994. *Charles Peirce's guess at the riddle*. Bloomington: Indiana UP.
Shklar, Judith. 1986. Legalism. *Law, morals, and political trials*. Cambridge, MA: Harvard UP(2).
Sonesson, Göran. 2004. The globalisation of ego and alter. An essay in cultural semiotics. *Semiotica* 148:153–73.
Stephen, Breyer. 2005. *Active liberty. Interpreting our Democratic constitution.* New York: Praeger Publishers.
Stjernfelt, Frederik. 2007. *Diagrammatology—An investigation on the borderlines of phenomenology, ontology, and semiotics*. Synthese library, 336. Dordrecht: Springer.
Taxidou, Olga. 2004. *Tragedy, modernity and mourning*. Edinburgh: Edinburg UP.
Uhr, Leonard. 1966. *Pattern recognition*. New York: Wiley.
Umberto, Eco. 1979. *A theory of semiotics*. Bloomington: Indiana University Press.
Umberto, Eco. 1979. *The role of the reader*. Bloomington: Indiana University Press.
Unger, Roberto M. 1983. *The critical legal studies movement.* Cambridge, MA: Harvard UP.
Unger, Roberto M. 1996. *What would legal analysis become?*. London: Verso.
Vanlandingham, R.C. 2010. Signs of law in student perspective. *IJSL* 23.
Welby, Lady Victoria. 1903. *What is meaning? Studies in the development of significance*. London: Semantics.
Welby, Lady Victoria. 1911. *Significs and language*. London: Macmillan.
Welby, Lady Victoria. 1911. Significs. *Encyclopedia Brittannica.*
Westbrook, David A. 2007. *Between citizen and state: An introduction to the corporation*. Boulder, CO: Paradigm Press.
White, James Boyd. 1984. *When words lose their meaning.* Chicago: Chicago UP.
Wiley, Norbert 1994. *The semiotic self.* Chicago: Chicago UP.
William, Gibson. 2005. *Pattern recognition.* Berkeley: Penguin.
Wirth, Michelle. 2009. Who's your daddy? or: Using semiotic tools to deconstruct legal determinations of who holds parenthood obligations and privileges. *International Journal for the Semiotics of Law* 22(1).

Wirth, Michelle L. 2011. Semiotics of parenthood in legal perspective. In *The semiotics of law in legal education,* eds. Jan M. Broekman, and Francis J. Mootz III. Dordrecht: Springer.
Wittgenstein, L. 1958. *Philosophical investigations*. Oxford: Blackwell.
Wolfgang, Blankenburg. 1971. *Der Verlust der natürlichen Selbstverständlichkeit*. Stuttgart: Enke.
Zamora, Melina M. 2010. A deeper understanding of law. *International Journal for the Semiotics of Law* 23.

Subject Index

J. M. Broekman, L. Catà Backer, *Lawyers Making Meaning*,
DOI 10.1007/978-94-007-5458-4, © Springer Science+Business Media Dordrecht 2013

Author Index

J. M. Broekman, L. Catà Backer, *Lawyers Making Meaning*,
DOI 10.1007/978-94-007-5458-4, © Springer Science+Business Media Dordrecht 2013

MIX
Papier aus verantwortungsvollen Quellen
Paper from responsible sources
FSC® C105338
FSC
www.fsc.org

If you have any concerns about our products,
you can contact us on
ProductSafety@springernature.com

In case Publisher is established outside the EU,
the EU authorized representative is:
Springer Nature Customer Service Center GmbH
Europaplatz 3, 69115 Heidelberg, Germany

Printed by Libri Plureos GmbH
in Hamburg, Germany